CBT: Science Into Practice

Series Editor

Nikolaos Kazantzis, Cognitive Behavior Therapy Research Unit, Melbourne, VIC, Australia

This series addresses topics that reflect current thinking in the field of cognitive behavior therapy, the most widely accepted form of therapy across mental health disciplines. Despite the consensus that CBT is an effective treatment modality, much of the existing clinical literature focuses on single facets, such as specific disorders or populations. Mostly it does not take into account the latest evidence for transdiagnostic change mechanisms and processes. This series provides guidance on how the latest evidence can be translated into practice. Volumes focus on enhancing flexibility in both the selection and delivery of techniques tailored to individual clients. Each provides clinical insights enhanced by case studies and vignettes to ensure relevance for the practicing professional.

Julian A. Rubel • Wolfgang Lutz
Editors

Feedback Informed Psychological Therapy

Science and Practice

Springer

Editors
Julian A. Rubel
Department of Psychotherapy Research
and Clinical Psychology
Osnabrueck University
Osnabrück, Germany

Wolfgang Lutz
Department of Clinical Psychology
and Psychotherapy
Trier University
Trier, Germany

ISSN 2946-5419 ISSN 2946-5427 (electronic)
CBT: Science Into Practice
ISBN 978-3-031-90427-1 ISBN 978-3-031-90428-8 (eBook)
https://doi.org/10.1007/978-3-031-90428-8

This Springer imprint is published by the registered company Springer Nature Switzerland AG
The registered company address is: Gewerbestrasse 11, 6330 Cham, Switzerland

Foreword

I am delighted that the book *Advances in the Science and Practice of Feedback-Informed Psychological Therapy* is being published in the **CBT: Science into Practice** book series. Cognitive-behavioral therapy (CBT) remains one of the most well-supported interventions for a range of psychological disorders, yet the challenge of improving outcomes for patients who do not respond adequately to standard treatments persists. Feedback-Informed Therapy (FIT) represents a critical innovation in addressing this challenge.

The practice of CBT is grounded in empiricism—not only in evaluating the overarching approach and modifications such as FIT, but also in generating within-patient data to evaluate individual progress and goal acquisition using FIT. By integrating routine outcome monitoring (ROM) into clinical practice, FIT offers a pathway to refine therapy in real time, tailoring interventions to individual patient needs and improving outcomes.

This edited volume, contributed by Dr. Julian A. Rubel and Dr. Wolfgang Lutz, two of the leading experts in the field, provides a comprehensive guide to the theoretical foundations, empirical evidence, and practical applications of FIT. This book synthesizes decades of research into a compelling and accessible guide—it is an essential resource for clinicians, researchers, and trainees who are committed to enhancing therapeutic outcomes and advancing personalized care.

In the introductory chapter, Dr. Rubel and Dr. Lutz offer an insightful overview of FIT as a transtheoretical approach that enriches clinical decision-making through the systematic use of patient progress data. They highlight the limitations of relying solely on clinician judgment, which is often subject to cognitive biases, and advocate for the integration of psychometric data to guide treatment adaptations. This approach is not only innovative but also deeply grounded in evidence, with over fifty studies demonstrating the efficacy of FIT in improving outcomes, particularly for patients at risk of treatment failure.

The editors' exploration of FIT systems is both broad and detailed throughout the volume. Across three well-structured sections, they examine the diversity of feedback systems, adaptations for specific clinical challenges, and the technological advancements that have propelled FIT into modern practice. Clinicians will appreciate the practical focus, with case studies and guidelines offering actionable strategies for integrating FIT into diverse therapeutic settings.

One of the most compelling aspects of this book is its emphasis on the mechanisms of change that make FIT effective. Beyond simply monitoring symptoms, FIT fosters a dynamic interplay between therapist and patient, strengthening the therapeutic relationship and enhancing shared decision-making. The inclusion of clinical support tools (CSTs) further amplifies these effects, providing therapists with targeted interventions to address emerging risks.

Dr. Rubel and Dr. Lutz also address the critical challenges associated with implementing FIT, from technical considerations to the need for cultural adaptations in diverse settings. Their discussion of the heterogeneity in feedback systems—ranging from session-by-session assessments to less frequent measures—underscores the flexibility of FIT while emphasizing the importance of tailoring its application to specific contexts.

This book serves not only as a guide for implementing FIT but also as a call to action for the field. As clinicians, we are tasked with constantly improving our practices to meet the needs of our patients. FIT represents a paradigm shift, offering a systematic, data-driven approach to achieve this goal. Rubel and Lutz's work challenges us to embrace this innovation while remaining attuned to the nuances of individual patient care.

The editors' expertise and dedication to advancing psychotherapy are evident throughout this volume. Dr. Rubel, a renowned clinical psychologist specializing in adult psychotherapy at the University of Osnabrück in Germany, brings his expertise in clinical psychology and psychotherapy, along with skill in advanced longitudinal data analysis. He is known for his rigorous approach to integrating empirical evidence into therapeutic practices. Dr. Lutz, a pioneer in patient-focused and feedback research at the University of Trier, has transformed the way therapy progress is measured through his concept of Expected Treatment Response, enabling providers worldwide to deliver personalized, empirically based treatment plans. With over 350 peer-reviewed articles to his name, Dr. Lutz's work continues to shape the future of psychotherapy.

With such distinguished backgrounds to draw on, Dr. Rubel and Dr. Lutz are eminently qualified to offer this book. They have produced a work with a rich synthesis of evidence to guide practice. The purpose of this book is to guide the use of FIT in everyday clinical practice, and they have performed exceptionally well in this regard.

This book is an invaluable contribution to the field and will undoubtedly inspire its readers to integrate FIT into their own practices. I applaud the authors and contributors for their exceptional work in bringing this volume to life.

Cognitive Behavior Therapy Research Unit
Melbourne, VIC, Australia
Beck Institute for Cognitive Behavior Therapy
Philadelphia, PA, USA

Nikolaos Kazantzis

Conflicts of Interest Kazantzis disclosed his royalties from the Guilford Press (Therapeutic Relationship in Cognitive Behavior Therapy; Cognitive and Behavior Theories in Clinical Practice), Routledge (Using Homework Assignments in Cognitive Behavior Therapy); SpringerNature publishers (CBT: Science into Practice Book Series; Handbook of Homework Assignments in Psychotherapy: Research, Practice, & Prevention). He also disclosed editor stipend from the Association for Behavioral and Cognitive Therapies for his role as Editor-in-Chief for Cognitive and Behavioral Practice (Elsevier).

Contents

Editors and Contributors

About the Editors

Wolfgang Lutz, PhD completed his doctorate in Psychology at the University of Heidelberg, Germany, a post-doctorate at Northwestern University, USA and a research professorship at the University of Berne (Switzerland). He is currently full professor and chair of Clinical Psychology and Psychotherapy at the University of Trier/Germany as well as director of the clinical training program and the outpatient research clinic. He is one of the pioneers of precision mental health and has worked in the field of routine outcome monitoring and measurement-based care for over 30 years. He has more than 400 publications (peer-reviewed papers, chapters, and books) including the 7th edition of the *Bergin & Garfield's Handbook of Psychotherapy and Behavior Change*, which he co-edited with Michael Barkham and Louis G. Castonguay. He is a past editor of *Psychotherapy Research,* a co-editor of the *Journal of Consulting and Clinical Psychology and Behavior Therapy* and serves on the editorial board of several leading journals in the field. He was president of the *Society for Psychotherapy Research* (SPR) and has been recognized by various awards and fellowships, including the SPR's *Early Career Contribution Award* and distinguished research and leader recognition from the *Association for Psychological Science (APS).*

Julian A. Rubel, PhD studied Psychology at the University of Trier (Germany) from 2007-2011. After his studies, he started his dissertation project in the group of Wolfgang Lutz in Trier focusing on patterns of change in psychotherapy. He finished his PhD in 2015 with honors and proceeded working at Trier University as a post-doc until 2019. From 2019-2021, he was an assistant professor and from 10/2021 to 02/2023 full professor for psychotherapy research at Justus Liebig University Giessen. Since 03/2023, he has been full professor and chair of the unit Psychotherapy Research and Clinical Psychology at Osnabrueck University. His research focuses on a broad range of topics aiming at improving our understanding of the mechanisms underlying psychotherapy and the development and evaluation of empirically supported tools to prevent treatment failure and premature termination.

Contributors

Michael Barkham School of Psychology, University of Sheffield, Sheffield, UK

Stephan Bartholdy Department of Clinical Psychology and Psychotherapy, University of Greifswald, Greifswald, Germany

Harald Baumeister Department of Clinical Psychology and Psychotherapy, Institute of Psychology and Education, University Ulm, Ulm, Germany

Mark E. Beecher Counseling and Psychological Services, Brigham Young University, Provo, UT, USA

Jana Bommer Department of Clinical Psychology and Psychotherapy, Trier University, Trier, Germany

Eva-Lotta Brakemeier Department of Clinical Psychology and Psychotherapy, University of Greifswald, Greifswald, Germany

Gary M. Burlingame Department of Psychology, Brigham Young University, Provo, UT, USA

Kim de Jong Institute of Psychology, Leiden University, Leiden, The Netherlands

Anne-Katharina Deisenhofer Department of Clinical Psychology and Psychotherapy, Trier University, Trier, Germany

Jaime Delgadillo Institute of Psychiatry, Psychology and Neuroscience, King's College London, London, United Kingdom

Selin Demir Department of Clinical Psychology and Psychotherapy, University of Greifswald, Greifswald, Germany

Susan Douglas Department of Leadership, Policy, and Organizations, Vanderbilt University, Peabody College, Nashville, TN, USA

Steffen T. Eberhardt Department of Clinical Psychology and Psychotherapy, Trier University, Trier, Germany

David M. Erekson Counseling and Psychological Services, Brigham Young University, Provo, UT, USA

Stian Sørheim Espevoll Helse Førde Hospital Trust, Førde, Norway

Department of Health and Caring Science, Western Norway University of Applied Science, Førde, Norway

Department of Psychiatry, Weill Cornell Medical Center, New York, NY, USA

Department of Behavioral Health, Reliant Medical Group, Worcester, MA, USA

Derek Griner Counseling and Psychological Services, Brigham Young University, Provo, UT, USA

Mila Hall Department of Clinical Psychology and Psychotherapy, Trier University, Trier, Germany

Miriam Hehlmann Department of Psychotherapy Research and Clinical Psychology, Osnabrueck University, Osnabrueck, Germany

Geoff R. Hooke Perth Clinic, Perth, WA, Australia

Amanda Jensen-Doss Department of Psychology, University of Miami, Coral Gables, FL, USA

Tim Kaiser Department of Education and Psychology, Free University of Berlin, Berlin, Germany

Johannes Knauer Department of Clinical Psychology and Psychotherapy, Institute of Psychology and Education, University Ulm, Ulm, Germany

Michael J. Kyron School of Psychological Science, University of Western Australia, Perth, WA, Australia

Michael J. Lambert Department of Psychology, Brigham Young University, Provo, UT, USA

Tasha Love Health Connect America, Columbia, TN, USA

Wolfgang Lutz Department of Clinical Psychology and Psychotherapy, Trier University, Trier, Germany

Andrew A. McAleavey Helse Førde Hospital Trust, Førde, Norway

Department of Health and Caring Science, Western Norway University of Applied Science, Førde, Norway

Department of Psychiatry, Weill Cornell Medical Center, New York, NY, USA

Fabienne Mink Department of Clinical Psychology and Psychotherapy, Trier University, Trier, Germany

Danilo Moggia Department of Clinical Psychology and Psychotherapy, Trier University, Trier, Germany

Christian Moltu Helse Førde Hospital Trust, Førde, Norway

Department of Health and Caring Science, Western Norway University of Applied Science, Førde, Norway

Sam Nordberg Department of Behavioral Health, Reliant Medical Group, Worcester, MA, USA

Benjamin M. Ogles Department of Psychology, Brigham Young University, Provo, UT, USA

Andrew C. Page School of Psychological Science, University of Western Australia, Perth, WA, Australia

Tate M. Paxton Department of Psychology, Brigham Young University, Provo, UT, USA

Harriëtte Riese Department of Psychiatry, University Medical Center Groningen, University of Groningen, Groningen, The Netherlands

Julian A. Rubel Department of Psychotherapy Research and Clinical Psychology, Osnabrueck University, Osnabrueck, Germany

Jana Schaffrath Department of Clinical Psychology and Psychotherapy, Trier University, Trier, Germany

Brian Schwartz Department of Clinical Psychology and Psychotherapy, Trier University, Trier, Germany

Michelle N. Servaas Department of Psychiatry, University Medical Center Groningen, University of Groningen, Groningen, The Netherlands

Yannik Terhorst Department of Psychological Methods and Assessment, Ludwigs-Maximilian University Munich, Munich, Germany

Markus Tewes Department of Clinical Psychology and Psychotherapy, University of Greifswald, Greifswald, Germany

Antonia Vehlen Department of Clinical Psychology and Psychotherapy, Trier University, Trier, Germany

Birgit Weinmann-Lutz Department of Clinical Psychology and Psychotherapy, Trier University, Trier, Germany

Grace Woodard Department of Psychology, University of Miami, Coral Gables, FL, USA

Jordan Zahora Department of Leadership, Policy, and Organizations, Vanderbilt University, Peabody College, Nashville, TN, USA

Chapter 1
Introduction to Feedback-Informed Psychological Therapy

Julian A. Rubel and Wolfgang Lutz

Introduction to Feedback-Informed Psychological Therapy

The present book describes a set of methods that are aimed at enhancing common cognitive-behavioral therapy (CBT) practices. Although CBT has been proven to be effective in numerous original studies and meta-analyses, a considerable amount of patients still do not benefit from this approach (e.g., Barkham & Lambert, 2021). This is especially problematic since the prediction and recognition of treatment non-response based on a purely clinical decision-making has long been identified as an Achilles heel of therapists and a task at which statistical algorithms tend to outperform biased human judgment (e.g., Hannan et al., 2004; Meehl, 1954; Walfish et al., 2012). As a consequence, one promising path to an enhancement of treatments and especially reduction of treatment failure is supporting clinical decision-making with psychometric data at the start and over the course of therapy (Lutz, Schwartz, & Delgadillo, 2022). In order to do so, the repeated assessment of patient outcomes, that is, routine outcome monitoring (ROM), is a necessary precondition. This information is then processed and fed back to clinicians in a visually appealing way. In order to support therapists in interpreting this information, patient data is often put in the context of empirical comparison data, for example, trajectories of previously successfully treated patients (e.g., Lutz et al., 2019). Based on this additional data, therapists can make a more empirically informed decision about whether or not this particular patient is progressing as expected and thus whether or not the

J. A. Rubel (✉)
Department of Psychotherapy Research and Clinical Psychology, Osnabrueck University, Osnabrueck, Germany
e-mail: julian.rubel@uni-osnabrueck.de

W. Lutz
Department of Clinical Psychology and Psychotherapy, Trier University, Trier, Germany
e-mail: lutzw@uni-trier.de

J. A. Rubel, W. Lutz (eds.), *Feedback Informed Psychological Therapy*, CBT: Science Into Practice, https://doi.org/10.1007/978-3-031-90428-8_1

approach applied so far is the most appropriate or if adaptations are needed. Treatments enhanced with ROM and feedback have been given multiple names over the years. Two regularly used ones are measurement-based care (MBC; e.g., Trivedi & Daly, 2007) and feedback-informed psychological therapies (FIT; e.g., Delgadillo et al., 2021). The term FIT embraces all treatments in which the decision-making process of clinicians is supported by a systematic, repeated assessment of psychometric progress data during the course of a psychological treatment. Although the clinical examples that are given in this book stem mainly from settings in which cognitive-behavioral treatments are provided, FIT in general is a transtheoretical approach (e.g., Barber & Resnick, 2023).

Effects of Feedback

With over 50 studies, progress monitoring and feedback based on session-level assessments has the best empirical evidence of its effects on clinical practice (e.g., Lutz, de Jong et al., 2021). Multiple systematic reviews and meta-analyses have demonstrated the effectiveness of FIT and ROM (FIT, ROM, and PFR are often used synonymously) on treatment progress and outcomes, suggesting a small overall effect of feedback (e.g., Barkham et al., 2023; de Jong et al., 2021; Rognstad et al., 2023). This effect is particularly pronounced in not-on-track (NOT) cases, indicating that patients at risk of treatment failure benefit significantly (e.g., Barkham et al., 2023; de Jong et al., 2021; Rognstad et al., 2022). The effect is amplified when feedback is combined with clinical support tools (CSTs; de Jong et al., 2021; Lambert et al., 2018; Shimokawa et al., 2010). CSTs are a set of materials comprising educational elements and intervention suggestions that are provided for NOT cases and selected based on the specific needs of a patient. In their review, Barkham et al. (2023) reported a statistically significant overall effect of feedback on patient outcome with an effect size (ES) of approximately $g \approx 0.15$. It is essential to remember that these effects add to the standard effects of psychological therapies and on average result in an $\approx 8\%$ advantage [success rate difference (SRD)] over standard care. Furthermore, the effect of feedback is augmented to $g \approx 0.36$–0.53 when CSTs are employed for NOT cases, resulting in an SRD of between $\approx 20\%$ and 29%. Therefore, FIT offers a cost-effective, patient-supported approach, which has the potential to improve existing treatment outcomes, especially for patients at risk for negative treatment outcomes. It also helps clinicians monitor patient progress and make treatment length decisions based on actual treatment progress (more sessions for patients in need or at higher risk) and perhaps fewer sessions for patients who are improving early, compared to a traditional determination of treatment length based on the average session calculations for patient cohorts (Lutz et al., 2021). However, there are still many challenges to face (Lutz et al., 2024). For example, the effective implementation and use of these new tools is a challenge for clinical training and practice that must be overcome to enable practitioners to make the most of these new decision-making techniques (Barkham et al., 2023). In order to enhance the routine use of measurements among psychologists, the APA has published a practice guideline in which they outline important issues that need to be considered when conducting FIT in practice (Jensen-Doss et al., 2024).

How Does Feedback Work?

FIT share three basic commonalities: (1) patient data is collected on a regular basis; (2) this data is fed back to therapists (and sometimes patients); and (3) it is assumed that therapists use this feedback in order to adapt their treatment if appropriate. However, besides these commonalities there is quite a bit of heterogeneity between different feedback systems. First, the frequency of assessments varies considerably between systems. While many systems include session-by-session assessments, some have less intensive (e.g., every 3 months) or more intensive (e.g., several measures per day) assessment schedules. Second, the content of the measures varies greatly. While many assess symptom impairment, more general constructs like well-being and functioning are also often included. Besides established psychometrically tested instruments, also idiographic questionnaires, in which new questions are developed for each individual patient, are used in some systems (e.g., Sales & Cooper, 2023). Also with regard to the feedback provided based on the repeatedly assessed data, there is some heterogeneity between systems. These differences start with the question who receives the feedback: therapists, patients, or both. The most usual approach is feedback given to therapists with the idea that they have the professional knowledge to decide which information should be passed on to the patients. Furthermore, the content of the feedback and how the data is processed varies between systems. Many systems provide graphical representations of the development of symptoms, etc., using line charts. Moreover, these curves are often accompanied by decision support tools that help interpret the trajectory of the patient currently being treated. These tools comprise, for example, expected treatment response curves of previously treated, similar patients (e.g., Lutz et al., 2006, 2019) or cut-offs that indicate whether observed scores are more likely in the range of a clinical or healthy norm population.

These differential approaches are closely connected with the hypotheses about the putative mechanisms through which feedback is assumed to exert its effects (Mc McAleavey et al., 2024). The most prevalent idea is that therapists are aided by feedback in the accurate assessment of their patients' progress (e.g., Herzog et al., 2023). Based on this knowledge, therapists can counteract negative developments that they would have overseen without feedback. This is why many systems include an alarm system, alerting therapists in case of an increased risk for treatment failure. Other theories emphasize the positive effects feedback has on the therapeutic alliance and postulate a feedback ⟶ alliance ⟶ outcome mediation model (e.g., Brattland et al., 2019).

Not much is known about the differential effects of these different variants of feedback systems. Only the person of the therapist (e.g., Simon et al., 2012) and the implementation of the feedback system (e.g., Brattland et al., 2018) have been repeatedly found to moderate the effects of feedback. Regarding therapist differences it has been found that the more therapists report to actually use the feedback, the more they benefit from feedback (de Jong et al., 2012). Predictors of feedback usage have been gender (female therapists tend to use feedback more than male therapists; de Jong et al., 2012) and attitudes toward feedback (therapists with more positive attitudes tend to use feedback more effectively than those with less positive attitudes; de Jong et al., 2012; Lutz et al., 2015; Lutz, Deisenhofer, et al., 2022). A further factor that is assumed on the therapist level is professional self-doubt (PSD; Nissen-Lie et al., 2017). That is, the tendency of therapists to critically reflect on their professional actions. Based on the contextual feedback intervention theory (CFIT; Sapyta et al., 2005) and the belief-updating model (Herzog et al., 2023), it is assumed that therapists who are more open to the perspective of their patients and are less convinced of the accuracy of their own perceptions tend to be more likely to revise their own view in favor of their patient's view. As such, therapists who show higher levels of PSD should be more likely to actually use feedback to update their own evaluation of how their patient is doing.

Outline of the Present Book

Given the aforementioned heterogeneity, the present book aims to provide an overview of feedback systems and their application for different settings and aims. The heart of this book lies in its practical application. Through case studies and detailed guidelines, it is illustrated in which ways feedback can be integrated into various therapeutic modalities, ranging from individual to group therapy. Moreover, we explore the technological advancements that have propelled feedback-informed therapy into the modern era. With the advent of digital tools and platforms, collecting and analyzing feedback has become more accessible and sophisticated, opening new possibilities for enhancing therapeutic practice.

The book is divided into three parts. In the first part (Chaps. 2–8), different feedback systems from different research teams around the world and their clinical applications are presented. In these chapters, a total of six different systems are presented with the focus on their clinical application. The second part of the book (Chaps. 9–11) focuses on specific settings or problems for which feedback may be adapted. These are the tracking of suicidal ideation, rehabilitation settings, and group settings. The last part (Chaps. 12–14) focuses on the issue of technology and implementation of feedback systems in clinical practice settings. These chapters address the challenges and nuances of implementing feedback systems, offering insights into overcoming common obstacles and maximizing the potential of this approach. Chapter 12 covers the technology needed to implement feedback systems and encourages practitioners, from mental health professionals in private practices to scientist-practitioners in research hubs, to engage in routine outcome monitoring. Chapter 13 deals with central steps and potential pitfalls in implementing FIT into clinical practice and shares lessons learned from the launch of a specific system, the Trier Treatment Navigator. Chapter 14 discusses implementation issues more generally.

References

Barber, J., & Resnick, S. G. (2023). Collect, Share, Act: A transtheoretical clinical model for doing measurement-based care in mental health treatment. *Psychological Services, 20*(2), 150–157. https://doi.org/10.1037/ser0000629

Barkham, M., de Jong, K., Delgadillo, J., & Lutz, W. (2023). Routine Outcome Monitoring (ROM) and Feedback: Research Review and Recommendations. *Psychotherapy Research, 33*(7), 841–855. https://doi.org/10.1080/10503307.2023.2181114

Barkham, M., & Lambert, M. J. (2021). The efficacy and effectiveness of psychological therapies. In M. Barkham, W. Lutz, & L. G. Castonguay (Eds.), *Bergin and Garfield's handbook of psychotherapy and behavior change* (7th ed., pp. 135–189). Wiley.

Brattland, H., Koksvik, J. M., Burkeland, O., Gråwe, R. W., Klöckner, C., Linaker, O. M., Ryum, T., Wampold, B., Lara-Cabrera, M. L., & Iversen, V. C. (2018). The effects of routine outcome monitoring (ROM) on therapy outcomes in the course of an implementation process: A randomized clinical trial. *Journal of Counseling Psychology, 65*(5), 641. https://doi.org/10.1037/cou0000286

Brattland, H., Koksvik, J. M., Burkeland, O., Klöckner, C. A., Lara-Cabrera, M. L., Miller, S. D., Wampold, B., Ryum, T., & Iversen, V. C. (2019). Does the working alliance mediate the effect of routine outcome monitoring (ROM) and alliance feedback on psychotherapy outcomes? A secondary analysis from a randomized clinical trial. *Journal of Counseling Psychology, 66*(2), 234. https://doi.org/10.1037/cou0000320

de Jong, K., Conijn, J. M., Gallagher, R. A. V., Reshetnikova, A. S., Heij, M., & Lutz, M. C. (2021). Using progress feedback to improve outcomes and reduce drop-out, treatment duration, and deterioration: A multilevel meta-analysis. *Clinical Psychology Review, 85*, 102002. https://doi.org/10.1016/j.cpr.2021.102002

de Jong, K., van Sluis, P., Nugter, M. A., Heiser, W. J., & Spinhoven, P. (2012). Understanding the differential impact of outcome monitoring: Therapist variables that moderate feedback effects in a randomized clinical trial. *Psychotherapy Research, 22*(4), 464–474. https://doi.org/10.1080/10503307.2012.673023

Delgadillo, J., McMillan, D., Gilbody, S., de Jong, K., Lucock, M., Lutz, W., Rubel, J., Aguirre, E., & Ali, S. (2021). Cost-effectiveness of feedback-informed psychological treatment: Evidence from the IAPT-FIT trial. *Behaviour Research and Therapy, 142*, 103873. https://doi.org/10.1016/j.brat.2021.103873

Hannan, C., Lambert, M. J., Harmon, C., Nielsen, S. L., Smart, D. W., Shimokawa, K., & Sutton, S. W. (2004). A lab test and algorithms for identifying clients at risk for treatment failure. *Journal of Clinical Psychology, 61*(2), 155–163. https://doi.org/10.1002/jclp.20108

Herzog, P., Kube, T., & Rubel, J. (2023). Why some psychotherapists benefit from feedback on treatment progress more than others: A belief updating perspective. *Clinical Psychology: Science and Practice, 30*(4), 468. https://doi.org/10.1037/cps0000174

Jensen-Doss, A., Barber, J., But, Z., Cooper, L., DuBois, R., Gato, A. J., Orimoto, T., Scot, K., & Wright, C. V. (2024). *Professional practice guidelines on measurement-based care*. APA Professional Practice Guidelines Committee.

Lambert, M. J., Whipple, J. L., & Kleinstäuber, M. (2018). Collecting and delivering progress feedback: A meta-analysis of routine outcome monitoring. *Psychotherapy, 55*(4), 520–537. https://doi.org/10.1037/pst0000167

Lutz, W., de Jong, K., Rubel, J. A., & Delgadillo, J. (2021). Measuring, predicting, and tracking change in psychotherapy. Bergin and Garfield's handbook of psychotherapy and behavior change: 50th anniversary edition (7th ed., pp. 89–133). Wiley.

Lutz, W., Deisenhofer, A. K., Rubel, J., Bennemann, B., Giesemann, J., Poster, K., & Schwartz, B. (2022). Prospective evaluation of a clinical decision support system in psychological therapy. *Journal of Consulting and Clinical Psychology, 90*(1), 90.

Lutz, W., Rubel, J., Schiefele, A. K., Zimmermann, D., Böhnke, J. R., & Wittmann, W. W. (2015). Feedback and therapist effects in the context of treatment outcome and treatment length. *Psychotherapy Research: Journal of the Society for Psychotherapy Research, 25*(6), 647–660.

Lutz, W., Rubel, J. A., Schwartz, B., Schilling, V., & Deisenhofer, A.-K. (2019). Towards integrating personalized feedback research into clinical practice: Development of the Trier Treatment Navigator (TTN). *Behaviour Research and Therapy, 120*, 103438. https://doi.org/10.1016/j.brat.2019.103438

Lutz, W., Saunders, S. M., Leon, S. C., Martinovich, Z., Kosfelder, J., Schulte, D., Grawe, K., & Tholen, S. (2006). Empirically and clinically useful decision making in psychotherapy: Differential predictions with treatment response models. *Psychological Assessment, 18*(2), 133–141. https://doi.org/10.1037/1040-3590.18.2.133

Lutz, W., Schwartz, B., & Delgadillo, J. (2022). Measurement-based and data-informed psychological therapy. *Annual Review of Clinical Psychology, 18*, 71–98. https://doi.org/10.1146/annurev-clinpsy-071720-014821

Lutz, W., Vehlen, A., & Schwartz, B. (2024). Data-informed psychological therapy, measurement-based care, and precision mental health. *Journal of Consulting and Clinical Psychology, 92*(10), 671–673. https://doi.org/10.1037/ccp0000904

McAleavey, A. A., de Jong, K., Nissen-Lie, H. A., et al. (2024). Routine outcome monitoring and clinical feedback in psychotherapy: Recent advances and future directions. *Administration and Policy in Mental Health, 51*, 291–305. https://doi.org/10.1007/s10488-024-01351-9

Meehl, P. E. (1954). *Clinical versus statistical prediction: A theoretical analysis and a review of the evidence*. University of Minnesota Press. https://doi.org/10.1037/11281-000

Nissen-Lie, H. A., Rønnestad, M. H., Høglend, P. A., Havik, O. E., Solbakken, O. A., Stiles, T. C., & Monsen, J. T. (2017). Love yourself as a person, doubt yourself as a therapist? *Clinical Psychology & Psychotherapy, 24*(1), 48–60. https://doi.org/10.1002/cpp.1977

Rognstad, K., Engell, T., Fjermestad, K., Wentzel-Larsen, T., & Kjøbli, J. (2023). Process and Implementation Elements of Measurement Feedback Systems: A Systematic Review. *Administration and Policy in Mental Health and Mental Health Services Research, 52*(1), 74–87. https://doi.org/10.1007/s10488-023-01325-3

Rognstad, K., Wentzel-Larsen, T., Neumer, S. P., & Kjøbli, J. (2022). A Systematic Review and Meta-Analysis of Measurement Feedback Systems in Treatment for Common Mental Health Disorders. *Administration and Policy in Mental Health and Mental Health Services Research, 50*(2), 269–282. https://doi.org/10.1007/s10488-022-01236-9

Sales, C. M. D., & Cooper, M. (2023). Special section: Idiographic tools for routine outcome monitoring in psychotherapy. *Journal of Clinical Psychology, 79*(3), 593–595. https://doi.org/10.1002/jclp.23489

Sapyta, J., Riemer, M., & Bickman, L. (2005). Feedback to clinicians: Theory, research, and practice. *Journal of Clinical Psychology, 61*(2), 145–153. https://doi.org/10.1002/jclp.20107

Shimokawa, K., Lambert, M. J., & Smart, D. W. (2010). Enhancing treatment outcome of patients at risk of treatment failure: Meta-analytic and mega-analytic review of a psychotherapy quality assurance system. *Journal of Consulting and Clinical Psychology, 78*(3), 298–311. https://doi.org/10.1037/a0019247

Simon, W., Lambert, M. J., Harris, M. W., Busath, G., & Vazquez, A. (2012). Providing patient progress information and clinical support tools to therapists: Effects on patients at risk of treatment failure. *Psychotherapy Research, 22*(6), 638–647. https://doi.org/10.1080/10503307.2012.698918

Trivedi, M. H., & Daly, E. J. (2007). Measurement-based care for refractory depression: A clinical decision support model for clinical research and practice. *Drug and Alcohol Dependence, 88*, S61–S71. https://doi.org/10.1016/j.drugalcdep.2007.01.007

Walfish, S., McAlister, B., O'Donnell, P., & Lambert, M. J. (2012). An Investigation of Self-Assessment Bias in Mental Health Providers. *Psychological Reports, 110*(2), 639–644. https://doi.org/10.2466/02.07.17.PR0.110.2.639-644

Chapter 2
Feedback-Informed Psychological Therapy in Practice: The Trier Treatment Navigator (TTN)

Wolfgang Lutz, Danilo Moggia, Jana Bommer, Jana Schaffrath, Anne-Katharina Deisenhofer, Steffen T. Eberhardt, Antonia Vehlen, Brian Schwartz, and Julian A. Rubel

Introduction

This chapter discusses the conceptual background of a comprehensive feedback and treatment navigation system that can form the basis of feedback-informed psychological therapy (FIT) and clinical training in cognitive-behavior therapy (CBT). We place this system in the context of measurement-based care (MBC), data-informed psychological therapy, and practice-based evidence (PBE). Therefore, we discuss new ways to implement routine outcome monitoring (ROM) and clinical support tools into clinical practice using modern technologies and software solutions. The main aim of this feedback system and the research behind it is to establish a data-driven approach to psychological therapy that allows clinical practice to be informed by ongoing research. Simultaneously, practice-based evidence is generated, which can be used to optimize clinical practice and training. This conceptualizes the mental health service system as a learning system, in which the delivery of psychological therapies can continually evolve and improve based on patient-level data and service-level evidence (Barkham & Lambert, 2021).

This work was supported by the German Research Foundation (DFG) under project nos. 493169211 and 504507043, 525286173, LU 660/10-1, and LU 660/8-1. The authors are most thankful for the very helpful proofreading by Kaitlyn Poster (Trier University).

W. Lutz (✉) · D. Moggia · J. Bommer · J. Schaffrath · A.-K. Deisenhofer · S. T. Eberhardt · A. Vehlen · B. Schwartz
Department of Clinical Psychology and Psychotherapy, Trier University, Trier, Germany
e-mail: lutzw@uni-trier.de; schaffrath@uni-trier.de

J. A. Rubel
Department of Psychotherapy Research and Clinical Psychology, Osnabrueck University, Osnabrueck, Germany

J. A. Rubel, W. Lutz (eds.), *Feedback Informed Psychological Therapy*, CBT: Science Into Practice, https://doi.org/10.1007/978-3-031-90428-8_2

More specifically, the main aim of such a feedback and navigation system is to provide timely feedback to clinicians and enable them to use data-informed decision-making in both research and clinical practice settings. This approach allows clinical work to be continuously informed by the latest research (including information on the case currently being treated), while also generating new practice-based evidence to further advance the field of psychotherapy research: research informs practice and practice informs research.

In this chapter, we describe the implementation of these concepts into a psychotherapy research and training clinic and provide recommendations for readers interested in setting up their own research clinic or private practice using a similar framework. We present examples from the outpatient clinic at the University of Trier to illustrate the concepts and research that led to its development.

Conceptual Foundations of Feedback-Informed Psychological Therapy and Clinical Training

In psychotherapy, or more precisely, psychological therapy (including the various newer theoretical concepts and developments), implementing research findings into clinical practice is often a lengthy process. Developing an evidence-based psychological treatment requires several time-consuming steps: (1) development over several years, (2) testing, initially with case examples and subsequently with randomized controlled trials (RCTs), and (3) training new clinicians in its application. After this extensive path from research to practice, the new psychological treatment is eventually implemented into clinical practice (Lutz, Castonguay, et al., 2021). Given the lengthy development process and the challenge new clinical developments face in demonstrating significant improvements over established methods, it is not surprising that a research–practice gap has emerged within the profession (e.g., Barkham & Lambert, 2021).

To address this gap, various research approaches have been developed to directly implement research findings into clinical practice and enhance clinical care. These approaches are described in the literature using various terms, including FIT, MBC, ROM, and PBE, as well as terms such as practice-oriented research (POR), patient-focused research (PFR), treatment personalization, data-informed clinical practice, and precision mental health (e.g., Barkham et al., 2010, 2023; Castonguay et al., 2013, 2021; Lutz, 2002; Lutz, de Jong, et al., 2021; Lutz, Rubel, et al., 2022). These concepts differ regarding the use of research results and empirically based algorithms to plan and monitor treatment on the patient and health care system level. However, they all share the common goal of using data from clinical practice to enhance clinical practice.

In such a context, clinical practice data can be collected at different times during treatment and at different frequencies: (a) before and after treatment with pre-post assessments, which is easy to administer, but only captures simple changes and is prone to missing data if patients drop out early; (b) throughout treatment with repeated measures, which can inform treatment decisions based on psychometric feedback on linear and nonlinear patterns of change; (c) session-by-session assessments, whose even higher resolution allows continuous tracking of individual treatment progress, allowing the activation of clinical support tools to help therapists to adjust treatment as needed; or even (d) intensive longitudinal assessments with multiple assessments per day or high-resolution video and text analysis using artificial intelligence tools (Lutz, Schwartz, & Delgadillo, 2022).

Expected Treatment Response and Clinical Decision Tools

In recent years, researchers have used large databases and advanced digital and statistical tools, such as machine learning algorithms, to improve empirically based decision-making in clinical practice. The development of clinical decision rules to identify those cases that do not benefit from treatment and to adjust treatments for those patients in order to achieve a favorable outcome garnered particular attention within FIT research. Two approaches to the identification of not-on-track patients (NOT) have been investigated extensively: rationally and empirically derived methods.

Rationally derived methods implement previously formalized criteria to classify patient progress in order to predict potential lack of or negative treatment response. These criteria are based on clinical cutoff scores of the administered instruments or on the concepts of reliable change and clinically significant improvement (Jacobson & Truax, 1991). Studies evaluating rationally derived methods show that these clinical decision rules provide reliable treatment response identification in various clinical populations and settings (e.g., Delgadillo et al., 2014; Lutz, Lambert, et al., 2006).

In contrast, empirically derived methods rely on data-based prediction models, often called expected treatment response (ETR) models in the research literature (Howard et al., 1996). ETR models go beyond average change patterns and capture individual patterns of change. Instead of assuming that each patient will gradually improve based on an average patient's progress, researchers began to calculate individual trajectories of change. To do this, patient characteristics such as problem chronicity, prior treatments, treatment expectations, and global assessment of functioning were used as predictors to construct ETR curves in growth curve models (Lutz et al., 1999).

These predictions and corresponding measures of variance (e.g., confidence intervals) were then used to identify patients at risk of deterioration (e.g., Finch et al., 2001; Lutz, Lambert, et al., 2006). With the increasing availability of machine learning algorithms, methods such as nearest neighbors (NN) have been applied to improve predictions (Lutz et al., 2005; Lutz, Saunders, et al., 2006).

Some recent advances incorporate prediction algorithms and critical failure boundaries (where the probability of a negative treatment outcome exceeds the probability of a positive outcome) tailored to individual patients (e.g., Bone et al.,

2021; Lutz et al., 2019). This customization is based on dynamically updating failure boundaries based on progress data from evaluations of previous therapy sessions.

Monitoring patient response against an ETR alone does not provide explicit information on *how* to adjust treatment if the patient is not progressing as expected. For this purpose, clinical support tools (CSTs) have been developed to alert therapists to potential barriers to improvement and recommend interventions for patients at risk of treatment failure. (e.g., Finch et al., 2001). For example, Lutz et al. (2019) incorporate the assessment of five domains that may represent obstacles to improvement: (a) risk/suicidality; (b) motivation/therapy goals; (c) therapeutic alliance; (d) social support and critical life events; and (e) emotion regulation/self-regulation. This feedback system prompts the therapist to assess these domains when the patient's response crosses the failure boundary. An examination of archival data from more than 400 patients who were monitored using this model revealed that those who crossed the failure boundary had significantly higher scores in the areas of risk/suicidality, social support, and critical life events (Schilling et al., 2021). Various studies demonstrated the effectiveness of CSTs and their additional effect beyond feedback (De Jong et al., 2021; Lambert et al., 2018). CSTs also appear to be helpful in the context of severe psychopathology (Errázuriz & Zilcha-Mano, 2018; van Oenen et al., 2016).

Early Response, Patterns of Change, and Sudden Gains and Losses

Early response refers to a significant decrease in symptoms in the early stages of treatment. Most patients who show substantial improvement early in treatment have better outcomes at termination and follow-up than those who improve later (Beard & Delgadillo, 2019). In other words, early responders require fewer sessions to achieve steady improvement and are, therefore, more likely to terminate treatment earlier (Haas et al., 2002). Indeed, these findings have been observed in samples differing in age, diagnosis, treatment approach, intensity, and modality (e.g., Gunlicks-Stoessel & Mufson, 2011; Lutz et al., 2014, 2017; Moggia et al., 2020; Nazar et al., 2017).

Sudden gains and sudden losses represent a sudden shift in the trajectory that the patient follows over relatively short intervals during treatment, resulting in a significant improvement (sudden gains) or worsening (sudden losses) of symptoms (e.g., Lutz et al., 2013). In most cases, sudden gains tend to occur early in treatment, suggesting an association with early response. However, sudden gains also appear in later sessions, with certain therapists demonstrating a talent for facilitating and initiating such improvements (Deisenhofer et al., 2021). A meta-analysis identified sudden gains in cases of major depressive disorder, anxiety disorders, and posttraumatic stress disorder (PTSD); and across different therapeutic approaches, including cognitive-behavioral therapy (CBT), interpersonal therapy (IPT), and supportive-expressive therapy. The study showed that sudden gains were associated with good treatment outcomes (Aderka et al., 2012).

There is limited research on sudden losses, as evidenced by the low number of studies (e.g., Krüger et al., 2014; Lutz et al., 2013). Patients who experience sudden losses appear to derive less benefit from treatment than those who experience sudden gains or those who do not experience abrupt changes. In addition, sudden losses are less frequent and show no tendency to occur at a particular time during treatment, in contrast to sudden gains.

Collectively, these studies indicate the usefulness of research on early response, sudden gains and losses, and patterns of change to develop decision rules and early indicators of negative change, which can then be used to provide feedback to clinicians to improve the likelihood of better outcomes.

Therapist Effects and Patient–Therapist Matching

Therapists differ in the outcomes their patients achieve. Some therapists are significantly better than average, and some therapists are worse than average (Baldwin & Imel, 2013; Johns et al., 2019; Wampold & Owen, 2021). They differ in terms of treatment outcome (Schiefele et al., 2017), treatment length (Lutz et al., 2015), dropout rates (Zimmermann et al., 2017), and sudden gains (Deisenhofer et al., 2022). It appears that the therapist effect is influenced by both patient and therapist characteristics. On the patient side, the therapist effect is particularly evident in highly distressed patients (Saxon & Barkham, 2012). On the therapist side, greater interpersonal skills are observable in more effective therapists (Heinonen & Nissen-Lie, 2020). Furthermore, the interaction of patient and therapist characteristics seems to be important as interpersonal skills are especially relevant in highly challenging situations (Anderson et al., 2016). Delgadillo et al. (2020) showed that there are effective and less effective therapist-patient dyads and that patient demographics and clinical characteristics appeared to play a role. Therefore, the matching of patients to therapists could be an effective method of treatment allocation. Constantino et al. (2021) matched patients to therapists based on the therapists' success rate with similar previously treated patients and found that matched patients had better outcomes than those assigned in the usual way. Matching patients seems especially relevant for highly distressed patients, for complex cases, and for racial/ethnic minority patients (Boswell et al., 2022).

Therapist effects are not only evident in treatment outcomes, but also in the implementation and the effectiveness of feedback. Therapists differ in the extent to which they implement feedback, with higher levels of feedback implementation associated with shorter treatment duration (Janse et al., 2020). They also differ in the effectiveness of feedback. Therapists with an open attitude toward feedback or showing a greater perceived usefulness of feedback achieve enhanced effects with their patients (De Jong et al., 2012; Lutz et al., 2015; Lutz, Deisenhofer, et al., 2022).

Prognostic Models: Tailoring Psychological Treatments

In recent years, the concepts of personalized mental health care and precision psychological therapy have become prominent (Delgadillo & Lutz, 2023; Lutz et al., 2024). Treatment responses vary widely among individual patients, so that a patient starting an evidence-based treatment may not necessarily achieve a successful outcome, even if the initial level of efficacy is average. Although therapists have always tailored treatments to individual patients as part of their daily work, this decision-making process can vary widely, as it may be based on intuitive judgments, theoretical models, evidence from clinical guidelines, or a combination of these sources. Clinical guidelines are often based on RCTs, which often neglect the heterogeneity of treatment effects (e.g., Kaiser et al., 2022) and thus often overlook individual characteristics (beyond the diagnostic category) that may be associated with treatment effects.

As a result, over the past decade, novel approaches using new digital and statistical tools have emerged, such as the application of machine learning algorithms on large databases, attempting to provide a more precise, data-driven strategy to tailor psychological therapy (Lutz, Schwartz, & Delgadillo, 2022). These approaches rely on predictive algorithms and feedback and include a broader range of patient characteristics (e.g., Delgadillo & Lutz, 2020).

Similar to the ETR, several additional indices have been applied to perform treatment selection in recent years, including the Prognostic Index (PI; e.g., Cohen et al., 2023; Lorenzo-Luaces et al., 2017), the Leeds Risk Index (LRI; e.g., Delgadillo et al., 2016), and the Personalized Advantage Index (PAI; e.g., DeRubeis et al., 2014; Cohen et al., 2021). Several of these studies were conducted by or in collaboration with our research group and were able to show a benefit in outcome or dropout rates for patients treated with their recommended treatment approach (package/protocol; e.g., Cohen et al., 2021, 2023; Deisenhofer et al., 2018; Delgadillo et al., 2016, 2022; Lorenzo-Luaces et al., 2017; Schwartz et al., 2021), strategy (modules/processes; e.g., Gómez Penedo et al., 2023; Lutz, Deisenhofer, et al., 2022; Moggia et al., 2023; Rubel et al., 2020), setting (online vs. face-to-face; e.g., Gonzalez Salas Duhne et al., 2022), or by a therapist who was matched to them (e.g., Constantino et al., 2021; Delgadillo et al., 2020; Lutz et al., 2007).

Feedback-Informed Psychological Therapy and Precision Mental Health: An Example

In summary, several key research findings described in the previous section are particularly relevant for feedback-informed psychological therapy and the development of clinical decision tools to support clinical practice: (a) patient baseline characteristics are better predictors of patient change, outcome, and dropout than diagnostic categories alone; (b) early treatment response, patterns of change, and sudden gains and losses research can be used to develop decision rules to identify patients at risk for negative outcome early in treatment; (c) therapist differences make feedback-informed psychological therapy especially valuable in routine care settings; and (d) enhancing outcome monitoring and feedback research with clinical support tools increases their positive effects on psychological therapy outcomes.

In the following, we introduce the Trier Treatment Navigator (TTN; Lutz, Deisenhofer, et al., 2022; Lutz et al., 2019), a comprehensive feedback system that integrates pretreatment strategies recommendations, dropout risk prognosis, and a monitoring system with clinical support tools for feedback-informed clinical practice. Chapter 3 will cover a concrete case example of how the TTN is used in clinical practice, training, and supervision. More recently, two additional versions of the system have been developed to improve the system's implementation, scalability, and precision. These developments are described in Chaps. 12 and 13.

The TTN was developed by the Department of Clinical Psychology and Psychotherapy at the University of Trier and its outpatient clinic. The clinic provides psychological therapy in southwest Germany. It comprises a therapist training program, research projects, and academic activities. The clinic follows a cognitive-behavioral approach that integrates strategies and techniques from other approaches under the framework of a transtheoretical treatment and training model (4TM; Lutz et al., 2024). Additionally, therapists plan and personalize the treatment based on the clinical recommendations provided by the TTN in a case conceptualization. Our method emphasizes monitoring patients' ongoing improvements and adjusting treatment accordingly to meet their individual needs (Lutz, Schwartz, & Delgadillo, 2022). As a result, our treatments incorporate a range of therapeutic principles, mostly cognitive-behavioral, but also interpersonal, emotion-focused, motivation-oriented, alliance-focused, mindfulness-based, and strength-based interventions.

Patients attending our clinic undergo an initial clinical intake interview. They are then assessed using the Structured Clinical Interview for DSM-5 Disorders (SCID-5; Beesdo-Baum & Zaudig, 2019) and a battery of psychometric instruments. These instruments cover a wide range of factors, including psychological and physical symptoms, common mental health problems, affective style, interpersonal problems, personality disorder traits, self-efficacy, self-perception, critical life events, the impact of mental disorders on daily functioning, hope for the future, expectations of treatment, and more.

Throughout the course of treatment, we administer brief psychometric instruments at the beginning and end of each session. Patients complete symptom and general psychological distress questionnaires at the beginning of the session. At the end of the session, patients and therapists respond to questionnaires focusing on the therapeutic alliance and the transtheoretical processes present during the session.

Every five sessions, patients also complete a questionnaire assessing critical aspects of their psychosocial functioning (e.g., risk of self-harm) and engagement in therapy (e.g., motivation for change). These areas may require immediate attention and have been associated with a lack of progress or deterioration in patients (White et al., 2015).

Throughout the treatment process, therapists are strongly encouraged to keep a close eye on their patient's progress in order to adapt treatment to their patients' specific needs. To achieve this goal, our therapists use the TTN.

The TTN is a comprehensive feedback and treatment navigation system that provides the results of the initial psychometric assessment of the patient, gives personalized pretreatment recommendations, and incorporates a feedback system that monitors treatment and provides clinical support tools for cases that do not respond as expected (NOT cases). Therapists learn to use and integrate the TTN into their practice at the beginning of their training. They acquire the skills to use the information provided by the TTN for case conceptualization at the beginning of treatment and treatment adaptation based on information received over the course of therapy.

The TTN includes several algorithms that compare the new patient's initial characteristics to the clinic's database of patients who have already been treated. Through these comparisons, the system generates personalized recommendations and provides a range of clinical tools. At the beginning of treatment, the TTN presents the results of the initial psychometric assessment. Then, based on these results, the TTN yields three predictions for the new patient. First, it calculates the probability of dropout and compares it to the clinic's average dropout rate (Fig. 2.1a). Second, it suggests the optimal therapeutic strategy, indicating which one (problem-solving, motivation-oriented, or mixed) has the highest probability of therapeutic success for the new patient (Fig. 2.1b). Finally, the TTN calculates an expected treatment response curve, representing the expected outcome trajectory the patient would follow if he or she were to progress to a good outcome (Fig. 2.2c).

Based on the patient's progress (Fig. 2.2a), the TTN estimates personalized and dynamic boundaries for the patient's outcome trajectory during treatment. These boundaries enable the identification of the patient's deviation from the expected treatment response curve and therefore their risk of deterioration (NOT; Fig. 2.2b). When a patient crosses this dynamic boundary, the TTN triggers an alert, signaling that the patient is "off track" (Fig. 2.2d) and highlighting critical clinical areas that require attention. These critical areas could include issues such as suicide risk, motivation to change, therapeutic alliance, significant life events, lack of social support, and emotion regulation problems. Different clinical support tools are activated depending on the specific critical area of concern.

Clinical support tools are educational resources. They are interactive clinical guidelines, including written materials, videos, and exercises. They serve as educational tools for therapists, teaching them how to approach and address critical clinical areas that may be challenging and associated with a patient not progressing as expected. For example, when the emotion-regulation/self-regulation alert is triggered, the interactive clinical guidelines provide didactic explanations on emotion regulation, which subscale is affected (acceptance, suppression, or reappraisal of emotions), and how to work on these areas (e.g., mindfulness-based exercises for emotional awareness or exercises to train reappraisal of situations). These explanations are supplemented by examples of therapeutic dialogues, demonstration videos, and exercises for the therapist.

In summary, the TTN presents the results of the initial psychometric assessment, estimates the likelihood of patient dropout, provides recommendations for

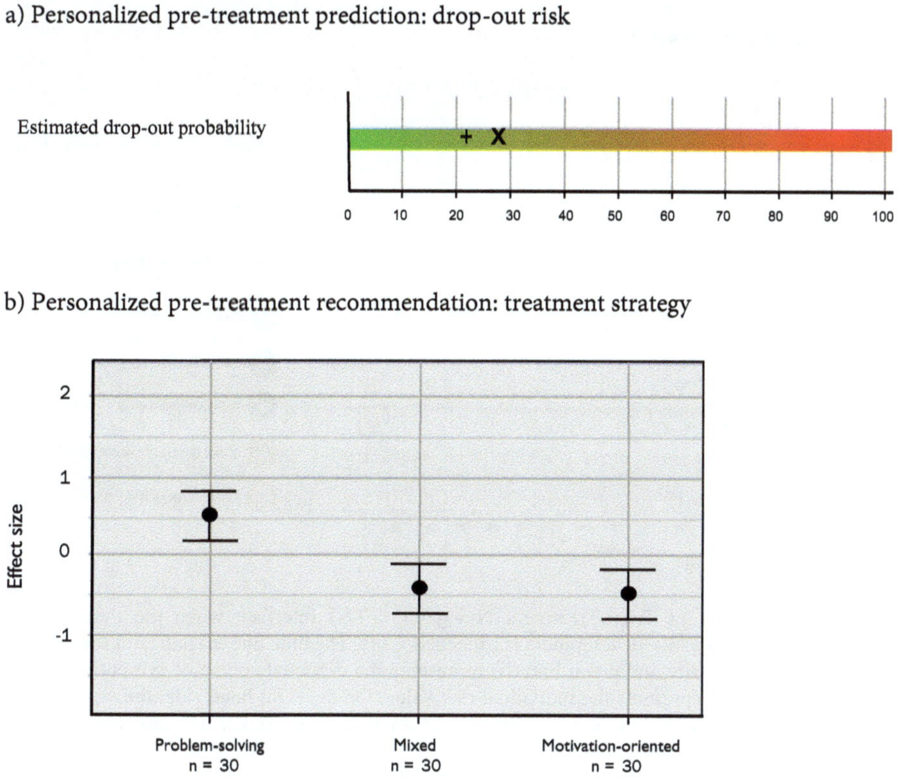

Fig. 2.1 Drop-out probability and optimal treatment strategy. *Note.* (**a**) shows the patient's drop-out risk (+ is the average dropout rate, X is the patient's dropout risk). (**b**) shows the treatment strategy recommendation for the first 10 sessions based on similar treated cases. Effect sizes are shown in Cohen's d of the particular treatment strategy. "n" indicates how many similar patients were used to calculate effect sizes in each treatment strategy

the optimal therapeutic strategy, and calculates an expected treatment response. During treatment, the TTN provides a feedback system that allows therapists to monitor their patient's progress in the context of the expected treatment response and dynamic boundaries. If the patient is not progressing as expected (crossing the dynamic boundary), the TTN assesses the risk of deterioration by evaluating critical clinical areas and provides therapists with various clinical support tools to address the issues at hand. With this information, therapists can dynamically adjust their treatment plans and effectively address factors that are impeding patient progress.

The TTN was evaluated in a prospective randomized controlled trial (RCT) in which therapists were randomly assigned to having access to the TTN or not (Lutz, Deisenhofer, et al., 2022). The prospective evaluation showed a differential effect size of about 0.3 when therapists followed the recommended treatment strategy in the first 10 sessions. Furthermore, therapists' confidence using the system and the perceived usefulness of feedback moderated the effect of feedback on outcomes.

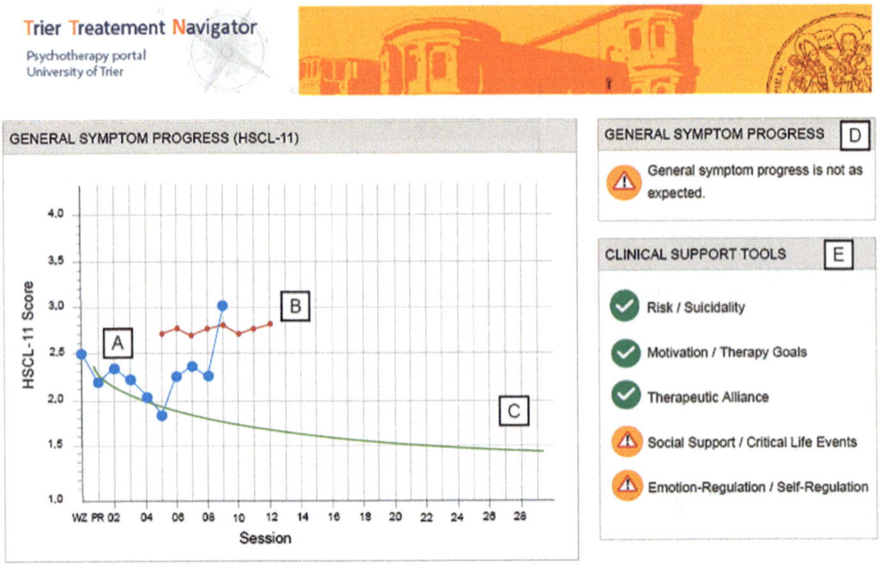

Fig. 2.2 Screenshot of Trier Treatment Navigator (TTN) Interface when the threshold for increased risk of a negative development is exceeded. *Note.* The blue line (**a**) indicates the patient's actual symptom severity, the green line (**b**) represents the expected course of symptom severity, and the red line (**c**) represents the individual risk value. On the right-hand side, the warning sign (**d**) and the domains relevant to the current problem are displayed (**e**). For this case, especially the domains "Social Support/Critical Life Events" and "Emotion-Regulation/Self-Regulation" seem to be affected. HSCL-11 = Hopkins Symptom Checklist-11; PR, pretreatment; WZ, waitlist

New Developments

Despite the successful implementation of feedback-informed psychological therapy in our clinic and training program for over 7 years, we recognize that further advancing the field of data-informed psychological therapy in CBT requires improving data assessment and analysis accuracy, as well as addressing implementation and dissemination issues. Therefore, our current research aims to refine the TTN into a practitioner version that will allow easy implementation into routine clinical care and large-scale dissemination. We aim to provide comprehensive support for therapists interested in integrating the TTN into their private practices. In contrast, an alternative development/advanced research version focuses on improving measurement and precision by testing new data assessment strategies and analysis techniques before they can be implemented into routine care.

Improving Implementation and Dissemination: Going Local and Global

The success of FIT and data-informed psychological therapy hinges on the commitment of all stakeholders, especially therapists and patients. While patients generally accept and embrace a more outcome-oriented approach, gaining clinicians' support remains challenging (e.g., Castonguay et al., 2021). Furthermore, research shows that therapists' attitudes significantly impact outcomes (Lutz, de Jong, et al., 2021). For example, in our study, therapists' perceived usefulness of feedback and therapists' positive attitudes toward feedback were significantly associated with improved effects (Lutz, Deisenhofer, et al., 2022).

Overall, FIT's implementation and dissemination face significant challenges due to human, organizational, and systemic factors. To address these obstacles, the recently published Implementing Precision Methods (IPM; Deisenhofer et al., 2023) framework provides valuable guidelines. This framework encompasses several core strategies aimed at facilitating successful implementation. These strategies include making cultural adjustments to prevent discrimination within clinical settings and identifying potential barriers early. The IPM framework also emphasizes the importance of ensuring adequate resource allocation and actively engaging clinicians in the development of computerized systems. Furthermore, it recommends implementing user-friendly systems that are easy to interpret, such as clear feedback signals. Lastly, the framework advocates for the use of short, robust, and relevant measures to garner organizational support and increase overall acceptance of PBE methods in clinical practice.

These are important steps to increase acceptance and organizational support from therapists and users, ultimately enhancing the effectiveness of FIT in clinical practice. Another very important aspect is the implementation of FIT into clinical training. It is critical for clinicians to learn a reflective professional approach to such models, integrating both clinical judgment and empirical information into their clinical identity and practice (e.g., Deisenhofer et al., 2024). Furthermore, it will be important to overcome the issue of measurement heterogeneity within and across countries. Often measures are only used in a few places, and it is hard to reach a consensus regarding the central measures.

To improve the current situation, efforts are being made to standardize data collection across institutions and broaden access to advanced algorithms like those embedded in the TTN. For example, the European Psychotherapy Consortium (EPoC), a network of European research outpatient clinics, is leading this initiative across Europe, with a parallel consortium recently established in Latin America (Gonçalves et al., 2024; Paz et al., 2025). This internationally coordinated collaboration in psychotherapy research has the potential to gather data from tens of thousands of patients annually and integrate PBE and FIT concepts, such as the TTN or similar systems, into clinical practice on a much larger scale. As Gonçalves et al. (2024) recently discussed, this approach could significantly advance the quality and scope of psychotherapy research and practice by providing a robust foundation for evidence-based treatment decisions and ongoing improvements in therapeutic care, even if it starts with a one-item measure and data exchange based on aggregated outcomes and common scales. By fostering a more standardized approach to data collection and analysis, these efforts could help create a more comprehensive understanding of therapeutic processes and outcomes, ultimately leading to more effective and personalized mental health interventions.

In another new research initiative, our research group at the University of Trier has launched a new FIT initiative to integrate the TTN into local private practices. We are collaborating with clinicians to adapt the system, ensuring it fits into and benefits their practice. This cooperative approach allows clinicians to actively participate and provide feedback on practical aspects like assessment time and desired measures, feedback graphics, and other features. In particular, clinicians with a research background are involved in the early development process, with plans to involve more colleagues after several feedback cycles. The goal is for successful early adopters to inspire their peers, creating an expanding network of scientist-practitioners using the TTN.

Improving Measurements and Precision: Machine Learning, Ecological Momentary Assessment, and Large Language Models

Prognostic models have a long history in psychological therapy, but recent advancements in machine learning (ML) algorithms have enhanced their capabilities (Delgadillo & Lutz, 2020). These algorithms can now handle complex data from advanced assessments and research designs. While the optimal ML algorithm for each situation is still being determined, initial methodological studies are examining various parameter settings for specific prediction problems (Bennemann et al., 2022; Giesemann et al., 2023; Moggia et al., 2023). Furthermore, early prospective studies have shown promise in testing the successful implementation of such models in routine care, but further validation is certainly needed (Deisenhofer et al., 2024; Delgadillo & Lutz, 2023). Recent research has further expanded beyond traditional cross-sectional data, incorporating innovative technologies like ecological momentary assessment (EMA). EMA employs methods such as self-reports and passive sensing to gather diverse datasets. Our team has begun using intensive longitudinal assessments to enhance predictive accuracy and treatment recommendations (Hehlmann et al., 2024; Husen et al., 2016; Lutz et al., 2018; Rubel, Bar-Kalifa, et al., 2018; Rubel, Fisher, et al., 2018). Video analysis of therapy sessions provides further opportunity to improve precision in measurement and feedback of clinical processes. Automated analysis of nonverbal synchrony between patient and therapist can potentially improve the assessment of social and emotional dynamics (Lutz et al., 2020; Paulick et al., 2018; Schwartz et al., 2022). Our recent studies have demonstrated the validity of these novel measures (Terhürne et al., 2022), including the use of natural language processing for sentiment analysis in therapy sessions (Eberhardt et al., 2024). These innovations have the potential to enhance our understanding of therapeutic processes and improve feedback procedures in the future (Atzil-Slonim, 2024). However, first they require further testing in real-world settings.

Discussion

FIT and precision mental health use data-informed feedback to tailor treatments to individual patients. They employ predictive algorithms, to consider individual differences, identify patients at risk for negative outcomes, and provide patient-specific supportive information to improve psychological interventions. The benefits of such low-intensity add-on interventions are improved treatment outcomes, especially for cases at risk of a negative outcome, better resource allocation, and reduced dropout rates. Of course, in the future further multicultural adaptations and testing in diverse settings are necessary to broaden the knowledge base about feedback-informed interventions. Furthermore, such systems require therapists to be skilled in the use of empirical feedback, making it essential to implement such topics into clinical training. It is crucial for therapists to learn to balance data-informed insights with clinical expertise and patient perspectives. Data-informed approaches should enhance, but not replace, clinical thinking. As the present book shows, the Trier Treatment Navigator is just one example of how the integration of data-informed feedback and personalization can be applied in clinical practice. FIT systems such as the TTN can provide empirically based guidelines and can work as supportive navigation systems when well implemented. However, they are not automated in the sense that they can provide psychological therapy autonomously. They can only be applied with the critical reflective ability of a clinically and scientifically well-trained therapist.

Finally, we believe it is a worthwhile endeavor to establish the implementation of FIT in practice-research networks, clinics, and private practices, collect information from clinical practice, and use that information to improve it. We hope that the future will see many such efforts and initiatives in different countries around the world. Such developments will help advance psychotherapy research as a field and ground psychological therapy in better science, leading to improved evidence-based training and clinical practice.

References

Aderka, I. M., Nickerson, A., Bøe, H. J., & Hofmann, S. G. (2012). Sudden gains during psychological treatments of anxiety and depression: A meta-analysis. *Journal of Consulting and Clinical Psychology, 80*(1), 93–101. https://doi.org/10.1037/a0026455

Anderson, T., McClintock, A. S., Himawan, L., Song, X., & Patterson, C. L. (2016). A prospective study of therapist facilitative interpersonal skills as a predictor of treatment outcome. *Journal of Consulting and Clinical Psychology, 84*(1), 57–66. https://doi.org/10.1037/ccp0000060

Atzil-Slonim, D., Penedo, J. M. G., & Lutz, W. (2024). Leveraging novel technologies and artificial intelligence to advance practice-oriented research. *Administration and Policy in Mental Health and Mental Health Services Research, 51*(3), 306–317. https://doi.org/10.1007/s10488-023-01309-3

Baldwin, S. A., & Imel, Z. E. (2013). Therapist effects: Findings and methods. *Bergin and Garfield's handbook of psychotherapy and behavior change* (6th ed., pp. 258–297).

Barkham, M., De Jong, K., Delgadillo, J., & Lutz, W. (2023). Routine outcome monitoring (ROM) and feedback: Research review and recommendations. *Psychotherapy Research, 33*(7), 841–855. https://doi.org/10.1080/10503307.2023.2181114

Barkham, M., Hardy, G. E., & Mellor-Clark, J. (2010). Improving practice and enhancing evidence. In M. Barkham, G. E. Hardy, & J. Mellor-Clark (Eds.), *Developing and delivering practice-based evidence* (1st ed., pp. 327–353). Wiley. https://doi.org/10.1002/9780470687994.ch13

Barkham, M., & Lambert, M. J. (2021). The efficacy and effectiveness of psychological therapies. In M. Barkham, W. Lutz, & L. G. Castonguay (Eds.), *Bergin and Garfield's handbook of psychotherapy and behavior change: 50th anniversary edition* (7th ed., pp. 135–189). John Wiley & Sons, Inc.

Beard, J. I. L., & Delgadillo, J. (2019). Early response to psychological therapy as a predictor of depression and anxiety treatment outcomes: A systematic review and meta-analysis. *Depression and Anxiety, 36*(9), 866–878. https://doi.org/10.1002/da.22931

Beesdo-Baum, K., & Zaudig, M. (2019). *SCID-5-CV Strukturiertes Klinisches Interview für DSM-5-Störungen–Klinische Version: Deutsche Bearbeitung des Structured Clinical Interview for DSM-5 Disorders–Clinician Version von Michael B. First, Janet BW Williams, Rhonda S. Karg, Robert L. Spitzer.* Hogrefe.

Bennemann, B., Schwartz, B., Giesemann, J., & Lutz, W. (2022). Predicting patients who will drop out of out-patient psychotherapy using machine learning algorithms. *The British Journal of Psychiatry, 220*(4), 192–201. https://doi.org/10.1192/bjp.2022.17

Bone, C., Delgadillo, J., & Barkham, M. (2021). A systematic review and meta-analysis of the good-enough level (GEL) literature. *Journal of Counseling Psychology, 68*(2), 219–231. https://doi.org/10.1037/cou0000521

Boswell, J. F., Constantino, M. J., & Coyne, A. E. (2022). What works in therapy when delivered by whom? *Clinical Psychology: Science and Practice, 29*(2), 137–139. https://doi.org/10.1037/cps0000072

Castonguay, L. G., Barkham, M., Lutz, W., & McAleavey, A. A. (2013). Practice-oriented research: Approaches and application. In M. J. Lambert (Ed.), *Bergin & Garfield's handbook of psychotherapy and behavior change* (6th ed., pp. 85–133). Wiley.

Castonguay, L. G., Barkham, M., Youn, S., & Page, A. C. (2021). Practice-based evidence—Findings from routine clinical settings. In M. Barkham, W. Lutz, & L. G. Castonguay (Eds.), *Bergin and Garfield's handbook of psychotherapy and behavior change* (50th Anniversary ed., pp. 191–222). Wiley.

Cohen, Z. D., Delgadillo, J., & DeRubeis, R. (2021). Personalized treatment approaches. In M. Barkham, W. Lutz, & L. G. Castonguay (Eds.), *Bergin and Garfield's handbook of psychotherapy and behavior change* (50th Anniversary ed., pp. 673–704). Wiley.

Cohen, Z. D., Barnes-Horowitz, N. M., Forbes, C. N., & Craske, M. G. (2023). Measuring the active elements of cognitive-behavioral therapies. *Behaviour Research and Therapy, 167*, 104364. https://doi.org/10.1016/j.brat.2023.104364

Constantino, M. J., Boswell, J. F., Coyne, A. E., Swales, T. P., & Kraus, D. R. (2021). Effect of matching therapists to patients vs assignment as usual on adult psychotherapy outcomes: A randomized clinical trial. *JAMA Psychiatry, 78*(9), 960. https://doi.org/10.1001/jamapsychiatry.2021.1221

De Jong, K., Conijn, J. M., Gallagher, R. A. V., Reshetnikova, A. S., Heij, M., & Lutz, M. C. (2021). Using progress feedback to improve outcomes and reduce drop-out, treatment duration, and deterioration: A multilevel meta-analysis. *Clinical Psychology Review, 85*, 102002. https://doi.org/10.1016/j.cpr.2021.102002

De Jong, K., Van Sluis, P., Nugter, M. A., Heiser, W. J., & Spinhoven, P. (2012). Understanding the differential impact of outcome monitoring: Therapist variables that moderate feedback effects in a randomized clinical trial. *Psychotherapy Research, 22*(4), 464–474. https://doi.org/10.1080/10503307.2012.673023

Deisenhofer, A.-K., Barkham, M., Beierl, E. T., Schwartz, B., Aafjes-van Doorn, K., Beevers, C. G., Berwian, I. M., Blackwell, S. E., Bockting, C. L., Brakemeier, E.-L., Brown, G., Buckman, J. E. J., Castonguay, L. G., Cusack, C. E., Dalgleish, T., De Jong, K., Delgadillo, J., DeRubeis, R. J., Driessen, E., et al. (2024). Implementing precision methods in personalizing psychological therapies: Barriers and possible ways forward. *Behaviour Research and Therapy, 172*, 104443. https://doi.org/10.1016/j.brat.2023.104443

Deisenhofer, A., Delgadillo, J., Rubel, J. A., Böhnke, J. R., Zimmermann, D., Schwartz, B., & Lutz, W. (2018). Individual treatment selection for patients with posttraumatic stress disorder. *Depression and Anxiety, 35*(6), 541–550. https://doi.org/10.1002/da.22755

Deisenhofer, A. K., Rubel, J. A., Bennemann, B., Aderka, I. M., & Lutz, W. (2021). Are some therapists better at facilitating and consolidating sudden gains than others? *Psychotherapy Research, 32*, 343. https://doi.org/10.1080/10503307.2021.1921302

Delgadillo, J., Branson, A., Kellett, S., Myles-Hooton, P., Hardy, G. E., & Shafran, R. (2020). Therapist personality traits as predictors of psychological treatment outcomes. *Psychotherapy Research, 30*(7), 857–870. https://doi.org/10.1080/10503307.2020.1731927

Delgadillo, J., & Lutz, W. (2020). A development pathway towards precision mental health care. *JAMA Psychiatry, 77*(9), 889. https://doi.org/10.1001/jamapsychiatry.2020.1048

Delgadillo, J., & Lutz, W. (2023). Precision mental health care for depression. In J. Pettit (Ed.), *APA handbook of depression*. American Psychological Association.

Delgadillo, J., McMillan, D., Lucock, M., Leach, C., Ali, S., & Gilbody, S. (2014). Early changes, attrition, and dose–response in low intensity psychological interventions. *British Journal of Clinical Psychology, 53*(1), 114–130. https://doi.org/10.1111/bjc.12031

Delgadillo, J., Moreea, O., & Lutz, W. (2016). Different people respond differently to therapy: A demonstration using patient profiling and risk stratification. *Behaviour Research and Therapy, 79*, 15–22. https://doi.org/10.1016/j.brat.2016.02.003

DeRubeis, R. J., Cohen, Z. D., Forand, N. R., Fournier, J. C., Gelfand, L. A., & Lorenzo-Luaces, L. (2014). The personalized advantage index: Translating research on prediction into individualized treatment recommendations. A demonstration. *PLoS One, 9*(1), e83875. https://doi.org/10.1371/journal.pone.0083875

Eberhardt, S. T., Schaffrath, J., Moggia, D., Schwartz, B., Jaehde, M., Rubel, J. A., Baur, T., André, E., & Lutz, W. (2024). Decoding emotions: Exploring the validity of sentiment analysis in psychotherapy. *Psychotherapy Research, 35*, 174. https://doi.org/10.1080/10503307.2024.2322522

Errázuriz, P., & Zilcha-Mano, S. (2018). In psychotherapy with severe patients discouraging news may be worse than no news: The impact of providing feedback to therapists on psychotherapy outcome, session attendance, and the alliance. *Journal of Consulting and Clinical Psychology, 86*(2), 125–139. https://doi.org/10.1037/ccp0000277

Finch, A. E., Lambert, M. J., & Schaalje, B. G. (2001). Psychotherapy quality control: The statistical generation of expected recovery curves for integration into an early warning system. *Clinical Psychology & Psychotherapy, 8*(4), 231–242. https://doi.org/10.1002/cpp.286

Giesemann, J., Delgadillo, J., Schwartz, B., Bennemann, B., & Lutz, W. (2023). Predicting dropout from psychological treatment using different machine learning algorithms, resampling methods, and sample sizes. *Psychotherapy Research, 33*(6), 683–695. https://doi.org/10.1080/10503307.2022.2161432

Gómez Penedo, J. M., Rubel, J., Meglio, M., Bornhauser, L., Krieger, T., Babl, A., Muiños, R., Roussos, A., Delgadillo, J., Flückiger, C., Berger, T., Lutz, W., & Grosse Holtforth, M. (2023). Using machine learning algorithms to predict the effects of change processes in psychotherapy: Toward process-level treatment personalization. *Psychotherapy, 60*(4), 536–547. https://doi.org/10.1037/pst0000507

Gonçalves, M. M., Lutz, W., Schwartz, B., Oliveira, J. T., Saarni, S. E., Tishby, O., Rubel, J. A., Boehnke, J. R., Montesano, A., Paiva, D., Ceridono, D., Zech, E., Willemsen, J., Saarni, S. I., Kompan Erzar, K., Janeiro, L., Gelo, O. C. G., Errázuriz, P., Holas, P., et al. (2024). Developing a European Psychotherapy Consortium (EPoC): Towards adopting a single-item self-report outcome measure across European countries. *PsychArchives, 6*, e13827. https://doi.org/10.23668/PSYCHARCHIVES.15081

Gonzalez Salas Duhne, P., Delgadillo, J., & Lutz, W. (2022). Predicting early dropout in online versus face-to-face guided self-help: A machine learning approach. *Behaviour Research and Therapy, 159*, 104200. https://doi.org/10.1016/j.brat.2022.104200

Gunlicks-Stoessel, M., & Mufson, L. (2011). Early patterns of symptom change signal remission with interpersonal psychotherapy for depressed adolescents. *Depression and Anxiety, 28*(7), 525–531. https://doi.org/10.1002/da.20849

Haas, E., Hill, R. D., Lambert, M. J., & Morrell, B. (2002). Do early responders to psychotherapy maintain treatment gains? *Journal of Clinical Psychology, 58*(9), 1157–1172. https://doi.org/10.1002/jclp.10044

Hehlmann, M. I., Siepe, B. S., Mink, F., Loray, J. S. P., Fritz, J., N. Danilo Moggia, … Lutz, W. (2024, August 27). Exploring the predictive value of different affect dynamics for psychological treatment outcome. Retrieved from https://osf.io/nhy9s/

Heinonen, E., & Nissen-Lie, H. A. (2020). The professional and personal characteristics of effective psychotherapists: A systematic review. *Psychotherapy Research, 30*(4), 417–432. https://doi.org/10.1080/10503307.2019.1620366

Howard, K. I., Moras, K., Brill, P. L., Martinovich, Z., & Lutz, W. (1996). Evaluation of psychotherapy: Efficacy, effectiveness, and patient progress. *American Psychologist, 51*(10), 1059–1064. https://doi.org/10.1037/0003-066X.51.10.1059

Husen, K., Rafaeli, E., Rubel, J. A., Bar-Kalifa, E., & Lutz, W. (2016). Daily affect dynamics predict early response in CBT: Feasibility and predictive validity of EMA for outpatient psychotherapy. *Journal of Affective Disorders, 206*, 305–314. https://doi.org/10.1016/j.jad.2016.08.025

Jacobson, N. S., & Truax, P. (1991). Clinical significance: A statistical approach to defining meaningful change in psychotherapy research. *Journal of Consulting and Clinical Psychology, 59*(1), 12–19. https://doi.org/10.1037/0022-006X.59.1.12

Janse, P. D., De Jong, K., Veerkamp, C., Van Dijk, M. K., Hutschemaekers, G. J. M., & Verbraak, M. J. P. M. (2020). The effect of feedback-informed cognitive behavioral therapy on treatment outcome: A randomized controlled trial. *Journal of Consulting and Clinical Psychology, 88*(9), 818–828. https://doi.org/10.1037/ccp0000549

Johns, R. G., Barkham, M., Kellett, S., & Saxon, D. (2019). A systematic review of therapist effects: A critical narrative update and refinement to review. *Clinical Psychology Review, 67*, 78–93. https://doi.org/10.1016/j.cpr.2018.08.004

Krüger, A., Ehring, T., Priebe, K., Dyer, A. S., Steil, R., & Bohus, M. (2014). Sudden losses and sudden gains during a DBT-PTSD treatment for posttraumatic stress disorder following childhood sexual abuse. *European Journal of Psychotraumatology, 5*(1), 24470. https://doi.org/10.3402/ejpt.v5.24470

Lambert, J. D., Greaves, C. J., Farrand, P., Price, L., Haase, A. M., & Taylor, A. H. (2018). Web-based intervention using behavioral activation and physical activity for adults with depression (the eMotion study): Pilot randomized controlled trial. *Journal of Medical Internet Research, 20*(7), e10112. https://doi.org/10.2196/10112

Lorenzo-Luaces, L., DeRubeis, R. J., Van Straten, A., & Tiemens, B. (2017). A prognostic index (PI) as a moderator of outcomes in the treatment of depression: A proof of concept combining multiple variables to inform risk-stratified stepped care models. *Journal of Affective Disorders, 213*, 78–85. https://doi.org/10.1016/j.jad.2017.02.010

Lutz, W. (2002). Patient-focused psychotherapy research and individual treatment progress as scientific groundwork for an empirically based clinical practice. *Psychotherapy Research, 12*(3), 251–272. https://doi.org/10.1080/713664389

Lutz, W., Arndt, A., Rubel, J., Berger, T., Schröder, J., Späth, C., Meyer, B., Greiner, W., Gräfe, V., Hautzinger, M., Fuhr, K., Rose, M., Nolte, S., Löwe, B., Hohagen, F., Klein, J. P., & Moritz, S. (2017). Defining and predicting patterns of early response in a web-based intervention for depression. *Journal of Medical Internet Research, 19*(6), e206. https://doi.org/10.2196/jmir.7367

Lutz, W., Castonguay, L. G., Lambert, M. J., & Barkham, M. (2021). Traditions and new beginnings: Historical and current perspectives on research in psychotherapy and behavior change. In M. Barkham, W. Lutz, & L. G. Castonguay (Eds.), *Bergin and Garfield's handbook of psychotherapy and behavior change* (7th ed., pp. 3–18). Wiley.

Lutz, W., de Jong, K., Rubel, J. A., & Delgadillo, J. (2021). Measuring, predicting, and tracking change in psychotherapy. In M. Barkham, W. Lutz, & L. G. Castonguay (Eds.), *Bergin and Garfield's handbook of psychotherapy and behavior change* (7th ed., pp. 89–134). Wiley.

Lutz, W., Deisenhofer, A.-K., Rubel, J., Bennemann, B., Giesemann, J., Poster, K., & Schwartz, B. (2022). Prospective evaluation of a clinical decision support system in psychological therapy. *Journal of Consulting and Clinical Psychology, 90*(1), 90–106. https://doi.org/10.1037/ccp0000642

Lutz, W., Ehrlich, T., Rubel, J., Hallwachs, N., Röttger, M.-A., Jorasz, C., Mocanu, S., Vocks, S., Schulte, D., & Tschitsaz-Stucki, A. (2013). The ups and downs of psychotherapy: Sudden gains and sudden losses identified with session reports. *Psychotherapy Research, 23*(1), 14–24. https://doi.org/10.1080/10503307.2012.693837

Lutz, W., Hofmann, S. G., Rubel, J., Boswell, J. F., Shear, M. K., Gorman, J. M., Woods, S. W., & Barlow, D. H. (2014). Patterns of early change and their relationship to outcome and early treatment termination in patients with panic disorder. *Journal of Consulting and Clinical Psychology, 82*(2), 287–297. https://doi.org/10.1037/a0035535

Lutz, W., Lambert, M. J., Harmon, S. C., Tschitsaz, A., Schürch, E., & Stulz, N. (2006). The probability of treatment success, failure and duration—What can be learned from empirical data to support decision making in clinical practice? *Clinical Psychology & Psychotherapy, 13*(4), 223–232. https://doi.org/10.1002/cpp.496

Lutz, W., Leach, C., Barkham, M., Lucock, M., Stiles, W. B., Evans, C., Noble, R., & Iveson, S. (2005). Predicting change for individual psychotherapy clients on the basis of their nearest neighbors. *Journal of Consulting and Clinical Psychology, 73*(5), 904–913. https://doi.org/10.1037/0022-006X.73.5.904

Lutz, W., Leon, S. C., Martinovich, Z., Lyons, J. S., & Stiles, W. B. (2007). Therapist effects in outpatient psychotherapy: A three-level growth curve approach. *Journal of Counseling Psychology, 54*(1), 32–39. https://doi.org/10.1037/0022-0167.54.1.32

Lutz, W., Martinovich, Z., & Howard, K. I. (1999). Patient profiling: An application of random coefficient regression models to depicting the response of a patient to outpatient psychotherapy. *Journal of Consulting and Clinical Psychology, 67*(4), 571–577. https://doi.org/10.1037/0022-006X.67.4.571

Lutz, W., Rubel, J., Deisenhofer, A., & Moggia, D. (2022). Continuous outcome measurement in modern data-informed psychotherapies. *World Psychiatry, 21*(2), 215–216. https://doi.org/10.1002/wps.20988

Lutz, W., Rubel, J., Schiefele, A.-K., Zimmermann, D., Böhnke, J. R., & Wittmann, W. W. (2015). Feedback and therapist effects in the context of treatment outcome and treatment length. *Psychotherapy Research, 25*(6), 647–660. https://doi.org/10.1080/10503307.2015.1053553

Lutz, W., Rubel, J. A., Schwartz, B., Schilling, V., & Deisenhofer, A.-K. (2019). Towards integrating personalized feedback research into clinical practice: Development of the Trier Treatment

Navigator (TTN). *Behaviour Research and Therapy, 120*, 103438. https://doi.org/10.1016/j.brat.2019.103438

Lutz, W., Saunders, S. M., Leon, S. C., Martinovich, Z., Kosfelder, J., Schulte, D., Grawe, K., & Tholen, S. (2006). Empirically and clinically useful decision making in psychotherapy: Differential predictions with treatment response models. *Psychological Assessment, 18*(2), 133–141. https://doi.org/10.1037/1040-3590.18.2.133

Lutz, W., Schwartz, B., Deisenhofer, A.-K., Schaffrath, J., Eberhardt, S. T., Bommer, J., Vehlen, A., Moggia, D., Poster, K., Weinmann-Lutz, B., Rubel, J. A., & Hehlmann, M. I. (2024). From theory to practice: A transtheoretical treatment and training model (4TM). *Clinical Psychology in Europe, 6*, 1–12. https://doi.org/10.32872/cpe.12421

Lutz, W., Schwartz, B., & Delgadillo, J. (2022). Measurement-based and data-informed psychological therapy. *Annual Review of Clinical Psychology, 18*(1), 71–98. https://doi.org/10.1146/annurev-clinpsy-071720-014821

Lutz, W., Schwartz, B., Hofmann, S. G., Fisher, A. J., Husen, K., & Rubel, J. A. (2018). Using network analysis for the prediction of treatment dropout in patients with mood and anxiety disorders: A methodological proof-of-concept study. *Scientific Reports, 8*(1), 7819. https://doi.org/10.1038/s41598-018-25953-0

Moggia, D., Lutz, W., Arndt, A., & Feixas, G. (2020). Patterns of change and their relationship to outcome and follow-up in group and individual psychotherapy for depression. *Journal of Consulting and Clinical Psychology, 88*(8), 757–773. https://doi.org/10.1037/ccp0000562

Moggia, D., Saxon, D., Lutz, W., Hardy, G. E., & Barkham, M. (2023). Applying precision methods to treatment selection for moderate/severe depression in person-centered experiential therapy or cognitive behavioral therapy. *Psychotherapy Research, 34*, 1–16. https://doi.org/10.1080/10503307.2023.2269297

Nazar, B. P., Gregor, L. K., Albano, G., Marchica, A., Coco, G. L., Cardi, V., & Treasure, J. (2017). Early response to treatment in eating disorders: A systematic review and a diagnostic test accuracy meta-analysis. *European Eating Disorders Review, 25*(2), 67–79. https://doi.org/10.1002/erv.2495

Paulick, J., Rubel, J. A., Deisenhofer, A. K., Schwartz, B., Thielemann, D., Altmann, U., et al. (2018). Diagnostic features of nonverbal synchrony in psychotherapy: Comparing depression and anxiety. *Cognitive Therapy and Research, 42*, 539–551.

Paz, C., Férnandez-Álvarez, J., Altimir, C., Gonçalves, M., Lutz, W., & Barkham, M. (2025). Fostering global collaboration in psychotherapy: The development of two regional consortia. *Psychotherapy Bulletin, 59*, 70–76.

Rubel, J. A., Bar-Kalifa, E., Atzil-Slonim, D., Schmidt, S., & Lutz, W. (2018). Congruence of therapeutic bond perceptions and its relation to treatment outcome: Within- and between-dyad effects. *Journal of Consulting and Clinical Psychology, 86*(4), 341–353. https://doi.org/10.1037/ccp0000280

Rubel, J. A., Fisher, A. J., Husen, K., & Lutz, W. (2018). Translating person-specific network models into personalized treatments: Development and demonstration of the dynamic assessment treatment algorithm for individual networks (DATA-IN). *Psychotherapy and Psychosomatics, 87*(4), 249–251. https://doi.org/10.1159/000487769

Rubel, J. A., Zilcha-Mano, S., Giesemann, J., Prinz, J., & Lutz, W. (2020). Predicting personalized process-outcome associations in psychotherapy using machine learning approaches—A demonstration. *Psychotherapy Research, 30*(3), 300–309. https://doi.org/10.1080/10503307.2019.1597994

Saxon, D., & Barkham, M. (2012). Patterns of therapist variability: Therapist effects and the contribution of patient severity and risk. *Journal of Consulting and Clinical Psychology, 80*(4), 535–546. https://doi.org/10.1037/a0028898

Schiefele, A.-K., Lutz, W., Barkham, M., Rubel, J., Böhnke, J., Delgadillo, J., Kopta, M., Schulte, D., Saxon, D., Nielsen, S. L., & Lambert, M. J. (2017). Reliability of therapist effects in practice-based psychotherapy research: A guide for the planning of future studies. *Administration and*

Policy in Mental Health and Mental Health Services Research, 44(5), 598–613. https://doi.org/10.1007/s10488-016-0736-3
Schilling, V. N. L. S., Zimmermann, D., Rubel, J. A., Boyle, K. S., & Lutz, W. (2021). Why do patients go off track? Examining potential influencing factors for being at risk of psychotherapy treatment failure. *Quality of Life Research, 30*(11), 3287–3298. https://doi.org/10.1007/s11136-020-02664-6
Schwartz, B., Cohen, Z. D., Rubel, J. A., Zimmermann, D., Wittmann, W. W., & Lutz, W. (2021). Personalized treatment selection in routine care: Integrating machine learning and statistical algorithms to recommend cognitive behavioral or psychodynamic therapy. *Psychotherapy Research, 31*(1), 33–51. https://doi.org/10.1080/10503307.2020.1769219
Schwartz, B., Rubel, J. A., Deisenhofer, A.-K., & Lutz, W. (2022). Movement-based patient-therapist attunement in psychological therapy and its association with early change. *Digital Health, 8*, 205520762211290. https://doi.org/10.1177/20552076221129098
Terhürne, P., Schwartz, B., Baur, T., Schiller, D., Eberhardt, S. T., André, E., & Lutz, W. (2022). Validation and application of the non-verbal behavior analyzer: An automated tool to assess non-verbal emotional expressions in psychotherapy. *Frontiers in Psychiatry, 13*, 1026015. https://doi.org/10.3389/fpsyt.2022.1026015
Van Oenen, F. J., Schipper, S., Van, R., Schoevers, R., Visch, I., Peen, J., & Dekker, J. (2016). Feedback-informed treatment in emergency psychiatry; a randomised controlled trial. *BMC Psychiatry, 16*(1), 110. https://doi.org/10.1186/s12888-016-0811-z
Wampold, B. E., & Owen, J. (2021). Therapist effects: History, methods, magnitude, and characteristics of effective therapists. In M. Barkham, W. Lutz, & L. G. Castonguay (Eds.), *Bergin and Garfield's handbook of psychotherapy and behavior change* (7th ed., pp. 297–326). John Wiley & Sons, Inc.
White, M. M., Lambert, M. J., Ogles, B. M., Mclaughlin, S. B., Bailey, R. J., & Tingey, K. M. (2015). Using the assessment for signal clients as a feedback tool for reducing treatment failure. *Psychotherapy Research, 25*(6), 724–734. https://doi.org/10.1080/10503307.2015.1009862
Zimmermann, D., Rubel, J., Page, A. C., & Lutz, W. (2017). Therapist effects on and predictors of non-consensual dropout in psychotherapy. *Clinical Psychology & Psychotherapy, 24*(2), 312–321. https://doi.org/10.1002/cpp.2022

Chapter 3
The TTN in Practice, Clinical Training, and Supervision

Miriam Hehlmann, Jana Schaffrath, Anne-Katharina Deisenhofer, Birgit Weinmann-Lutz, and Wolfgang Lutz

This chapter highlights the use of the TTN in clinical practice, clinical training, and supervision and emphasizes implementation content. Clinicians as well as experienced supervisors provide insights into their work with the TTN through a case study.

Description of the Patient and Their Problems

This clinical case example highlights the implementation of the Trier Treatment Navigator (TTN; Lutz et al., 2019) in an outpatient clinic to treat Ms. Miller,[1] a 32-year-old patient diagnosed with a moderate episode of recurrent depressive disorder and a suspected post-traumatic stress disorder (PTSD). The clinic employs a cognitive-behavioral approach, integrating techniques from various frameworks within a transtheoretical treatment model (4TM; Lutz et al., 2024). Therapists personalize care based on TTN recommendations and case conceptualization, continuously monitoring progress to adjust treatment to individual needs (see Chap. 2). This approach incorporates cognitive-behavioral, interpersonal, emotion-focused, motivation-oriented, alliance-focused, mindfulness, and strength-based

[1] This case is based on real patient experiences but has been anonymized and modified to protect the confidentiality of the individuals involved.

M. Hehlmann (✉)
Department of Psychotherapy Research and Clinical Psychology, Osnabrueck University, Osnabrueck, Germany
e-mail: miriam.hehlmann@uni-osnabrueck.de

J. Schaffrath · A.-K. Deisenhofer · B. Weinmann-Lutz · W. Lutz
Department of Clinical Psychology and Psychotherapy, Trier University, Trier, Germany

J. A. Rubel, W. Lutz (eds.), *Feedback Informed Psychological Therapy*, CBT: Science Into Practice, https://doi.org/10.1007/978-3-031-90428-8_3

interventions. This chapter will examine the benefits and challenges of the TTN system using the case example.

Ms. Miller registered for outpatient psychotherapeutic treatment at the psychotherapy outpatient clinic on her own initiative and was treated between 2019 and 2021. In the initial interview, she reports suffering from a depressive mood, a lack of drive, a reduction of energy, and a decrease in enjoyment, interest, and concentration, while her appetite increased. In addition, she complains of feeling worthlessness and guilt, low self-esteem, and sleep disturbances. Moreover, she describes latent suicidal thoughts from which she can distance herself and states that she feels no urge to act. Ms. Miller began experiencing symptoms at the age of 10, with various mild episodes lasting several weeks during adolescence. At 26, she experienced a prolonged moderate episode that lasted several months. The current episode had developed slowly, whereupon she had registered for outpatient psychotherapy in 2019. Her depressive symptoms became more severe following her partner's cancer diagnosis, and after he passed away later in 2019, she has been experiencing a deep sense of loss and overwhelming grief. Furthermore, Ms. Miller expresses feeling weighed down by memories of violent incidents that occurred during her childhood and adolescence. She was frequently physically abused by her parents and usually tries to avoid thinking about or confronting the emotions associated with those experiences.

Following the initiation of treatment, the second session involved administering the Structured Clinical Interview for Diagnostic and Statistical Manual of Mental Disorders-IV Axis I Disorders (SCID-I, Wittchen et al., 1997) to determine the patient's diagnoses. According to the International Statistical Classification of Diseases and Related Health Problems (ICD-10, Dilling & Freyberger, 2019), criteria for a moderate episode of a recurrent depressive disorder (F33.1) were met and a suspected PTSD (F43.1) was diagnosed.

Ms. Miller grew up with her parents until she was 17 years old, together with her sister, who is 2 years younger. She described her relationship with her parents as strained and lacking closeness. The mother was not very affectionate, showed depressive and narcissistic behavior, and was overwhelmed with the upbringing of her two children. Ms. Miller was subjected to regular physical abuse by her mother starting from the fourth grade. The beatings were often a consequence of her poor academic performance. In addition to this, Ms. Miller was also punished for her sister's misconduct as her mother believed it was the patient's job to monitor and control the sisters' doings. The most recent incident of physical abuse occurred when Ms. Miller was 18 years old. Although her mother was primarily responsible for the beatings, there were instances where she involved the father and encouraged him to participate in the abuse. Ms. Miller describes her father as a workaholic, disorganized, and chaotic. Her relationship with him is rather distant and lacks a personal connection as his frequent absences left her feeling as though she did not truly know him. From an early age, Ms. Miller had to take responsibility for herself and her younger sister, including tasks such as preparing meals and managing the household. This was necessary because her mother frequently stayed in bed until noon and spent afternoons lying on the couch. Ms. Miller's relationship with her sister was strained during their childhood and teenage years, although it has since improved, they only maintain sporadic contact. Initially, Ms. Miller's school years were a positive experience, but this changed due to the punishments she received for receiving poor grades. Throughout her school years and beyond, she was able to cultivate some close and supportive friendships. However, she also endured some incidents of bullying and social exclusion by her peers, which made her feel unloved. In terms of romantic relationships, Ms. Miller has been involved in three serious partnerships. Unfortunately, her first two partners were unfaithful to her. Her third partner, whom she met when she was 20 years old, passed away from cancer in 2019. Regarding her professional life, the patient expresses high levels of satisfaction as an office administrator, finding her work to be personally fulfilling due to the sense of being essential to the organization. Overall, Ms. Miller has endured a number of challenging experiences throughout her life, including episodes of violence during her childhood and teenage years, social exclusion in school, and the death of her partner. Among these, the most significant violent event happened when she was 10 years old, when her parents beat her and confined her to her room for a period of 1.5 days. Additionally, her partner's cancer diagnosis and eventual passing were highly distressing experiences for her.

Following the initial interview and diagnostic session, the TTN provided the therapist with an overview of Ms. Miller's symptom severity and the calculated risk behavior such as suicidality and dropout. The Brief Symptom Inventory (BSI, Franke, 2000) was used to assess the symptom severity, which indicated elevated a high overall score regarding physical and psychological symptoms. Furthermore, she showed severe distress scores on the subscale Depressiveness and moderate distress scores on the subscales Somatization, Obsessiveness, Insecurity, Aggressiveness, Paranoid Thinking, and Strangeness. According to the results of the Inventory for the Assessment of Interpersonal Problems (IIP-32, Horowitz et al., 2016), there were strong indications of being "too introverted/socially avoidant," "too self-confident/submissive," as well as "too exploitable/yielding" and "too caring/kind." The overall score of 1.91 suggested high total stress. The Beck Depression Inventory (BDI-II, Hautzinger et al., 2006) yielded a total score of 33, indicating severe depression. The Problem Check List for PTSD (PCL-C, Weathers et al., 1994) revealed medium distress scores in the areas of intrusions, increased arousal and high distress in the area of avoidance behavior.

Furthermore, the calculated individual risk behavior and dropout indicated that Ms. Miller was at increased risk of suicide. However, there was no risk of increased consumption of drugs. Additionally, the dropout risk was lower than the average dropout rate in the outpatient clinic (Fig. 3.1a). Ultimately, the TTN recommended a motivation-oriented treatment strategy for the first 10 sessions (Fig. 3.1b).

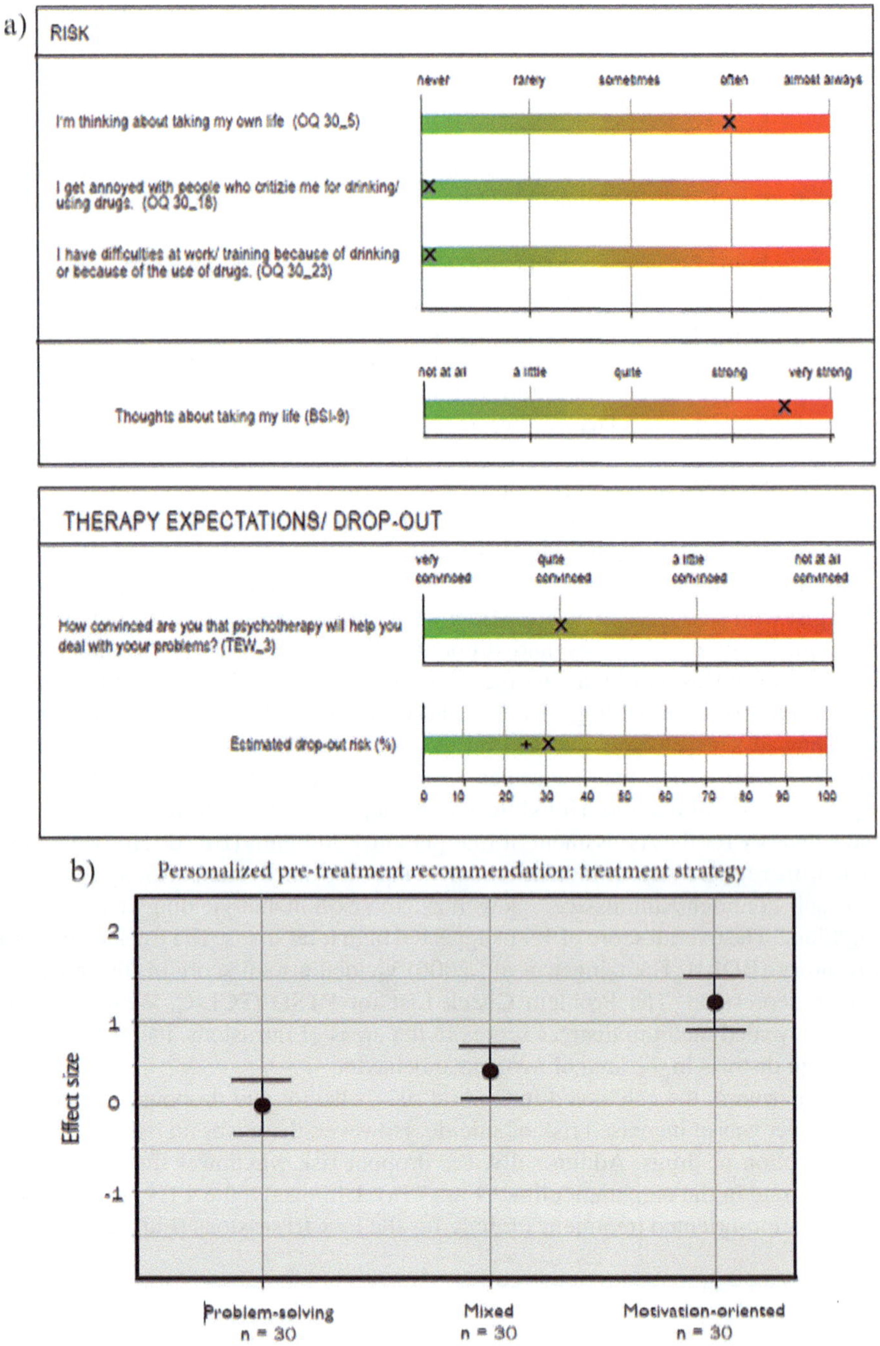
a)
RISK
never
rarely
sometimes
often
almost always
I'm thinking about taking my own life (OQ 30_5)
I get annoyed with people who critizie me for drinking/ using drugs. (OQ 30_18)
I have difficulties at work/ training because of drinking or because of the use of drugs. (OQ 30_23)
not at all
a little
quite
strong
very strong
Thoughts about taking my life (BSI-9)
THERAPY EXPECTATIONS/ DROP-OUT
very convinced
quite convinced
a little convinced
not at all convinced
How convinced are you that psychotherapy will help you deal with yoour problems? (TEW_3)
Estimated drop-out risk (%)
0 10 20 30 40 50 60 70 80 90 100
b)
Personalized pre-treatment recommendation: treatment strategy
Effect size
2
1
0
-1
Problem-solving
n = 30
Mixed
n = 30
Motivation-oriented
n = 30

Case Conceptualization

The information gathered during the indication and diagnostic phase was subsequently integrated into the case formulation. In relation to Ms. Miller's case formulation, the notion of life history is relevant and encompasses the multiple and prolonged violations of essential psychological needs (Grawe, 2004). Her parents' failure to appreciate and acknowledge her, as well as her mother's frequent belittling and her father's lack of interest, frustrated her attachment needs and hindered the development of her self-esteem. Additionally, the various instances of violence she experienced during her formative years had a detrimental impact on her need for attachment and her sense of control and security. As a result of these experiences, Ms. Miller learned to avoid drawing attention to herself, remain in the background, and prioritize her duties to prevent punishment. Therefore, the dysfunctional relational schema "*If I don't stand out, nothing will happen to me*" was reinforced. In addition, punishments for poor grades, unfinished household chores, or bad behavior by her sister contributed to the development of the basic assumption that "*I have to function to survive*" and further reinforced the idea that performance is linked to rejection or punishment. Ms. Miller's experiences with bullying at school also hindered her ability to form bonds with peers and limited opportunities for corrective experiences that could have helped to improve her self-perception and sense of self-worth. At the cognitive level, dysfunctional self-schemas ("*I am worthless*," "*I am not good enough*"), relationship schemas ("*I will be abandoned*"), plans ("*I must always function*"), automatic thoughts ("*I can't do it*"), and unfavorable, stable, and internal attributions ("*They don't have time because they don't want anything to do with me*") are relevant. Furthermore, on the competence level, Ms. Miller's social and interactive skills, such as the tendency to do everything for others, difficulty accepting or asking for help, and difficulty expressing one's own needs, as well as a lack of ability to regulate stress and reliance on dysfunctional emotion regulation strategies (e.g., eating), contribute to the development of her depressive mood. The TTN's portrayal of Ms. Miller's IIP-32 (Fig. 3.2) supports the hypotheses about her interpersonal styles. The IIP graph illustrates a clear inclination toward the submissive side of the circumplex model, leading to behaviors that are either overly dependent and exploitable or excessively avoidant of social situations.

On the activity level, her monotonous daily structure with few positive activities and reinforcing experiences, and a high degree of adaptation to others at the expense of her own desires and needs, further promote her depression. The reinforce-deficit

Fig. 3.1 Pretreatment Recommendations and Risk Factors in the TTN. *Note.* Ms. Miller's individual risk factors (suicidality, substance abuse), her treatment expectations, her dropout risk compared with the average dropout rate in the outpatient clinic (**a**), and the recommendation of treatment strategy (**b**). (**a**) + is the average dropout rate, X is Ms. Miller's dropout risk, based on different variables found to be significant predictors of dropout (e.g., education, Hopkins Symptom Checklist [HSCL] score, therapist's expectations). (**b**) Recommendation of treatment strategy for the first 10 sessions, based on similar cases. "n" indicates how many similar patients the calculation of effect size for this particular strategy is based on

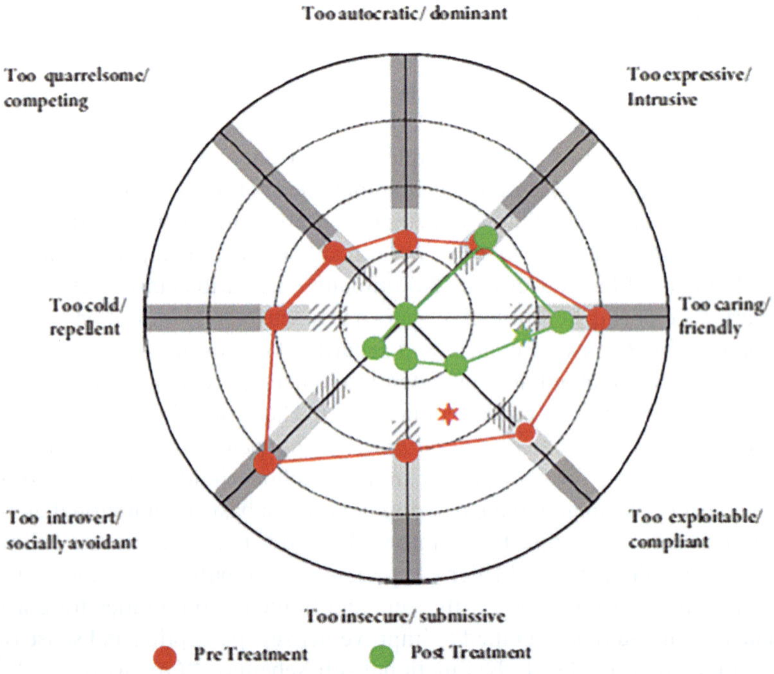

Fig. 3.2 Ms. Miller's pre- and post-treatment interpersonal styles. *Note.* Interpersonal styles were reported on the Inventory for the Assessment of Interpersonal Problems (IIP-32; Horowitz et al., 2016)

model suggests that depression can be triggered and maintained by low rates of positive reinforcement for one's behavior. In the case of Ms. Miller, she exhibits behaviors that foster her depression in two ways. On one hand, she avoids new social contacts to protect herself from exclusion, and withdraws from existing friendships, reducing opportunities for positive social reinforcement. On the other hand, she engages in few behaviors that she perceives as rewarding or meaningful, further reducing the potential for positive reinforcement. Moreover, because of avoidance and safety behaviors, she denies herself the opportunity for corrective experiences, which could challenge her dysfunctional cognitions. The triggers of her depressive symptoms can be attributed to her psychosocial stressors, including cancer and the loss of her partner, as well as the lack of positive activities and resources, and social isolation.

Based on these reflections, a treatment plan was developed, starting with the establishment of a sustainable therapeutic relationship. The focus was to cope with grief, stabilize mood, reduce withdrawal from friends, and take up activities to improve positive reinforcement. Dysfunctional thoughts and behaviors were to be identified and modified, and long-term mood stabilization was achieved through biography work and processing traumatic experiences. The goal was to promote the abandonment of negative self-concepts, strengthen confidence in her own strengths, and establish self-care activities to prevent further relapses and maintain mental health.

In response to the increased risk of suicidality, the therapist focused intensely on building a positive therapeutic alliance and carefully assessing the risk for suicidal behavior. During the therapy sessions, the therapist openly discussed the topic of suicide, aimed to promote mixed feelings about suicide, and encouraged the use of self-control strategies. These approaches were effective in reinforcing the patient's commitment to choosing life and in preparing them to handle future crises that may arise.

Treatment Course

At the beginning of treatment, the focus was on establishing a therapeutic relationship that met Ms. Miller's needs for bonding (empathy, acceptance, appreciation) and control (transparency, clear structure) based on Grawe's complementary relationship design (2004). The emphasis was on conducting structured psychodiagnostics, establishing the anamnesis, and clarifying and operationalizing therapy goals using the Goal Attainment Scaling (GAS; Kiresuk et al., 1994). A shared understanding of Ms. Miller's disorders was developed, which integrated both her biographical and current stress factors. This was done in an exemplary microanalytic manner, such as examining her increasing social isolation. The therapy goals that Ms. Miller and her therapist agreed upon were addressing her grief, regulating her emotions, and enhancing self-care/self-esteem. Furthermore, the suspected diagnosis of post-traumatic stress disorder (F43.1) was evaluated and revised. Ms. Miller described highly stressful and potentially traumatizing experiences of violence, as well as increased arousal and vigilance for potential threats. Despite this, she did not report experiencing flashbacks or nightmares about the traumatic events.

The depressed underlying mood persisted in the subsequent sessions, which was also evident in the TTN progression graph (Fig. 3.3). During supervision, strategies to help Ms. Miller overcome her affect rigidity and depressed mood were discussed. One suggestion was to use the final minutes of therapy to create positive experiences, such as through visualization exercises. In the subsequent phase of therapy, the therapist provided psychoeducation on the development of mental illness, such as the vulnerability-stress model, and explained key aspects of depressive disorders and their treatment. Ms. Miller also gained an understanding of how thoughts, emotions, physical sensations, and behaviors are interrelated, and learned how her increased appetite and eating were connected to her grieving process. With the therapist's guidance, she was able to identify the contributing factors to her depressive episode. In this context, grief work became the focus of the therapy. During this phase, Ms. Miller expressed her desire to cope with her grief, while also feeling pressure to maintain her connection to her deceased partner through her strong grief reaction.

While working through her grief, Ms. Miller's latent suicidal tendencies became apparent since she expressed a strong longing to be reunited with her partner. In line with the clinical impression, the HSCL values crossed the risk values at session

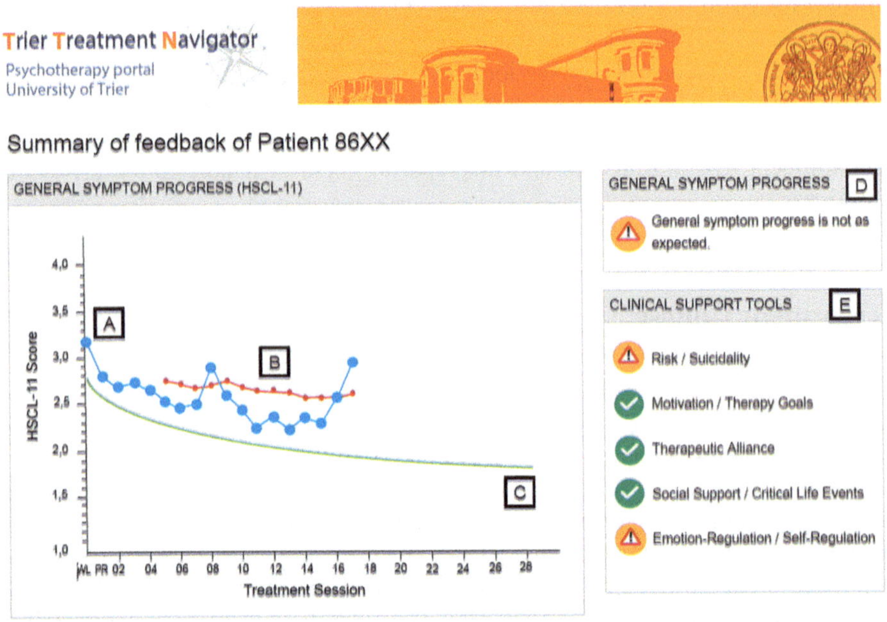

Fig. 3.3 Screenshot of the Trier Treatment Navigator (TTN) interface as Ms. Miller's therapist sees it. Note. The blue line (**a**) indicates the actual symptom severity, the green line (**b**) represents the expected course of symptom severity and the red line (**c**) represents the individual risk value. On the right-hand side, the warning sign (**d**) and the domains relevant to the current problem are displayed (**e**). For this case, especially the domains "Risk/Suicidality" and "Emotion Regulation/ Self-Regulation" seem to be affected. *HSCL* Hopkins Symptom Checklist, *PR* pretreatment, *WL* waitlist

eight calculated by the TTN indicating strong likelihood of a negative development (see Fig. 3.3). Accordingly, the TTN suggested the implementation of a clinical support tool for addressing suicidality. This tool provides the therapist with resources to effectively manage suicidal thoughts, including guidance on actions to take and whom to contact within the outpatient center in case the patient is unable to distance themselves from these thoughts and requires hospitalization. Additionally, the tool offers suggestions for exploring suicidality, as well as strategies for enhancing self-control and promoting ambivalent feelings toward suicide. The supervision session was utilized to discuss the next steps in Ms. Miller's treatment. Ms. Miller's progress was reviewed along with the proposed clinical support tools. Additionally, the supervisor encouraged the therapist to delve deeper into the conflict between Ms. Miller's desire to cope with her grief and her wish to keep her partner's memory alive. Subsequently, the therapist explored suicidality openly within the next session. Ms. Miller assured the therapist that she was not currently considering any plans of that nature. Additionally, the therapist helped her explore alternative ways of coping with her grief and maintaining her relationship with her partner. Some of the strategies they discussed included creating a memorial or writing a letter to her deceased loved one. The therapist also used Socratic dialogue to challenge Ms. Miller's negative thinking, such as the belief that she had to suffer in order to avoid disappointing her partner. This process was effective and brought Ms. Miller a sense of relief.

In the following sessions, the therapist and patient collaborated to identify and address several dysfunctional thought patterns. The therapist provided psychoeducation on common cognitive distortions, which helped Ms. Miller recognize that she frequently relied on her emotions rather than factual evidence to make decisions. As a result of this insight, she was able to identify several dysfunctional thoughts and even made connections to her upbringing and early life experiences. After reviewing her early life experiences, Ms. Miller became highly aware of the problems affecting her in subsequent therapy sessions. This newfound awareness enabled her to gain a deeper understanding of how her past experiences were impacting her current behavior. The therapist viewed this as a significant breakthrough. Despite the therapist's belief that the patient was making good progress, the TTN results suggested otherwise. It again showed a high likelihood of negative development and recommended clinical tools to assist with suicide risk and emotional regulation. To reconcile this discrepancy, the therapist showed Ms. Miller a graph of her progress and asked whether it aligned with her feelings. Ms. Miller acknowledged that she was gaining insight into her present state, but was also struggling with intense frustration related to her difficult childhood and adolescence, which continued to influence her. These intense feelings were challenging for her to handle. As a result, the therapy shifted toward a more problem-solving and resource activation approach. Ms. Miller's traumatic experiences were addressed using imaginary rescripting. At the same time, efforts were made to enhance the patient's resources, such as assisting her in creating a list of enjoyable and positive activities. They collaboratively planned her daily and weekly schedule, incorporating these activities and emphasizing self-care. This included creating a physical space for relaxation and well-being. Additionally, the therapist introduced the concept of mindfulness, which was practiced in therapy sessions. Furthermore, the focus on self-improvement was intensified during Ms. Miller's therapy sessions. As she often expressed feelings of self-deprecation, the therapist encouraged her to adopt a new perspective and introduced the concept of metacognition. Initially, Ms. Miller was guided to observe and identify her thoughts and various aspects of herself. This practice gradually became integrated into her daily routine with the aid of reminders, and a collection of prompts was created to help her challenge negative self-talk.

Using the techniques learned in therapy, Ms. Miller's symptoms gradually decreased and remained at a low level of severity for several sessions. Once the therapist and Ms. Miller confirmed that their therapy goals had been met, they agreed to gradually transition out of therapy. During the final sessions, they evaluated the progress made and documented the most significant successes. Additionally, they concentrated on developing strategies to prevent relapse by creating a folder of effective coping mechanisms. They analyzed Ms. Miller's unique early warning signs and potential crisis situations and identified suitable coping strategies to address them.

The therapy was successful, as evidenced by positive psychometric changes, clinical impressions, and the patient's self-report. The patient's distress levels decreased from very high at the start of therapy to low at the end, as indicated by the HSCL-11 scale. The therapy focused on addressing the patient's grief, dysfunctional cognitions (particularly self-deprecating thoughts), and self-regulation skills. Positive activities and self-care were incorporated into the patient's daily routine, resulting in sustained mood stabilization. Regular contact and expansion of the patient's social network contributed to an increase in quality of life. Throughout the therapy, Ms. Miller became more aware of her own needs and values in life. By the end of the therapy, she was able to critically question her own dysfunctional thoughts and make needs-oriented demands appropriately. At the end of treatment, Ms. Miller expressed great satisfaction with the therapy outcome. Her recurrent depressive disorder, currently in a moderate episode (F33.1), was considered remitted. All formulated goals in the Goal Attainment Scale were achieved according to clinical impression (Fig. 3.4).

Based on the results of the test-diagnostic assessment at the end of therapy, it was found that Ms. Miller exhibited lower levels of expressions in the IIP-32 axes of *too cold/rejective, too introverted/socially avoidant, too self-confident/submissive*, and *too exploitive/yielding*, in comparison to the beginning of therapy. The overall score showed significant improvement, decreasing from a very severe load to a low load (refer to Fig. 3.2). Furthermore, the BSI assessment showed improvement across all subscales, with particular improvement observed on the *Depressiveness* scale (PR > 80 to PR < 20) and on the *Obsessiveness, Insecurity*, and *Strangeness* scales (PR > 75 to PR < 20). In addition, the BDI-II assessment indicated a decrease in distress levels from predominantly severe at baseline to low at post-measurement (BDI-II score of 1).

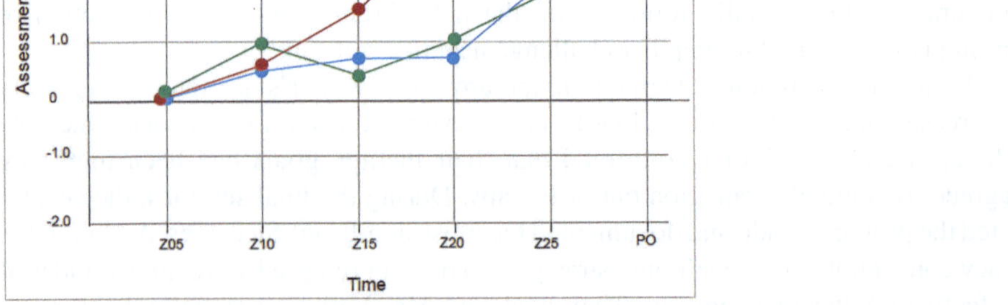

Fig. 3.4 Ms. Miller's goal attainment throughout treatment. *Note.* Ms. Miller was asked to assess the level of goal attainment for her individually formulated goals every five sessions. Z05 = session 5, Z10 = session 10, and so on. "0" indicates the state at the beginning of therapy, "−2" represents the worst imaginable state, and "4" would be that the goal was achieved

Critical Reflection

In summary, the TTN proved to be a valuable resource for the therapist in multiple aspects. Before treatment onset, the TTN highlighted Ms. Miller's suicidal ideation so that the therapist could address this topic openly and work on reinforcing Ms. Miller's commitment to choosing life and on preparing her to handle future crises that may arise. The evidence-based recommendation for a motivation-oriented strategy, as well as the representation of Ms. Miller's interpersonal style on the IIP informed the therapist's case conceptualization and treatment planning.

Throughout the course of therapy, the TTN played a pivotal role in supporting the therapist during several critical moments. In session 8, when Ms. Miller's HSCL score crossed the critical threshold, signaling increased suicidal tendencies and increased risk of worse treatment outcome, the TTN suggested the implementation of a clinical support tool. This tool assisted with suicide risk and emotional regulation and was subsequently discussed during supervision, allowing the therapist to effectively address Ms. Miller's ambivalence between coping with grief and preserving the memory of their partner. In session 18, the therapist initially perceived a breakthrough after reviewing Ms. Miller's early life experiences and understanding how these experiences influenced her current behavior and believed that the patient was making good progress. However, at the same time, the TTN revealed a high likelihood of negative development, prompting a discussion with the patient and leading to a shift toward a more problem-oriented strategy because she was experiencing overwhelmingly intense frustration related to her difficult childhood and adolescence, which continued to influence her. Without the feedback from the TTN on the HSCL and given the submissive interpersonal style of the patient, the therapist might have overlooked the worsening of symptoms in her enthusiasm about the breakthrough in therapy or only later wondered why the patient was no longer making any progress. The feedback gave her the opportunity to discuss the issue transparently with the patient and jointly decide on an adjustment to the treatment strategy in the sense of shared decision-making and increasing self-efficacy. At the end of therapy, the feedback played a crucial role in helping both Ms. Miller and the therapist reflect on the challenges encountered and the progress achieved throughout the sessions. This reflective process boosted the therapist's confidence in her ability to support Ms. Miller more effectively and address any negative developments promptly. She felt that her decisions were more grounded in evidence, and she appreciated the ability to adjust her strategy quickly thanks to the real-time feedback. Overall, the recommendations from the TTN were considered highly valuable. Additionally, Ms. Miller evaluated the feedback after therapy using a standardized questionnaire. She recognized the importance of monitoring treatment outcomes through these questionnaires and found that the feedback deepened her engagement in therapy, offering her a new perspective on her concerns.

As Ms. Miller was treated as part of a training outpatient clinic, the supervisor also had access to the feedback from the TTN. From a supervisor's perspective, a feedback system as the TTN offers several key advantages. It provides objective, data-driven insights, enabling more informed decision-making and early detection of potential issues such as stagnation or deterioration in the patient's condition. By identifying specific areas where therapists may need support, the system facilitates targeted supervision and enhances communication between therapists and supervisors. Moreover, it promotes continuous quality improvement and accountability, ensuring that therapy remains patient-centered and effective. Overall, such a system allows supervisors to offer more precise and proactive guidance, ultimately improving therapy outcomes.

Nevertheless, we have to bear in mind that there is a long tradition of feedback in the outpatient clinic where Ms. Miller was treated and that this is well embedded in the theoretical and practical training of therapists. In terms of the Contextual Feedback Intervention Theory (Sapyta et al., 2005), the context of the feedback in the outpatient clinic hence was relatively good, ensuring that the feedback here can have a positive effect on the effectiveness of the treatment. Consequently, these contextual factors can be quite diverse in clinical practice, which may pose challenges to the implementation of such precision methods in personalizing psychological therapies (Deisenhofer et al., 2024).

Despite the feedback-supportive environment in this outpatient clinic, therapists' attitudes toward feedback can vary significantly, impacting how feedback influences therapy outcomes. Research suggests that not all therapists benefit equally from receiving feedback (e.g., De Jong et al., 2012). Specific therapist characteristics, such as satisfaction with the feedback system, female gender, stronger commitment to integrating feedback, and active utilization of the feedback, have been identified as predictors of feedback engagement (De Jong et al., 2012; Lutz et al., 2015; Simon et al., 2012). However, while these factors are known to influence feedback use, what exactly makes feedback truly effective in improving therapy outcomes remains unclear. Further research is needed to gain deeper insights into how feedback works and its optimal use. One area to explore is the timing of feedback; for instance, delivering feedback to therapists at the beginning of a session may enhance its utility. Additionally, it is worth considering the potential benefits of providing patients with feedback about the therapeutic process to foster more collaborative and informed engagement (Bos et al., 2022; Von Klipstein et al., 2023).

In summary, this case study illustrates how sophisticated feedback systems like the TTN can assist psychotherapists by providing insights from patient-centered psychotherapy research, thereby enhancing therapy outcomes. Such systems offer therapists an additional source of information that can be integrated with their clinical expertise and experience. This evidence-based foundation supports the personalization of treatment—a process that therapists already undertake daily—and is particularly valuable for patients at risk of adverse outcomes. This approach not only benefits therapists but also addresses patient interests by ensuring a more tailored and informed therapeutic process.

References

Bos, F. M., Von Klipstein, L., Emerencia, A. C., Veermans, E., Verhage, T., Snippe, E., Doornbos, B., Hadders-Prins, G., Wichers, M., & Riese, H. (2022). A web-based application for personalized ecological momentary assessment in psychiatric care: User-centered development of the PETRA application. *JMIR Mental Health, 9*(8), e36430. https://doi.org/10.2196/36430

De Jong, K., van Sluis, P., Nugter, M. A., Heiser, W. J., & Spinhoven, P. (2012). Understanding the differential impact of outcome monitoring: Therapist variables that moderate feedback effects in a randomized clinical trial. *Psychotherapy Research, 22*(4), 464–474. https://doi.org/10.1080/10503307.2012.673023

Deisenhofer, A. K., Barkham, M., Beierl, E. T., Schwartz, B., Aafjes-van Doorn, K., Beevers, C. G., et al. (2024). Implementing precision methods in personalizing psychological therapies: Barriers and possible ways forward. *Behaviour Research and Therapy, 172*, 104443. https://doi.org/10.1016/j.brat.2023.104443

Dilling, H., & Freyberger, H. J. (2019). *Taschenführer zur ICD–10–Klassifikation psychischer Störungen* (9th ed.). Hogrefe.

Franke, G. (2000). *BSI: Brief symptom inventory von L.R. Derogatis (Kurzform der SCL-90-R)—Deutsche Version.* Beltz Test GmbH.

Grawe, K. (2004). *Psychological therapy*. Hogrefe Publishing.

Hautzinger, M., Keller, F., & Kühner, C. (2006). *Beck-depressions-inventar: Revision.* Harcourt Test Services.

Horowitz, L. M., Strauß, B., Thomas, A., & Kordy, H. (2016). *IIP-D - Inventar zur Erfassung interpersonaler Probleme—Deutsche Version* (3rd ed.). Hogrefe.

Kiresuk, T., Smith, A., & Cardillo, J. (1994). *Goalattainment scaling: Applications, theory, and measurement.* Erlbaum.

Lutz, W., Rubel, J., Schiefele, A.-K., Zimmermann, D., Böhnke, J. R., & Wittmann, W. W. (2015). Feedback and therapist effects in the context of treatment outcome and treatment length. *Psychotherapy Research, 25*(6), 647–660. https://doi.org/10.1080/10503307.2015.1053553

Lutz, W., Rubel, J. A., Schwartz, B., Schilling, V., & Deisenhofer, A. K. (2019). Towards integrating personalized feedback research into clinical practice: Development of the Trier Treatment Navigator (TTN). *Behaviour Research and Therapy, 120*, 103438. https://doi.org/10.1016/j.brat.2019.103438

Lutz, W., Schwartz, B., Deisenhofer, A.-K., Schaffrath, J., Eberhardt, S. T., Bommer, J., Vehlen, A., Moggia, D., Poster, K., Weinmann-Lutz, B., Rubel, J. A., & Hehlmann, M. I. (2024). From theory to practice: A transtheoretical treatment and training model (4TM). *Clinical Psychology in Europe, 6*, 1–12. https://doi.org/10.32872/cpe.12421

Sapyta, J., Riemer, M., & Bickman, L. (2005). Feedback to clinicians: Theory, research, and practice. *Journal of Clinical Psychology, 61*(2), 145–153. https://doi.org/10.1002/jclp.20107

Simon, W., Lambert, M. J., Harris, M. W., Busath, G., & Vazquez, A. (2012). Providing patient progress information and clinical support tools to therapists: Effects on patients at risk of treatment failure. *Psychotherapy Research, 22*(6), 638–647. https://doi.org/10.1080/10503307.2012.698918

Von Klipstein, L., Servaas, M. N., Schoevers, R. A., Van Der Veen, D. C., & Riese, H. (2023). Integrating personalized experience sampling in psychotherapy: A case illustration of the Therap-i module. *Heliyon, 9*(3), e14507. https://doi.org/10.1016/j.heliyon.2023.e14507

Weathers, F. W., Litz, B. T., Herman, D., Huska, J., & Keane, T. (1994). *The PTSD checklist-civilian version (PCL-C)* (p. 10). National Center for PTSD.

Wittchen, H. U., Wunderlich, U., Gruschwitz, S., & Zaudig, M. (1997). SKID. In *Strukturiertes klinisches interview für DSM IV. Achse I.* Hogrefe.

Chapter 4
Advances in Routine Outcome Monitoring and Feedback Systems: Insights from the Greifswald Psychotherapy Navigation System (GPNS)

Selin Demir, Stephan Bartholdy, Markus Tewes, Eva-Lotta Brakemeier, and Tim Kaiser

The Greifswald Psychotherapy Navigation System (GPNS) is a digital application that aims to support the work of psychotherapists and increase its effectiveness with a combination of psychometric assessments, statistical and machine learning models, as well as feedback that facilitates the adoption of evidence-based practice by supplying data-driven clinical decision-making. The system follows the basic concepts of the tradition of dose–response-based feedback systems assuming a positive correlation between session number and outcome, as presented by Howard et al. (1986), supplemented by decision rule-based clinical support tools as proposed, for example, by Harmon et al. (2005). The "Outcome Questionnaire System" was later developed and marketed based on this work and is now one of the most widely used feedback systems (Lambert et al., 2010).

The basic approach is to carry out regular (usually weekly) surveys of therapy progress in the form of symptom burden and other constructs. The time series obtained in this way are interpreted as therapy progressions and compared with databases of previously collected progressions. Statistical methods are used to select the courses of patients who are particularly similar to the target case. Deviations from the expected course of therapy are reported back to therapists and patients. A similar tool, the Trier Treatment Navigator (Lutz et al., 2019), follows the same approach but incorporates an elaborate set of support tools and uses a somewhat different statistical approach.

S. Demir · S. Bartholdy · M. Tewes · E.-L. Brakemeier (✉)
Department of Clinical Psychology and Psychotherapy, University of Greifswald, Greifswald, Germany
e-mail: selin.demir@uni-greifswald.de; eva-lotta.brakemeier@uni-greifswald.de

T. Kaiser
Department of Education and Psychology, Free University of Berlin, Berlin, Germany
e-mail: tim.kaiser@fu-berlin.de

J. A. Rubel, W. Lutz (eds.), *Feedback Informed Psychological Therapy*, CBT: Science Into Practice, https://doi.org/10.1007/978-3-031-90428-8_4

Despite these systems already available, the authors identified the need for a new development. There were three main reasons for this. Firstly, the average additional therapeutic benefit of feedback systems is now very robust and has been demonstrated in some high-quality studies (De Jong et al., 2021). Using feedback systems was found to have a small, additive effect ($d = 0.15$) on average, whereas cases at risk of treatment failure showed somewhat stronger effects ($d = 0.22$). However, it is unclear why exactly feedback systems are useful and what are the components that make them effective. Our goal was to start the development of the GPNS by establishing a basic functionality and test every new component empirically. Second, therapists' needs regarding feedback systems are diverse and can vary depending on the therapeutic approach and the service context it is used in. Adaptions should therefore be easy to implement, so we aimed for a system that is modular and rapidly adaptable. The GPNS was developed mainly using Gnu R (R Core Team, 2024), which is very widespread in the psychological sciences and related disciplines. Finally, the new development of the GPNS aimed to provide a system supervised by academically oriented psychotherapy researchers for locally working psychotherapists in private practice. This is to take place within the framework of a researcher-practitioner network, which is facilitated by the closest possible support with specially developed software developed at a local research institution (Castonguay et al., 2015; Castonguay & Muran, 2015; Rief et al., 2024).

Technical Implementation

The GPNS was designed as a modular data collection and evaluation system for the psychotherapy processes and outcomes. Similar to earlier work by one of the authors (Kaiser & Laireiter, 2017), the GPNS consists of a data collection module and an evaluation module. It was designed to be run on a Linux server.

The data collection module provides an interface to the user. Psychometric data is collected from the patient via a web-based questionnaire system and stored in a database. Currently, the Open Source survey application LimeSurvey (LimeSurvey Development Team, 2012) is used. At the outpatient clinic, tablet computers are operated to access personalized survey links (see section "Clinical Implementation" in this chapter).

The feedback module consists of a Shiny web application (Chang et al., 2024) that processes the psychometric data in such a way that it can be used clinically. This is done by generating "expected treatment response" (ETR) curves, which make it possible to compare the observed course of a given patient with the expected course of similar patients. The ETR approach generally uses data on previously assessed symptom trajectories over the course of therapy as a basis for interpreting the symptom progress of new patients. A statistical model [e.g., a generalized linear mixed model (GLMM)] incorporates this longitudinal data, as well as potentially relevant predictive and moderating variables. This model can then be applied to estimate averaged, expected symptom courses for individual patients, given their pretreatment characteristics and, usually, their symptom changes during the first few sessions of therapy (e.g., see Lutz et al., 2019).

Through regular (e.g., weekly) symptom assessments and ETR curves within ROM systems, it is possible for clinicians to interpret "predicted differences" in symptom scores throughout therapy. For a comprehensive overview over different approaches to monitor symptom changes, see Langkaas et al. (2018). As an essential part of the GPNS and other common ROM systems, these predicted differences try to answer the questions *"Does a specific case progress as expected?"* and *"What is the most likely outcome for this case?"*. Similar to other ROM systems, the GPNS also includes individual thresholds for reliable and clinically significant change (RCSI), as well as for remission (e.g., see Barkham et al., 2023; McAleavey et al., 2024).

Psychometric Instruments

The psychometric instruments used in the GPNS are divided into process and outcome scales. The chronological sequence of the survey is divided into a "pre-session questionnaire," which refers to the time that has passed since the last therapy session, followed by a "feedback screen" that summarizes the newly entered data for a quick collaborative review, and a "post-session questionnaire," which refers to the session that has just taken place. The procedure, which on average takes 3–5 min before and after session to complete, is summarized in Table 4.1.

Short Emotional Disorder Inventory

The Short Emotional Disorder Inventory (SEDI; Kaiser et al., in preparation) is used as the main outcome instrument and is part of the pre-session survey. The SEDI is a short and simplified form of the Multidimensional Emotional Disorder

Table 4.1 Summary of GPNS assessments as implemented at the University of Greifswald outpatient clinic

Time	Location	Action	Instruments
5 min before the session starts	Waiting area	Patient is handed the tablet computer by a student assistant and proceeds to fill out pre-session questionnaire	SEDI, Intersession Process Scale, both referring to the time since the last session
During the session	Therapy room	Patient takes the tablet, proceeds to therapy room	–
After the session	Therapy room or waiting area	Patient fills out the post-session questionnaire. Student assistant takes the tablet	Therapeutic alliance and insight scale

Note*: SEDI* Short Emotional Disorder Inventory

Inventory (MEDI; Bartholdy et al., 2025; Rosellini & Brown, 2019). It was developed with the goal of obtaining a short, clinically broad scale that can still be scored to represent a single underlying construct. This way, the items have some relevance for all patients and their general symptom severity can be mapped on one score. Another important criterion was the sensitivity to change in long-term measurements, in which therapists can quickly and reliably distinguish random fluctuations in the measured values from clinically significant changes.

To achieve this, a three-step item reduction approach based on Item Response Theory (IRT) models was used. A diverse sample of treatment-seeking adults ($N = 1713$) from the outpatient clinic of the University of Greifswald was available to perform the analyses. First, a "Mokken scale" of 28 items was obtained using a genetic algorithm (Straat et al., 2013). This unidimensional scale consists of hierarchically ordered items that measure the same underlying, latent construct. Next, items with similar item information curves were eliminated. The resulting scale has 15 items. The original nine-point Likert format of the MEDI was reduced to a four-point format by merging two points of the nine-point scale. The GPNS scores the SEDI from an IRT model and rescales the scores to the original scale range (1–4).

A multilevel generalizability analysis (Shrout & Lane, 2012) performed to assess the reliability of within-person change of the SEDI showed promising results. The reliability of change was estimated as $Rc = 0.77$. This value indicates that, under the assumption that patients answer all questionnaires at fixed time points (i.e., before every therapy session), 77% of the variation of change in SEDI values represents true within-person change of symptom severity over time. As determined from a latent variable model for ordinal indicators, the SEDI had a Cronbach alpha of 0.89, and a McDonald's Omega of $\omega = 0.88$.

To maximize the clinical utility of the SEDI, we determined anchor-based cut-off values. These cut-offs represent clinically significant improvement, clinically significant deterioration, and recovery. During the surveys in the pilot phase, a "Global Rating of Change" (GROC; Kamper et al., 2009) scale was included in addition to the SEDI. On this 11-point scale, patients were asked to indicate how they would describe themselves in relation to their mental health problems compared to before therapy. The scale ranged from "extremely worsened" to "fully recovered," but for the anchoring it was simplified into "improved," "unchanged," and "deteriorated." We linked SEDI percentage change scores to the GROC scale in a receiver operating characteristic (ROC) analysis to obtain cut-off values for self-rated "improvement" and "deterioration." We found that a reduction of 12.5% compared to the baseline value can be considered "improvement" and a 12.5% increase a "deterioration."

We have defined "remission" as a state in which the patient's mental health problems no longer interfere significantly with everyday behavior. The three core domains of everyday behavior were determined as work, interpersonal relationships, and the general range of motion. If a patient reported no impairment in at least one of these domains and only little impairment in the two others after therapy, this was classified as "remission." The optimal cut-off value for the SEDI associated with this state was 1.52. Based on these threshold values, auxiliary lines are drawn in the feedback graphic, making it easy to see whether the respective status has been reached.

Process Scales

The authors are convinced that the regular assessment of therapy processes is an important addition to the monitoring of symptoms. Research on process–outcome associations is diverse and has been conducted on many different features of the therapeutic process. During the development phase, we had to make a selection to ensure economic assessments with maximum clinical utility. The scales used in the GPNS were developed from a data set of process questionnaire assessments (Kaiser, 2014). Similar to the SEDI, we used a Mokken scale search procedure and subsequent pairwise item elimination to extract short, unidimensional scales. The two scales resulting from this process relate to well-known correlates of psychotherapy outcomes. They were named "alliance" and "insight/understanding."

Therapeutic Relationship Given the very strong evidence of an association of the therapeutic alliance with the outcome (e.g., Flückiger et al., 2018) and, more importantly, of deterioration of the alliance preceding symptom deterioration (e.g., Flückiger et al., 2020), it seems important to conduct regular assessments of this process. Our goal was to obtain a scale that focuses on the interpersonal aspects of the alliance, such as the feeling of appreciation and support that the client receives from their therapist. The resulting scale is, conceptually, closer to the "real relationship" (Gelso, 2002) than to the "working alliance" (Bordin, 1979). It is asking patients to describe the quality of the therapeutic relationship, including the feeling of being understood and valued, as well as the perception of the therapist's support and openness. The scale had acceptable within-person reliability (Rc = 0.67), good between-person reliability (McDonald's omega = 0.90) and internal consistency (Cronbach alpha = 0.88). We attribute the relatively low within-person reliability to reduced within-person variance due to ceiling effects. The distribution of alliance scores was heavily skewed (skewness = −1.17).

Insight/Understanding Another important aspect at the process level is the extent of subjectively experienced insight. This term refers to the patient's understanding of the conditions that cause and maintain their psychological problems. As Jennissen et al. (2018) demonstrated, insight is another strong correlate of therapeutic outcome with effects on par with the therapeutic alliance. The effect is robust across different theoretical orientations, although it appears to be somewhat larger in psychodynamic therapies.

The content of the items was kept such that they do not presuppose a theoretical model of change. Generally, they refer to various aspects of insight, understanding, and self-awareness that a client might achieve through psychotherapy. The items cover recognizing and understanding one's problems, experiencing self-efficacy in previously challenging situations, recognizing areas for personal growth, understanding reactions to others, and comprehending the underlying reasons for one's behavior.

The insight scale demonstrates very good reliability on the between-person level (McDonald's omega = 0.92), good within-person reliability (Rc = 0.79), and very good internal consistency (Cronbach's alpha = 0.92).

Intersession Processes Based on the fundamental assumption that psychotherapy should also have an effect outside the therapy sessions and should thus be reflected in the patient's everyday behavior, a short scale was developed for therapy-related activity between sessions. In contrast to the other two process scales, this scale is part of the pre-session assessment and relates to the time since the last session.

Theoretically, this part of the assessment is based on the concept of intersession processes (ISP; Gablonski et al., 2023; Hartmann et al., 2011; Stewart & Schröder, 2015) and therapy representations (Orlinsky et al., 1993). As a working hypothesis, it was proposed that recurring interactional sequences, behaviors, and other in-session experiences are the building blocks of mental models of their psychotherapy. In general, ISP include thoughts, feelings, and behaviors that concern one's own psychotherapy or the therapist and take place between sessions. ISP can be of varying sensory quality and involve visual, auditory, and tactile sensations (Knox et al., 1999). They are more likely to occur when patients are in distress (Kaiser & Laireiter, 2018) and certain constellations were shown to be predictive of therapeutic outcomes (Hartmann et al., 2010, 2016). The Intersession Short Scale used in the GPNS was designed as a behavioral, economic scale for the core aspects of ISP: intensity of ISP (how frequently and vividly therapy content is remembered), instrumental recall (successfully applying therapy content to solve problems or enhance subjective well-being), and therapy-related emotional experiences. Feedback on this scale is currently given on the item level. An evidence-based feedback module is currently in development, based on Bayesian Networks of the intersession processes in relation to the therapeutic outcome (Demir et al., in prep.).

Clinical Support Tools

Expected Treatment Response Curves

The GPNS uses "expected treatment response" (ETR) curves to compare individual patients' symptom progression to that of similar cases. In this way, feedback can be provided on the extent to which a patient deviates from the expected course of treatment. The procedure consists of two steps. First, a multilevel model was calculated in which the SEDI values are predicted from the logarithm of the number of sessions. Random effects were included so that the intercept and the regression coefficient may vary between individuals. To obtain an ETR curve, patients' observed SEDI scores are compared with a continuously growing database of completed cases.[1] The 30 most similar cases based on the Euclidean distance are selected. For these cases, intercept and slope coefficients are taken from the multilevel model. The predictions based on these coefficients are then averaged, so that an ETR curve based on similar cases is obtained. As depicted in Fig. 4.1, the ETR curve is a solid, gray line. It is plotted with a 90% confidence interval (Fig. 4.1: 3) that serves as an individual not-on-track limit. The system issues a warning if the current SEDI value exceeds this boundary. It indicates that the patient is currently not on track to making significant changes in therapy. This statistically determined "not-on-track" (NOT) status was shown to be predictive of therapy outcomes using similar methodologies (Hannan et al., 2005). Additionally, NOT cases are those who profit most when outcome monitoring and feedback systems are used (De Jong et al., 2021). In addition to the individual boundary, group-based statistics on clinically meaningful improvement (Fig. 4.1: 5), deterioration (Fig. 4.1: 4), as well as remission (Fig. 4.1: 6) are included. These are based on the aforementioned SEDI cut-off values.

In the near future, the nearest neighbor search will be supplemented by further variables that are predictive of the therapy outcome. Also, it is important to note that logarithmic ETR curves are theoretically grounded in the phase model of therapeutic change, which states that there are three sequential phases in a patient's change process, each focusing on different problem dimensions and causing symptom reduction at different rates (Howard et al., 1986). Although there is evidence supporting this theoretical model (Stulz & Lutz, 2007), there are competing models that

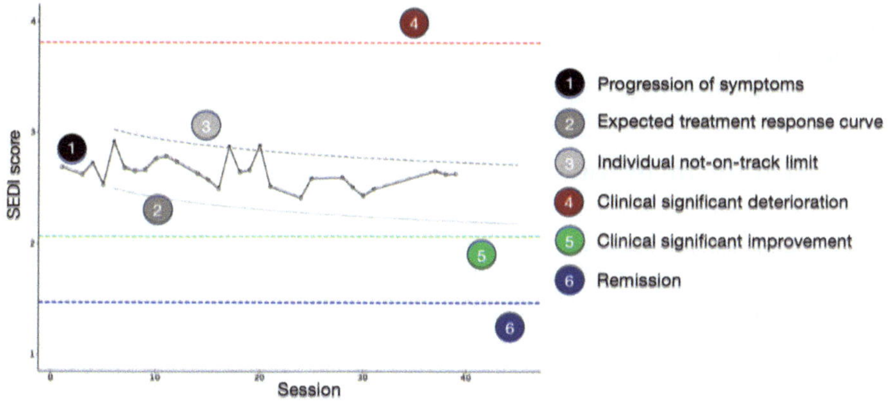

Fig. 4.1 Expected treatment response (ETR) curve with interpretation aids. *Note.* SEDI: Short Emotional Disorder Inventory

---

[1]The first 200 cases in this database were obtained from a publicly available data set constructed from cases who have used the Trier Treatment Navigator (https://github.com/Psykli/Trier_Treatment_Navigator). It is continuously updated with completed cases.

➢ Symptoms	Not on track	The patient deviates from the expected treatment response.
➢ Therapeutic Relationship	Good	The patient reports an appropriate quality of the therapeutic relationship.
➢ Insight / understanding	Good	The patient reports an adequate understanding of the conditions that cause and maintain their problems.

Fig. 4.2 Example for the GPNS pre-session feedback table

explain the curvilinear data patterns through statistical artifacts created by aggregating data (Baldwin et al., 2009). Thus, other alternatives to logarithmic ETR curves that do not assume a specific course of symptom reduction over time are currently tested.

Pre-Session Feedback

Before the start of each therapy session, a feedback screen is displayed on the tablet that patients use to answer the questionnaires. It contains the key information from the most recent measurements in a very concise format. This includes the current ETR curve, as well as a color-coded table showing the OT/NOT status, and whether the alliance and insight/understanding scales were rated below average. The screen is intended to be viewed and discussed collaboratively by the patient and therapist, although it is up to the therapist whether this is actually done. An example is given in Fig. 4.2, which shows the pre-session feedback of a NOT patient who still scores average on the process scales.

Clinical Implementation

Several studies have shown significant differences in how effectively individual therapists are utilizing ROM and feedback systems (De Jong, 2012; Herzog et al., 2023; McAleavey et al., 2024). Therefore, it appears crucial to focus on adequate clinical training and support when introducing these systems to new treatment centers. Furthermore, evidence suggests that therapists increase their use of ROM systems in psychotherapy after receiving proper training (Brattland et al., 2018; Lewis et al., 2019) and that the therapist-rated usefulness of feedback is a significant moderator of feedback outcome associations (Lutz et al., 2022). Thus, investing sufficient resources into implementation strategies is of high importance. These strategies can be divided into three categories: (1) creating the structural requirements for implementing ROM systems into routine care, (2) providing sufficient clinical training for the therapists, and (3) monitoring the adaptation of the system. Overall, it appeared helpful for the effective implementation of our GPNS to focus on improving the communication between researchers, therapists, and patients, as well as maintaining a continuous focus on the feasibility and clinical use of the system.

Structural Requirements

For the implementation of a ROM system at a new treatment center, it is recommended to assign an implementation team with a designated leader and a preplanned implementation strategy. The team should allocate sufficient resources for the coordination, clinical training, communication, maintenance, technical support (if the monitoring system functions digitally), and lastly, conducting the measurements.

In our case, we opted for more efficient digital measurements via tablets, which also allows therapists to view a quick feedback screen before each session. These tablets are prepared and handed out by our student staff to ensure that the correct patient pseudonym and session number are put into the system. Patients complete the measurements while they are in the waiting area before and after each session, which takes an approximate amount of 3 min. During the session, clinicians can view the feedback that already includes the current measurement and choose whether they want to discuss the content of the feedback in the session. Afterward, patients return the tablet to the student staff.

The main advantage of using student staff is that a high number of patients (in our case, around 60–90 per week) can be monitored without placing an additional burden on our clinicians, therefore enabling seamless integration into routine care and decreasing the risk of missing data. Additionally, technical and other support from our student staff is available at all times for the clinicians that improves the processes in our routine care immensely. As staff has to be present around the working hours at our treatment center (from 8 AM until 5 PM), the students are organized in shifts of around 4 h per week at the same time each week, according to their time preferences each semester. Here, it is important to note that the preparation of the tablets only takes around 10–15 min of each hour, leaving enough time for other supporting tasks at our treatment center regarding several research projects and clinical processes in our routine care. All of our student staff are closely coordinated and supported by the first author, Selin Demir.

Clinical Training

When conducting formal training for clinicians, several goals need to be addressed simultaneously: providing sufficient information on the psychometric instruments and their relevance for psychotherapeutic treatments, facilitating skills to understand feedback, utilizing the data for clinical decision-making making, and discussing the information with the patient in a constructive way, as well as addressing further attitudinal and competency-related barriers. Additionally, an established contact person should be available, and an environment of psychological safety should be maintained to allow clinicians to voice any concerns they might have.

During the implementation phase, at our treatment center in Greifswald, two of our authors, Tim Kaiser and Selin Demir, were available at all times for any questions and feedback the clinicians might have. They conducted training sessions regularly and provided easy-access material that included (1) training videos explaining the theoretical background, instruments, and interface of the system; (2) a GPNS wiki summarizing this information, the updated routine processes at our treatment center, and FAQs; and (3) helpful documents such as guidelines for discussing feedback. In the beginning, training sessions were provided monthly with a focus on navigating the ROM systems, utilizing feedback in therapy and supervision and answering to all questions and concerns the clinicians had. Later on, training sessions were provided every 6 months to 1 year, and clinicians were able to request help from our staff and/or a personal, short training at any time.

During the initial training sessions, it became apparent that simply providing clinicians with these clinical support tools was insufficient without first addressing attitude-related barriers and demonstrating how ROM systems can improve psychotherapies. This was necessary as some clinicians can be dismissive of these systems due to the (unfortunately incorrect) belief that clinical judgment is the most accurate one (De Jong et al., 2023). Following these beliefs, the repeated measurements first seemed like a burden on the patient to some of the therapists at our treatment center. Here, it appeared helpful to further explain the rationale and summarize the current evidence in favor of ROM systems regarding the robust, additive effect on the reduction of symptoms and dropout rates (Barkham et al., 2023; McAleavey et al., 2024) as well as illustrate case examples on how ROM systems are enabling data-driven personalization and fostering a transparent, collaborative therapeutic alliance (i.e., Demir et al., 2022). Ideally, this information is delivered by not only the researchers and developers involved with ROM systems, but also scientist-practitioners, who can integrate both perspectives and therefore narrow the research–practice gap.

As our treatment center is also providing therapist training, a large part of the treatments is being conducted under regular supervision that takes place at least every fourth session. Due to the important role that the supervisors play in our treatments, it was a central concern of ours to motivate them also to use the GPNS and include it as a further source of information in the work with our therapists in training. It has been shown that the inclusion of client feedback in supervision can increase the satisfaction of supervisees and help to decide which patient should be discussed (Grossl et al., 2014). Furthermore, our supervisors were informed about the general benefits of incorporating feedback into therapy and received a detailed introduction to the use of the GPNS, as well as recommendations and handout materials for implementing the GPNS into their supervision. We recommend focusing on specific aspects and items of the GPNS during supervision in addition to the regular assessment of the symptom progression. "Not-on-track" patients in particular should be discussed and possibilities for data-supported personalization and adaptation should be determined together with the supervisees. "On-track"-patients can in turn be used to emphasize the supervisees' effective approach and therapeutic successes. If a lack of response to therapy is possibly attributed to skill deficits on the part of the supervisee, these skills should be practiced regularly in supervision following the deliberate practice approach (Rousmaniere et al., 2017). Finally, our supervisors are reminded that the GPNS should only be used as one possible source of information and not as the sole criterion for treatment progression. Overall, the possibility of incorporating the GPNS into supervision was favorably received by our supervisors and is used to varying degrees depending on the personal style of supervision.

By involving all parties in the implementation process and constructively addressing reservations about our system, we were able to create an environment of participative research that led to a higher acceptance and compliance, as well as an improved, updated version of our GPNS, which is described in the following.

Monitoring and Enhancing the Adaption of the System

After the successful implementation of the GPNS, the main focus of our team were further developments and updates to improve the clinical utilization of the system, provide technical maintenance, and ensure a high compliance and quality of data. One of the earliest updates to our system was inspired by our therapists, who mentioned that they often forgot or lacked the time to look into their feedback in between sessions and requested a more efficient way to use the system. In response, we implemented a feedback screen that appeared directly before each session on the tablet, which significantly increased the usage of the GPNS due to its immediate availability.

Furthermore, we provided more information, learning resources and specific courses on monitoring and feedback in general for university students and psychotherapists in training in Greifswald. These materials and courses offered further insight into the purpose of feedback and the structured use of ROM systems in psychotherapy. As a result, the newer cohorts of clinicians were more open and accepting of the GPNS and able to utilize the feedback more effectively with their patients.

Additionally, we have continuously monitored the quality of data since the initial stages of the implementation and identified common risks for missing or unclear data, as sometimes sessions were canceled last minute, patients forgot to fill out the instruments after the session or students mixed up a pseudonym or session number. To counter these risk factors, we created a corrective filter to the system that also provided the students with the last six session numbers to avoid any confusion. Moreover, clear reminders for therapists and patients were included in the system itself as well as every therapy room. With these reminders and the help of student staff, the compliance and data quality improved greatly.

It should be also noted that the GPNS, like all digital applications in the healthcare sector, involves a certain amount of maintenance. Although this has so far been minimal in day-to-day operation, further developments require expertise in statistical programming, database management, and server administration. The most feasible way to operate a digital feedback system is therefore likely to remain the connection via user accounts to an instance that is managed by a cooperating university.

After a successful technical and clinical implementation, the use of a monitoring and feedback system such as the GPNS can enhance several different aspects of the therapeutic process, as illustrated in the following case example at our treatment center.

Clinical Use of the GPNS: A Case Example

Meet Julie

Julie*, a 43-year-old mother of a daughter and a son, working as a technical assistant, has struggled with persistent depressive disorder and social anxiety since her childhood. When she contacted our university's outpatient clinic, her depression had reached a further low point: she had been on sick leave for half a year, only leaving the house when she had to, and her mood was consistently irritated, anxious, or dysphoric. Adding onto that, she had trouble sleeping and her low levels of energy made it difficult to complete basic household tasks. All of her responsibilities regarding her family, the farm she and her husband purchased together, and her work had become too much to handle, especially considering her adverse childhood experiences. Like many patients with persistent depressive disorder (Brakemeier et al., 2018), Julie had experienced severe childhood maltreatment in the form of physical and emotional abuse as well as emotional neglect, causing her to fall into spirals of negative self-talk and retreat socially, avoiding any real connection to other people.

As a child, Julie grew up in a strict household with her parents and a 4-year older sister on her father's farm, where she was expected to help out substantially with all the various (and often tedious) tasks around the farm. It was not uncommon for her to receive physical abuse from her parents, which she interpreted as justified at that time. While growing up, more often than not, Julie felt rejected, misunderstood, and criticized by both her mother and her older sister. Her relationship with her father however was characterized by ambivalence: on the one hand, Julie felt most understood by him out of all her family members, and she idealized him and his work ethic. On the other hand, her father developed severe alcohol abuse issues over time that had often affected her negatively since she was 12 years old. To protect herself from further harm, Julie began to develop a deep distrust toward others, often reacting distant or impulsively to "push others away before they can hurt me." This coping mechanism further intensified when Julie endured severe bullying during her years in middle and high school and, as a result, became more socially anxious with an intense fear of rejection. When she was 17, her father died of suicide during an alcoholic episode, causing her to spiral into a major depressive episode with recurring thoughts of suicide. A part of her blamed her mother and the recurring conflicts between her parents in an attempt to deal with her grief, but deep down she already knew that no one could be blamed for such a tragedy.

The following 4 years she suffered from a major depressive episode, often considering suicide as well after losing the one person in her family who truly understood her. During that time, she managed to finish her education and also completed her training as a tailor, but was instead offered a job in a different field of expertise as a technical assistant. At the end of these 4 years, she met her now husband and considers him and the way he loved her the sole reason she survived after losing her father. Together, they built the home she had always dreamt of: with an (almost) self-sustainable farm and a variety of animals. However, even though Julie was able to fulfill this dream, her childhood experiences had left her with a chronic feeling of helplessness regarding her own life, low self-esteem and a difficulty to connect. She also felt trapped at her current job, but her fear of rejection kept her from applying to any alternatives in her actual field of expertise. The thought of "who would even want me?" was all-pervasive in her personal and professional life, causing Julie to feel afraid of any change. Her feelings of hopelessness intensified even further after the birth of her second child. While caring for her firstborn had been manageable to her thus far, her state worsened significantly with the increased workload of two children at home and she became increasingly isolated and exhausted.

One way Julie tried to deal with these chronic feelings of helplessness was a need to control her environment regarding cleanliness, order, and punctuality. If other people failed to meet these expectations, she reacted with anger and frustration. Soon, the mental load of caring for her family, the farm, and her job on top of maintaining a perfect home overwhelmed her, resulting in another major depressive episode. Her irritation and hostility started to cause conflicts not only at home, but also at her workplace, leading her to avoid work and take sick leave for several months. Although she remained pessimistic about the possibility of getting better, Julie at last decided to seek psychological help and contacted the center for psychological therapy in Greifswald, where she was diagnosed with persistent depressive disorder and social anxiety disorder and started her treatment with modern cognitive-behavioral therapy (CBT) as well as the cognitive-behavioral system of psychotherapy (CBASP).

Case Conceptualization

At the start of her first sessions with her therapist, it became evident how Julie struggled to express her emotions and needs constructively: She was either keeping them to herself or acting distant and provocative toward the people around her. Like many patients with persistent depressive disorder, Julie was stuck in a cycle of learned helplessness and an inability to reflect on the impact of her actions on her environment, resulting in a re-enactment of her childhood memories of rejection and distance. This in turn intensified her depressive episode and her coping mechanisms of controlling her environment, which was further emphasized by her psychometric data at the start of her treatment: Julie's BDI-II score (Beck's Depression Inventory; Beck et al., 1996) reached 43, indicating a severe case of depression. She also scored highly on the Multidimensional Inventory of Emotional Disorders (MEDI; Rosellini & Brown, 2019) with a moderate value on depressive mood as well as a severe value on neurotic temperament. In Fig. 4.3, the results of the Brief Symptom Inventory (BSI; Franke, 2000) are presented*.

Together, Julie and her therapist reflected on these cycles with a behavioral analysis and identified potential points of change together, resulting in three main treatment goals: (1) enable Julie to have healing, corrective relationship experiences regarding her maladaptive beliefs; (2) foster interpersonal skills such as considering the perspectives of other people or constructively voicing her needs; and (3) expand her flexibility in behavior by reducing social avoidance and rigid behavior patterns while increasing her acceptance as well as value-oriented behavior. To achieve these goals, several well-established methods and techniques of cognitive-behavioral therapy, such as exposure techniques, parts of the Acceptance and Commitment Therapy (ACT), and integrative psychotherapy methods such as the

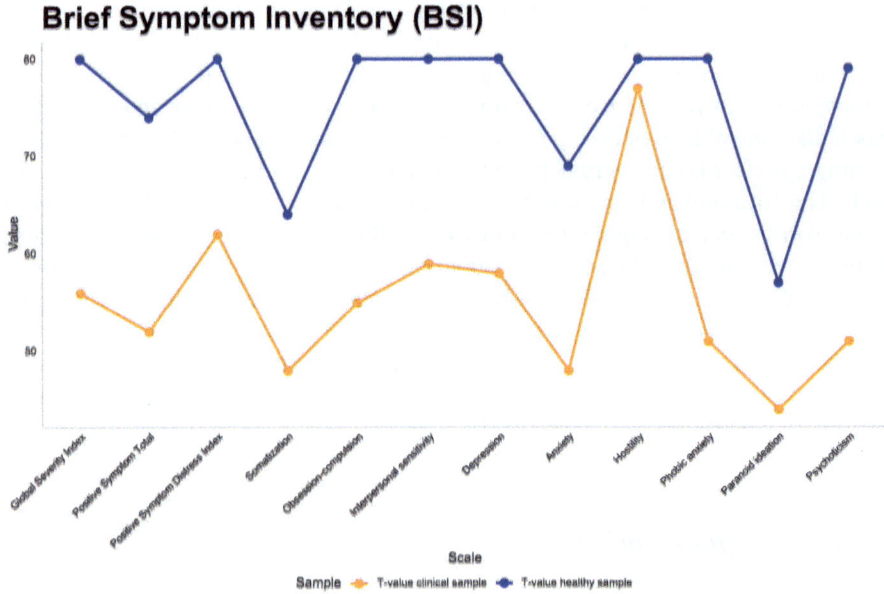

Fig. 4.3 Brief Symptom Inventory (BSI) score of the patient Julie. *Notes.* T-values for a clinical sample (orange) and T-values for a healthy sample (blue) are shown. T-scores that exceed 80 are set to the value of 80 (Derogatis, 1982)

Cognitive-Behavioral Analysis System of Psychotherapy (CBASP) were included in the treatment plan. Furthermore, starting with her first session, the GPNS was used to enhance the therapeutic outcome and allow for a data-driven personalization during the ongoing treatment.

Treating Julie with the Support of the GPNS

In light of Julie's treatment goals and her primary diagnosis of persistent depressive disorder (PDD), the first sessions were focused on the CBASP as CBASP is the only method specifically developed for chronic cases of depression (McCullough, 2000). After introducing the explanatory model of CBASP, the "interpersonal wall," her therapist administered the Significant Other History, an interpersonal-emotional history procedure to identify the "stamps" of Julie's childhood experiences and develop a transference hypothesis (McCullough et al., 2011). The main goal of this procedure is to increase the awareness of Julie's (maladaptive) interpersonal expectations and enable healing, corrective relationship experiences within the therapeutic dyad, which can then in turn be generalized to her other relationships. In these early stages of therapy, creating a warm, safe, and empathic environment is key to building trust after her negative childhood experiences. Therefore, the GPNS feedback regarding the therapeutic alliance was of special importance to Julie's therapist. Overall, Julie's rating of the therapeutic alliance remained "good" according to the GPNS, with her answering "often" on items such as "my therapist and I understood one another," "I felt valued by my therapist," and "I felt supported and backed up by my therapist" during the first six sessions. By session 7, her trust in her therapist grew, and Julie started to report "always" to these items, indicating an established alliance, which in turn reassured her therapist and also served as a confirmation of her clinical judgment. When they discussed the feedback together, Julie reported that she was able to dissolve her "interpersonal wall" with her therapist, although opening up to other people remained challenging.

Additionally, the feedback system did not only help in monitoring the therapeutic alliance—Julie's therapist noticed that the underlying message of implementing feedback and discussing it was helpful in itself to strengthen their bond, which Julie confirmed: to her, the feedback discussions had demonstrated that her therapist was willing to adapt to Julie, that her thoughts and feelings were valued in the therapeutic relationship and how she cared about her progress. This posed a stark contrast to Julie's learning history and her interpersonal beliefs, which they summarized as "other people will either criticize, hurt or leave me, so I will not let them get close to me." At this point during her first six sessions of treatment, Julie started connecting more to her therapist, but remained skeptical and pessimistic about whether or not true change was possible.

Here, the visualization of her progression of symptoms had proven especially useful in discussing her achievements, building upon them during the ongoing treatment and making collaborative, clinical decisions with statistical aid, for example,

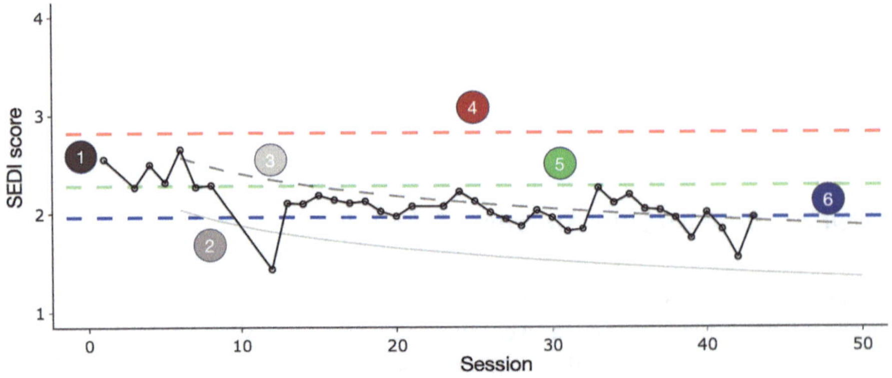

Fig. 4.4 GPNS feedback screen of the patient Julie. *Notes.* (1) Julie's SEDI score with (2) the expected treatment response curve, (3) the individual not-on-track limit, (4) clinically significant deterioration, (5) clinically significant improvement, and (6) remission

regarding the frequency of their sessions or when to change the focus from CBASP to treating her social anxiety later during treatment. In Fig. 4.4, Julie's SEDI score is shown with her boundaries for clinically significant improvement (green), deterioration (red), and remission (blue), as well as her individual expected treatment response curve (gray) and individual "Not-on-track"- boundary (gray, dotted line). As her treatment is still ongoing (as of August 8, 2024) and currently in the phase of relapse prevention, the measurements of 43 sessions are shown here.

As illustrated in Fig. 4.4, her first six sessions did not lead to a significant change in symptoms yet. This was to be expected, as CBASP patients first revisit their adverse childhood memories during the Significant Other History, oftentimes leading to stagnation or even slight deterioration of their symptoms before they can begin their healing process (Herzog et al., 2021; McCullough, 2000). Afterward, the tools of the Situational Analysis, the Interpersonal Discrimination Exercise, the Disciplined Personal Involvement and the Kiesler Circle are applied to improve their interpersonal skills and enable corrective, healing relationship experiences (McCullough, 2000).

In Julie's case, she reported feeling seen and validated by her therapist when talking about her biography and the impact her experiences had on her. However, the first hurdles appeared when her therapist encouraged her to try out new thought patterns and behavior in therapy to solve the current problems she faced. More often than not, Julie would opt out, saying that she "does not see the point" and she "does not believe that this would work" when they discussed reducing her mental and actual workload and new interpersonal strategies. This was also reflected on the GPNS scale that tracked insight: although no warning was present, a look at the single items revealed that Julie failed to understand the point of some of these interventions, causing her therapist to invest more time in psychoeducation and repeating some of the explanatory models to increase Julie's insight and motivation.

Furthermore, while recognizing that change can be scary and validating her doubts, her therapist also gently reminded Julie of the fact that at least a part of her already appeared to believe in some sort of change, otherwise she would not have started therapy in the first place. Additionally, by using the CBASP-specific technique of the Disciplined Personal Involvement, the therapist was able to show how these suggestions were not meant as criticism and instead support.

After questioning some of the mental barriers that Julie faced through Socratic dialogue, Julie came up with the idea to attempt taking each Friday off and focus on self-care to be more emotionally balanced. In therapy, they worked on difficult interpersonal situations occurring at work and at home, often using the Situational Analysis, Kiesler Circle, role-plays, and the Interpersonal Discrimination Exercise. The main goals were to foster skills such as flexibility in interpersonal behavior, considering the perspectives of others, and communicating her wishes cooperatively. Finally, Julie started to break out of her cycle of learned helplessness, and soon enough, after applying the techniques she learned, a significant change in symptoms was visible on the GPNS screen by session 11.

The resolution of some of her conflicts served as a great motivator for Julie to continue her active work in therapy. This effect further increased when she could also see her improvement clearly visualized on the GPNS curve and acknowledged by her therapist. Afterward, a slight increase on the insight scale was noticeable—while it was always rated as "good" overall, looking into the single items revealed how Julie started to understand the cause of her problems more and reported an increased awareness of a way to solve them than before.

Here, the monitoring system functioned more as an "amplifier" instead of its alerting function by enabling Julie and her therapist to track her progress and increase already helpful therapeutic processes. With the support of the GPNS, they continued to work on Julie's interpersonal skills and while starting to increase her acceptance and value-based actions by applying techniques derived from the Acceptance and Commitment Therapy. At this stage in her treatment, they discussed the feedback every three to five sessions to reflect on the ongoing treatment, their goals, and the intention behind the psychotherapeutic interventions. By session 20, Julie reported feeling happier and having increased energy. As her symptoms with the most intense burden had therefore now improved, Julie's focus in therapy shifted to her social anxiety and her negative self-talk that was related to her social fears. With her newfound confidence that change was indeed possible, she asked her therapist to focus the interventions on her social fears. As they were both used to a collaborative process of clinical decision-making due to the regular feedback discussions, Julie had felt safe enough in the therapeutic relationship to voice these wishes directly. Her therapist in turn was happy to comply and reinforced Julie's trust by using the Disciplined Personal Involvement and Interpersonal Discrimination Exercise, highlighting that she gladly supported Julie's wishes and needs. Together, after satisfactory cognitive preparation and an explanation of the rationale, they planned several sessions of exposure therapy for her social anxiety.

In these exposure sessions, Julie learned to confront her fear of meeting new people and was able to correct her negative expectations as to how other people will perceive her. Contrary to her belief, people were neither criticizing her, nor paying attention to any of the characteristics she was insecure about. Instead, she was able to engage in pleasant conversations and received warm and accepting responses. In this phase of her treatment, Julie's therapist paid special attention to the intersession progress scale, as it indicated how Julie fared in social situations outside of therapy and whether or not she was able to recall helpful in-session processes during her everyday life. Here, the previous work regarding Julie's motivation paid off: in between their sessions, she frequently tried to apply the newly learnt skills and reported being satisfied with the results. When her therapist brought these promising results up to further encourage her, Julie mentioned how she had been able to generalize the helpful experiences to her everyday life and use more positive self-talk when meeting unfamiliar people.

All these changes started to become more and more visible around sessions 29 and 30: Julie's mood and energy level had improved significantly, she felt more relaxed in several social situations and her relationships at home as well as at work (while still not free of conflict) seemed more harmonious than before. Eventually, Julie reached a point of improvement where she wanted to try out reducing the frequency of their sessions to every 2–3 weeks. For the final decision, Julie and her therapist took her wishes, the therapist's clinical impression, as well as the feedback data into account as recommended for evidence-based practice. Since Julie's progress had been close to the line of remission in the GPNS for several sessions (25–32), her therapist agreed to try out the new frequency and see how it would affect her progress.

Unfortunately, due to a combination of Julie falling physically ill and her therapist's vacation soon afterward, their next session took place 4 weeks later instead of 2. In the span of these 4 weeks, Julie had experienced a deterioration and went "off-track" according to the GPNS. While her symptoms were still considered to be clinically significantly improved at session 33 compared to the start of her treatment, this new development surprised her therapist. When discussing the feedback screen, Julie opened up about the cause of her minor setback: at her work, the pressure and workload had increased immensely and Julie found herself slipping into old habits, neglecting her self-care, lashing out at colleagues, and engaging in negative thought processes. Together, they figured out that although Julie had previously improved, she had not built up the resilience to remain stable during stressful episodes yet. Therefore, her therapist proposed a change of plan, focusing on building psychological and interpersonal flexibility and creating an intervention plan for early warning signals of depressive episodes. Furthermore, both agreed to change the frequency of their sessions to at least every other week, if not weekly. In this instance, the GPNS not only helped in signaling that a change of the treatment intensity was warranted, but also visualized the correct context of her progression of symptoms. For Julie, it was a relief to see that her current state was not as big of a setback as she feared since she could still be considered as "improved" compared to the start of her treatment. This reinforced her trust in her ability to "get back on track," validated the efforts she had already made in therapy, and motivated her for the upcoming sessions.

Here they focused on exercises and techniques from the Acceptance and Commitment Therapy (ACT; Hayes, 1999) to increase psychological flexibility, cognitive defusion, and value-oriented behavior. Soon enough at session 38, Julie was "back on track" and reported increased calmness as well as the ability to take action and shape her life in a way that was meaningful to her. During this time, she mustered up the courage to apply for a different job that would be a better fit for her. Up until then, beliefs such as "no one would want to hire me anyway" had stopped her, but with the techniques of cognitive defusion, she learned to take action despite these thoughts. Her courage paid off almost immediately: Julie received two job offers in a short amount of time, one of which was promising to be much calmer and less stressful than her current one. Finally, she began changing her life in significant ways,and in turn, became more hopeful regarding the rest of her life. At the start of her treatment, Julie would have never imagined that these changes were possible. While her treatment is still ongoing, together they had again reached a point of improvement that was considered a remission on the feedback screen at session 39, and this time, the trend appeared much more stable. As of right now, the goal of Julie's treatment can be summarized as amplifying these successes by revisiting and changing her "stamps," increasing her well-being, and providing relapse prevention. At this point, the GPNS might have already fulfilled its functions in (1) alerting the therapists about important therapeutic processes, (2) tracking Julie's change, (3) aiding both of them in strengthening their therapeutic alliance, and (4) enabling data-driven, adaptive clinical decisions. Nevertheless, they plan on continuing their treatment with the support of the GPNS until a stable remission is achieved, which will then determine the point of time at which the treatment can be terminated in good conscience.

Discussion of Feedback in Psychotherapy: Chances and Limitations

As illustrated in this case report, the GPNS can assist the therapeutic process at several points by enabling data-driven clinical decision-making and promoting a collaborative process and therefore improved alliance. Still, it is important to highlight potential barriers as well as the chances of using ROM systems in therapy. For this reason, further insights are drawn from a recent qualitative study focusing on therapist-patient dyads (Demir, Wrase, Brakemeier & Kaiser; in prep.) as an addition to this case. In this study, several advantages of the GPNS were found, which were also relevant in this particular clinical case: patients as well as therapists agreed that the joint discussion of therapy progress via the feedback screen at the beginning of the session appears to be particularly helpful. The therapeutic dyad can compare the measured therapy progress with their own subjective impression and reflect on the course of the therapy, as was the case between Julie and her therapist. Here, it can often be clarified whether deterioration or lack of progress can actually be attributed to the therapy or to factors outside the therapy. This clinical approach to the causal attribution of symptom changes is essential as long as no estimate of what the current symptom state at the present time without psychotherapy would be (Langkaas et al., 2018). This way, patients also learn to make connections between their psychological stress and events inside and outside therapy. Some patients reported that they felt motivated by the regular assessment of their progress because they got a clearer picture of the progress they have already made. This was reported by Julie as well, and especially important during her small deterioration at session 33: while she felt as if she had failed, the feedback screen helped her in realizing that she was still significantly improved compared to the beginning of her treatment.

Regarding the monitoring of the therapeutic relationship, therapists in the qualitative study noticed that dissatisfaction with the relationship seemed easier for patients to report. By evaluating the interaction with the therapist, patients would also be able to better reflect on their own communication behavior in the sessions and thus question the authenticity of their appearance. Subjective reports of improvements in the therapeutic bond were reported, as patients had the impression that the weekly surveys were taken seriously instead of only serving the internal quality assurance procedures. While reporting dissatisfaction had not been of importance for Julie, she and her therapist also noticed an improved bond as the discussion of feedback demonstrated how her therapist cared about her views and needs.

The intersession activity items were perceived as a way to supplement the symptom-focused SEDI questionnaire with information about the internalization of the therapeutic process. This was especially important in the case of Julie when her exposure sessions for social anxiety had begun as the application of the therapeutic content in between sessions was highly relevant to the success of her treatment. Some authors from the psychodynamic tradition have recognized the value of this additional information on intersession activity, which is often represented as a kind of bridge between of within-session processes and therapy outcome (Freedman et al., 2011). However, the GPNS is the first feedback system explicitly asking for intersession activity employed in a cognitive-behavioral therapy context.

Finally, the feedback process was perceived as supporting self-awareness and self-reflection by both therapists and patients. Therapists use the assessments as a way to critically examine their clinical expression and reconcile both perspectives. While Julie did not directly report an improved self-awareness as well, her therapist did notice how especially the insight scale helped her realize that further psychoeducation was needed at the beginning of their treatment to motivate Julie. At this point, it should be mentioned that the surveys are by no means regarded as a benchmark to which the clinical impression should be adjusted. There can often be a mismatch between these sources of information because the psychometric surveys do not fully reflect what takes place at the process level. Nevertheless, the surveys should always be included as they include information that goes beyond the clinical impression, which is always available anyway.

While we believe that the feedback system and approach is promising and clinically useful, some limitations need to be acknowledged. Despite the many positive aspects of the GPNS described above, not all of them are perceived equally by all patients and therapists. For example, it was critically noted that patients were sometimes not sufficiently informed about the rationale of the GPNS, or that at least a certain familiarization period was necessary to understand the mode of operation and the benefits. Particularly at the beginning of therapy, no progress can be interpreted due to the limited data basis, which is why the usefulness of the system only becomes apparent in the course of therapy. A lack of knowledge regarding the benefits of the GPNS in the context of therapy as well as hindering application aspects could lead to patients completing the pre- and post-treatment questionnaires in a stereotypical and unmotivated manner. In addition, response tendencies occur when patients fill out the questionnaire under the aspect of social desirability in order to please the therapist or to signal an improved symptom course. It therefore seems particularly important that therapists are trained to explain the GPNS well and discuss it regularly with patients in order to maximize the positive effects, which we have continued to work on in the ongoing implementation process. This was also shown in Julie's case: since she was treated by the first author of this chapter, she received a detailed introduction to the monitoring system and its benefits, which could be why she they were able to use the system effectively. Another important point to consider is that there is only limited time in each therapy session and discussing the current feedback takes away time from the treatment itself. We therefore usually recommend only discussing the feedback together in a session if the patient is currently NOT or any other warnings occurred, or every 5–8 sessions to amplify successes in treatment, and to otherwise use the time to directly work on the therapeutic tasks. Finally, a specific limitation of the currently implemented clinical feedback is the low psychometric sensitivity of the scale used to assess the quality of the therapeutic relationship, resulting in warnings in only 1.5% of the sessions. Therefore, this part of the information included in the feedback table is not useful in most sessions. The assumed reason for this problem are ceiling effects within the scale. Our goal and a work in progress regarding this problem is to develop more sensitive and differentiated feedback on the therapeutic alliance, with a focus on rupture and repair episodes. Considering all these advantages and limitations, the use of the GPNS appears to enhance ongoing psychotherapeutic treatments as long as enough knowledge of the system can be achieved for therapists and patients alike. Recent advances, especially regarding the sensitivity and details of the process scales and the provided clinical support tools, could further increase these effects and allow for an optimized, data-driven personalization of psychotherapy.

References

Baldwin, S. A., Berkeljon, A., Atkins, D. C., Olsen, J. A., & Nielsen, S. L. (2009). Rates of change in naturalistic psychotherapy: Contrasting dose–effect and good-enough level models of change. *Journal of Consulting and Clinical Psychology, 77*(2), 203. https://doi.org/10.1037/a0015235

Barkham, M., De Jong, K., Delgadillo, J., & Lutz, W. (2023). Routine outcome monitoring (ROM) and feedback: Research review and recommendations. *Psychotherapy Research, 33*(7), 841–855. https://doi.org/10.1080/10503307.2023.2181114

Bartholdy, S., Zimmer, R.I., Hermann, A., Stark, R., Brakemeier, E.-L., & Kaiser, T. (2025). Validation of the factor structure and psychometric and clinical properties of the Multidimensional Emotional Disorder Inventory (MEDI) - German Version. Preprint available at https://osf.io/j4xdc/ (in press).

Beck, A. T., Steer, R. A., & Brown, G. (1996). Beck depression inventory–II (BDI-II) [database record]. *APA PsycTests*. https://doi.org/10.1037/t00742-000

Bordin, E. S. (1979). The generalizability of the psychoanalytic concept of the working alliance. *Psychotherapy: Theory, Research & Practice, 16*(3), 252.

Brakemeier, E.-L., Dobias, J., Hertel, J., Bohus, M., Limberger, M. F., Schramm, E., Radtke, M., Frank, P., Padberg, F., Sabass, L., Jobst, A., Jacob, G. A., Struck, N., Zimmermann, J., & Normann, C. (2018). Childhood maltreatment in women with borderline personality disorder, chronic depression, and episodic depression, and in healthy controls. *Psychotherapy and Psychosomatics, 87*(1), 49–51. https://doi.org/10.1159/000484481

Brattland, H., Koksvik, J. M., Burkeland, O., Gråwe, R. W., Klöckner, C., Linaker, O. M., Ryum, T., Wampold, B., Lara-Cabrera, M. L., & Iversen, V. C. (2018). The effects of routine outcome monitoring (ROM) on therapy outcomes in the course of an implementation process: A randomized clinical trial. *Journal of Counseling Psychology, 65*(5), 641–652. https://doi.org/10.1037/cou0000286

Castonguay, L. G., & Muran, J. C. (2015). Fostering collaboration between researchers and clinicians through building practice-oriented research: An introduction. *Psychotherapy Research, 25*(1), 1–5. https://doi.org/10.1080/10503307.2014.966348

Castonguay, L. G., Youn, S. J., Xiao, H., Muran, J. C., & Barber, J. P. (2015). Building clinicians-researchers partnerships: Lessons from diverse natural settings and practice-oriented initiatives. *Psychotherapy Research, 25*(1), 166–184. https://doi.org/10.1080/10503307.2014.973923

Chang, W., Cheng, J., Allaire, J. J., Sievert, C., Schloerke, B., Xie, Y., Allen, J., McPherson, J., Dipert, A., & Borges, B. (2024). shiny: Web application framework for R. R package version 1.8.1.1. https://CRAN.R-project.org/package=shiny

De Jong, K. (2012). *A chance for change: Building an outcome monitoring feedback system for outpatient mental health care*. Leiden University.

De Jong, K., Conijn, J. M., Gallagher, R. A. V., Reshetnikova, A. S., Heij, M., & Lutz, M. C. (2021). Using progress feedback to improve outcomes and reduce drop-out, treatment duration, and deterioration: A multilevel meta-analysis. *Clinical Psychology Review, 85*, 102002. https://doi.org/10.1016/j.cpr.2021.102002

De Jong, K., Delgadillo, J., & Barkham, M. (2023). *Routine outcome monitoring and feedback in psychological therapies*. McGraw-Hill Education.

Demir, S., Schwarz, F., & Kaiser, T. (2022). Therapy from my point of view: A case illustration of routine outcome monitoring and feedback in psychotherapeutic interventions. *Journal of Clinical Psychology, 78*, 1–12. https://doi.org/10.1002/jclp.23408

Derogatis, L. R., & Spencer, M. S. (1982). The Brief Symptom Inventory (BSI): Administration, scoring, and procedures manual - 1. Baltimore: Johns Hopkins University School of Medicine, Clinical Psychometrics Research Unit.

Flückiger, C., Del Re, A. C., Wampold, B. E., & Horvath, A. O. (2018). The alliance in adult psychotherapy: A meta-analytic synthesis. *Psychotherapy, 55*(4), 316–340. https://doi.org/10.1037/pst0000172

Flückiger, C., Rubel, J., Del Re, A. C., Horvath, A. O., Wampold, B. E., Crits-Christoph, P., Atzil-Slonim, D., Compare, A., Falkenström, F., Ekeblad, A., Errázuriz, P., Fisher, H., Hoffart, A., Huppert, J. D., Kivity, Y., Kumar, M., Lutz, W., Muran, J. C., Strunk, D. R., et al. (2020). The reciprocal relationship between alliance and early treatment symptoms: A two-stage individual participant data meta-analysis. *Journal of Consulting and Clinical Psychology, 88*(9), 829–843. https://doi.org/10.1037/ccp0000594

Franke, G. H. (2000). *Brief symptom inventory (BSI) von LR derogatis—Deutsche Version*. Beltz Test.

Freedman, N., Hurvich, M., Ward, R., Geller, J. D., & Hoffenberg, J. (Eds.). (2011). *Another kind of evidence: Studies on internalization, annihilation anxiety and progressive symbolization in the psychoanalytic process*. Karnac Books.

Gablonski, T. C., Herrmann, P. L., Lüdemann, J., & Andreas, S. (2023). Intersession experiences and internalized representations of psychotherapy: A scoping review. *Journal of Clinical Psychology, 79*(8), 1875–1901. https://doi.org/10.1002/jclp.23502

Gelso, C. J. (2002). Real relationship: The "something more" of psychotherapy. *Journal of Contemporary Psychotherapy, 32*(1), 35–40. https://doi.org/10.1023/A:1015531228504

Grossl, A. B., Reese, R. J., Norsworthy, L. A., & Hopkins, N. B. (2014). Client feedback data in supervision: Effects on supervision and outcome. *Training and Education in Professional Psychology, 8*(3), 182–188. https://doi.org/10.1037/tep0000025

Hannan, C., Lambert, M. J., Harmon, C., Nielsen, S. L., Smart, D. W., Shimokawa, K., & Sutton, S. W. (2005). A lab test and algorithms for identifying clients at risk for treatment failure. *Journal of Clinical Psychology, 61*(2), 155–163. https://doi.org/10.1002/jclp.20108

Harmon, C., Hawkins, E. J., Lambert, M. J., Slade, K., & Whipple, J. S. (2005). Improving outcomes for poorly responding clients: The use of clinical support tools and feedback to clients. *Journal of Clinical Psychology, 61*(2), 175–185. https://doi.org/10.1002/jclp.20109

Hartmann, A., Orlinsky, D., Weber, S., Sandholz, A., & Zeeck, A. (2010). Session and intersession experience related to treatment outcome in bulimia nervosa. *Psychotherapy: Theory, Research, Practice, Training, 47*(3), 355–370. https://doi.org/10.1037/a0021166

Hartmann, A., Orlinsky, D., & Zeeck, A. (2011). The structure of intersession experience in psychotherapy and its relation to the therapeutic alliance. *Journal of Clinical Psychology, 67*, 1044–1063. https://doi.org/10.1002/jclp.20826

Hartmann, A., Zeeck, A., Herzog, W., Wild, B., de Zwaan, M., Herpertz, S., Burgmer, M., von Wietersheim, J., Tagay, S., Dinkel, A., Löwe, B., Resmark, G., Orlinsky, D., & Zipfel, S. (2016). The intersession process in psychotherapy for anorexia nervosa: Characteristics and relation to outcome. *Journal of Clinical Psychology, 72*(9), 861–879. https://doi.org/10.1002/jclp.22293

Hayes, S. C., Strosahl, K. D., & Wilson, K. G. (1999). Acceptance and commitment therapy (Vol. 6). New York: Guilford Press.

Herzog, P., Häusler, S., Normann, C., & Brakemeier, E.-L. (2021). Negative effects of a multimodal inpatient CBASP program: Rate of occurrence and their impact on treatment outcome in chronic and treatment-resistant depression. *Frontiers in Psychiatry, 12*, 575837. https://doi.org/10.3389/fpsyt.2021.575837

Herzog, P., Kube, T., & Rubel, J. (2023). Why some psychotherapists benefit from feedback on treatment progress more than others: A belief updating perspective. *Clinical Psychology: Science and Practice, 30*(4), 468–479. https://doi.org/10.1037/cps0000174

Howard, K. I., Kopta, S. M., Krause, M. S., & Orlinsky, D. E. (1986). The dose–effect relationship in psychotherapy. *American Psychologist, 41*(2), 159–164. https://doi.org/10.1037/0003-066X.41.2.159

Jennissen, S., Huber, J., Ehrenthal, J. C., Schauenburg, H., & Dinger, U. (2018). Association between insight and outcome of psychotherapy: Systematic review and meta-analysis. *American Journal of Psychiatry, 175*(10), 961–969. https://doi.org/10.1176/appi.ajp.2018.17080847

Kaiser, T. (2014). Bedeutung und Zusammenhänge psychotherapeutischer Intra- und Intersessionprozesse. https://doi.org/10.13140/RG.2.1.4838.9609

Kaiser, T., & Laireiter, A. R. (2017). DynAMo: A modular platform for monitoring process, outcome, and algorithm-based treatment planning in psychotherapy. *JMIR Medical Informatics, 5*(3), e6808. https://doi.org/10.2196/medinform.6808

Kaiser, T., & Laireiter, A.-R. (2018). Process-symptom-bridges in psychotherapy: An idiographic network approach. *Journal for Person-Oriented Research, 4*(2), Article 2. https://doi.org/10.17505/jpor.2018.06

Kamper, S. J., Maher, C. G., & Mackay, G. (2009). Global rating of change scales: A review of strengths and weaknesses and considerations for design. *Journal of Manual & Manipulative Therapy, 17*(3), 163–170. https://doi.org/10.1179/jmt.2009.17.3.163

Knox, S., Goldberg, J. L., Woodhouse, S. S., & Hill, C. E. (1999). Clients' internal representations of their therapists. *Journal of Counseling Psychology, 46*(2), 244–256. https://doi.org/10.1037/0022-0167.46.2.244

Lambert, M. J., Hansen, N. B., & Harmon, S. C. (2010). Outcome Questionnaire System (The OQ System): Development and practical applications in healthcare settings. In T. Trauer (Hrsg.), Outcome measurement in mental health: Theory and practice (1. publ). Cambridge University Press.

Langkaas, T. F., Wampold, B. E., & Hoffart, A. (2018). Five types of clinical difference to monitor in practice. *Psychotherapy, 55*(3), 241–254. https://doi.org/10.1037/pst0000194

Lewis, C. C., Boyd, M., Puspitasari, A., Navarro, E., Howard, J., Kassab, H., Hoffman, M., Scott, K., Lyon, A., Douglas, S., Simon, G., & Kroenke, K. (2019). Implementing measurement-based care in behavioral health: A review. *JAMA Psychiatry, 76*(3), 324–335. https://doi.org/10.1001/jamapsychiatry.2018.3329

LimeSurvey Development Team. (2012). *LimeSurvey—The free and open source survey software tool!* LimeSurvey Development Team. limesurvey.org

Lutz, W., Deisenhofer, A.-K., Rubel, J., Bennemann, B., Giesemann, J., Poster, K., & Schwartz, B. (2022). Prospective evaluation of a clinical decision support system in psychological therapy. *Journal of Consulting and Clinical Psychology, 90*(1), 90–106. https://doi.org/10.1037/ccp0000642

Lutz, W., Rubel, J. A., Schwartz, B., Schilling, V., & Deisenhofer, A.-K. (2019). Towards integrating personalized feedback research into clinical practice: Development of the Trier Treatment Navigator (TTN). *Behaviour Research and Therapy, 120*, 103438. https://doi.org/10.1016/j.brat.2019.103438

McAleavey, A. A., de Jong, K., Nissen-Lie, H. A., Boswell, J. F., Moltu, C., & Lutz, W. (2024). Routine outcome monitoring and clinical feedback in psychotherapy: Recent advances and future directions. *Administration and Policy in Mental Health and Mental Health Services Research, 51*, 291. https://doi.org/10.1007/s10488-024-01351-9

McCullough, J. P., Jr. (2000). *Treatment for chronic depression: Cognitive behavioral analysis system of psychotherapy (CBASP)*. Guilford Press.

McCullough, J. P., Lord, B. D., Martin, A. M., Conley, K. A., Schramm, E., & Klein, D. N. (2011). The significant other history: An interpersonal-emotional history procedure used with the early-onset chronically depressed patient. *American Journal of Psychotherapy, 65*(3), 225–248. https://doi.org/10.1176/appi.psychotherapy.2011.65.3.225

Orlinsky, D. E., Geller, J. D., Tarragona, M., & Farber, B. (1993). Patients' representations of psychotherapy: A new focus for psychodynamic research. *Journal of Consulting and Clinical Psychology, 61*(4), 596–610. https://doi.org/10.1037/0022-006X.61.4.596

R Core Team. (2024). *R: A language and environment for statistical computing [computer software]*. R Foundation for Statistical Computing. https://www.R-project.org/

Rief, W., Asmundson, G. J. G., Bryant, R. A., Clark, D. M., Ehlers, A., Holmes, E. A., McNally, R. J., Neufeld, C. B., Wilhelm, S., Jaroszewski, A. C., Berg, M., Haberkamp, A., & Hofmann, S. G. (2024). The future of psychological treatments: The Marburg declaration. *Clinical Psychology Review, 110*, 102417. https://doi.org/10.1016/j.cpr.2024.102417

Rosellini, A. J., & Brown, T. A. (2019). The multidimensional emotional disorder inventory (MEDI): Assessing transdiagnostic dimensions to validate a profile approach to emotional disorder classification. *Psychological Assessment, 31*(1), 59–72. https://doi.org/10.1037/pas0000649

Rousmaniere, T., Goodyear, R., Miller, S. D., & Wampold, B. E. (2017). The Cycle of Excellence: Using Deliberate Practice to Improve Supervision and Training. John Wiley & Sons. https://doi.org/10.1002/9781119165590

Shrout, P., & Lane, S. P. (2012). Psychometrics. In M. R. Mehl & T. S. Conner (Eds.), *Handbook of research methods for studying daily life* (pp. 302–320). Guilford Press.

Stewart, S., & Schröder, T. (2015). Emotional homework: A systematic literature review of patients' intersession experiences. *Journal of Psychotherapy Integration, 25*(3), 236–252. https://doi.org/10.1037/a0039639

Straat, J. H., Van Der Ark, L. A., & Sijtsma, K. (2013). Comparing optimization algorithms for item selection in Mokken scale analysis. *Journal of Classification, 30*(1), 75–99. https://doi.org/10.1007/s00357-013-9122-y

Stulz, N., & Lutz, W. (2007). Multidimensional patterns of change in outpatient psychotherapy: The phase model revisited. *Journal of Clinical Psychology, 63*(9), 817–833. https://doi.org/10.1002/jclp.20397

Chapter 5
The OQ® Analyst

David M. Erekson, Benjamin M. Ogles, and Michael J. Lambert

The OQ feedback system and clinical support tools, now known as the OQ® Analyst, was the first scientifically validated, structured program for conducting routine outcome monitoring (ROM) in both inpatient and outpatient psychotherapy. The system was originally developed as part of a consulting contract from a behavioral health care company to Dr. Michael J. Lambert. Lambert had long-standing interests in both measuring the outcome of psychotherapy (see Lambert et al., 1983) and understanding and reducing client deterioration in psychotherapy (e.g., see Lambert et al., 1977), a phenomenon he later documented as occurring 8% of the time in well-controlled clinical trials and up to 40% of the time in some routine clinical settings (Hansen et al., 2003). As a result, he was a good fit for the expectations of the consulting contract that focused on measuring outcome to reduce "over-managing" clinicians and cases (Lambert, 2015, p. 381). The behavioral health company's idea was that identifying and focusing case management on covered individuals in therapy who were not making progress as expected could result in greater efficiency and reduced costs. Additionally, this could also reduce micromanagement of providers for their cases that were improving as expected.

With this target in mind, the goal was to develop a measurement system that could both track client progress and compare that progress with expected rates of improvement to identify individuals not making progress as expected—what came to be known as "signal" or "not-on-track" (NOT) cases (Lambert et al., 2001). Lambert, along with colleagues and students at Brigham Young University, accepted the challenge and set out to create a brief instrument that could be used to track

D. M. Erekson (✉)
Counseling and Psychological Services, Brigham Young University, Provo, UT, USA
e-mail: david_erekson@byu.edu

B. M. Ogles · M. J. Lambert
Department of Psychology, Brigham Young University, Provo, UT, USA
e-mail: ben_ogles@byu.edu; michael_lambert@byu.edu

J. A. Rubel, W. Lutz (eds.), *Feedback Informed Psychological Therapy*, CBT: Science Into Practice, https://doi.org/10.1007/978-3-031-90428-8_5

symptoms through routine administration and monitoring concurrent with treatment; thus arose the Outcome Questionnaire—45 (OQ-45). During the evolution of the system, a second, supplementary instrument was developed to help assess the potential reasons for clients' failure to progress as expected: the Assessment for Signal Clients (OQ®-OQ®-ASC). This instrument is used within the OQ® Analyst system to provide clinical support tools for the clinician as they decide how to address flagging client progress in treatment (Lambert et al., 2015).

Description and Brief History of the OQ® Analyst

The OQ® Analyst system includes a measure for monitoring client progress (OQ-45), a computerized scoring system that uses algorithms to assess client progress and produce reports for both client and therapist. In addition, it includes clinical support tools (CSTs) that were developed to help therapists organize and target potential problems that might account for deterioration or lack of progress in therapy. The core of CST feedback is the Assessment for Signal Clients (OQ®-ASC), a measure designed to determine the potential reasons for lack of progress in signal cases. We provide brief descriptions of each of the components of the OQ® Analyst system below.

OQ®-45.2 Instrument

To track client progress, the OQ-45 was developed to be a brief (5–7 min), self-report measure of client functioning that could be administered at each therapy session (typically before each session). The 45 items on the survey are rated on a 5-point scale from 0 (*never*) to 4 (*almost always*) and include 36 negatively worded items (e.g., Item 15, "I feel worthless") and 9 positively worded items (e.g., Item 20, "I feel loved and wanted"). Items are summed to produce a total score that ranges from 0 to 180. Higher scores reflect higher levels of distress/disturbance. Total scores are valid if fewer than five items are left unanswered (i.e., if 41 items are answered, the OQ® Analyst system will calculate a total score).

The OQ-45 has adequate internal consistency ($r = 0.93$) and 3-week test–retest reliability ($r = 0.84$). Concurrent validity is moderate to high ($r = 0.50$–0.85) when correlated with measures most often used to assess psychotherapy outcome in clinical trials (e.g., Beck Depression Inventory, Symptom Checklist 90). In addition, OQ scores vary as expected when compared across student, community, and clinical populations (Lambert et al., 2013). Importantly, the OQ-45 is sensitive to change in clients who are being treated while remaining stable in untreated individuals (Vermeersch et al., 2000; Vermeersch et al., 2004).

Normative data for the OQ-45 have been analyzed to provide cutoff scores for both a Reliable Change Index (RCI) and clinically significant change (Jacobson &

Truax, 1991). Using normative data from community nonclients ($N = 1353$) and clients entering treatment ($N = 1476$), the RCI was estimated to be 14 points (Lambert et al., 2013). Clients who change in a positive or negative direction by at least 14 points are regarded as having made reliable change (improvement or deterioration depending on the direction of change). The clinical cutoff on the OQ-45 is 64, which is about a standard deviation higher than the mean of the nonclient sample ($M = 45.31$, $SD = 19.42$). When a client's score falls at 63 or below, it is considered to be more like nonclients than clients (Lambert et al., 2013). When the client improves (decreases) by 14 or more points and passes below 64, the client meets both criteria necessary for categorization as clinically significant (i.e., meaningful) change.

Finch et al. (2001) developed the first algorithms to identify cases at risk for deterioration based on a US sample ($N > 11,000$) of patients receiving treatment. The actuarial method developed for the OQ-45 has been successfully tested in several studies (e. g., Ellsworth et al., 2006; Lambert, Whipple, Bishop, et al., 2002; Spielmans et al., 2006), where algorithms identified 80–100% of clients who are deteriorated rather than improved at the end of therapy.

The 45 items were initially written to cover four broad areas or categories of mental health (Lambert, 2015): symptomatic distress (especially depression and anxiety), interpersonal problems, social role functioning, and well-being (positive functioning). However, the OQ® Analyst system now scores three subscales: symptom distress, interpersonal relations, and social role functioning. Factor analyses of the OQ-45 generally find different factors than suggested by the conceptually created subscales. For example, the factor analysis included in the OQ-45 manual reports preference for a unidimensional factor structure and notes that multifactorial models had high correlations between the factors. Later factor analyses of OQ data (e.g., Howland, 2021) have found that a unidimensional model is unsatisfactory and that best fit was identified when exploratory structural equation modeling (ESEM) using target rotation was applied to the bifactor model with one general factor and the three subscales. This bifactor model has been supported by another independent investigation (Arader, 2021) and in the Spanish version of the OQ-45 (Iraurgi & Penas, 2021; Silva et al., 2016). These most recent factor analyses suggest that, in line with practice, the OQ-45 total score is suitable for monitoring change. In addition, Howland (2021) found measurement invariance in factor structure through the first five sessions for clients participating in treatment, supporting an earlier study that found general temporal invariance in pre-post OQ-45 measurements (Jabrayilov et al., 2017). Silva et al. (2016) also examined invariance between men and women, and found the OQ-45 to be invariant between genders. Thus, use of the total score in practice is the most justified empirically and conceptually, across time and gender. At the same time, the potential for developing alternative subscales based on empirical dimensions of relationships among the items may be a fruitful source of future work.

Assessment for Signal Clients (OQ®-OQ®-ASC)

The OQ®-OQ®-ASC is a 40-item self-report measure that clients rate using a five-point scale, with anchors ranging from strongly agree to strongly disagree. It has four subscales: Therapeutic Alliance (11 items), Motivation for Therapy (9 items), Social Support (11 items), and Life Events (9 items). Therapeutic Alliance items inquire about the therapeutic bond, shared goals, and agreement on therapeutic tasks, as well as any rupture in the Therapeutic Alliance. Motivation items focus on low or inadequate motivation for treatment, negative expectations for treatment, or negative reactions to the treatment process. Social Support items cover the degree to which individuals feel that their family and close friends can be counted on. Finally, life event items focus on recent negative Life Events related to loss and illness and are intended to alert therapists to life crises that might need to be addressed in therapy.

According to Kimball (2010), the Cronbach alpha coefficient for each subscale is Therapeutic Alliance (0.87), Motivation for Therapy (0.81), Social Support (0.88), and Life Events (0.81). Similarly, Probst et al. (2013) found comparable values in Germany, with Cronbach alphas ranging from 0.89 to 0.71. Confirmatory factor analysis suggested the factor structure was consistent with the content of the designed scales. A more detailed presentation of the theoretical background of the OQ®-ASC subscales can be found in the manual and other publications (Lambert et al., 2015; White et al., 2015).

OQ® Analyst System

Initial tracking or monitoring of client progress is captured as the client completes the OQ-45 before each session. Initial reports, produced after the first administration, provide the therapist with clinically relevant information that can be used for treatment planning. For example, client's responses to critical items are provided to clinicians to highlight any needs that may require immediate attention (Item 8, Suicidal thoughts; Item 11, Alcohol, drugs to get going; Item 26, Criticized for substance use; Item 32, Substance use affects daily functioning; and Item 44, Workplace conflict). In addition, subscale scores and individual items with high endorsement provide information about potential areas of focus in treatment.

The OQ® Analyst system then uses session-by-session tracking data to compare client treatment trajectories with algorithms (rational or empirical) of expected change. Reports are provided to clinicians regarding client progress, including a categorical signal, or alert status, that is, white, green, yellow, or red. A white signal indicates that the client's score falls in the range in which it can be considered part of a nonclinical population. Depending on the circumstances, this may be an indication that the clinician can consider ending treatment. A green signal indicates that the client is improving as expected compared to the change trajectories of other similar clients. A yellow signal indicates that the client is not improving at the same rate as might be expected compared to the trajectories of other similar clients. Finally, a red signal indicates that the client is at risk for deterioration or worsening of symptoms at the conclusion of treatment. In addition, a client may have a secondary alert status of blue, indicating that they have improved at a faster rate than expected for 90% of clients. A blue signal has been associated with a high likelihood of reliable and clinically significant change at the end of treatment (Erekson et al., 2018; Erekson et al., 2020; Haas et al., 2002).

When cases are identified for potential treatment failure or lack of progress, the OQ®-ASC can be administered to the client to help provide clinical support for the therapist. The OQ®-ASC targets general areas that are important in outpatient psychotherapy across types of therapy and client presentations. The software uses a decision tree to organize and support therapist problem-solving (see Lambert et al., 2018 for a brief example of the decision tree). Therapists are directed first to consider the strength of the therapeutic relationship, then motivation, then Social Support, followed by negative Life Events (subscales of the OQ®-ASC). The decision tree then directs therapists to reconsider the patient's diagnosis and the need for potential referral for medication and/or reconsideration of the treatment method. Potential interventions are also presented for consideration of the therapist. Clinicians have found the CST feedback to be useful in their work and experimental data demonstrated reduced deterioration rates in predicted treatment failures from a baseline of 20% to 5.5%, and the rate of positive outcomes from 22% to 50.5% (Shimokawa et al., 2010).

The OQ®-ASC feedback report is given to the therapist after a session is completed. Total scores are first presented for each of the subscales along with comparison to a cutoff that indicates any problem areas. Individual item feedback is also provided for items that are endorsed by 20% or fewer clients. This helps make the feedback more specific and enhance clinician problem-solving.

OQ® Analyst offers the OQ-45 in over 40 languages, including "English, Spanish, Spanish (Chilean), Spanish (Colombian), French (Canadian), French (European), Arabic, Armenian, Bosnian, Cambodian, Chinese Simplified, Chinese Traditional, Danish, Dari, Dutch, Farsi, Finnish, Frysk, German, Hebrew, Hungarian, Italian, Japanese, Korean, Lithuanian, Norwegian, Philippines, Polish, Portuguese (Brazilian), Portuguese (European), Punjabi, Romanian, Russian, Slovak, Slovene, Somali, Swedish, Tagalog, Taiwanese, Thai, Turkish, Ukrainian, Vietnamese and Visually Impaired" (OQ Measures, 2023a). The OQ®-ASC, while having fewer translations, is available in six languages, including "English, Spanish, French (Canadian), Finnish, German and Swedish" (OQ Measures, 2023b).

Brief Review of the Empirical Evidence

Most of the early research using the OQ was focused on providing the background and context for the measure's psychometric properties (e.g., Umphress et al., 1997; Vermeersch et al., 2000) and algorithms (e.g., Finch et al., 2001; Lambert, Whipple,

Bishop, et al., 2002). Later research began to experimentally examine the treatment benefits of using ROM to provide feedback to clinicians regarding client progress using the OQ® Analyst compared to treatment as usual with no feedback.

Lambert et al. (2001) conducted the first study to examine the utility of providing feedback to clinicians about client progress using the OQ® Analyst signal alarm system. They found that providing feedback reduced the chance of end-of-treatment deterioration and improved efficiency for clients who were making progress as expected. Subsequent studies focused on replicating those findings (e.g., Lambert et al., 2001; Whipple et al., 2003), added components such as the clinical support tools (e.g., Harmon et al., 2007; Slade et al., 2008), used the system for feedback in supervision (e.g., Lambert & Hawkins, 2001), or investigated applications of the ROM system in different clinical settings (e.g., Probst et al., 2013; Simon et al., 2013). In addition, later research focused on validation of the instruments (e.g., Coco et al., 2008; de Jong et al., 2007) or applications of the OQ® Analyst system in other countries using translations of the scales (e.g., Amble et al., 2015; Bovendeerd et al., 2022; Hansson et al., 2013). Enough research has been conducted using the OQ® Analyst system that two meta-analyses reviewed the findings across primary studies (Lambert et al., 2018; Shimokawa et al., 2010). In the 8 years between the first and second meta-analysis, the number of studies directly comparing feedback to no feedback conditions using the OQ® Analyst system doubled to 15. [The second review also included studies using the Partners for Change Outcome Management System (PCOMS; Miller et al., 2005).] When summarizing the findings from the 15 studies of the OQ® Analyst system, Lambert et al. (2018) concluded that "the results of examining effect sizes across the published studies suggest a very small effect of 0.14 for feedback on the whole sample, a larger effect (0.33) for feedback on NOT [Not on Track] clients, and a still larger effect (0.49) when CSTs are provided to therapists" (p. 530).

In addition, de Jong et al. (2021) reviewed the ROM literature more broadly including studies using several different feedback approaches, of which the OQ® Analyst was one. Consistent with other primary studies and meta-analyses, they found a small and consistent effect for feedback that can be implemented at low cost to the clinician. Overall, the findings of these and other studies are sufficiently consistent that some scholars have suggested that routine outcome monitoring is an evidence-based approach to treatment that should be more widely implemented in practice (e.g., Boswell et al., 2015; Boswell et al., 2023). For example, the second Task Force on Evidence-Based Therapy Relationships (Norcross & Wampold, 2011) concluded that "collecting client feedback" was one of several elements of the therapeutic relationship that are "demonstrably effective" (p. 99).

Case Example

To illustrate how the OQ® Analyst system might function in clinical practice, we present the following case example. The client in this example is an amalgam of several clients and bears a fictitious name to protect anonymity. We will begin by presenting the client's history and presenting problem, initial assessment data, and case conceptualization. We will then present the course of treatment, focusing particularly on how OQ® Analyst facilitated therapist responsiveness within the treatment model and led to better treatment outcome.

Presenting History and Problem

Elizabeth is a 21-year-old, single, Mexican American, cisgender woman. She identifies as bisexual, and at the time of intake, had recently begun dating a man for the first time. She also identifies as Christian, noting that religion is "very important" to her. Elizabeth presented at her university clinic in late December during her fourth and final academic year. She was self-referred for therapy, and expressed that she would like to work on "anxiety" that seemed to be affecting her ability to engage in relationships, particularly romantic relationships. Elizabeth also noted that, as a university student, she often felt overwhelmed by her academic work and unable to engage with it.

In the first session, Elizabeth denied a history of psychological diagnosis, indicating that her family generally "did not believe" in psychotherapy and that she did not want to reveal to them that she was currently seeking therapy. She denied a family history of formal mental health diagnosis, but noted that she believed she saw symptoms of anxiety in her father and her sister. She denied any current or historical use of psychotropic medications, as well as any current or historical use of substances. She denied a history of physical, sexual, and verbal abuse, as well as symptoms of mania or psychosis. When the therapist asked about potential symptoms of post-traumatic stress, Elizabeth indicated that she had had an experience that still caused significant anxiety in her daily life, including flashbacks and occasional nightmares. She did not immediately disclose the nature of the experience. She attended her first session well-groomed and oriented to time, person, and place.

Initial Assessment and Case Conceptualization

In addition to the history noted above, Elizabeth completed the Counseling Center Assessment of Psychological Symptoms 62 (CCAPS-62; Locke et al., 2011; McAleavey et al., 2012) and the OQ-45 at intake. The CCAPS-62 is a 62-item measure, where each item is considered over the last 2 weeks and is rated on a Likert-type scale, from 0 (i.e., *not at all like me*) to 4 (i.e., *extremely like me*). The CCAPS-62 has eight symptom-specific subscales and one overall distress scale. The seven specific subscales include depression, generalized anxiety, social anxiety, academic distress, eating concerns, family distress, frustration/anger, and substance use. Current norms for the CCAPS-62 are based on 388,266 university students seeking therapy in university-based clinics across the United States (Center for Collegiate

Mental Health, 2023). The CCAPS-62 has good reliability, with a Cronbach's alpha ranging from 0.78 to 0.91 across the eight subscales, and test–retest reliability ranging from 0.78 to 0.93 (Locke et al., 2011).

Elizabeth's scores on this measure indicated elevated symptoms in depression, generalized anxiety, social anxiety, and academic distress. She indicated low symptoms in eating concerns, family distress, frustration/anger, and substance use. Her overall distress index (a scale derived from specific items across each subscale) was at the 74th percentile, where she was experiencing more overall distress than 74% of her peers attending therapy in counseling centers across the United States (and less distress than 26%).

Elizabeth's total score on the OQ-45 (see details of the measure discussed above) was 69, indicating moderate distress consistent with students presenting at university counseling centers. This is above the 63/64 cutoff point that was empirically derived to differentiate between a clinical and a nonclinical population. OQ® Analyst presents the clinician with a graph of the current score (and previous scores, as therapy progresses), recent critical items, and a way to quickly view items endorsed at any specific level of the Likert scale (see Fig. 5.1 for an example of the clinician report at session 10). Her initial report indicated no endorsement of the critical items (i.e., the suicide item, three substance use items, and the work/school violence item). It also indicated that she endorsed "almost always" for the following items: *I blame myself for things, I feel weak, I feel fearful, I feel nervous,* and *I feel blue*.

Elizabeth's scores on each of these questionnaires were discussed with her in the intake session. She reported feeling that the CCAPS-62 was generally congruent with her experience, though she expressed some surprise at her elevated social anxiety scale. She noted that she feels naturally extraverted and friendly, but that she has recently also noticed that it has felt harder to feel close to others. She also expressed a sense of relief in understanding how her symptoms compared to others', reporting that she often wonders if it is "all in her head" and something she should "just feel differently" about. She noted that seeing her scores classified as elevated helped her feel like it was more "okay" to be seeking treatment, and she experienced more relief in having started therapy.

When presenting the OQ-45 to Elizabeth, the therapist discussed how the measure would be used throughout therapy—that Elizabeth would be given the opportunity to take it before each session and then she and the therapist would review the results together. The therapist noted that this was a standardized way to better understand Elizabeth's experience during the week, and that research indicated that looking at it increased the chances of therapy having a positive effect. Elizabeth agreed to take the questionnaire each week and expressed interest in watching her progress over time.

The therapist and Elizabeth collaboratively discussed her presenting problems and decided to focus on working with her symptoms of anxiety as they applied to relationships and school (though they also discussed how these goals may shift and develop over the course of therapy based on the client's experience and wishes). The therapist conceptualized these symptoms in the context of a biopsychosocial model,

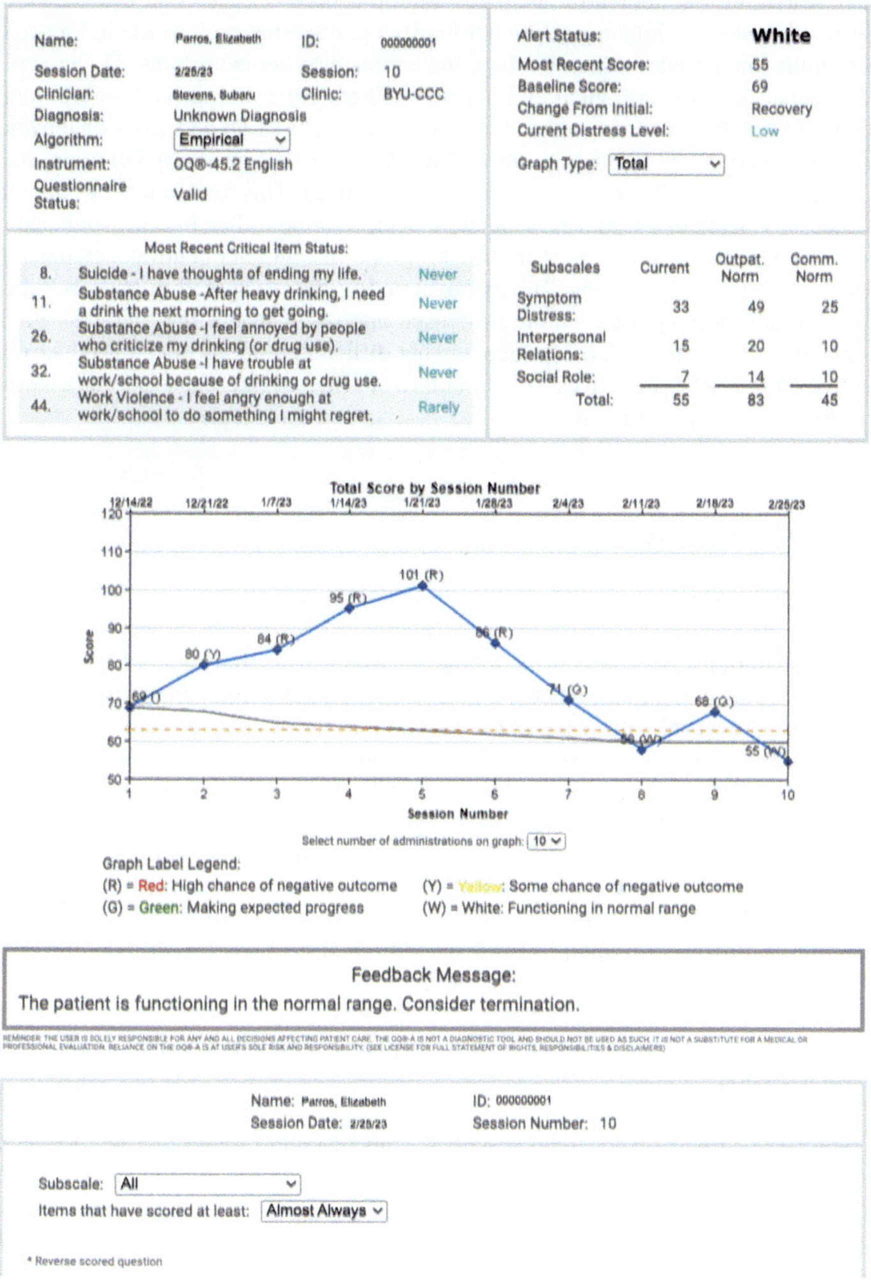

Name: Parros, Elizabeth ID: 000000001
Session Date: 2/25/23 Session: 10
Clinician: Stevens, Subaru Clinic: BYU-CCC
Diagnosis: Unknown Diagnosis
Algorithm: Empirical
Instrument: OQ®-45.2 English
Questionnaire Status: Valid

Alert Status: White
Most Recent Score: 55
Baseline Score: 69
Change From Initial: Recovery
Current Distress Level: Low
Graph Type: Total

Most Recent Critical Item Status:

8.	Suicide - I have thoughts of ending my life.	Never
11.	Substance Abuse -After heavy drinking, I need a drink the next morning to get going.	Never
26.	Substance Abuse -I feel annoyed by people who criticize my drinking (or drug use).	Never
32.	Substance Abuse -I have trouble at work/school because of drinking or drug use.	Never
44.	Work Violence - I feel angry enough at work/school to do something I might regret.	Rarely

Subscales	Current	Outpat. Norm	Comm. Norm
Symptom Distress:	33	49	25
Interpersonal Relations:	15	20	10
Social Role:	7	14	10
Total:	55	83	45

Select number of administrations on graph: 10

Graph Label Legend:
(R) = Red: High chance of negative outcome
(Y) = Yellow: Some chance of negative outcome
(G) = Green: Making expected progress
(W) = White: Functioning in normal range

Feedback Message:
The patient is functioning in the normal range. Consider termination.

REMINDER: THE USER IS SOLELY RESPONSIBLE FOR ANY AND ALL DECISIONS AFFECTING PATIENT CARE. THE OQ®-A IS NOT A DIAGNOSTIC TOOL AND SHOULD NOT BE USED AS SUCH. IT IS NOT A SUBSTITUTE FOR A MEDICAL OR PROFESSIONAL EVALUATION. RELIANCE ON THE OQ®-A IS AT USER'S SOLE RISK AND RESPONSIBILITY. (SEE LICENSE FOR FULL STATEMENT OF RIGHTS, RESPONSIBILITIES & DISCLAIMERS)

Name: Parros, Elizabeth ID: 000000001
Session Date: 2/25/23 Session Number: 10

Subscale: All
Items that have scored at least: Almost Always

* Reverse scored question

Fig. 5.1 Clinician feedback report generated by OQ® Analyst for the OQ-45

acknowledging the potential genetic and epigenetic effects (as evidenced by Elizabeth's observations regarding her family members) as well as the influence of her family and broader culture on how she approached her symptoms. The therapist approached the psychological components of her symptoms through an emotion-focused conceptualization, noting that Elizabeth's behavioral and emotional avoidance may perpetuate her symptoms and mask core social needs to feel connected, accepted, and safe (Timulak & Pascual-Leone, 2015). This avoidance was demonstrated in Elizabeth's initial reluctance to seek treatment, her initial avoidance of detail in her description of post-traumatic symptoms, and her cautious approach to revealing emotion in therapy. The therapist and Elizabeth agreed to approach therapy through an integrative emotion-focused approach, where the therapist would help guide Elizabeth toward experiencing her difficult emotions, then introduce corrective emotional experiences to help bolster a sense of internal wisdom, adaptive meaning, and empowerment.

Treatment Course

Session 1: Intake

When the initial session began, the therapist asked Elizabeth what it was like for her coming in for therapy and what she was feeling in the present moment. Elizabeth noted that she wasn't sure what to expect and felt a little anxious, and that she also felt relieved that she was starting to work on her mental health. The therapist reflected and normalized these emotions, and outlined the potential structure of their first session, including the initial logistical information and assessment, and the subsequent more open format. The initial part of the first session was then used to discuss confidentiality, gather information, and come to a consensus on therapeutic goals. The therapist also described what Elizabeth could expect from him, including empathy, genuineness, and unconditional positive regard; noticing emotions and facilitating experiencing them; and collaborating with the client on how they would like to engage with therapy between sessions. As noted above, the therapist included a discussion of intake measures and continued outcome measurement in each session.

In the second half of the first session, the therapist asked Elizabeth what she would like to focus on for today's session, and Elizabeth stated that her academic anxiety was feeling most pressing. She described her anxiety in vague terms, noting that she felt unsure about when or why she felt more or less anxious. The therapist reflected her frustration regarding her anxiety, and mentally noted that Elizabeth engaged in little elaboration or deepening. The therapist attempted to help Elizabeth become more attuned to her emotions by asking her what it was like to try to talk about her anxiety in session. Elizabeth stated that she was unsure. At the end of the session, the therapist and Elizabeth agreed that she would pay attention to her emotions throughout the week and journal about them at the end of each day.

Sessions 2 and 3: OQ® Analyst Alerts

In the second session, Elizabeth's OQ score (taken just before the session started) rose from a 69 to an 80, and OQ® Analyst's alert status indicated "yellow" (i.e., based on an initial score of 69, Elizabeth was at risk of deviating significantly from her algorithmically derived treatment trajectory and may be at risk for deterioration; note session 2 in Fig. 5.1). At the beginning of the session, the therapist showed Elizabeth her OQ® Analyst output and noted that her OQ score had increased, potentially indicating more distress. The therapist asked Elizabeth if this fit her experience during the week. Elizabeth stated that things had felt more stressful with school and that she was unable to journal about her emotions during the week due to time constraints. She asked for "tips" regarding coping with anxiety and the therapist responded with a reflection: "Your anxiety has really been difficult lately, and here, after your first session of therapy, it's only increasing. It would really feel nice if I could just hand over some tips that you could apply and this would go away." Elizabeth agreed that this would be nice and shifted the conversation to anxiety around relationships. She noted that she often feels perfectionistic with herself and worries that she may be too "picky" when it comes to pursuing romantic relationships. The therapist expressed empathy for her experience and facilitated an exploration of her high expectations for herself and others in order to feel safe. The therapist noted aloud that it seemed difficult for Elizabeth to connect with her emotions as she talked about her difficulties, and Elizabeth agreed. At the end of this session, Elizabeth and the therapist agreed again on journaling about her emotions, specifically including her emotions around relationships.

In the third session, Elizabeth's OQ score rose again to 84, and OQ® Analyst's alert status indicated "red" (i.e., Elizabeth's trajectory indicated a high likelihood that she would deteriorate [and not improve] in therapy; note session 3 in Fig. 5.1). The therapist showed Elizabeth her OQ® Analyst graph and asked if it fit her experience. He also discussed that she had signaled red, relating that this may indicate that something about therapy wasn't working well for her and that they could evaluate different ways of moving forward together. Elizabeth reported feeling uncertain about therapy and discussed her family of origin that discouraged speaking about emotions or seeking professional help. The therapist expressed hope that they could find an approach that would work better and reflected the bravery it took to for her to even approach therapy. Elizabeth noted that she would prefer to not feel like she had an assignment after therapy, so they agreed to forgo formulating work she might do between sessions. The therapist ended the session by introducing the OQ®-ASC as another way of gathering information to help direct their therapy, and Elizabeth agreed to take it after her session. The OQ®-ASC was sent via electronic link after the session, and Elizabeth completed it. The therapist reviewed the results (see Fig. 5.2) and noted that Elizabeth was experiencing the most difficulty in the Therapeutic Alliance, then motivation, and finally Social Support.

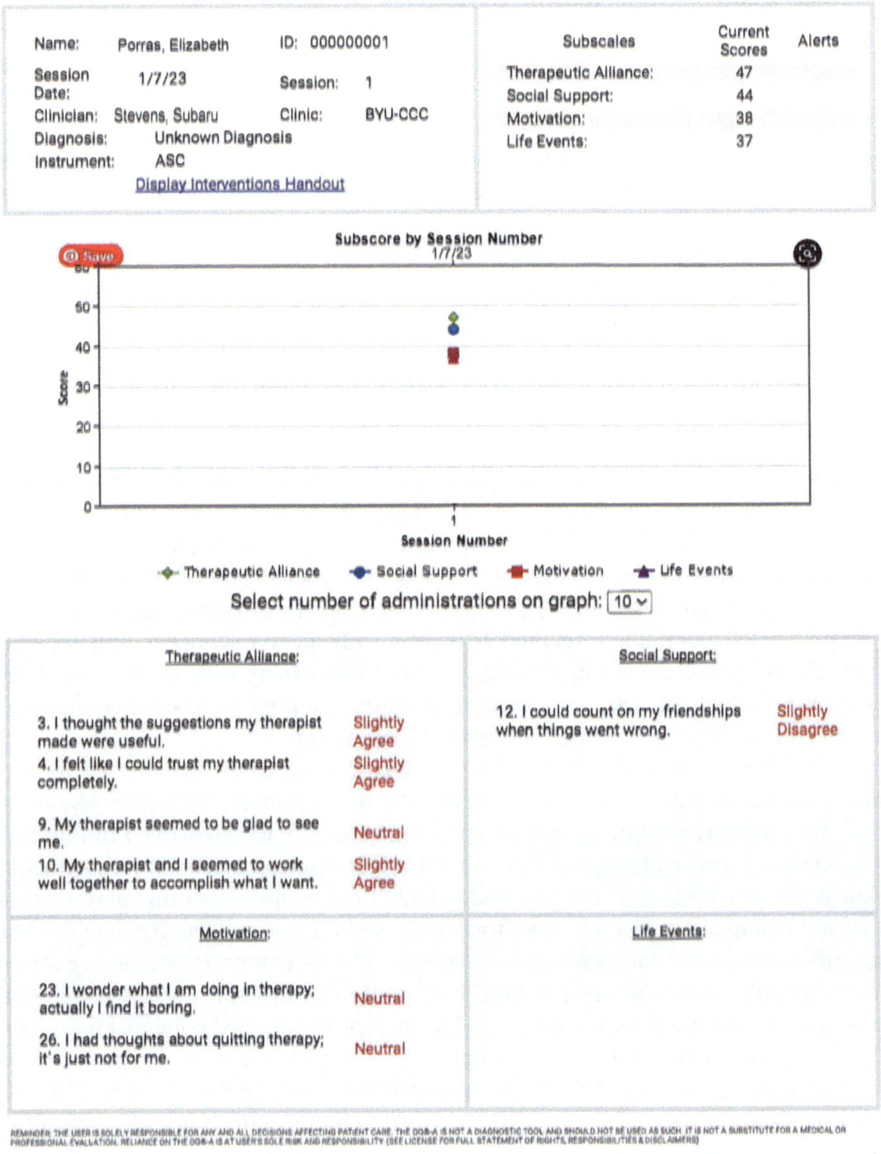

Fig. 5.2 Clinician feedback report generated by OQ® Analyst for the OQ®-ASC at first administration

Sessions 4 and 5: Responding Using the OQ®-ASC

In the fourth session, Elizabeth's OQ score rose to 95 and continued to signal "red" (see session 4 in Fig. 5.1). The therapist began by showing Elizabeth her score and also sharing the results of the OQ®-ASC from the previous session. The therapist introduced a discussion on the Therapeutic Alliance, reflecting the client's responses on the OQ®-ASC regarding the difficulty feeling like what they were doing was useful and the difficulty trusting the therapist. The therapist reflected "Part of you is really unsure if this can be helpful—if I can be helpful; and another part of you keeps showing up for appointments." The therapist introduced a two-chair exercise, where Elizabeth was asked to embody the part that did not want to be in therapy and have a conversation with the other part of her that felt motivated to come to therapy. After this exercise, the therapist and Elizabeth processed the experience, noting her fear around vulnerability and how the cynical part of her was trying to protect her from potentially getting hurt. They related this to her broader experiences in relationships outside of the therapy. They decided to not formulate a concrete task to work on during the week, but rather to continue to think about the parts of the session that stood out to her. The therapist asked Elizabeth to complete the OQ®-ASC again; results indicated improvement in Social Support and motivation, with some limited improvement in alliance (see Fig. 5.3).

In the fifth session, Elizabeth began the session feeling tearful and reported that she had received difficult news. Her OQ had risen to 101. She recounted, with some difficulty, that several years ago she had been sexually assaulted by someone she believed to be a friend, and that she found out this individual had returned to the university after being away for 2 years. The therapist helped Elizabeth feel grounded while also processing her emotions around this news. They discussed beginning to approach her traumatic experience in writing, paying attention to her emotions that came up as she wrote and allowing herself to journal about those as well. They also discussed a plan for if she happened to see him on campus. The therapist asked Elizabeth to take the OQ®-ASC after this session and sent an electronic link; the OQ®-ASC indicated even more improvement in the Therapeutic Alliance with no items flagged on any subscale except for Life Events: *I received bad news that was difficult for me* (see Fig. 5.4).

Sessions 6–10: Deepening and Concluding

The remaining five sessions focused on exposing Elizabeth to her trauma and helping her create a coherent narrative while processing and shaping her emotional experience around it. Between sessions, she engaged in writing the details of her traumatic experience each day. The therapist helped Elizabeth explore and process her anger at her assaulter and anger at God. The therapist also used chairwork to help Elizabeth incorporate compassionate voices into her difficult experiences—specifically the voice of her grandmother who had passed away several years ago. Elizabeth grew more accepting of her emotions and more able to engage with them, and also became more capable of self-soothing. She began to feel more confident in her ability to turn inward to find ways forward that would be helpful for her. She also bolstered her Social Support and opened up to her parents and one friend about her experience. Elizabeth's OQ scores decreased over these sessions from 101 to 55 in her final session (see Fig. X). In her last session, Elizabeth noted that she felt

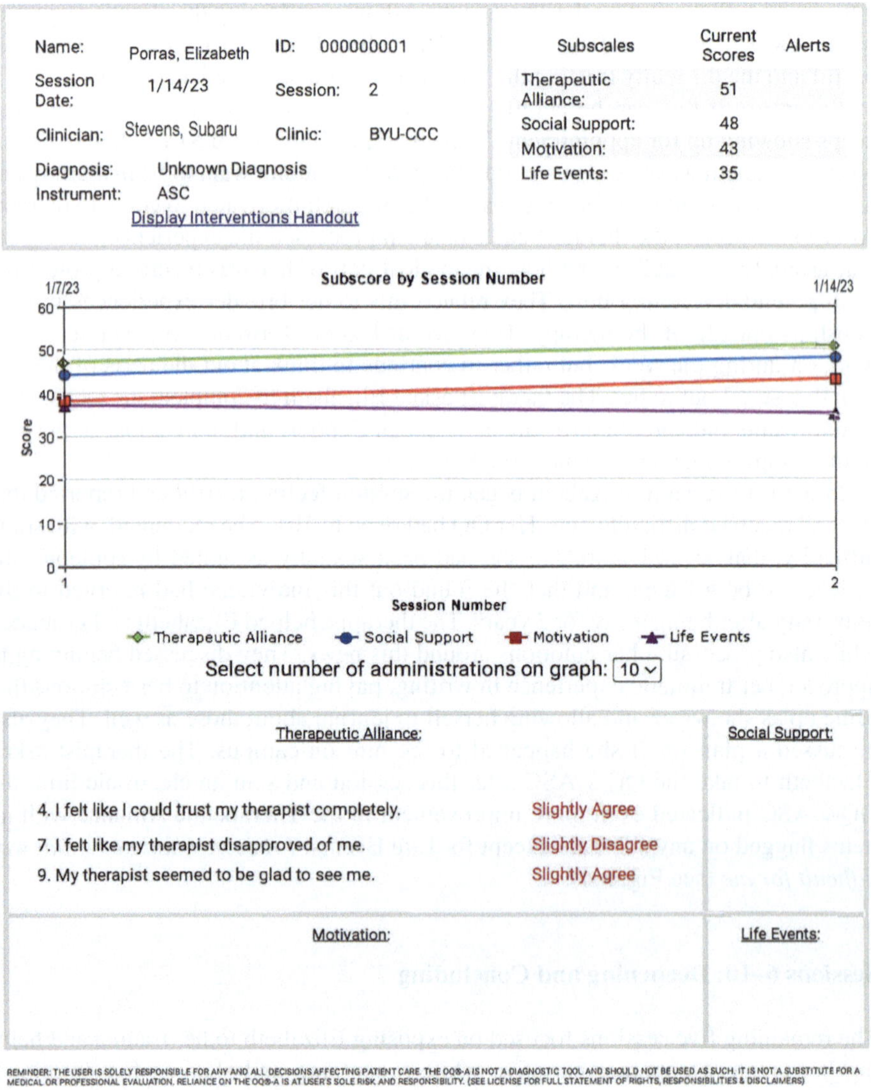

Fig. 5.3 Clinician feedback report generated by OQ® Analyst for the OQ®-ASC at second administration

that her sleep was much better, that her anxiety around schoolwork had decreased, that she felt less pressure to pursue a romantic relationship immediately, and that she could continue working on her mental health on her own for the time being. She noted still feeling concerned about seeing the perpetrator of her assault, but felt that it wasn't affecting her daily functioning. The therapist invited her to return at any point if she felt that she needed additional support.

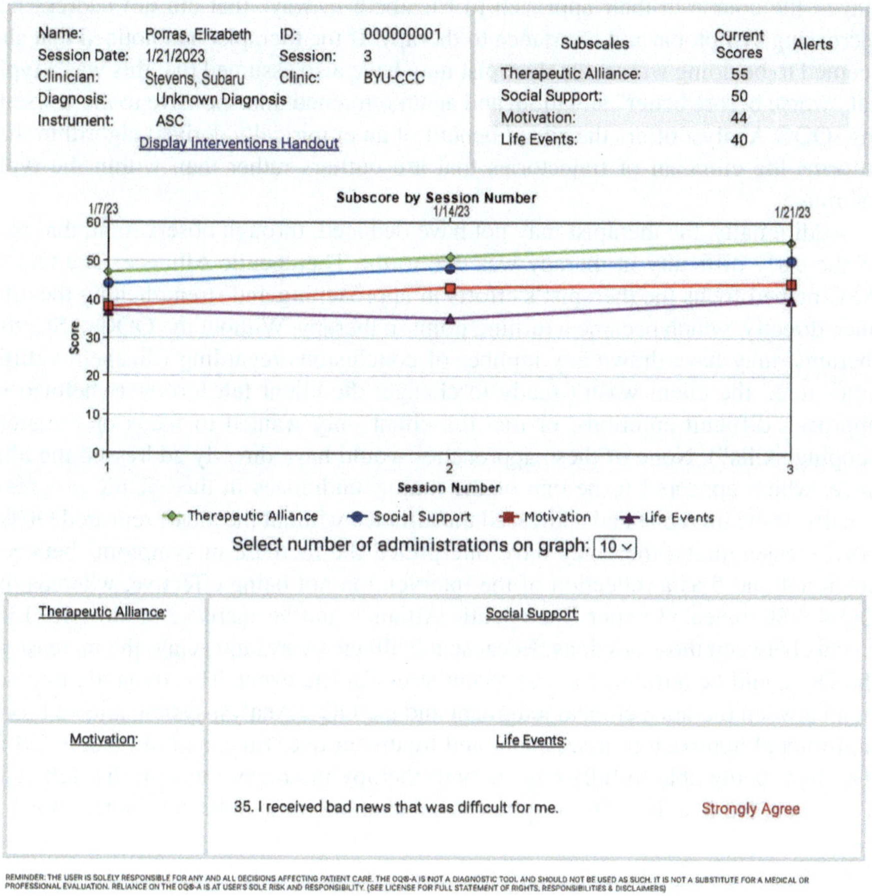

Fig. 5.4 Clinician feedback report generated by OQ® Analyst for the OQ®-ASC at third administration

Case Reflection

This type of experience with routine outcome monitoring and feedback is not uncommon and speaks to the utility of measuring outcome each week and considering those measures in session and in treatment planning. There are several points in therapy throughout that the therapist may have missed (or misinterpreted) without the aid of the OQ-45 and the OQ®-ASC. For example, in the early stages of treatment, Elizabeth presented relatively consistently. The therapist may have concluded, based on observed presentation, that Elizabeth had not started improving yet (and missed that Elizabeth was, in fact, deteriorating). This would align with previous research that has confirmed that therapists are not able to accurately predict when their clients are deteriorating (Hannan et al., 2005). The therapist may have then stayed the course in their approach to Elizabeth in ways that did not address her increasing symptoms and resistance to therapy. If the therapist had noticed that she seemed to be doing worse, the therapist may have also assumed that this was a typical "worse before better" situation, and again remained unresponsive to the worsening. OQ® Analyst offers the added benefit of an empirically derived algorithm that informs the clinician of trajectories that are outliers rather than within the typical range.

Additionally, the therapist may not have deduced, through observation, that part of the early difficulty in therapy was due to the Therapeutic Alliance. The OQ®-ASC helped focus the therapist's efforts in approaching and strengthening the alliance directly, which became a turning point in therapy. Without the OQ®-ASC, the therapist may have drawn any number of conclusions regarding Elizabeth's difficulty (e.g., the client wasn't ready to change, the client felt too overwhelmed to approach difficult emotions, or that the client only wanted to focus on concrete "coping skills"). None of these approaches would have directly addressed the alliance, which appeared to be one of the major hindrances in therapeutic progress. Finally, if the therapist had addressed the alliance without the aid of repeated OQ®-ASC measurement, they may have interpreted the increase in symptoms between session 4 and 5 as a reflection of the intervention not being effective, whereas the OQ®-ASC revealed better Therapeutic Alliance and an increase in stressful Life Events between those sessions. Because the alliance was improving, the increase in the OQ could be attributed to the recent stressful life event. This dynamic interaction between therapist clinical judgment and the OQ® Analyst system allowed for a multimodal approach to assessment and treatment over time, and ultimately led to the client being able to fully engage with therapy in an environment that felt safe. This, then, led to a decrease in symptoms and an increase in healthy functioning.

Critical Reflection of the OQ® Analyst System

The OQ® Analyst system (comprised of the OQ-45, the OQ®-ASC, and clinical support tools) offers an integrated feedback system that can have a significant impact on clients, clinicians, and clinics. After having described the system, a brief review of the research, and a case example, we now present several strengths as well as potential difficulties that are worthy of consideration.

Strengths

The OQ-45 provides a consistent, quantitative approach that allows for multimethod ongoing assessment throughout the course of therapy. While this is not unique to the OQ-45 (and cognitive behavioral therapy has long included repeated measurement in therapeutic interventions), the OQ-45 has several advantages over many traditional measures. First, it was designed to be a transdiagnostic measure of global psychological functioning rather than a diagnosis-specific measure of symptom severity. This indicates two strengths—first, the measure can be used broadly in a clinic across all clients and diagnoses; and second, it includes not only measures of symptoms, but also interpersonal and social role functioning. This breadth of application and content allows for simpler integration into a clinical system and a richer definition of psychotherapy outcomes than more narrow measures.

Second, the measure was designed to detect change over time in treatment and includes empirically derived algorithms that signal to therapists whether their client is "on-track" (i.e., following the expected trajectory of change based on their initial score) or "not-on-track" (i.e., following unexpected and deteriorating trajectories of change). Without these signals, a clinician would have significant difficulty accurately interpreting change in a measure and how their client's scores relate to the final psychotherapy outcome. Unfortunately, therapists appear to be blinded by their optimistic positive view of their own effectiveness, perhaps even to the extreme of interpreting negative outcomes as a positive development.

Third, there is significant research evidence (noted above) that using the OQ-45 and accompanying clinical support tools is associated with better outcomes for clients. As noted above, this appears to be particularly true of clients who are likely to deteriorate in therapy. There is also evidence that using the OQ-45 as a feedback tool is associated with diminishing variance in outcomes between therapists—in other words, therapists are more likely to do equally well with clients if feedback is employed (Delgadillo et al., 2022).

Fourth, the OQ-45 has recently demonstrated invariance across gender and time (Howland, 2021; Silva et al., 2016), and has shown relatively robust psychometrics, particularly when considering the total score rather than subscales.

Fifth, OQ® Analyst is a relatively convenient system that allows for flexible delivery and immediate feedback. This is essential for working clinics and clinicians that cannot sustain implementing a burdensome outcome monitoring protocol. OQ® Analyst is simple to access online, and clients are able to quickly and easily complete questionnaires through the client-facing portal.

Potential Difficulties

Despite the convenience of OQ® Analyst, implementing a new system in an established psychotherapy practice can be difficult logistically and financially. Wampold and Miller (2023) emphasize that focusing on training individual therapists is similar to "looking for the keys where the light is." It can be convenient to focus on the easiest point of implementation, but it likely misses the broader context that leads to the effectiveness of the approach—a strong clinic culture around feedback-informed treatment and monitoring outcomes, with strong administrative support.

In addition to the difficulties at the clinic level, it can be difficult for individual therapists who were not trained in graduate programs that emphasized the use of routine outcome monitoring to begin to use weekly outcome measurements. Therapists may believe that the repeated use of a measure is too onerous a task for clients who are already coming in distressed, or that the measure doesn't capture the parts of psychotherapy outcome that they value. They may also find it threatening to have their psychotherapy outcomes measured and worry that administrators may use the data to compare employees or determine pay or rank advancement (for further discussion of these obstacles, see Boswell et al., 2015). In the presence of all these potential impediments, OQ® Analyst relies on individual therapists to view the feedback—something that the first author has informally examined in his own clinic and found that about half of the therapists rarely or never access OQ® Analyst reports for their clients. Though perhaps obvious, if the therapist does not view the feedback (which can be a common occurrence in practice), the system cannot have an effect.

While implementation concerns loom as the largest difficulties associated with OQ® Analyst, two other concerns bear mentioning. First, the factor structure of the OQ has been relatively inconsistent across the literature (as noted above) and it appears that the individual subscales reported in OQ® Analyst are less easily interpretable than the total score. That said, recent analyses have supported the structure in a bifactor model, where the subscales primarily contribute to a shared "general" factor but also separate neatly into the originally designed subscales (see Arader, 2021; Howland, 2021).

Second, while OQ® Analyst includes both a measure of outcome (the OQ-45) and a measure of process (the OQ®-ASC), it likely does not capture every component of psychotherapy outcome that may be important to a client or a clinician. This has been more recently recognized in the literature and efforts have been made to create measures that capture a broader view of outcome, including changes in insight, changes in the client's relationship to self, and changes in a sense of agency or empowerment (see Chui et al., 2021; Levitt et al., 2023). Studies by Ogles et al. (2022) and Ghelfi (2021) have also explored discrepancies between client's retrospective evaluations of their psychotherapy and their OQ-45 trajectories. For example, some clients report feeling that they had recovered when their OQ-45 scores suggested they had deteriorated. These disparities merit further research and represent a practical limitation of the OQ® Analyst system.

Conclusion

Despite the limitations listed above, the OQ® Analyst system represents one of the first developed and best-researched psychotherapy feedback systems available. The system is designed to facilitate clinical judgment using empirically derived algorithms and provide a clinician with tools for addressing psychotherapy process difficulties (particularly when the client is predicted to deteriorate). Decades of research support its use in improving the delivery of psychotherapy across a diverse array of therapeutic orientations, clinical settings, and populations. In an era of multiplying therapeutic theories, techniques, and strategies, OQ® Analyst represents one of the simplest and most effective tools available to broadly improve psychotherapy outcomes.

References

Amble, I., Gude, T., Stubdal, S., Andersen, B. J., & Wampold, B. E. (2015). The effect of implementing the Outcome Questionnaire-45.2 feedback system in Norway: A multisite randomized clinical trial in a naturalistic setting. *Psychotherapy Research, 25*(6), 669–677. https://doi.org/10.1080/10503307.2014.928756

Arader, L. L. (2021). *The OQ-45: The structure of mental health symptoms during psychotherapy* [Doctoral dissertation, St. John's University]. St. John's Scholar. https://scholar.stjohns.edu/theses_dissertations/254/

Boswell, J. F., Hepner, K. A., Lysell, K., Rothrock, N. E., Bott, N., Childs, A. W., Douglas, S., Owings-Fonner, N., Wright, C. V., Stephens, K. A., Bard, D. E., Aajmain, S., & Bobbitt, B. L. (2023). The need for a measurement-based care professional practice guideline. *Psychotherapy, 60*(1), 1–16. https://doi.org/10.1037/pst0000439

Boswell, J. F., Kraus, D. R., Miller, S. D., & Lambert, M. J. (2015). Implementing routine outcome monitoring in clinical practice: Benefits, challenges, and solutions. *Psychotherapy Research, 25*(1), 6–19. https://doi.org/10.1080/10503307.2013.817696

Bovendeerd, B., de Jong, K., de Groot, E., Moerbeek, M., & de Keijser, J. (2022). Enhancing the effect of psychotherapy through systematic client feedback in outpatient mental healthcare: A cluster randomized trial. *Psychotherapy Research, 32*(6), 710–722. https://doi.org/10.1080/10503307.2021.2015637

Center for Collegiate Mental Health. (2023, November 7). Counseling Center Assessment of Psychological Symptoms (CCAPS) instruments. https://ccmh.psu.edu/ccaps-34-62

Chui, H., Chong, E. S., Atzil-Slonim, D., Sahin, Z., Solomonov, N., Minges, M. V., Kuprian, N., & Barber, J. P. (2021). Beyond symptom reduction: Development and validation of the complementary measure of psychotherapy outcome (COMPO). *Journal of Counseling Psychology, 68*(5), 550. https://doi.org/10.1037/cou0000536

Coco, G. L., Chiappelli, M., Bensi, L., Gullo, S., Prestano, C., & Lambert, M. J. (2008). The factorial structure of the Outcome Questionnaire-45: A study with an Italian sample. *Clinical Psychology & Psychotherapy, 15*(6), 418–423. https://doi.org/10.1002/cpp.601

de Jong, K., Conjin, J. M., Gallagher, R. A. V., Reshetnikova, A. S., Heij, M., & Lutz, M. C. (2021). Using progress feedback to improve outcomes and reduce drop-out, treatment duration, and deterioration: A multilevel meta-analysis. *Clinical Psychology Review, 85*, 102002. https://doi.org/10.1016/j.cpr.2021.102002

de Jong, K., Nugter, M. A., Polak, M. G., Wagenborg, J. E. A., Spinhoven, P., & Heiser, W. J. (2007). The Outcome Questionnaire (OQ-45) in a Dutch population: A cross-cultural validation. *Clinical Psychology & Psychotherapy, 14*(4), 288–301. https://doi.org/10.1002/cpp.529

Delgadillo, J., Deisenhofer, A. K., Probst, T., Shimokawa, K., Lambert, M. J., & Kleinstäuber, M. (2022). Progress feedback narrows the gap between more and less effective therapists: A therapist effects meta-analysis of clinical trials. *Journal of Consulting and Clinical Psychology, 90*(7), 559. https://doi.org/10.1037/ccp0000747

Ellsworth, J. R., Lambert, M. J., & Johnson, J. (2006). A comparison of the Outcome Questionnaire-45 and Outcome Questionnaire-30 in classification and prediction of treatment outcome. *Clinical Psychology & Psychotherapy: An International Journal of Theory & Practice, 13*(6), 380–391.

Erekson, D. M., Clayson, R., Park, S. Y., & Tass, S. (2020). Therapist effects on early change in psychotherapy in a naturalistic setting. *Psychotherapy Research, 30*(1), 68–78.

Erekson, D. M., Horner, J., & Lambert, M. J. (2018). Different lens or different picture? Comparing methods of defining dramatic change in psychotherapy. *Psychotherapy Research, 28*(5), 750–760.

Finch, A. E., Lambert, M. J., & Schaalje, B. G. (2001). Psychotherapy quality control: The statistical generation of expected recovery curves for integration into an early warning system. *Clinical Psychology & Psychotherapy: An International Journal of Theory & Practice, 8*(4), 231–242.

Ghelfi, E. A. (2021). *When clients who got worse believe they got better: A qualitative analysis of OQ-deteriorators reporting improvement in therapy* [Doctoral dissertation, Brigham Young University]. ScholarsArchive. https://scholarsarchive.byu.edu/etd/9259

Haas, E., Hill, R. D., Lambert, M. J., & Morrell, B. (2002). Do early responders to psychotherapy maintain treatment gains? *Journal of Clinical Psychology, 58*(9), 1157–1172.

Hannan, C., Lambert, M. J., Harmon, C., Nielsen, S. L., Smart, D. W., Shimokawa, K., & Sutton, S. W. (2005). A lab test and algorithms for identifying clients at risk for treatment failure. *Journal of Clinical Psychology, 61*(2), 155–163.

Hansen, N. B., Lambert, M. J., & Forman, E. M. (2003). An evaluation of the dose-response in naturalistic treatment settings using survival analysis. *Mental Health Services Research, 5*(1), 1–12.

Hansson, H., Rundberg, J., Österling, A., Öjehagen, A., & Berglund, M. (2013). Intervention with feedback using Outcome Questionnaire 45 (OQ-45) in a Swedish psychiatric outpatient population. A randomized controlled trial. *Nordic Journal of Psychiatry, 67*(4), 274–281. https://doi.org/10.3109/08039488.2012.736534

Harmon, S. C., Lambert, M. J., Smart, D. M., Hawkins, E., Nielsen, S. L., Slade, K., & Lutz, W. (2007). Enhancing outcome for potential treatment failures: Therapist-client feedback and clinical support tools. *Psychotherapy Research, 17*(4), 379–392. https://doi.org/10.1080/10503300600702331

Howland, S. M. (2021). Longitudinal measurement invariance of the Outcome Questionnaire-45. [Doctoral dissertation, Brigham Young University]. ScholarsArchive. https://scholarsarchive.byu.edu/etd/9694/

Iraurgi, I., & Penas, P. (2021). Outcomes assessment in psychological treatment: Spanish adaptation of OQ-45 (outcome questionnaire). *Revista Latinoamericana de Psicología, 53*, 56–63. https://doi.org/10.14349/rlp.2021.v53.7

Jabrayilov, R., Emons, W. H., de Jong, K., & Sijtsma, K. (2017). Longitudinal measurement invariance of the Dutch Outcome Questionnaire-45 in a clinical sample. *Quality of Life Research, 26*, 1473–1481. https://doi.org/10.1007/s11136-017-1500-1

Jacobson, N. S., & Truax, P. (1991). Clinical significance: A statistical approach to defining meaningful change in psychotherapy research. *Journal of Consulting and Clinical Psychology, 59*, 12–19.

Kimball, K. L. (2010). *Toward determining best items for identifying therapeutic problem areas* [Doctoral dissertation, Brigham Young University]. ProQuest Dissertations & Theses Global.

Lambert, M. J. (2015). Progress feedback and the OQ-system: The past and the future. *Psychotherapy, 52*(4), 381–390. https://doi.org/10.1037/pst0000027

Lambert, M. J., Bailey, R. J., White, M., Tingey, K. M., & Stevens, E. (2015). *Clinical support tool manual—Brief version-40*. OQMeasures.

Lambert, M. J., Bergin, A. E., & Collins, J. L. (1977). Therapist induced deterioration in psychotherapy patients. In A. S. Gurman & A. M. Razin (Eds.), *Effective psychotherapy: A handbook of research* (pp. 452–481). Pergamon Press.

Lambert, M. J., Christensen, E. R., & DeJulio, S. S. (1983). *The assessment of psychotherapy outcome*. Wiley and Sons.

Lambert, M. J., & Hawkins, E. J. (2001). Using information about patient progress in supervision: Are outcomes enhanced? *Australian Psychologist, 36*(2), 131–138. https://doi.org/10.1080/00050060108259645

Lambert, M. J., Kahler, M., Harmon, C., Burlingame, G. M., Shimokawa, K., & White, M. M. (2013). *Administration and scoring manual: Outcome Questionnaire OQ®-45.2*. OQMeasures.

Lambert, M. J., Whipple, J. L., & Kleinstäuber, M. (2018). Collecting and delivering progress feedback: A meta-analysis of routine outcome monitoring. *Psychotherapy, 55*(4), 520–537. https://doi.org/10.1037/pst0000167

Lambert, M. J., Whipple, J. L., Smart, D. W., Vermeersch, D. A., Nielsen, S. L., & Hawkins, E. J. (2001). The effects of providing therapists with feedback on patient progress during psychotherapy: Are outcomes enhanced? *Psychotherapy Research, 11*(1), 49–68. https://doi.org/10.1093/ptr/11.1.49

Lambert, M. J., Whipple, J. L., Vermeersch, D. A., Smart, D. W., Hawkins, E. J., Nielsen, S. L., & Goates, M. (2002). Enhancing psychotherapy outcomes via providing feedback on client progress: A replication. *Clinical Psychology & Psychotherapy, 9*(2), 91–103. https://doi.org/10.1002/cpp.324

Levitt, H. M., Grabowski, L. M., Minami, T., & Morrill, Z. (2023). An initial validation of the clients' experience of therapy scale (CETS): Assessing the quality of psychotherapy process and outcome from clients' perspectives. *Counselling Psychology Quarterly, 37*, 1–25. https://doi.org/10.1080/09515070.2023.2191171

Locke, B. D., Buzolitz, J. S., Lei, P. W., Boswell, J. F., McAleavey, A. A., Sevig, T. D., Dowis, J. D., & Hayes, J. A. (2011). Development of the Counseling Center Assessment of Psychological Symptoms-62 (CCAPS-62). *Journal of Counseling Psychology, 58*(1), 97. https://doi.org/10.1037/a0021282

McAleavey, A. A., Nordberg, S. S., Hayes, J. A., Castonguay, L. G., Locke, B. D., & Lockard, A. J. (2012). Clinical validity of the Counseling Center Assessment of Psychological Symptoms-62 (CCAPS-62): Further evaluation and clinical applications. *Journal of Counseling Psychology, 59*(4), 575. https://doi.org/10.1037/a0029855

Miller, S. D., Duncan, B. L., Sorrell, R., & Brown, G. S. (2005). The partners for change outcome management system. *Journal of Clinical Psychology, 61*(2), 199–208.

Norcross, J. C., & Wampold, B. E. (2011). Evidence-based therapy relationships: Research conclusions and clinical practices. *Psychotherapy, 48*(1), 98.

Ogles, B. M., Goates-Jones, M. K., & Erekson, D. M. (2022). Treatment success or failure? Using a narrative interview to supplement ROM. *Journal of Clinical Psychology, 78*(10), 1986–2001.

OQ Measures. (2023a, November 21). OQ-45.2. https://www.oqmeasures.com/oq-45-2/

OQ Measures. (2023b, November 21). OQ-OQ®-ASC. https://www.oqmeasures.com/oq-asc/

Probst, T., Lambert, M. J., Loew, T. H., Dahlbender, R. W., Göllner, R., & Tritt, K. (2013). Feedback on patient progress and clinical support tools for therapists: Improved outcome for patients at risk of treatment failure in psychosomatic in-patient therapy under the conditions of routine practice. *Journal of Psychosomatic Research, 75*(3), 255–261. https://doi.org/10.1016/j.jpsychores.2013.07.003

Shimokawa, K., Lambert, M. J., & Smart, D. W. (2010). Enhancing treatment outcome of patients at risk of treatment failure: Meta-analytic and mega-analytic review of a psychotherapy quality assurance system. *Journal of Consulting and Clinical Psychology, 78*(3), 298–311. https://doi.org/10.1037/a0019247

Silva, S. M. D., Alves, I. C. B., Peixoto, E. M., Rocha, G. M. A., & Nakano, T. D. C. (2016). Outcome Questionnaire (OQ-45.2): Assessment of the psychometric properties using bifactor model and IRT. *Psico, 47*(4), 298–308. https://doi.org/10.15448/1980-8623.2016.4.24600

Simon, W., Lambert, M. J., Busath, G., Vazquez, A., Berkeljon, A., Hyer, K., Granley, M., & Berrett, M. (2013). Effects of providing patient progress feedback and clinical support tools to psychotherapists in an inpatient eating disorders treatment program: A randomized controlled study. *Psychotherapy Research, 23*(3), 287–300. https://doi.org/10.1080/10503307.2013.787497

Slade, K., Lambert, M. J., Harmon, S. C., Smart, D. W., & Bailey, R. (2008). Improving psychotherapy outcome: The use of immediate electronic feedback and revised clinical support tools. *Clinical Psychology & Psychotherapy, 15*(5), 287–303. https://doi.org/10.1002/cpp.594

Spielmans, G. I., Masters, K. S., & Lambert, M. J. (2006). A comparison of rational versus empirical methods in the prediction of psychotherapy outcome. *Clinical Psychology & Psychotherapy, 13*(3), 202–214. https://doi.org/10.1002/cpp.491

Timulak, L., & Pascual-Leone, A. (2015). New developments for case conceptualization in emotion-focused therapy. *Clinical Psychology & Psychotherapy, 22*(6), 619–636. https://doi.org/10.1002/cpp.1922

Umphress, V. J., Lambert, M. J., Smart, D. W., Barlow, S. H., & Clouse, G. (1997). Concurrent and construct validity of the Outcome Questionnaire. *Journal of Psychoeducational Assessment, 15*(1), 40–55.

Vermeersch, D. A., Lambert, M. J., & Burlingame, G. M. (2000). Outcome questionnaire: Item sensitivity to change. *Journal of Personality Assessment, 74*(2), 242–261.

Vermeersch, D. A., Whipple, J. L., Lambert, M. J., Hawkins, E. J., Burchfield, C. M., & Okiishi, J. C. (2004). Outcome Questionnaire: Is it sensitive to changes in counseling center clients? *Journal of Counseling Psychology, 51*(1), 38–49. https://doi.org/10.1037/0022-0167.51.1.38

Wampold, B. E., & Miller, S. D. (2023). Measurement-based care professional practice guideline: Fine, but guidelines do not make good therapy. *Psychotherapy, 60*(1), 17–19. https://doi.org/10.1037/pst0000450

Whipple, J. L., Lambert, M. J., Vermeersch, D. A., Smart, D. W., Nielsen, S. L., & Hawkins, E. J. (2003). Improving the effects of psychotherapy: The use of early identification of treatment and problem-solving strategies in routine practice. *Journal of Counseling Psychology, 50*(1), 59–68. https://doi.org/10.1037/0022-0167.50.1.59

White, M. M., Lambert, M. J., Ogles, B. M., McLaughlin, S. B., Bailey, R. J., & Tingey, K. M. (2015). Using the assessment for signal clients as a feedback tool for reducing treatment failure. *Psychotherapy Research, 25*, 724–734. https://doi.org/10.1080/10503307.2015.1009862

Chapter 6
Clinical Support Tools for Treatment Adaptation in Non-improving Cases

Jaime Delgadillo, Kim de Jong, and Michael Barkham

Introduction

Routine outcome monitoring involves the regular and systematic collection of psychometric measures that index a patient's ongoing response to treatment. This process can be supplemented by computerised feedback systems, which automatically identify patients at risk of treatment failure, so-called 'not-on-track' cases, whose trajectory of change is poor compared to most other patients. In these cases, usual psychological procedures are insufficient to effect change, which warrants considering some adaptations of the treatment plan to prevent poor treatment outcomes (Lambert et al., 2002). Logically, the questions that follow are twofold: Why is the therapy not-on-track? What can be done to rectify this? This chapter aims to provide

JD and KdJ receive royalties from a book on routine outcome monitoring and feedback. MB has no financial or other conflicts of interest to disclose. Abridged versions of the content in this chapter are used by the authors for teaching, training and clinical supervision. Correspondence concerning this article should be addressed to Jaime Delgadillo, Institute of Psychiatry, Psychology and Neuroscience, King's College London, De Crespigny Park, London SE5 8AF, United Kingdom. Email: jaime.delgadillo@kcl.ac.uk

J. Delgadillo (✉)
Institute of Psychiatry, Psychology and Neuroscience, King's College London, London, United Kingdom
e-mail: jaime.delgadillo@kcl.ac.uk

K. de Jong
Institute of Psychology, Leiden University, Leiden, The Netherlands

M. Barkham
School of Psychology, University of Sheffield, Sheffield, UK

J. A. Rubel, W. Lutz (eds.), *Feedback Informed Psychological Therapy*, CBT: Science Into Practice, https://doi.org/10.1007/978-3-031-90428-8_6

some evidence-based answers to these questions and supplement this with clinical support tools that therapists can use to adapt treatment for not-on-track cases.

The chapter is organised into four sections. The first section provides a brief case vignette to illustrate how treatment non-response can be examined from two different—albeit complementary—perspectives: *idiographic* and *nomothetic* approaches. The second section summarises empirical research examining the most common obstacles to improvement that occur in not-on-track cases. The third section summarises empirical research on treatment adaptations used to support not-on-track cases. The fourth section presents a series of evidence-based clinical support tools, providing practical clinical instructions and worksheets that can be integrated into feedback-informed treatment.

Two Perspectives to Understand Treatment Non-Response: A Case Vignette

An Idiographic Perspective

An idiographic approach assumes that the course of a mental health condition is influenced by individually relevant variables that characterise each patient's unique biopsychosocial circumstances at a given point in time. Such an approach requires

Box 1. Clinical Case Vignette

Sam,[1] a 51-year-old female patient with angina symptoms related to coronary artery disease, was referred by her physician to psychological services for the treatment for panic disorder. She had no prior history of mental health problems until she experienced an episode of chest pains which led to a hospital visit and subsequent treatment with statins. This event precipitated intense and recurrent panic attacks, which deteriorated to a state of agoraphobic avoidance over the course of 5 years. Whenever the patient noticed chest discomfort, this triggered catastrophic thoughts about an impending heart attack, resulting in intense panic attacks and a tendency to escape and avoid any physical exertion. In turn, a lack of physical exertion over time contributed to poor fitness and a chronic course of coronary artery disease, thus resulting in a vicious cycle where physical and mental health problems interacted.

Sam was offered cognitive behavioural therapy following a treatment protocol that involved psychoeducation about panic, case formulation and interoceptive exposure-based behavioural experiments which aimed to modify

(continued)

[1] Pseudonym.

Box 1. (continued)
catastrophic misinterpretations of somatic sensations (Clark & Salkovskis, 2009). Using a computerised feedback system to monitor the patient's treatment response with repeated measurements of anxiety symptoms (GAD-7; Spitzer et al., 2006), the therapist became aware that the trajectory of anxiety symptoms was not-on-track.

Upon discussion with the patient about the feedback and lack of improvement, it became clear that the patient's distress was intensified by events and activities that led her to notice her heart palpitations or to become exhausted. She also tended to hyper-focus on bodily sensations when she was idle, for instance, during days when she felt excessively tired and avoided activities. Moreover, she explained that she avoided engaging with interoceptive exposure tasks discussed with her therapist due to fear that this might provoke a heart attack.

Based on this information, the case formulation was modified to promote greater insight into the key obstacles that were interfering with progress: Distress fluctuated alongside angina symptoms, which triggered catastrophic beliefs and avoidant behaviours. Avoidance of activities made her overall fitness worse and resulted in a habit of selective attention to somatic sensations due to inactivity and lack of mental stimulation. The patient was also highly reluctant to make changes to her routine.

The solution involved a combination of three strategies: [1] symptom-induction tasks were carried out within therapy sessions to learn that angina-like symptoms can be induced and tolerated in a way that is not dangerous. [2] Attention-training experiments were practised in session to learn that selective attention to any bodily sensation has a magnifying and anxiety-inducing effect. [3] A decisional-balance exercise was used to increase motivation to change, which supported the patient to gradually improve her fitness through a graded activity schedule, enabling her to have greater sources of mental and physical stimulation.

The patient's anxiety symptoms improved over the course of the following 10 sessions, resulting in a full remission of panic attacks and a restoration of usual activities and social functioning.

identifying the variables that are relevant for that individual and understanding their history of progression and interrelations with treatment outcomes. For instance, a patient's anxiety symptoms could be exacerbated by fluctuations in other health problems, as illustrated in the case vignette described in Box 1.

In order to decide on how to conceptualise and resolve the lack of improvement in this patient's case, the therapist had to consider questions such as:

- What are the obstacles to improvement in this case?
- How might these obstacles make it difficult to cope with daily stressors?

- How might they interfere with hypothesised change mechanisms for panic disorder?
- Are these obstacles modifiable and how?
- How should the treatment plan be adapted to ensure that these obstacles do not lead to further deterioration in mental health and well-being?

A thorough understanding of the time course, risk and mitigating factors for the patient's angina were important additions to the clinical case formulation and treatment plan in these circumstances. A collaborative exploration of the above questions between the therapist and patient helped generate ideas for treatment adaptations—changes to the goals and/or tasks of the treatment—designed to improve clinical outcomes. It was not certain that the planned treatment adaptations would have the intended effect, so the therapist and patient approached this as an experiment: based on their understanding of relevant complicating factors, they formed a hypothesis that making some adaptations to the treatment plan might lead to improvements, which could be confirmed or disconfirmed using routine outcome monitoring after implementing the agreed changes. In this case, the adaptations worked, and the patient's anxiety and panic symptoms subsided after adapting the treatment plan.

The approach outlined above is an idiographic method that we call *clinical troubleshooting*. We refer readers to related book chapters that provide clinical guidelines (de Jong et al., 2023) and case examples illustrating how to implement this idiographic approach (Barkham et al., 2023).

A Nomothetic Perspective

A nomothetic approach assumes that the course of a mental health condition can be influenced by biopsychosocial variables that are known predictors of treatment response in clinical samples of treatment-seeking patients. Such an approach assumes that there are common and generalisable 'obstacles' that could be relevant to many not-on-track cases, despite their many idiographic differences. Hence, the answer to the question about why a case is not-on-track could be gleaned from the empirical literature on psychological therapies. This approach requires understanding which variables have been shown to be associated with not-on-track signals and which related intervention strategies have been shown to be effective treatment adaptations. As it turned out, the patient described above had not been adhering to homework assignments and had been avoiding both interoceptive exposures as well as exposures to daily life situations that were consistent with the patient's stated goals (e.g. avoiding going for a morning walk). Even though angina is not a condition that affects all panic disorder patients (it is a relevant idiographic factor in this particular case), homework non-adherence is common and detrimental to treatment outcomes (Kazantzis et al., 2016). In turn, homework adherence is at least partly influenced by individual differences in motivation to change (Detweiler & Whisman, 1999) and expectations of improvement (Westra et al., 2007).

From an idiographic perspective, the patient's angina was a unique complicating factor that exacerbated her distress and avoidant tendencies. From a nomothetic perspective, it could be said that the patient's non-improvement was related to homework non-adherence, poor expectations related to exposure tasks, and low motivation to change. Ultimately, the adapted treatment plan required the patient to see the connections between both levels of explanation: angina-related fears made her avoidant, and improving this situation required a willingness to approach rather than to avoid exposure tasks that have been shown to help other people to overcome their panic disorder. Hence, the therapist decided to introduce a motivational enhancement technique as a treatment adaptation, which would be warranted from a nomothetic perspective.

In our view, nomothetic and idiographic approaches are not competing nor incompatible perspectives. They examine the problem from equally valid vantage points. Moreover, we cannot be sure that either perspective is truly accurate in clinical practice. This is why we approach clinical troubleshooting as a hypothesis-testing endeavour: the clinical utility of an adaptation to treatment becomes evident once we test it out, much in the same way that a scientific hypothesis is tested using experiments. Still, ethical practice requires a therapist to be cautious in the selection of treatment strategies, especially if they deviate from treatment protocols that have well-established empirical support. Under what circumstances is it appropriate to adapt treatment, and what types of adaptations work? These questions are pertinent to the nomothetic perspective.

The present chapter focuses largely on the nomothetic approach to treatment adaptation, and it is intended to complement the idiographic clinical troubleshooting method that we have elaborated elsewhere (de Jong et al., 2023). In the following sections, we will discuss the obstacles to clinical improvement and the treatment adaptation strategies that have been examined by research in the field of feedback-informed treatment.

Research on Obstacles to Clinical Improvement

Lambert and colleagues pioneered the clinical implementation of feedback based on routine outcome measures, as well as the investigation of plausible obstacles that impeded progress in cases classed as not-on-track. In the studies advanced by Lambert's research group, the 45-item patient-reported *Outcome Questionnaire* (OQ-45) was applied as an outcome measure, which includes items covering three domains of symptoms, interpersonal problems and social functioning (OQ-45; Lambert et al., 2004). In these studies, patients completed the OQ-45 on a session-by-session basis and their responses were classed as on-track or not-on-track using a computerised feedback system called OQ-Analyst (Lambert, 2012). Evidence from clinical trials using this system indicates that providing feedback about the patient's treatment progress improved clinical outcomes in comparison to usual therapy control groups (Shimokawa et al., 2010). Lambert and colleagues also developed the *Assessment for Signal Cases* (ASC), a 40-item patient-reported questionnaire which covers four domains: therapeutic alliance, social support, motivation and negative life events (Lambert et al., 2007). Psychometric studies have supported the four-domain factor structure of the ASC measure (Probst et al., 2020). These domains were selected with reference to the psychotherapy process literature and intended to capture the fewest number of transtheoretical factors that might be relevant to a wide clinical population, and which are amenable to change. The reasoning behind the ASC was that an extreme score denoting a problem in one or more of these domains could be associated with poor treatment response, and hence could be a target for treatment adaptation. The studies described below collected both routine outcome monitoring data as well as the ASC in the same sample, allowing for an investigation of the prognostic value of these hypothetical obstacles to improvement.

White et al. (2015) analysed data from 107 cases classed as not-on-track using the OQ-Analyst system during hospital-based outpatient therapy for common mental health problems (mood, anxiety and substance use disorders) and who completed the ASC questionnaire. Applying a cluster analysis to responses in the ASC resulted in a three-cluster solution: [1] patients with alliance and motivational difficulties; [2] patients with social support and life event difficulties and [3] patients who had an indistinguishable and generally elevated pattern across the ASC domains. A relatively higher percentage of not-on-track cases had extreme scores (alerts) in the social support domain, followed by the motivation and alliance domains.

Probst et al. (2015) analysed data for 271 patients treated in a psychosomatic inpatient clinic who participated in a randomised controlled trial of feedback-informed therapy using the OQ-Analyst system, and who completed the ASC questionnaire. They investigated associations between ASC domain scores and extreme positive and negative deviations from the clinical norms in the OQ-45 outcome measure. Results indicated that only responses to the social support and life events scales were significantly associated with extreme negative deviations (not-on-track signals). In a reanalysis of this dataset, Probst et al. (2020) examined item-level associations between ASC questionnaire responses and not-on-track signals using a variable selection method to exclude items that did not significantly improve predictive value. The results indicated that interpersonal problems captured by specific ASC items (not feeling able to speak about problems with family members; feeling rejected or betrayed) were the most reliable predictors of not-on-track status. Furthermore, not-on-track signals were significantly associated with aggregated domain scores for social support, motivation and life event domains, but not with the alliance domain.

Schilling et al. (2021) analysed data from 413 patients who received cognitive behavioural therapy for common mental disorders as part of a randomised clinical trial of feedback-informed treatment. The primary outcome and feedback measure, completed on a session-by-session basis, was the Hopkins Symptom Checklist-11 (HSCL-11; Lutz et al., 2006). In addition, patients completed three questionnaires at every fifth session: the ASC, the 30-item version of the OQ-45 and the Affective

Style Questionnaire (ASQ; Hofmann & Kashdan, 2010). The analysis examined associations between not-on-track status and measures covering the following domains: alliance, motivation, social support, life events, risk/suicidality and emotion regulation styles (emotional avoidance/suppression; acceptance; reappraisal). Results indicate that social support, life events and motivation problems were often endorsed by not-on-track cases, with the latter two being the most reliable predictors of not-on-track status.

Using a different design intended to capture idiographic and other factors not encompassed in the ASC paradigm, Williams et al. (2025) analysed qualitative clinical case notes for 192 therapy sessions sampled from electronic health records pertaining to 44 cases classed as not-on-track using a computerised feedback system that included automated alerts based on depression (PHQ-9; Kroenke et al., 2001) and anxiety (GAD-7; Spitzer et al., 2006) measures. Participating therapists were trained to use the clinical troubleshooting method described by de Jong et al. (2023) and primed to be open to identifying both idiographic and nomothetic domains described by the ASC literature. Clinical case notes captured information about therapist–patient dialogues concerning potential obstacles to improvement. Case notes were analysed using a topic modelling approach that identifies semantically similar topics (e.g. themes) in qualitative data. Common topics that occurred in case notes referring to obstacles to improvement included [1] the impact of adverse past experiences (e.g. trauma, attachment difficulties); [2] indicators of resistance (e.g. avoidance, low expectations, lack of focus); [3] social and interpersonal problems (e.g. conflicts, isolation); [4] stressful life events (e.g. financial, occupational matters) and [5] therapy process problems (e.g. motivational deficits, poor treatment adherence on part of therapists and patients).

Taken together, evidence across these studies provides support for most of the assumptions underpinning Lambert's ASC model. Replicated evidence indicates that problems (e.g. extreme negative scores) across three domains have been found to co-occur with not-on-track signals: social support, life events and motivation. The study by Williams et al. (2025) also found that instances of social support deficits, stressful life events and motivational deficits commonly occurred in clinical case notes reflecting the content of therapist–patient dialogues in not-on-track cases. Related to the latter domain (motivation), a common topic in case notes referred to as *resistance* included instances of low expectations often related to avoidance of therapy tasks, as well as instances of a lack of focus on a specific problem or therapy goal.

A theoretically and clinically interesting finding concerns the role of the therapeutic alliance. Although alliance problems seem to correlate with motivational deficits as shown by White et al. (2015), there is no consistent evidence that the alliance domain is directly associated with not-on-track signals when controlling for the other ASC domains. This may seem contradictory to the well-established association between patient-rated alliance and clinical outcomes (Flückiger et al., 2018). However, while a strong alliance has been found to have a beneficial effect on symptomatic changes in cases with milder symptoms (Flückiger et al., 2020), it does not necessarily follow that a poor alliance rating is causally associated with not-on-track signals. Recent evidence indicates that improvements in alliance from one session to the next are usually followed by lower symptom scores by the next session, but the reverse is not true, as alliance deteriorations are not consistently followed by symptomatic deteriorations (Sun et al., 2021). Hence, focusing on the alliance as an area for repair may not necessarily be an empirically supported solution in not-on-track cases.

The uncertainty about the role of the alliance in not-on-track cases is also evident in the results of a meta-analysis of clinical trials that applied the *Partners for Change Outcome Management System* (PCOMS; Miller & Duncan, 2004). This routine outcome monitoring system includes patient-reported measures of the alliance (SRS) and psychological distress (ORS), which are used to provide continuous feedback to therapists. In the meta-analysis by Østergård et al. (2020) including data from 18 studies, feedback was significantly associated with better treatment outcomes relative to usual therapy without feedback. However, removing samples from studies that did not provide feedback on the alliance (SRS) did not change the overall effects. Furthermore, there were no significant differences between feedback versus control groups in the subgroup of cases classed as not-on-track, indicating that this system with a particular emphasis on the alliance did not help to improve outcomes for patients at the highest risk of treatment failure. These sources of evidence do not altogether rule out alliance ruptures as relevant targets for feedback-informed treatment (this could be relevant in rare cases), but rather shift the focus onto the collaborative aspects of the alliance: goals and tasks. Hence, we caution against jumping to the conclusion that not-on-track signals are necessarily due to some alliance rupture, and we recommend a careful consideration of the other domains as initial hypotheses to guide treatment adaptation.

Overall, current evidence in the field of feedback-informed treatment indicates that not-on-track cases usually present problems in the following domains: [1] social and interpersonal problems; [2] stressful life events and [3] therapy process problems and resistance (low expectations, low motivation, low focality, avoidance).

Research on Treatment Adaptations

Having surveyed the types of obstacles that are most likely to be relevant to not-on-track cases, in this section we will describe treatment adaptations that have been tested in clinical trials of feedback-informed treatment.

Lambert and colleagues developed clinical support tools (CST) to guide therapists on how to address common problem domains that are identified using the ASC measure described above (Harmon et al., 2005; Lambert et al., 2007). This CST method has been implemented in several clinical trials in the USA and other countries. Meta-analytic evidence (including ~50 studies, of which at least 8 included CST) indicates that supplementing feedback with the above CST method was associated with significantly greater improvement in clinical outcomes compared to feedback without CST and usual psychological treatment without feedback (de Jong et al., 2021).

In Lambert's CST method, the recommendations regarding the alliance domain draw on the rupture–repair literature (Safran et al., 2002) and include both attention to the *bond*, as well as the *goals* and *tasks* of therapy, for example:

- Discuss the here-and-now relationship with your client.
- Allow the client to assert his/her negative feelings about the relationship.
- Process transference and be aware of countertransference.
- Pay careful attention to the agreement between you and your client concerning the overall goals of treatment and the tasks necessary to achieve those goals.
- Provide a rationale for your techniques, actions, and/or behaviours.

Regarding motivation to change, the recommendations draw on the motivational interviewing literature (Prochaska & Norcross, 1999) and involve exploring and resolving ambivalence by considering the costs and benefits of current (no change) versus alternative behaviours (change). Regarding social support, the recommendations include practical strategies to map the patient's social network and to support them to re-establish social contact and activities, for example:

- Discuss the client's social network.
- Encourage activities that promote contact with people.
- Process concerns related to trusting others.
- Utilise desensitisation to aid client in overcoming social anxieties.

Regarding stressful life events, the recommendations involve problem-solving (e.g. evaluating possible sources of help, alternative actions/options and their respective pros/cons). Furthermore, this process of treatment adaptation also considered the possibility of reviewing the diagnostic formulation to aid the selection of an empirically supported treatment for the target problem and/or a referral for pharmacotherapy in cases of treatment-resistant symptoms.

Delgadillo et al. (2018) developed a training course that included an idiographic clinical troubleshooting method (summarised above), supplemented by clinical support tools structured as four worksheets, informed by research by Lambert et al. (2007) and wider psychological therapies literature. This feedback-informed treatment method was found to improve clinical outcomes in comparison to a usual psychological therapy control group (Delgadillo et al., 2018).

- Worksheet 1, based on cognitive behavioural theories, targets stressful life events that are difficult or impossible to control. It emphasises acceptance and directing one's energy towards value-driven and controllable actions, to compensate for uncontrollable problems.
- Worksheet 2, based on problem-solving therapy, targets controllable problems and involves drawing up a cost–benefit analysis of a series of possible solutions/options.
- Worksheet 3, based on motivational interviewing, targets motivational deficits and includes a decisional balance exercise to resolve ambivalence about change.

- Worksheet 4, based on cognitive and interpersonal theories, supports the therapist and patient to develop an interpersonal formulation based on a specific event (e.g. an interpersonal situation, rupture or experience).

Lutz et al. (2019) developed clinical support tools targeting five problem areas, informed by research by Lambert et al. (2007) and wider psychological therapies literature. In a randomised controlled trial that implemented a feedback system including these clinical support tools, treatment outcomes were improved when therapists followed the recommended treatment strategy in the first 10 sessions (Lutz et al., 2022).

- Tool 1 provides recommendations for risk management concerning suicidal and substance use-related risks, guiding the therapist on how to generate a safety plan.
- Tool 2 focuses on clarifying therapy goals and enhancing motivation to change.
- Tool 3 focuses on rupture–repair strategies targeting problems in the therapeutic alliance.
- Tool 4 focuses on problem-solving to improve social support and critical life events.
- Tool 5 focuses on identifying emotion regulation deficits/problems and serves as a guide to correct problems in self-regulation skills measured by the Affective Style Questionnaire (Hofmann & Kashdan, 2010) including emotional avoidance/suppression, acceptance and reappraisal.

In summary, all three CST methods described in this section have been tested in clinical trials and cover similar target domains and treatment adaptation methods (e.g. motivational enhancement, alliance rupture–repair, problem-solving). Some of these CST manuals cover domains that are not featured in manuals by other authors, and the evidence supporting the inclusion of some domains is more robust than others (as discussed in the previous section). Drawing on this literature, the next section presents an updated and empirically supported series of CST, including practical instructions on how to implement them in therapy.

Clinical Support Tools: An Evidence-Based Toolkit

The accumulation of research evidence generated in different countries and clinical settings over the last 20 years now permits us to draw general deductions about the factors that commonly interfere with treatment progress and the clinical support tools that may help to adapt treatment for not-on-track cases. Following the principle of parsimony, we have chosen to present the minimum number of least complicated strategies that are likely to help to address a range of commonly encountered obstacles. This encompasses five clinical support tools that include practical

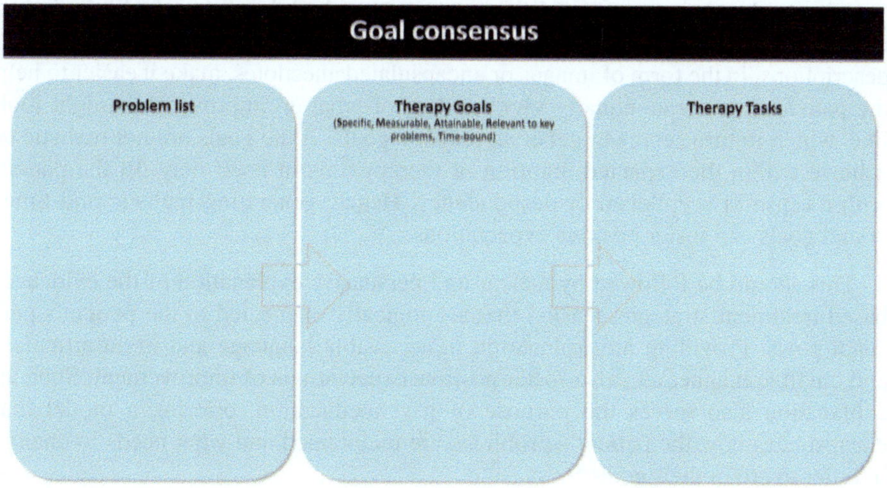

Worksheet 6.1 Goal-consensus

instructions and visual aids presented in the style of worksheets (available as supplemental appendices) that can support the therapy process.

CST 1: Goal-Consensus (See Worksheet 6.1)

Target Obstacles This CST helps to address obstacles related to a lack of focus and clarity about the goals and tasks of therapy. It could help to rectify common sources of *resistance*, such as low expectations of improvement, misunderstandings about how therapy works, poor engagement, avoidance and drift away from evidence-based treatment strategies.

Relevant Theory and Evidence A clear agreement on the goals and tasks of therapy is central to the formation of a working alliance (Bordin, 1979). In turn, goals and tasks are logically articulated based on specific problems that bring the patient to therapy. Generating a list of goals is in itself positively associated with clinical outcomes (Gates et al., 2021), and so is fostering a process characterised by collaboration (Tryon et al., 2018). Moreover, homework compliance in cognitive behavioural therapy—facilitated by an agreement on the tasks of therapy—is associated with treatment outcomes (Kazantzis et al., 2016).

Procedure This task involves generating (for the first time) or revising (at later sessions) the patient's list of key problems that led them to seek treatment. The list should be as specific as possible, preferring vivid and concrete descriptions (e.g.

'arguing with my spouse several times per week, which leaves me feeling rejected and hurt') rather than vague labels (e.g. 'relationship problems'). More vivid descriptions, in the form of images or encapsulated anecdotes, make it easier to help the patient to generate equally vivid images of what an improvement might look like, which in turn serves to generate realistic goals. If the goals are not realistic to achieve within the expected duration of therapy, this in itself may fill the patient with a sense of scepticism or despondency. Hence, generating realistic and time-bound goals can foster positive expectations.

This should be followed by a clear and persuasive explanation of the evidence-based treatment strategies (tasks) that are logically connected to the patient's personal goals. Providing an explanation in accessible language and in an articulate and credible manner can also foster positive expectations of improvement. Such an explanation also serves the purpose of psychoeducation, offering a model that encapsulates how the patient's problems are maintained and what needs to change in order to attain their goals.

In summary, this CST has three steps: [1] specify concrete problems, [2] generate realistic goals and [3] provide a credible explanation of evidence-based treatment strategies and therapy tasks that are coherently linked to the latter two lists.

CST 2: Acceptance and Compensation (See Worksheet 6.2)

Target Obstacles Stressful life events that are not easily controllable or that are impossible to change or control. Some idiographic examples include chronic illnesses, disabling injuries, irrevocable losses (e.g. by death, separation), societal and

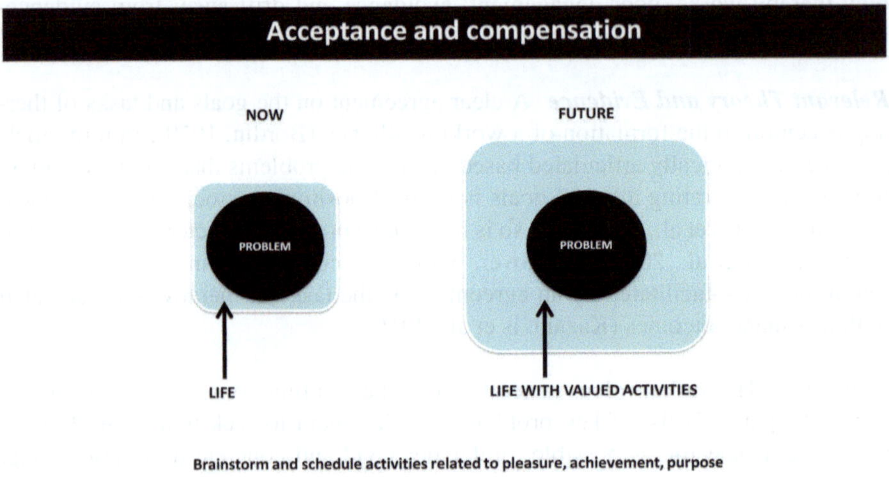

Worksheet 6.2 Acceptance and compensation

worldwide events (e.g. social injustices, conflicts, natural disasters), events that occurred in the past and which cannot be rectified or changed.

Relevant Theory and Evidence Perseverant rumination about problems that cannot be controlled or changed is associated with increased distress, hopelessness and a low sense of self-efficacy (Watkins & Roberts, 2020). Accepting that some problems are unsolvable and turning one's attention and energy towards more controllable and goal-congruent activities can be an effective way of coping with difficult circumstances.

Acceptance as a coping strategy has been popularised by contemporary approaches such as acceptance and commitment therapy (ACT; Hayes et al., 2006) and emotion regulation theory (Gross, 2008). The therapeutic use of acceptance can in fact be traced back to earlier cognitive behavioural therapy protocols (see Beck et al., 2005—first published in 1985), where it was described as a 'paradoxical intervention': by giving up the idea of control, the patient can be taught to control their anxiety and distress. Such an outcome may come about through attaining a sense of mastery or solace through the solution of other—more tractable—problems, or by gaining some respite from pleasant activities.

According to meta-cognitive therapy (Wells, 2011), patients can be driven to ruminate about unsolvable problems because they might have positive beliefs about rumination, such as 'dwelling about this awful situation means that I care, that I'm a moral person, that I am atoning for my mistakes, etc.' Accepting to give up on an uncontrollable problem, while shifting effort towards other personally congruent goals can help to resolve this dilemma (e.g. 'focusing my energy on X instead of dwelling on this awful situation still fits with my goal of being a moral person').

Procedure This task is based on a visual metaphor illustrated in Worksheet 6.2, which guides the patient–therapist dialogue. The dialogue starts with focusing on the uncontrollable problem, describing its history, its associated emotions, its current consequences and the way that it affects the person's life. The left-side figure is then pointed out as a metaphor for the problem: it is at the centre of attention, dominating their thoughts and energy, taking up most of the space in their life, disrupting and cancelling most other things. This part of the dialogue enables the therapist to recognise the person's plight, validate their feelings and empathise with the desperateness of the situation.

The next step involves drawing attention to the right-side figure. The circle representing the problem is still in the centre, it is just as large as the one on the left, but it no longer takes up the whole rectangular frame, as the frame has expanded around it. This figure is taken to represent a metaphor of the future. The patient is invited to imagine a future where the problem remains unsolved, but their life activities have expanded around it.

The patient is then guided to brainstorm ideas about valued activities that they might like to build into their routine. The patient is prompted to come up with ideas for activities related to three areas: pleasure, achievement and purpose. These can be written down and rated according to how realistic it would be to schedule such activities in the short term as a means of compensating for the fact that they have to accept and tolerate an unsolvable problem.

CST 3: Problem-Solving (See Worksheet 6.3)

Target Obstacles Problems that are more realistic to control, which could be of a practical nature (e.g. a financial problem, a difficult decision to make) or which could be interpersonal (e.g. a conflict or dispute with others).

Relevant Theory and Evidence This strategy is drawn from problem-solving therapy (D'Zurilla & Nezu, 2010), a technique that is commonly featured in cognitive behavioural therapy treatment protocols for depression and anxiety problems. Problem-solving therapy is an efficacious intervention for a wide range of mental and physical health problems (Malouff et al., 2007). Often patients are so distressed and demoralised that they cannot fathom a way to solve their problems as they hyper-focus on the worst-case scenario. Or they may be stuck with a single, habitual, but ineffective option to deal with the problem. This technique enables the patient to adopt a flexible perspective towards problem-solving by mapping out more than one option and carefully weighing up the pros and cons of each potential solution.

Procedure Worksheet 6.3 serves as a blueprint to guide the patient through a four-step process. First, the problem is specified in concrete and descriptive terms, taking

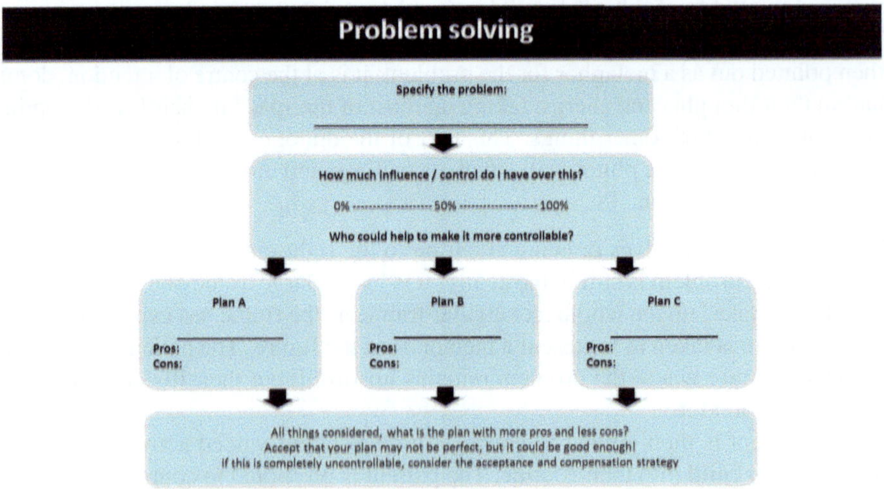

Worksheet 6.3 Problem solving

care to formulate abstract or vague problems (e.g. 'my partner says I'm scatty') in concrete ways (e.g. 'I get into arguments with my partner at least twice a week when I fail to get my chores organised and done on time').

Second, the patient is invited to consider how much influence or control they have regarding this problem. This part of the task enables the person to consider if eliciting social support or gathering certain resources or knowledge may be helpful as part of their options, and it can help them to feel less overwhelmed by a perception of complete uncontrollability.

Next, the patient is prompted to generate and write down some alternative options, no matter how unrealistic or implausible these might seem at first. It can actually be helpful to write down an implausible option among other options on the list because more plausible options that the person may have been ambivalent to try may suddenly seem more realistic in contrast.

Next, lists of pros and cons for each option are noted down and compared across. Finally, the patient is guided to reflect on all the information discussed so far in order to select a solution to try out.

CST 4: Decisional Balance (See Worksheet 6.4)

Target Obstacles Low motivation to change, poor engagement with therapy tasks or homework assignments. Associated problems impinging on low motivation could be low expectations, low sense of self-efficacy and competence, failure aversion or catastrophic fears about imagined negative consequences of trying.

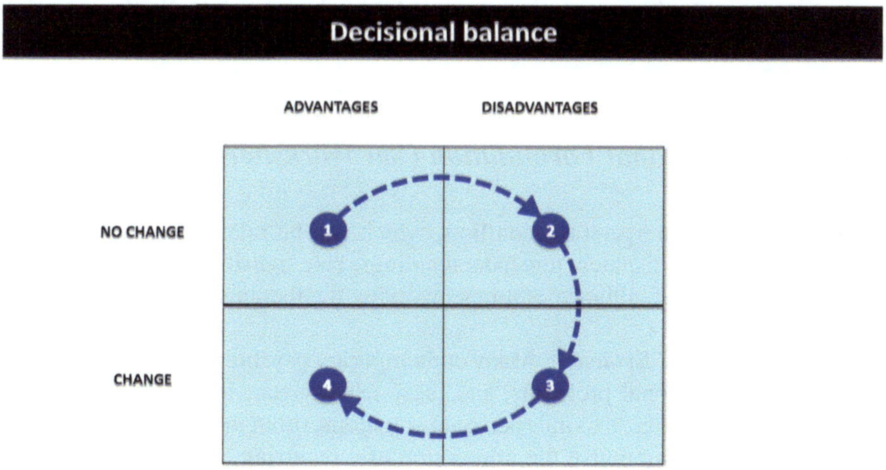

Worksheet 6.4 Decisional balance

Relevant Theory and Evidence The decisional balance is a well-established technique related to the Transtheoretical Stages of Change Model (Prochaska et al., 1994). Originally based on the conflict theory of decision-making (Janis & Mann, 1968), this strategy serves to induce a sense of cognitive dissonance by contrasting two competing sets of decisions: a 'no change' versus a 'change' option. By amplifying the salience of a set of positive (pros) attributes of the 'change' option and the negative (cons) aspects of the 'no change' option, the process is intended to foster motivation to change, thus resolving the cognitive dissonance.

Evidence from the field of psychological therapies indicates that augmenting treatment with motivational techniques such as the decisional balance improves treatment attendance (Lawrence et al., 2017) and clinical outcomes (Marker & Norton, 2018).

Procedure As illustrated by the clockwise cycle in Worksheet 6.4, this strategy involves the patient in a structured dialogue that has four parts. First, the therapist acknowledges and validates the patient's current struggles to make changes to their situation, inviting them to recognise and list some of the advantages (pros) of not making any changes and instead using their usual ways of coping.

Next, the patient is guided to reflect on any disadvantages (cons) of their current situation, habits and ways of coping, with an emphasis on imaging what might be the longer-term consequences of 'no change'.

The third part involves tentatively considering the alternative option of 'change', initially recognising some of the drawbacks, uncertainties, concerns and worries. Special emphasis could be devoted to thinking about any mitigating factors for these worries (e.g. skills, strengths, sources of support, past history of successes).

Finally, the dialogue moves towards considering the potential advantages of change, vividly imagining what such a future could look like, and connecting this to the patient's personally relevant goals. This step of the process naturally serves as a connecting point to the first clinical support tool, which helps to clarify and refine key goals and tasks for therapy.

CST 5: Interpersonal Formulation (See Worksheet 6.5)

Target Obstacles Interpersonal conflicts, which can be related to any number of situations including disputes, misunderstandings, role transitions, unfinished business, unresolved grief, alliance ruptures involving the therapist, etc.

Relevant Theory and Evidence Many contemporary psychological therapies focus on solving interpersonal problems, and these usually start by promoting insights into how the patient reacts to interpersonal situations, often influenced by relational blueprints that over time give the impression of a recurring cycle. Such blueprints contain core assumptions or intuitive models about oneself in relation to other peo-

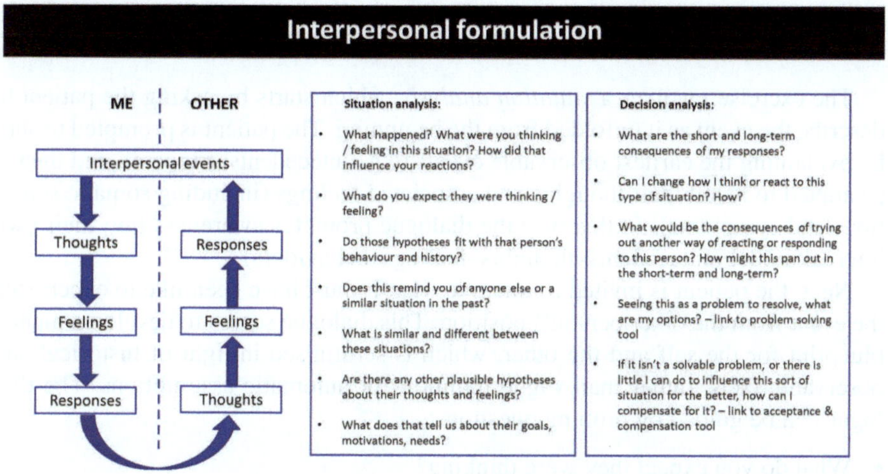

Worksheet 6.5 Interpersonal formulation

ple. This idea is central to attachment theory (Bowlby, 1975) and psychodynamic approaches, for example, reflected in the concepts of *transference* (Freud, 1920), the *core conflictual relationship theme* (CCRT; Luborsky, 1997) and the notion of *mentalisation* (Fonagy & Adshead, 2012).

Contrary to popular lore, attention to interpersonal dynamics is not the sole purview of psychodynamic, attachment-oriented or interpersonal psychotherapies. In cognitive behavioural therapies, interpersonal blueprints are featured in the concepts of *core beliefs* (Beck et al., 1979), *schema modes* (Young, 1999) and transference *hotspots* (McCullough, 2000). Integrative therapies such as cognitive analytic therapy (CAT; Ryle, 1997) approach these phenomena through concepts such as *reciprocal roles*.

Despite the diversity of concepts found across these traditions, a common principle involves promoting insight into the interpersonal blueprint, as a dialectical process that involves two agents, who may actually have an incomplete and even erroneous model of each other's minds.

This clinical support tool promotes insight into this dialectical process, following practical and uncomplicated techniques such as *situation analysis* (cognitive behavioural analysis system of psychotherapy), *communication* and *decision analysis* (interpersonal psychotherapy). Such strategies count with empirical support as part of clinical trials of interpersonally oriented psychotherapies (Cuijpers et al., 2016; Negt et al., 2016).

Procedure Worksheet 6.5 visually represents the dialectical process where two people are involved in an interpersonal situation and they react to each other in a cyclical way. The people can only observe each other's overt behaviours, and the motivations underlying such behaviours are not immediately obvious. The diagram explicitly draws attention to the fact that both people have an internal world characterised by associated thoughts and feelings, which in turn influence their observable behaviour.

The exercise involves a *situation analysis*, which starts by asking the patient to describe the event as it unfolded from the beginning. The patient is prompted to start by explaining the earliest observable events (e.g. antecedents, triggers), and then is prompted to recall their thoughts and associated feelings (including somatic sensations and symptoms). In this way the dialogue promotes awareness into their own internal model (antecedents–thoughts–feelings–behaviours).

Next, the patient is invited to imagine what it must have been like to experience the event from the other person's position. This dialogue serves to develop a mental blueprint for the self and the other, which is scrutinised in light of historical and observable facts, rather than vague intuitions or automatic assumptions. The dialogue can be guided by probing questions:

- What do you expect they were thinking?
- How do you expect they were feeling?
- Do those hypotheses fit with that person's behaviour and history?
- Does this remind you of anyone else or a similar situation in the past?
- What is similar and different between these situations?
- Are there any other plausible hypotheses about their thoughts and feelings?
- What does that tell us about their goals, motivations, needs, interests?

Next, the exercise shifts onto a *decision analysis*, considering alternative ways of reacting and the possible costs and benefits. This could involve role-playing exercises with the therapist to enable the patient to 'try out' different ways of interacting and to get feedback from the therapist on the cognitive-emotional impact of such interactions. Furthermore, this could logically connect to some of the other clinical support tools described above: acceptance and compensation (for intractable interpersonal problems) or problem-solving (for more controllable situations).

Concluding Remarks

The clinical support tools presented in this chapter should be seen as optional tools to aid the therapeutic process if and only when required. As a general principle, we do not believe that technical eclecticism is an empirically supported or parsimonious approach to therapy. Feedback-informed treatment is an effective approach to personalise and adjust therapy when evidence-based protocols fall short of their utility in cases that present some of the obstacles described above. This approach illustrates a philosophy of *flexible fidelity*: implementing evidence-based protocols as a first line of intervention for most patients, but having the flexibility to adapt treatment with empirically supported tools when progress is evidently not-on-track.

References

Barkham, M., De Jong, K., Delgadillo, J., & Lutz, W. (2023). Routine outcome monitoring. In C. E. Hill & J. C. Norcross (Eds.), *Psychotherapy skills and methods that work* (pp. 429–471). Oxford University Press.

Beck, A. T., Emery, G., & Greenberg, R. L. (2005). *Anxiety disorders and phobias: A cognitive perspective*. Basic Books.

Beck, A. T., Rush, A. J., Shaw, B. F., & Emery, G. (1979). *Cognitive therapy of depression*. Guilford Press.

Bordin, E. S. (1979). The generalizability of the psychoanalytic concept of the working alliance. *Psychotherapy: Theory, Research & Practice, 16*(3), 252–260. https://doi.org/10.1037/h0085885

Bowlby, J. (1975). *Attachment theory, separation anxiety, and mourning*. Basic Books.

Clark, D. M., & Salkovskis, P. M. (2009). Panic disorder. In K. Hawton, P. M. Salkovskis, J. Kirk, & D. M. Clark (Eds.), *Cognitive behaviour therapy: A practical guide* (2nd ed.). Oxford University Press.

Cuijpers, P., Donker, T., Weissman, M. M., Ravitz, P., & Cristea, I. A. (2016). Interpersonal psychotherapy for mental health problems: A comprehensive meta-analysis. *American Journal of Psychiatry, 173*(7), 680–687. https://doi.org/10.1176/appi.ajp.2015.15091141

D'Zurilla, T. J., & Nezu, A. M. (2010). Problem-solving therapy. In K. S. Dobson (Ed.), *Handbook of cognitive-behavioral therapies* (3rd ed., pp. 197–225). The Guilford Press.

de Jong, K., Conijn, J. M., Gallagher, R. A., Reshetnikova, A. S., Heij, M., & Lutz, M. C. (2021). Using progress feedback to improve outcomes and reduce drop-out, treatment duration, and deterioration: A multilevel meta-analysis. *Clinical Psychology Review, 85*, 102002. https://doi.org/10.1016/j.cpr.2021.102002

de Jong, K., Delgadillo, J., & Barkham, M. (2023). *Routine outcome monitoring and feedback in psychological therapies*. Open University Press.

Delgadillo, J., de Jong, K., Lucock, M., Lutz, W., Rubel, J., Gilbody, S., et al. (2018). Feedback-informed treatment versus usual psychological treatment for depression and anxiety: A multisite, open-label, cluster randomised controlled trial. *The Lancet Psychiatry, 5*(7), 564–572. https://doi.org/10.1016/S2215-0366(18)30162-7

Detweiler, J. B., & Whisman, M. A. (1999). The role of homework assignments in cognitive therapy for depression: Potential methods for enhancing adherence. *Clinical Psychology: Science and Practice, 6*(3), 267–282. https://doi.org/10.1093/clipsy.6.3.267

Flückiger, C., Del Re, A. C., Wampold, B. E., & Horvath, A. O. (2018). The alliance in adult psychotherapy: A meta-analytic synthesis. *Psychotherapy, 55*(4), 316–340. https://doi.org/10.1037/pst0000172

Flückiger, C., Rubel, J., Del Re, A. C., Horvath, A. O., Wampold, B. E., Crits-Christoph, P., Atzil-Slonim, D., Compare, A., Falkenström, F., Ekeblad, A., Errázuriz, P., Fisher, H., Hoffart, A., Huppert, J. D., Kivity, Y., Kumar, M., Lutz, W., Muran, J. C., Strunk, D. R., et al. (2020). The reciprocal relationship between alliance and early treatment symptoms: A two-stage individual participant data meta-analysis. *Journal of Consulting and Clinical Psychology, 88*(9), 829–843. https://doi.org/10.1037/ccp0000594

Fonagy, P., & Adshead, G. (2012). How mentalisation changes the mind. *Advances in Psychiatric Treatment, 18*(5), 353–362. https://doi.org/10.1192/apt.bp.108.005876

Freud, S. (1920). Transference. In I. S. Freud (Ed.), *A general introduction to psychoanalysis* (pp. 372–387). Horace Liveright. https://doi.org/10.1037/10667-026

Gates, V., Hsiao, M., Zieve, G. G., Courry, R., & Persons, J. B. (2021). Relationship to CBT outcome and dropout of decision support tools of the written case formulation, list of treatment goals and plot of symptom scores. *Behaviour Research and Therapy, 142*, 103874. https://doi.org/10.1016/j.brat.2021.103874

Gross, J. J. (2008). Emotion and emotion regulation: Personality processes and individual differences. In O. P. John, R. W. Robins, & L. A. Pervin (Eds.), *Handbook of personality: Theory and research* (3rd ed., pp. 701–724). The Guilford Press.

Harmon, S. C., Hawkins, E. J., Lambert, M. J., Slade, K., & Whipple, J. S. (2005). Improving outcomes for poorly responding clients: The use of clinical support tools and feedback to clients. *Journal of Clinical Psychology, 61*, 175–185. https://doi.org/10.1002/jclp.20109

Hayes, S. C., Luoma, J. B., Bond, F. W., Masuda, A., & Lillis, J. (2006). Acceptance and commitment therapy: Model, processes and outcomes. *Behaviour Research and Therapy, 44*(1), 1–25. https://doi.org/10.1016/j.brat.2005.06.006

Hofmann, S. G., & Kashdan, T. B. (2010). The affective style questionnaire: Development and psychometric properties. *Journal of Psychopathology and Behavioral Assessment, 32*, 255–263. https://doi.org/10.1007/s10862-009-9142-4

Janis, I. L., & Mann, L. (1968). A conflict theory approach to attitude and decision making. In A. Greenwald, T. Brook, & T. Ostrom (Eds.), *Psychological foundations of attitudes* (pp. 327–360). Academic Press.

Kazantzis, N., Whittington, C., Zelencich, L., Kyrios, M., Norton, P. J., & Hofmann, S. G. (2016). Quantity and quality of homework compliance: A meta-analysis of relations with outcome in cognitive behavior therapy. *Behavior Therapy, 47*(5), 755–772. https://doi.org/10.1016/j.beth.2016.05.002

Kroenke, K., Spitzer, R. L., & Williams, J. B. W. (2001). The PHQ-9: Validity of a brief depression severity measure. *Journal of General Internal Medicine, 16*, 606–613. https://doi.org/10.1046/j.1525-1497.2001.016009606.x

Lambert, M. J. (2012). Helping clinicians to use and learn from research-based systems: The OQ-analyst. *Psychotherapy, 49*(2), 109–114. https://doi.org/10.1037/a0027110

Lambert, M. J., Bailey, R., Kimball, K., Shimokawa, K., Harmon, S. C., & Slade, K. (2007). *Clinical support tools manual-brief Version-40*. OQ Measures.

Lambert, M. J., Morton, J. J., Hatfield, D., Harmon, S. C., Hamilton, S., Reid, R. C., & Burlingame, G. M. (2004). *Administration and scoring manual for the Outcome Questionnaire-45*. American Professional Credentialing Services.

Lambert, M. J., Whipple, J. L., Bishop, M. J., Vermeersch, D. A., Gray, G. V., & Finch, A. E. (2002). Comparison of empirically-derived and rationally-derived methods for identifying patients at risk for treatment failure. *Clinical Psychology & Psychotherapy, 9*(3), 149–164. https://doi.org/10.1002/cpp.333

Lawrence, P., Fulbrook, P., Somerset, S., & Schulz, P. (2017). Motivational interviewing to enhance treatment attendance in mental health settings: A systematic review and meta-analysis. *Journal of Psychiatric and Mental Health Nursing, 24*(9–10), 699–718. https://doi.org/10.1111/jpm.12420

Luborsky, L. (1997). The core conflictual relationship theme: A basic case formulation method. In T. D. Eells (Ed.), *Handbook of psychotherapy case formulation* (pp. 58–83). Guilford Press.

Lutz, W., Rubel, J. A., Schwartz, B., Schilling, V., & Deisenhofer, A. K. (2019). Towards integrating personalized feedback research into clinical practice: Development of the Trier Treatment Navigator (TTN). *Behaviour Research and Therapy, 120*, 103438. https://doi.org/10.1016/j.brat.2019.103438

Lutz, W., Deisenhofer, A.-K., Rubel, J., Bennemann, B., Giesemann, J., Poster, K., & Schwartz, B. (2022). Prospective evaluation of a clinical decision support system in psychological therapy. *Journal of Consulting and Clinical Psychology, 90*(1), 90–106. https://doi.org/10.1037/ccp0000642

Lutz, W., Tholen, S., Schürch, E., & Berking, M. (2006). Die Entwicklung, Validierung und Reliabilität von Kurzformen gängiger psychometrischer Instrumente zur Evaluation des therapeutischen Fortschritts in Psychotherapie und Psychiatrie. *Diagnostica, 52*(1), 11–25. https://doi.org/10.1026/0012-1924.52.1.11

Malouff, J. M., Thorsteinsson, E. B., & Schutte, N. S. (2007). The efficacy of problem solving therapy in reducing mental and physical health problems: A meta-analysis. *Clinical Psychology Review, 27*(1), 46–57. https://doi.org/10.1016/j.cpr.2005.12.005

Marker, I., & Norton, P. J. (2018). The efficacy of incorporating motivational interviewing to cognitive behavior therapy foranxiety disorders: A review and meta-analysis. *Clinical Psychology Review, 62*, 1–10. https://doi.org/10.1016/j.cpr.2018.04.004

McCullough, J. P. (2000). Treatment for chronic depression. In *Cognitive behavioral analysis system of psychotherapy*. Guilford Press.

Miller, S. D., & Duncan, B. L. (2004). *The outcome and session rating scales: Administration and scoring manual*. Institute for the Study of Therapeutic Change.

Negt, P., Brakemeier, E. L., Michalak, J., Winter, L., Bleich, S., & Kahl, K. G. (2016). The treatment of chronic depression with cognitive behavioral analysis system of psychotherapy: A systematic review and meta-analysis of randomized-controlled clinical trials. *Brain and Behavior, 6*(8), e00486. https://doi.org/10.1002/brb3.486

Østergård, O. K., Randa, H., & Hougaard, E. (2020). The effect of using the Partners for Change Outcome Management System as feedback tool in psychotherapy—A systematic review and meta-analysis. *Psychotherapy Research, 30*(2), 195–212. https://doi.org/10.1080/10503307.2018.1517949

Probst, T., Kleinstäuber, M., Lambert, M. J., Tritt, K., Pieh, C., Loew, T. H., et al. (2020). Why are some cases not on track? An item analysis of the assessment for signal cases (ASC) during inpatient psychotherapy. *Clinical Psychology and Psychotherapy, 27*(4), 559–566. https://doi.org/10.1002/cpp.2441

Probst, T., Lambert, M. J., Loew, T., Dahlbender, R. W., & Tritt, K. (2015). Extreme deviations from expected recovery curves and their associations with therapeutic alliance, social support, motivation, and life events in psychosomatic in-patient therapy. *Psychotherapy Research, 25*, 714–723. https://doi.org/10.1080/10503307.2014.981682

Prochaska, J. O., & Norcross, J. C. (1999). Stages of change. In J. C. Norcross (Ed.), *Psychotherapy relationships that work*. Oxford University Press.

Prochaska, J. O., Velicer, W. F., Rossi, J. S., Goldstein, M. G., Marcus, B. H., Rakowski, W., Fiore, C., Harlow, L. L., Redding, C. A., Rosenbloom, D., & Rossi, S. R. (1994). Stages of change and decisional balance for 12 problem behaviors. *Health Psychology, 13*(1), 39–46. https://doi.org/10.1037/0278-6133.13.1.39

Ryle, A. (1997). *Cognitive analytic therapy and borderline personality disorder: The model and the method*. John Wiley & Sons.

Safran, J. D., Muran, J. C., Samstang, L. W., & Stevens, C. (2002). Repairing alliance ruptures. In J. C. Norcross (Ed.), *Psychotherapy relationships that work*. Oxford University Press.

Schilling, V. N., Zimmermann, D., Rubel, J. A., Boyle, K. S., & Lutz, W. (2021). Why do patients go off track? Examining potential influencing factors for being at risk of psychotherapy treatment failure. *Quality of Life Research, 30*, 3287–3298. https://doi.org/10.1007/s11136-020-02664-6

Shimokawa, K., Lambert, M. J., & Smart, D. W. (2010). Enhancing treatment outcome of patients at risk of treatment failure: Meta-analytic and mega-analytic review of a psychotherapy quality assurance system. *Journal of Consulting and Clinical Psychology, 78*, 298–311. https://doi.org/10.1037/a0019247

Spitzer, R. L., Kroenke, K., Williams, J. B., & Lowe, B. (2006). A brief measure for assessing generalized anxiety disorder: The GAD-7. *Archives of Internal Medicine, 166*, 1092–1097. https://doi.org/10.1001/archinte.166.10.1092

Sun, Q., Holmqvist Larsson, M., & Falkenström, F. (2021). Separating the effects of improvements and deteriorations in mechanisms on outcome using the asymmetric effects model. *Journal of Counseling Psychology, 68*(6), 696–704. https://doi.org/10.1037/cou0000569

Tryon, G. S., Birch, S. E., & Verkuilen, J. (2018). Meta-analyses of the relation of goal consensus and collaboration to psychotherapy outcome. *Psychotherapy: Theory, Research, & Practice, 55*(4), 372–383. https://doi.org/10.1037/pst0000170

Watkins, E. R., & Roberts, H. (2020). Reflecting on rumination: Consequences, causes, mechanisms and treatment of rumination. *Behaviour Research and Therapy, 127*, 103573. https://doi.org/10.1016/j.brat.2020.103573

Wells, A. (2011). *Metacognitive therapy for anxiety and depression*. Guilford press.

Westra, H. A., Dozois, D. J. A., & Marcus, M. (2007). Expectancy, homework compliance, and initial change in cognitive-behavioral therapy for anxiety. *Journal of Consulting and Clinical Psychology, 75*(3), 363–373. https://doi.org/10.1037/0022-006X.75.3.363

White, M. M., Lambert, M. J., Ogles, B. M., Mclaughlin, S. B., Bailey, R. J., & Tingey, K. M. (2015). Using the assessment for signal clients as a feedback tool for reducing treatment failure. *Psychotherapy Research, 25*, 724–734. https://doi.org/10.1080/10503307.2015.1009862

Williams, E., Christensen, H., Aguirre, E., Wheatley, J., Corfe, A., Thomson, J., & Delgadillo, J. (2025). Why are some cases not on track? An investigation of common obstacles and solutions during feedback-informed psychological therapy (in press).

Young, J. E. (1999). *Cognitive therapy for personality disorder: A schema-focused approach* (3rd ed.). Professional Resource Press/Professional Resource Exchange.

Chapter 7
A Dynamic Feedback Tool for Clinical Practice: Norse Feedback

Andrew A. McAleavey, Stian Sørheim Espevoll, Sam Nordberg, and Christian Moltu

Introduction

What Is the Norse Feedback?

The Norse Feedback (NF) is a *multidimensional, dynamic, digital self-report* assessment tool, designed for the needs of psychotherapists, other mental and behavioral healthcare providers, and their patients. Though this one-sentence description may sound overly complex and jargony, each part of it is important to fully understand the role of the NF in a clinical application.

The NF is *multidimensional*: While some measurement tools used in psychology measure a single factor and provide a single summary score (e.g., the Patient Health Questionnaire-9; PHQ-9; Kroenke et al., 2001), others tools measure several factors

A. A. McAleavey (✉)
Helse Førde Hospital Trust, Førde, Norway

Department of Health and Caring Science, Western Norway University of Applied Science, Førde, Norway

Department of Psychiatry, Weill Cornell Medical Center, New York, NY, USA
e-mail: andrew.athan.mcaleavey@helse-forde.no

S. S. Espevoll
Øygarden kommune, Øygarden, Norway

S. Nordberg
Department of Behavioral Health, Reliant Medical Group, Worcester, MA, USA

C. Moltu
Helse Førde Hospital Trust, Førde, Norway

Department of Health and Caring Science, Western Norway University of Applied Science, Førde, Norway
e-mail: Christian.Moltu@hvl.no

J. A. Rubel, W. Lutz (eds.), *Feedback Informed Psychological Therapy*, CBT: Science Into Practice, https://doi.org/10.1007/978-3-031-90428-8_7

and provide several scores (e.g., the Symptom Checklist-90; SCL-90; Derogatis, 2017). The NF is the latter. Each type of system has a set of benefits and costs, which have been discussed extensively already (e.g., McAleavey et al., 2012; McAleavey et al., 2021). Unidimensional measures can be quite useful as brief snapshots for the overall impact of problems in patients' lives and capturing the most common problems in a population, like negative affect, making them good at administrative levels of analysis (Herdman et al., 2011). Their biggest cost is in missing concerns that are not common in the population but might be important to several individuals therein. For example, Sales et al. (2018) found that 95% of patients wanted a measure to track at least one topic not covered by the PHQ-9 and 71% wanted to track at least one topic not covered by another common unidimensional scale, the CORE-OM. Multidimensional scales have the advantage of greater breadth than most unidimensional scales since they can include questions on less common but important issues, which might not make sense to include in a single-scale score. However, they usually come with the cost of greater length and added complexity.

The current version of the NF used in most psychotherapeutic settings (as of fall 2023) includes 96 items scored as 18 scale scores, several single-item indicators, 2 psychotherapy process concepts (alliances and preferences), and a 4-item screening for suicidal thoughts. Each of these scales is fairly narrow in focus: rather than assessing, say, depression, the NF includes separate scales for Sad Affect, Hopelessness, Anger, Suicidal thoughts, and Sleep disturbances. Each of these scores may be relevant to patients with depressive disorders, but they are not automatically combined. The purpose of this is to highlight the specific concerns that each patient experiences individually.

The NF is *dynamic*: The NF is highly multidimensional: A patient report includes more than 25 indicators of potentially important topics. We are not aware of any other measurement feedback systems that attempt to measure as many constructs as the NF. However, this breadth is grounded in an important assumption, commonly applied in semi-structured interviews and clinical assessments more broadly: not every question is relevant to every patient. That is, of the 18 scale scores on the NF, we expect that only a small number are relevant or important to a particular patient at a given time.

Which scales are most important will depend primarily on the patient, and secondarily where they are in their treatment process. To operationalize this, the NF changes person-to-person and time-to-time. Patients are automatically asked more questions from the scales on which we expect clinically relevant responses and are asked fewer questions when the scale is expected to be irrelevant. This is primarily accomplished using an algorithm that considers the patient's previous response pattern for the scale and their response to a single key item from the scale in the present administration (for details, see Nordberg et al., 2021). Clinicians can also choose to override the algorithm, to require that a patient complete a particular scale in full. This system means that patients either complete a full scale when (a) they have reported the concern previously, (b) their response in the current administration indicates a relevant current concern, or (c) the clinician has decided that completing the scale would be helpful. The dynamic adaptation to patient and clinician needs allows the NF to include multidimensional scale scores without undue burden to patients. Most patients complete the first NF in under 8 min, with subsequent administrations requiring significantly less time.

The NF is *digital*: In order to accomplish the dynamic adaptation to patient responses, the NF needs to be a digital-only tool. There is no paper-and-pencil version. To support the digital technology, the NF is supported by a health technology company, spun off from the Helse Førde Hospital Trust, in Førde, Norway. Technology is, therefore, an integrated and essential component of the NF. The NF is designed to be completed by patients on their personal devices, often mobile telephones, prior to clinical encounters. Patients receive a notification to complete the measure 48 h before a planned encounter, and clinicians are encouraged to review their responses prior to sessions. Because it is digital and geographically widely distributed, there must be live computer servers operating 24 h a day, with integration into electronic medical records systems, and a staff capable of managing technological challenges that arise.

Despite its complexity, the NF remains a *self-report* tool. We do not claim that it discovers anything about patients that they themselves do not already know: In fact, one of the priorities during the development of the NF has been matching the patients' experience of their own problems to the text of the items on the NF. However, the questions on the NF might trigger insights and experiences that expand the patients' awareness of their own situation (Solstad et al., 2021). Based on the findings that feedback questions have an effect on the therapeutic process in addition to just measuring it (Börjesson & Boström, 2020), the overarching goal for the NF is to facilitate communication between patients and therapists (Hovland et al., 2020). Often, this means providing an opportunity for patients to send a clear communicative message to their therapist, so if the feedback is surprising to the therapist, it should not be surprising to the patient. At times, the feedback could surprise patients by highlighting experiences that they consider normal but are highly unusual compared to others. In both cases, the goal of the NF is to highlight the key parts of a patient's experience and enable a new understanding thereof, generally through in-session dialogue (Solstad et al., 2021). Like any self-report tool, it should not be used as a diagnosis or case formulation on its own, but requires thoughtful application from a skilled clinician to provide value.

Development of the Norse Feedback: Continuous Improvement

The Norse Feedback was developed from a desire to implement routine outcome monitoring in psychotherapy, while addressing two important concerns. First, while much of the research on ROM and clinical feedback is responsive to therapist and/or clinical administrator needs, several steps of the process seem to lack direct input from patient stakeholders (Moltu et al., 2025). We believed that this limits engagement from patients and misses key opportunities to measure important constructs.

Second, we felt that existing measurement tools were not sufficiently flexible and responsive to developments in research and practice, making them suboptimal in the long term. While there is value in using well-established measures, a more agile solution that could change over time would better respond to emerging research and treatment needs. The NF is therefore developed with the explicit intention of continuous improvement (Nordberg et al., 2021). Regular revision rounds based on clinical and empirical evaluation are integral, and the measurement tool is expected to change over time.

In order to prioritize patient stakeholders, one of the very first steps was to conduct a study of participants' needs from measurement tools. Moltu et al. (2018) provided a qualitative analysis of the shared and distinct needs of therapists and patients when considering a feedback system. Unsurprisingly, therapists frequently described needing a measurement tool that was valid and useful for assessment and diagnosis, which most measurement tools have tried to accomplish. Additionally, therapists wished to have a measurement that mirrored typical clinical conversations, in that it was broad and covered more than symptoms: they wanted a tool to help them understand and talk to patients, not merely diagnose them. This meant that the measure would need to include questions about the problems in patients' lives, underlying features of patients' presentation, and also strengths and points of resilience.

Patients wanted to feel sure that their responses on items would not be misinterpreted by their therapists, and that the measure would accurately capture and express their own experiences in a personal way. Overly vague or simplistic questions would not be sufficient. In other words, they were asking for very broad measurement, but also only personally relevant items. This balance is difficult for traditional paper-and-pencil measures because the most relevant question for one patient may be completely irrelevant to another patient, and asking too many irrelevant questions is frustrating. However, using digital assessment methods only, a patient-adaptive measure could be constructed that assigned different patients different combinations of questions. Simultaneously, a fully computer-adaptive test with hundreds of possible questions might be frustrating for clinicians, who rely on a given scale being consistent over time and across patients: therapists want to know that each patient will get the same basic assessment, and they want to know that the same questions are being asked over time. To resolve these tensions, the digital adaptive nature of the NF was developed. The complete logic has been described elsewhere (Nordberg et al., 2021).

The NF has changed considerably over its lifespan, as described in McAleavey et al. (2021), Moltu et al. (2021), and Nordberg et al. (2021). The major determinations in developing the NF have come from user feedback (patient and clinician) and psychometric evaluation. Briefly, we have elicited patient feedback in several ways, including in formal research projects, self-report user surveys, and the inclusion of a routine item on the perceived value of the NF in practice. Clinician feedback has similarly been collected in multiple ways, including formal research studies, in-person workshops, and online feedback. The psychometric data derives from routine practice. In psychometric development, each scale of the NF has primarily been treated as an independent test. This means that we have prioritized evaluating the reliability and validity of each scale, rather than the NF as a whole. In principle, this should help identify when a particular scale score should have a particular clinical meaning, especially because each scale should be able to be administered independently. In concert, the user feedback and psychometric evidence are used by a central group of clinicians, researchers, and technology developers to prioritize changes. This continuous improvement process thus includes substantial content expert input, empirical evaluation, and feasibility evaluations as standard practice.

Recommended Use Strategies

Lately, feedback in psychotherapy is explored and discussed as a clinical skill that therapists must master (Brooks Holliday et al., 2021), but we have yet to fully understand what this skill refers to concretely. In our implementation experience, the key to using the system successfully in psychotherapy is to ensure that the focus of its use is on facilitating patient–clinician communication (Hovland et al., 2020). Therefore, the appropriate uses of the NF are centered on clinical exploration, collaborative interpretation and focused intervention. Therapists should consider a few central questions when working with the NF, and, we would argue, other feedback systems as well.

What Is the Patient Trying to Communicate? As described by Låver et al. (2023), there is clear evidence from qualitative studies that patients use questionnaires for more than just accurately reporting their responses to items. Notably, they also use questionnaires to communicate with their therapists and achieve certain goals, sometimes causing them to emphasize or under-report certain experiences. Therefore, when reviewing responses to any self-report measure to be used as feedback in ongoing treatment, a key task of the therapist is to explore what the patient may be trying to communicate, either directly or indirectly. The NF process scales exist to facilitate direct communication of this nature: the Therapy Alliance scale is very similar to other alliance scales, and the Therapy Preferences scale includes items that ask patients to explicitly tell their therapist if they prefer the current focus of the treatment, or if they would like it to change. We encourage therapists to review these scores each week since any negative trends or sudden changes on these scales likely reflect a conscious communication from patients to therapists.

Beyond these explicit communications, therapists should also consider parallel implicit communications. This is important in every kind of treatment, even when therapists are not intentionally identifying subconscious implicit messaging as a key treatment technique, because the NF does not limit itself to symptoms. For instance, each item on the NF has the option to respond with "Prefer not to answer" and a separate option, "Not relevant to me." While both could mean the same thing to some patients, the choice between them may say something about how the therapist should assess the topic further tactfully. Additionally, should the patient choose not to respond to crucial risk assessment items—such as those on suicidal thoughts—the therapist absolutely must at least consider inquiring further in the session. There could be important clinical material to discuss, like very uncomfortable feelings or anxious avoidance, or the patient might be simply trying to help treatment focus on other topics. The clinical skill referred to in this context is thus the skill to explore the meaning of patient responses safely in dialogue, in line with the general clinical skill of making implicit meanings constructively explicit.

What Does the Clinician Know That the Patient Does Not? Once the clinician receives a patient's NF report and has considered what the patient might want to communicate directly or indirectly, they should then consider if there is anything in the report of which the patient should be made aware. This does not have to be completely new to patients—as any self-report form, the patient will know how they responded—but clinicians have a different perspective and context for this information, which may be useful to patients. This could be as simple as showing the patient the historical overview graph and noting that there has been substantial improvement in one or two scales. Doing so not only provides a sense of tangible progress to patients, but also shows patients that the clinician actively uses the measure and increases buy-in for future administrations. Another contextualizing use could be showing the patient that their scores on a certain scale are rather typical in a patient population, so that they might feel assured that they are not "going crazy." Exploration, validation, and attentiveness to the patient's situation are parts of the contextualizing skill involved in MBC.

Clinicians are also frequently able to make connections between scales based on their case formulation and understanding of the patient's problem, in ways that may not be easy for the patient. For instance, if the item for sleep disturbance is endorsed at a high level and the Anger scale is also high, the therapist may hypothesize that the patient's lack of sleep has made them more irritable than usual. Since patients are not always aware of the link between sleep and wakeful moods, this connection may be useful to explore. However, we stress that the therapist's inferences about their patients' responses are fallible, both because therapists make mistakes and because all self-report questionnaires include measurement error and can be interpreted by patients in different ways. Thus, this second clinical skill involves exploring contexts and interactions as hypotheses in collaboration with the patient.

How to Bring Feedback into Sessions, Explicitly and Implicitly? We recommend recognizing the NF report with patients each time the NF has been completed, but to be clinically sensitive on how it is used in the session. As a baseline, patients should be shown the full report, or at least some of their data, on some occasions when this is helpful to their process. Probably the most important period for this is the start of therapy. A patient, new to therapy and having given the therapist a lot of information about themselves, may be apprehensive about the therapist's evaluation. Not being transparent and explicit in this situation is potentially damaging. We encourage clinicians to not only come to some tentative inferences based on the report prior to the session (e.g., this patient is feeling better than they were last week), but to check in with the patient to establish whether these inferences are accurate and expand both participants' understanding of the scores (e.g., "Do you think it's correct that you've been doing a bit better this week? What do you think has been driving that change?"). Sometimes, patients will disagree with the conclusion therapists have drawn. This is an opportunity for therapists to demonstrate understanding and flexibility, while also seeking to relate the patient's in-session descriptions to their NF scale scores. Doing so can improve the therapeutic relationship and patient engagement with the measurement process, improving their shared understanding in future sessions.

Later in treatment when the report has been reviewed in detail on some occasions and when therapist and client are mutually engaged in a productive psychotherapeutic process, the therapist's method of discussing the NF can change. In many cases, it may be optimal for the therapist to implicitly refer to the feedback, stating: "I looked and it seems from your NF report that you are working hard and feeling some positive results, would you like to explore that or do you just want us to continue where we ended last time?" Such comments can communicate a shared understanding, reinforce the patient's autonomy in steering the process, and maximizes in-session time devoted to productive psychotherapy techniques. A key example would be time-consuming and emotionally difficult in-session exposures: therapists should not discuss feedback for too long before initiating exposures because they do not want to accidentally reinforce avoidance patterns.

Actively discussing the NF in sessions demonstrates to the patient that the NF is potentially useful in treatment and helps engage patients in future administrations, if the use is in line with the patient's needs and preferences. Importantly, we view this method of flexible in-session use a best practice in clinical feedback, not only with the NF: the therapist must use the feedback explicitly and often, but avoid spending so much time on feedback that it distracts from other productive clinical tasks. As discussed earlier, addressing the patient's NF scores in session should be considered a clinical skill, and knowing how and when to do it is another skill that can be improved with practice (McAleavey et al., 2024). Of course, it is important to remember that the more common danger is therapists ignoring the feedback report. Failing to address the NF in session can lead to the opposite: suspicion and distrust from patients, and an unwillingness to engage in sharing information during treatment since the therapist is not clear how that information is being used (Börjesson & Boström, 2020; Solstad et al., 2021). We denote this third clinical skill a timing and process integration skill, and it is aligned with the general skill of empathetic attunement to patient needs.

What Phases of Treatment Is the Patient In? Although there has not been much research on the subject, clinical experience suggests that the optimal application of the NF changes as psychotherapy progresses. Given that some treatments in which the NF is used can be quite lengthy, we generally do not recommend or require that every patient complete the NF at every session for the full duration of treatment. Instead, we typically recommend that in the early stages of long-term treatment, or for the full-length of short-term treatment, frequent and regular (e.g., every outpatient session) completion of the NF will be useful. If treatment is to last longer than 2–3 months, however, it may be prudent to reduce the frequency of assessment in the middle phase, after the therapist has established a trusting relationship with the patient and better understands the formulation. Some dyads find it useful to continue frequent assessments during this phase, but not all. Finally, toward the end of a planned treatment course, we recommend including a few weeks of regular assessment again, to track any changes in typical problems and mark progress for patients. These schedule changes correspond to different clinical benefits of measurement across treatment phase, and we encourage individual therapists to discuss these decisions explicitly with their patients. And to be clear, given the evidence that every-session assessment is often simpler to implement, does not detrimentally affect patient attitudes toward measurement (Cooper et al., 2021) and may lead to faster improvements in patient symptoms as a result of measurement (Janse et al., 2017), weekly measurements should probably be the default until a given therapist–patient dyad decides that it is not providing benefit.

Case Example

Patient Description

Here, we present the case of Anthony, a 48-year-old heterosexual married man, married with two teenage children and employed in a professional role in the public sector. Anthony contacted the municipal psychological services of the public health sector of Norway in fall 2023 with the primary complaints of sleep difficulties. He had previously completed three separate courses of psychological treatment in his life. Two of those, both while the patient was under 25 years old, were a specialized obsessive-compulsive disorder treatment due to strong checking and hand-washing compulsive behaviors. Positive treatment response was apparent from the clinical documentation, indicating that he had engaged well with exposure-based treatment and improved during each treatment course, although the second treatment course was required to address residual symptoms that had worsened after the first treatment ended. More recently, Anthony had completed a CBT for Insomnia (CBT-I) group-based online treatment 6 months prior to accessing services. His treatment response was positive in this instance as well: he was noted for positive contributions to group process and a high degree of adherence to the behavioral treatment interventions. At the termination of that treatment, he reported large improvements in sleep duration and quality.

Anthony's stated reason for accessing care was sleep loss due to work-related stress. He had received a promotion earlier in the year, which included new supervisory responsibilities over a small work team. Unfortunately, in the months leading to treatment, a majority of this team went on medical leave. The causes of his coworkers' absences were varied, but Anthony blamed himself for their challenges, without evidence to support such blame. He felt that he had not performed well as a supervisor, and that someone else could have helped them maintain working roles despite their difficulties. As a result, after only a few months in this new role Anthony asked his supervisor for another change in position to a role without personnel management responsibilities—effectively declining the promotion he had received. Even after this change was granted, Anthony continued to have challenges with sleep, however, reporting difficulty both in falling asleep and early wakefulness. Upon waking, he often felt intense tightness and sharp pains in his chest, which he described as a "large claw" on his stomach. This sensation of weight, pressure, and sharpness seemed apt to convey the intense physiological anxiety Anthony experienced in the early morning.

Upon presentation in fall 2023, Anthony was assigned to the short-term treatment service, a system designed to identify and treat patients amenable to time-limited anxiety and depression treatments, similar to the Talking Therapies for Anxiety and Depression service in the United Kingdom (Lervik et al., 2020). The assigned therapist was a 38-year-old male licensed psychologist with 10 years of experience providing psychotherapy and specialized training in the treatment of adult anxiety and depression. All treatment sessions were conducted in-person.

Importantly, the therapist had been one of two therapists who provided the group CBT-I intervention to Anthony previously. While that group treatment had been primarily skills-based and educational, the two had a positive working relationship and the therapist expected a positive relationship in individual psychotherapy as well. He noted that the patient has a relaxed interpersonal presentation and tends to make others feel at ease, generally being very easy to get along with.

Case Formulation and Relevant Measurement Evidence

Initially, the therapist began treatment with the conceptualization of Anthony's problems as a recurrence of the primary insomnia that had been the focus of treatment previously. The first two sessions proceeded with this understanding, reinitiating behavioral strategies from this treatment, particularly restarting more stringent sleep-related stimulus controls. However, after having the patient monitor and closely report patterns of sleep disturbance, Anthony reported that the "claw" feeling was primarily present on weekdays when he was going to work, and released over the course of the morning. It tended not to be present on weekends and holidays, and would usually subside by lunchtime. Since this pattern is tied to his work schedule, and the work-related stress seemed to indicate a tendency for the patient to blame himself, the therapist was forced to reconsider the case formulation and treatment plan.

Coincidentally, but fortuitously, the healthcare system in which the therapist worked began to roll out the Norse Feedback at this early stage of treatment. This particular therapist had already used the NF for more than a year at a different clinical setting, so was able to begin implementation right away with Anthony. Thus, the first two sessions of Anthony's treatment did not have an NF, but after that the therapist asked him to complete it prior to each session.

The patient's first NF report is shown in Fig. 7.1. The report clearly indicated two scales of the NF that were considerably elevated: Physical Anxiety and Worry. The single-item indicator for physical health was also elevated, indicating that the patient might have complaints about his physical well-being as well. Interestingly, the indicator for sleep problems did not suggest the patient was suffering from poor sleep at present, possibly because the first two sessions had included skill-refreshing elements and reminders for how to control sleep-related behaviors. There were almost no other scores in the clinical range, which is important information in itself. While the "clinical range" is not diagnostic on the NF, it is intended to indicate a level at which many therapists would want to assess further. Because no other scales than Worry and Physical Anxiety were elevated, this meant that the NF was implicitly telling the therapist to assess these more, and focus less on other subjects.

The NF report suggested that worry—conscious negative expectations—were a major feature of Anthony's problems, more so than he had indicated during their sleep-focused treatment. This suggested to the therapist that case formulation should center on a diagnosis of generalized anxiety disorder, which had not been the focus of any of Anthony's previous treatments. It is important to remember that the NF is not a diagnostic test, but rather intended to facilitate communication between the patient and therapist. As such, the therapist printed out the NF report and brought it

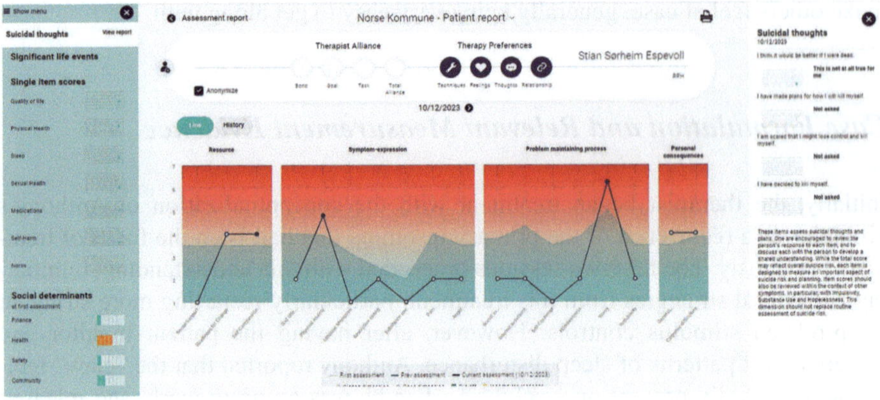

Fig. 7.1 Anthony's first Norse Feedback patient report. Note. In the central panel, scale scores on 18 scales of the NF are presented, with higher values indicating more severe problems. The shaded green area is the norm-derived level for each scale above which the patient may require additional assessment. In Anthony's case, the scales Readiness for change, Self-compassion, Physical Anxiety, Worry, General functioning, and Cognitive problems were above this threshold. The side panels include additional information on individual items and data completeness. The alliance and therapy preferences are not included in patients' first NF report. Note that this is a static screenshot, while the therapist used an interactive website to examine item responses. Additional information is also obscured for anonymization. Some text was inadvertently deleted as a result of the display used to capture this image

into the session with the patient. Here is a version of this conversation, as recalled by the therapist:

Therapist: I was thinking earlier today about that "claw" feeling you have in the mornings, and then when I got your Norse report I wanted to see what stood out. I really see the Worry score stick out, do you see that?

Anthony: Yeah, definitely. I feel like the questions about worries were right on for me, especially with work.

Therapist: I see that. I also note that this distressing claw sensation in your body is happening especially on weekdays prior to work, and you have been having quite a lot of distressing thoughts about work. That, combined with this (NF) report of high worries, makes me think that we might need to slightly change focus. It would be interesting to see how focusing more on these worries about work in therapy might affect your negative thoughts and how we can help you shift your cognitions to target those bodily feelings you're having. If we do that, I would teach you some techniques that we know have an impact on the way we think and feel, and that I think would be useful for you to apply in your daily life. So, I think that you would most likely experience an effect on your daily life if we do that, what do you think?

Anthony: Sure, absolutely. Sounds like a good idea to me, this work thing has really been getting to me, I guess.

While there are many successful ways to introduce a shift in treatment, this approach has some clear strengths. First, it empowers the patient by providing information, including a clear recommendation, but also explicitly and earnestly seeking the patient's consent. This particular treatment requires that the therapist be an expert in some ways while also respecting the patient's autonomy and expertise in his own feelings. It also demonstrates a good framing for data from the NF: the NF report exists in the context of previous treatment conversations and should always be understood as a part of the ongoing treatment. The NF is not intended to provide out-of-the-blue feedback or completely unexpected information. Finally, the NF information is linked to a plan for treatment and the hoped-for impact on the patient's specific treatment goals. In this way, data from the NF is part of a longer story of the patient's treatment and progress toward his goals, but the NF is not seen as the spark or end goal of treatment.

Having received the patient's permission to shift the focus of treatment, the therapist began right away to establish a basic foundation of cognitive theory. The therapist has found that it is often best to move energetically and quickly in these moments, to strike while the iron is hot and the patient is most open to new perspectives. In this case, the therapist had decided to provide a GAD-focused treatment in an integrative mode, using more traditional Cognitive interventions alongside those from Metacognitive Therapy (MCT), in which the therapist had also trained. The reason for this integration was that the patient had extensive experience in CBT-based treatment, but MCT has demonstrated excellent efficacy in GAD treatments (Nordahl et al., 2018). Within this session, the therapist introduced both relaxation methods—a simple mindful breathing exercise and progressive muscle relaxation—and thought-sorting techniques from MCT.

It is worth considering how similar and different this approach was to the patient's past treatments. Similar anxious thought processes had been partially the focus of

Anthony's earlier OCD treatments, though those treatments had been much more behavioral and limited in focus to specific compulsive behaviors. The CBT-I intervention had similarly drawn too small a target by focusing only on one, albeit major, problem in Anthony's life: sleep. With this focus on worry and GAD symptoms, the therapist and Anthony both believed that they had identified a central pattern of catastrophic thinking, which tended to make all of his struggles appear more problematic to him than they often were. The MCT approach in particular differed significantly from the patient's prior treatments, which had been quite practical and behavioral in their approach, while MCT allows for a more introspective approach.

The therapist also explored the patient's endorsement of problems with his physical health. Though he appeared physically healthy and had no history of medical illness, Anthony had responded to that question in order to indicate that in the past he had been much more active and hoped to achieve that level of physical fitness again. However, he rarely had the energy or felt a desire to exercise. While the dyad agreed this was not central to their care and did not require separate focus in sessions, it is worth observing that Anthony responded to this item in a somewhat self-blaming way, consistent with the formulation that he is quick to identify problems that he perceives he should be able to address on his own.

Treatment Course with an Emphasis on Monitoring Strategies

Soon after identifying worry and GAD as central concerns, the therapist began to identify behavioral tasks to expose the patient to anxiety and limit the impact of anxiety on other aspects of the patient's life. This began with some psychoeducational content, to describe the mechanisms of worry in general and identify the specific experiences for the patient that fit this conceptualization. Anthony was particularly appreciative of some early discussions about worry maintaining rather than relieving anxiety in the long term and was quick to understand this paradoxical relationship. A specific feature that several clinicians have reported using on the NF is the division of scores into four domains, as shown in Fig. 7.1. These are Symptom Expression, Problem maintaining Processes, Resources, and Personal consequences. Within this system, Worry is a problem maintaining process. This categorization was decided based on the theoretical understanding that while worries may be the presenting concern and central symptom of GAD, they often serve to maintain anxiety through complex avoidance processes, and they generally make other problems worse by occupying patients' thoughts and emotions. This rationale was very resonant for Anthony and fit the therapist's formulation: Anthony's worries were serving to make other problems worse. In this case, by including relaxation methods early, the therapy enabled Anthony to practice physical self-soothing, exert greater control over his thought processes, and develop a skill for relaxation that he could apply throughout treatment and afterward. The first worry-focused homework were relatively straightforward practice and anxiety monitoring tasks designed to encourage the patient to experience mastery of this skill.

At the next session, the therapist again printed and reviewed the patient's NF report. It showed small improvements to both Worry and Physical Anxiety scales. Anthony confirmed that this decrease felt accurate to him: even just 1 week of focus on relaxation and thinking of worries as modifiable targets of change—rather than immutable experiences due to external causes—had lightened his load. Though he was still worrying, as noted by his monitoring worksheets, he reported feeling that the worries were already somewhat easier to control. The patient had also indicated on the NF that he felt answering the NF items could be helpful for him in treatment, another indicator that the responses on the NF should be taken seriously. This is important because some patients express uncertainty or even suspiciousness about measurement tools being used in treatment, and there is good reason to think that responses from such patients should be treated with less certainty. However, when patients believe that the measurement tool can be useful, they will likely respond honestly and with careful consideration, which means therapists would be wise to pay close attention to their responses.

After establishing the basic case formulation and some initial shared understanding of the goals for treatment, the therapist began to introduce more interventions targeted at the patient's specific concerns and presentation. One such intervention that was very helpful for Anthony was the introduction of a scheduled worry time: setting aside a given amount of time each day when worries are permitted, and at other times, redirecting focus to the here-and-now whenever worries are noticed. Thought stopping also proved quite helpful to Anthony, because he was able to quickly identify worries and redirect his focus relatively quickly, compared to some patients with even more severe anxieties. The dyad worked on these skills over two sessions, with Anthony experiencing greater mastery and control over his worries, exactly as hoped. The NF showed near-linear improvements in the key scales that had been identified earlier: Worry and Physical Anxiety.

Given the progress, the therapist felt that successful treatment was highly likely. The patient's responses to the NF's alliance scale overall indicated that he felt they had a strong bond and agreement on the tasks and goals of treatment (see Fig. 7.2). Slight deviations of these items over time should be expected, but the patient began and ended treatment at the ceiling of the measure, which confirmed the therapist's sense of their positive working relationship. However, the patient at various points did use the NF process scales to indicate some desire for changes in treatment. The NF Therapy Preferences scale include four items that ask patients to rate how they would like their therapist to adjust treatment. In practice, these items are used in diverse ways by patients. Many patients choose not to endorse any particular changes to treatment, either because they do not know how they would like their therapist to change, defer to the therapist's decisions, would like to ensure the therapist knows they enjoy treatment, or any number of other reasons. Thus, when patients who are highly engaged in the measurement and treatment processes do endorse a desire for any change in treatment, even at a comparatively low level, it may be important to address in-session. Anthony specifically reported that he would like the therapist to focus more on the patient's feelings and thoughts, while not requesting changes to how they discussed their own relationship or the frequency of

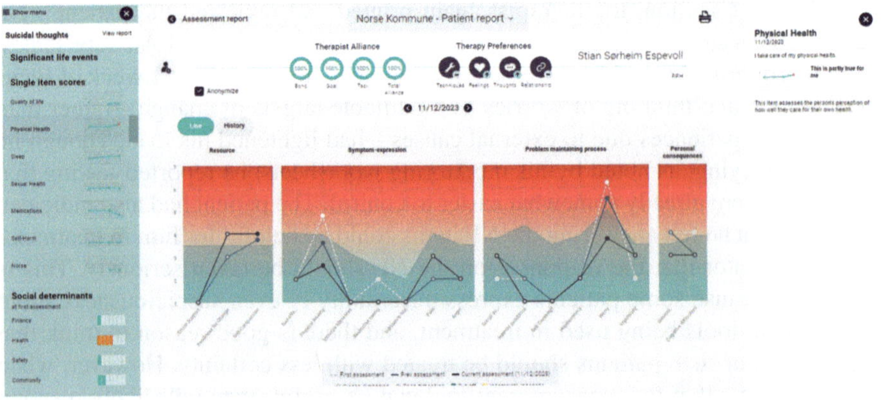

Fig. 7.2 Anthony's third NF report, from mid-treatment. Note. Up to three administrations of the NF are displayed in this view, with different colored lines indicating different administrations. At this administration, the only scale scores that remained above the clinical relevance cutoff were Readiness for Change and Self-compassion. The alliance, displayed at the top, indicated the patient's full endorsement of all alliance questions. However, the Needs in Treatment items, displayed in the icons to the top right, indicated that the patient did wish for some changes to treatment, to which the therapist responded in care. Some text was inadvertently deleted as a result of the display used to capture this image

techniques and exercises. This suggested a desire for deeper cognitive work in treatment. The dyad explicitly agreed that more cognitive therapy techniques, especially exploratory work, might complement their behavioral progress.

Midway through treatment, with significant progress already made but new tasks to consider, Anthony's score on the Self-Compassion scale was noted to still be elevated. This scale includes questions about intentionally being kind and caring for oneself, and elevated scores may indicate that a patient does not prioritize their own well-being in comparison to others' needs or reactions. Another scale on the NF that pertain to self-image, Self-Contempt, was not elevated, indicating that although Anthony was not generally treating himself positively, he did not feel that he was worthless or detestable. This observation helped facilitate some of the therapist's cognitive exploration with Anthony. One of the key insights during this exploration phase was that the feeling of having a claw on his chest, which Anthony still reported occurring upon waking sometimes, reminded him of his father. Anthony reported that his father had been quick to blame and short-tempered, and that small problems that did not seem to be Anthony's fault were often treated as though he had caused them.

Although the treatment was intended to be brief and CBT does not generally focus on historical or family-of-origin explanations for anxiety, the therapist did reflect these observations to Anthony, framing them as a contributor to his current pattern of anxiety. Specifically, the therapist stated that many of Anthony's worries seemed related to his own competence and the consequences of his anxiety, and that these reflected a sense of self-blame that might have some roots in the way his father treated him as a child. Anthony found this explanation relieving, and he appreciated having an explanation for his symptoms that was connected to the past. Though this was indeed helpful to the patient in this way, the therapist continued to focus on the patient's current worries and avoidance behavior.

A range of behavioral interventions tied to reaffirming the patient's skills to expose himself to anxiety-provoking situations—not exclusive to worry—was also introduced. Given the patient's history of OCD and insomnia, it is not surprising that some obsessive thoughts occasionally bothered him despite mostly feeling they were manageable. In particular, the therapist worked with Anthony on a brief hierarchy of exposures, focused on a particular obsession with parking his car. The task of treatment here was to not just discourage obsessive thoughts and compulsive checking, but also to help Anthony redevelop the skills needed to recognize and address such problems for when they might recur outside of treatment.

Already after five sessions of worry-focused treatment, the patient had reported significant improvements in his own sense of well-being. This was confirmed by the continued improvement in Worry and Physical Anxiety scores on the NF. Just as importantly, the patient's significant other reported a marked improvement in his demeanor and mood. This was particularly important to the patient, as it seemed to validate that not only was he experiencing improvement, but the work and effort that he and the therapist had put in was providing benefit to others in his life. After seven sessions, the therapist and Anthony agreed that they had achieved their goals, and that Anthony had enough skills and exercises to navigate any recurrence of worry and anxiety independently. This mutual termination was marked on the NF with scale scores that were all in the below-threshold range, meaning that his reported concerns were lower than the vast majority of all treatment seekers in this context, and that clinicians should generally not need to assess any particular area in more detail (see Fig. 7.3). The lone exception to this on the NF was Self-Compassion,

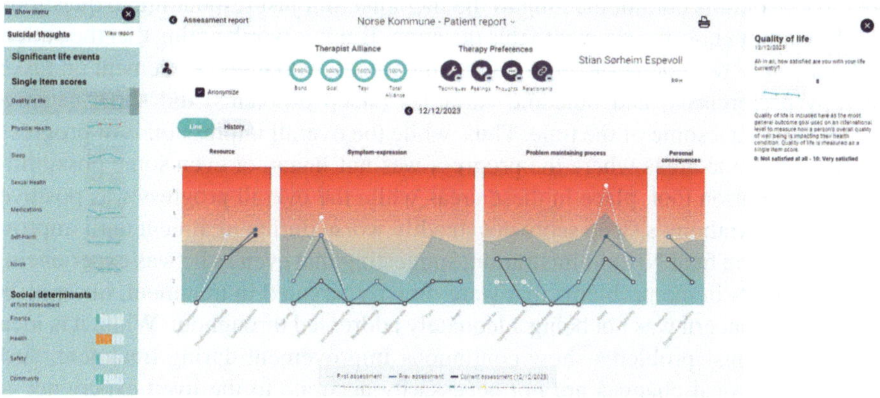

Fig. 7.3 Anthony's final NF report. Note. At the end of this treatment course, Anthony had experienced treatment as helpful, and reported improvements on almost all of the relevant scales of the NF, including Physical Anxiety and Worry, which were the primary focus of treatment during this phase. In both cases his responses to the items went down 3 scale points on average, indicating a quite meaningful change. Self-compassion, however, did not change much during treatment. Some text was inadvertently deleted as a result of the display used to capture this image

which continued to be a bit over this threshold, but the participants agreed that this was manageable. Additionally, while they had not used them for measurement-based care during treatment, the patient had completed the PHQ-9 and GAD-7 a few times during treatment. These measures were exactly in line with the NF Worry scale: They were both moderately elevated at the start, but by the end of treatment documented minimal residual symptoms.

Upon reflecting on this brief treatment several months after it ended, the therapist noted mostly positive aspects and one or two missed opportunities or ways he might change in the future. Overall, the therapist believed that looking at the NF provided an accurate account of their time together: the NF seemed to identify key areas of distress and relationship that were useful at the time, but also allow for reinterpretations with the benefit of hindsight. In particular, the therapist wondered to what degree Anthony's tendency to self-blame and relatively weaker Self-Compassion might have affected their work and the patient's responses. On the one hand, he did truly seem to have a good relationship with Anthony, the process of treatment was smooth, and the outcome was highly productive. On the other hand, Anthony certainly may tend to over-please in social relationships, given his tendency to accept more responsibility and blame than others might in his shoes. The therapist wondered if, paradoxically, overly high scores on alliance and overt progress on self-report scores might hide deeper dissatisfaction with treatment and/or larger issues that would make Anthony vulnerable to recurrence of anxiety in the future. It is certainly possible that another treatment provider would have explored these themes in greater depth, or perhaps sought to concretize this core relational pattern for Anthony by finding the ways in which his relation to the therapist mirrored his relationships to other people in his life. It is possible that doing so might have helped. While the NF cannot say exactly what should be discussed, perhaps therapists should consider extremely positive responses and outcomes in their relational context: the patient is communicating to the therapist, not just responding to questions.

We cannot know the answer to this question. But it is worth noting that the patient did not solely provide perfect ratings. Some process variables (agreement on tasks, therapy preferences) and outcome variables (sleep problems) did show negative progress at least some of the time. Thus, while the overall impression is of progress, there were some areas where the progress was not linear, or even some possibility that deterioration took place in these areas while the overall progress was positive. Noticeably, Anthony's sleep score got steadily worse during treatment until improving again at the final NF administration, suggesting that even as he was experiencing improvements in the problems that were directly targeted in treatment, his specific presenting concern was not being adequately addressed throughout. While it is ideal that all patients' problems show continuous improvement during treatment, such clear unequivocal changes are not necessarily accurate to the lived experience of patients even when quantitative measures indicate they have had the best psychotherapy outcomes (De Smet et al., 2020). It is realistic to believe that even patients who improve overall may have areas or specific problems in their life that do not improve. In fact, it might be preferable to show patients that they can tolerate slight deviations from perfect trajectories of care, as occur during normal life, it helps build resilience. In general, this is one advantage of multidimensional measurement: rather than obscuring or oversimplifying the complex change process, having multiple indicators allows for such in-depth investigations.

Strengths and Limitations of the NF

As with any tool, the NF has some strengths and other areas of weakness. It is important to consider when the NF is a useful tool and when it may not provide sufficient value.

The NF's most distinguishing strength is probably its particular combination of breadth and depth. While many other tools and systems cover a wide variety of symptoms, few systems cover as broad an array of symptoms while also assessing psychotherapy process variables, social/environmental variables, and clinically derived nonsymptomatic factors as well. By including all of these factors in the self-report questionnaire, the NF can capture something important about many patients, while also avoiding problems of oversimplifying patient responses or overburdening patients with assessment length. In the case of Anthony, the NF allowed for a relatively simple assessment and monitoring process by identifying Worry and Physical Anxiety problems as central to his case. This meant that the therapist could quickly see which concerns were relevant, and that Anthony never had to complete questions that he would be extremely unlikely to endorse. It also allowed for tracking of the alliance and preferences in treatment, which were meaningful even though they did not alert the therapist to any major challenges in this case.

The NF probably does not work well for all patients. Some items require a fairly advanced reading comprehension level and a capacity to introspect, given their focus on personal experience. The digital nature of the tool requires fluency with technology as well, and an available smartphone, tablet, or computer. The benefits of broad assessment are most notable when patients may have many overlapping concerns or when the focus of treatment is not known in advance. This is often true in many primary and secondary mental health treatment centers, because patients must be triaged, assessed, and assigned to one of many possible types of care, but means that the NF may not be ideal for disorder-specific treatment clinics where a specific condition is required and only one or two treatment options are available. In its present version, the NF also does not excel at identifying meaningful changes over time either retrospectively or predictively: therapists and patients should determine whether any changes observed on the NF are meaningful for them, rather than relying on predetermined effect size or cut score metrics. Future analytic work should address this weakness.

Summary and Conclusions

The NF is an adaptive multidimensional self-report tool to help facilitate communication between therapists and patients during mental health treatments. Its unique digital-only structure is beneficial because it enables a broad array of specific scales with relatively limited time commitment from patients. While the NF may be complex compared to some other systems, it has been successfully implemented in diverse treatments, showing that therapists are able to identify key areas of patient need during treatment. This includes both long-term and short-term care, as demonstrated by the case presented here. The NF is also a living document: future revisions and improvements to the NF are planned to ensure it continues to expand its validity and appropriate uses, and to support clinicians and patients in their treatment courses.

References

Börjesson, S., & Boström, P. K. (2020). "I want to know what it is used for": Clients' perspectives on completing a routine outcome measure (ROM) while undergoing psychotherapy. *Psychotherapy Research : Journal of the Society for Psychotherapy Research, 30*(3), 337–347. https://doi.org/10.1080/10503307.2019.1630780

Brooks Holliday, S., Hepner, K. A., Farmer, C. M., Mahmud, A., Kimerling, R., Smith, B. N., & Rosen, C. (2021). Discussing measurement-based care with patients: An analysis of clinician-patient dyads. *Psychotherapy research : journal of the Society for Psychotherapy Research, 31*(2), 211–223. https://doi.org/10.1080/10503307.2020.1776413

Cooper, L. D., Murphy, H. G., Delk, L. A., Fraire, M. G., Van Kirk, N., Sullivan, C. P., Waldron, J. C., Halliburton, A. E., Schiefelbein, F., & Gatto, A. (2021). Implementing routine outcome monitoring in a psychology training clinic: A case study of a process model. *Training and Education in Professional Psychology, 15*(2), 87. https://doi.org/10.1037/tep0000298

De Smet, M. M., Meganck, R., De Geest, R., Norman, U. A., Truijens, F., & Desmet, M. (2020). What "good outcome" means to patients: Understanding recovery and improvement in psychotherapy for major depression from a mixed-methods perspective. *Journal of Counseling Psychology, 67*(1), 25–39. https://doi.org/10.1037/cou0000362

Derogatis, L. R. (2017). Symptom checklist-90-revised, brief symptom inventory, and BSI-18. In *Handbook of psychological assessment in primary care settings* (pp. 599–629).

Herdman, M., Gudex, C., Lloyd, A., Janssen, M. F., Kind, P., Parkin, D., Bonsel, G., & Badia, X. (2011). Development and preliminary testing of the new five-level version of EQ-5D (EQ-5D-5L). *Quality of Life Research, 20*(10), 1727–1736. https://doi.org/10.1007/s11136-011-9903-x

Hovland, R. T., Ytrehus, S., Mellor-Clark, J., & Moltu, C. (2020). How patients and clinicians experience the utility of a personalized clinical feedback system in routine practice. *Journal of Clinical Psychology, 79*, 711. https://doi.org/10.1002/jclp.22992

Janse, P. D., De Jong, K., Van Dijk, M. K., Hutschemaekers, G. J. M., & Verbraak, M. (2017). Improving the efficiency of cognitive-behavioural therapy by using formal client feedback. *Psychotherapy Research, 27*(5), 525–538. https://doi.org/10.1080/10503307.2016.1152408

Kroenke, K., Spitzer, R. L., & Williams, J. B. W. (2001). The PHQ-9: Validity of a brief depression severity measure. *Journal of General Internal Medicine, 16*(9), 606–613.

Låver, J., McAleavey, A., Valaker, I., Castonguay, L., & Moltu, C. (2023). Therapists' and patients' experiences of using patients' self-reported data in ongoing psychotherapy processes—A systematic review and meta-analysis of qualitative studies. *Psychotherapy Research, 34*, 1–18. https://doi.org/10.1080/10503307.2023.2222896

Lervik, L. V., Knapstad, M., & Smith, O. R. F. (2020). Process evaluation of Prompt Mental Health Care (PMHC): The Norwegian version of improving access to psychological therapies. *BMC Health Services Research, 20*(1), 437. https://doi.org/10.1186/s12913-020-05311-5

McAleavey, A. A., de Jong, K., Nissen-Lie, H. A., Boswell, J. F., Moltu, C., & Lutz, W. (2024). Routine outcome monitoring and clinical feedback in psychotherapy: Recent advances and future directions. *Administration and Policy in Mental Health and Mental Health Services Research, 51*, 291. https://doi.org/10.1007/s10488-024-01351-9

McAleavey, A. A., Nordberg, S. S., Kraus, D., & Castonguay, L. G. (2012). Errors in treatment outcome monitoring: Implications for real-world psychotherapy. *Canadian Psychology/Psychologie Canadienne, 53*(2), 105–114. https://doi.org/10.1037/a0027833

McAleavey, A. A., Nordberg, S. S., & Moltu, C. (2021). Initial quantitative development of the Norse Feedback system: A novel clinical feedback system for routine mental healthcare. *Quality of Life Research, 30*, 3097–3115.

Moltu, C., McAleavey, A. A., Helleseth, M. M., Møller, G. H., & Nordberg, S. S. (2021). How therapists and patients need to develop a clinical feedback system after 18 months of use in a practice-research network: A qualitative study. *International Journal of Mental Health Systems, 15*(1), 1–9.

Moltu, C., Nordberg, S. S., & McAleavey, A. A. (2025). Collaborating with patients and therapists in practice-research networkds: The Norse Feedback Action Research Program. In L. G. Castonguay, D. Atzil-Slonim, M. Barkham, & W. Lutz (Eds.), *Practice-based evidence in the psychological therapies: Towards clinical, training, and public policy guidelines*. Oxford University Press. (in press).

Moltu, C., Veseth, M., Stefansen, J., Notnes, J. C., Skjolberg, A., Binder, P. E., Castonguay, L. G., & Nordberg, S. S. (2018). This is what I need a clinical feedback system to do for me: A qualitative inquiry into therapists' and patients' perspectives. *Psychotherapy Research, 28*(2), 250–263. https://doi.org/10.1080/10503307.2016.1189619

Nordahl, H. M., Borkovec, T. D., Hagen, R., Kennair, L. E., Hjemdal, O., Solem, S., Hansen, B., Haseth, S., & Wells, A. (2018). Metacognitive therapy versus cognitive–behavioural therapy in adults with generalised anxiety disorder. *BJPsych open, 4*(5), 393–400.

Nordberg, S. S., McAleavey, A. A., & Moltu, C. (2021). Continuous quality improvement in measure development: Lessons from building a novel clinical feedback system. *Quality of Life Research, 30*(11), 3085–3096. https://doi.org/10.1007/s11136-021-02768-7

Sales, C. M., Neves, I. T., Alves, P. G., & Ashworth, M. (2018). Capturing and missing the patient's story through outcome measures: A thematic comparison of patient-generated items in PSYCHLOPS with CORE-OM and PHQ-9. *Health Expectations, 21*(3), 615–619. https://doi.org/10.1111/hex.12652

Solstad, S. M., Kleiven, G. S., Castonguay, L. G., & Moltu, C. (2021). Clinical dilemmas of routine outcome monitoring and clinical feedback: A qualitative study of patient experiences. *Psychotherapy Research, 31*(2), 200–210. https://doi.org/10.1080/10503307.2020.1788741

Chapter 8
Advances in ESM-Derived Feedback Integrated into Psychotherapy

Mila Hall, Michelle N. Servaas, and Harriëtte Riese

Advances in ESM-Derived Feedback Integrated into Psychotherapy

This chapter describes developments in the usability of the Experience Sampling Method (ESM) in mental health care. ESM involves repeated sampling, which is filling out the same questions, typically on one's own smartphone, for multiple times a day, over the course of several days or weeks, on experienced momentary affect, cognitions, behavior, and (social) context (e.g., "at the moment I feel sad" or "at the moment I am alone"). ESM is an established scientific method, designed for time-series data collection (Csikszentmihalyi & Larson, 1987) but has also shown potential in psychological treatments (deVries et al., 1992; Daniëls et al., 2023; Linardon et al., 2024; Myin-Germeys et al., 2018; Myin-Germeys & Kuppens, 2022; Shiffman et al., 2008; Simons et al., 2017; Trull & Ebner-Priemer, 2009; Wichers, 2014). A first question that may arise is why we would consider ESM as a tool to be used in clinical practice?

The idea of using ESM clinically is not novel (deVries et al. 1992). Recent technological innovations provide new opportunities for ESM data collection and implementation into clinical practice. To explain why a clinical application of ESM deserves our attention, we need to understand current developments in the field of psychiatry and psychotherapy. The effect size of pharmacological and psychotherapeutic treatments has been shown to vary greatly among individuals with

M. Hall (✉)
Department of Clinical Psychology and Psychotherapy, Trier University, Trier, Germany
e-mail: hall@uni-trier.de

M. N. Servaas · H. Riese
Department of Psychiatry, University Medical Center Groningen, University of Groningen, Groningen, The Netherlands
e-mail: m.n.servaas@umcg.nl; h.riese@umcg.nl

J. A. Rubel, W. Lutz (eds.), *Feedback Informed Psychological Therapy*, CBT: Science Into Practice, https://doi.org/10.1007/978-3-031-90428-8_8

(long-term) effects remaining relatively small to moderate (Cuijpers et al., 2014). Thus, a portion of patients experience little to no sustainable benefits due to psychotherapy, as it is currently practiced, with some even having adverse experiences and worsening symptomatology (Strauss et al., 2021). Furthermore, pharmacological and psychotherapeutic treatments (the combination seems to provide a slight advantage) have not been shown more effective than alternative therapies or active intervention controls (Cuijpers et al., 2013; Khan et al., 2012). As average treatment effects do not provide a convincing rationale for choosing one treatment modality over another (Zuidersma et al. fact & fictions paper), it is important to consider preferences of individuals and to investigate patient profiles for different treatment modalities (Khan et al., 2012). The persistent dearth of understanding about treatment nonresponse and what works for whom, despite many decades of in-depth research, needs further attention in clinical research.

With examples from our own work, we would like to argue that ESM can potentially bridge this gap by fulfilling a role as a useful tool to obtain person specific, dynamic, and ecologically valid information on psychiatric complaints that can inform and tailor psychotherapy. After an introduction of two specific clinical research projects, the potential benefits of using ESM in clinical practice will be discussed. We close with recommendations for clinical researchers interested in using ESM, implementation-level difficulties and considerations to keep in mind in this regard, and what a potential ideal research design could entail.

Introduction to ESM

ESM provides an ecologically valid way of monitoring dynamics in psychiatric complaints and resilience in individual patients during their normal daily lives (see Hall et al., 2021 and Riese et al., 2021 for examples of ESM protocols for momentary mood or anxiety, and see Kirtley et al., 2020 for more information about the ESM Item Repository). ESM offers a range of advantages over static cross-sectional symptom assessment questionnaires (i.e., Routine Monitoring Assessments, ROM), which we summarize below in five points.

First, ESM has a higher sampling frequency compared to symptom assessment questionnaires. Traditional questionnaires often require participants to retrospectively report on their subjective experiences over longer periods of time, such as "the last two weeks." With ESM, patients rate momentary affective states or report retrospectively about a much shorter time period, such as "in the last three hours." In this way, ESM may be less prone to recall bias than traditional retrospective questionnaires (Ebner-Priemer et al., 2006; Schuler et al., 2019; Stone et al., 1998).

Second, daily fluctuations in affect are not easily assessed with cross-sectional symptom questionnaires. ESM allows for capturing change processes that are highly time-varying and dynamic. Observing fluctuations on an individual level with assessments at a higher sampling frequency allows researchers to test inter- and intra-individual variability in reactions to different contexts and stress levels

(Hehlmann et al., 2021) in a way that mirrors functional analyses of problem behaviors in clinical practice (Hanley et al., 2003). Also, with ESM, the dynamic interplay between affect and triggering factors (e.g., activities or social contexts) can be visualized, and order effects can even be tested. It is helpful to know, for example, whether reduced physical activity triggers depressive feelings, or vice versa (Solhan et al., 2009; Rosmalen et al., 2012). A recent survey on therapists and clinical researchers found ESM to be a useful clinical tool, particularly for gaining insight into context specificity of psychiatric complaints (Piot et al. 2022).

Third, filling out ESM questions appears to promote a patients' ability to differentiate and reflect on their negative emotions, cognitions, and behaviors through the intensive self-monitoring involved (Bos et al., 2019; Widdershoven et al., 2019). Thereby, ESM stimulates and supports awareness of, insights in, and self-management of psychiatric complaints (Bos et al., 2019). In this way, ESM monitoring is an intervention in itself, comparable with the traditional registration tasks used in psychotherapy.

Fourth, systematic ESM-derived time-series data can be summarized into feedback reports with intuitive visualizations of item or scale values over time to facilitate shared decision-making (Bartels et al., 2023; Kramer et al., 2014). Moreover, if and when patients prefer, can also share the feedback reports and insights, obtained from discussing the feedback, with significant others or other health care providers.

Fifth, ESM provides a unique tool for idiographic clinical research, also in single-case experimental designs (Tanious et al., 2024). Ultimately, in scientific research, both idiographic and nomothetic approaches are valuable and needed (Lamiell, 1998; Zuidersma et al., 2020). The nomothetic research approach focuses on finding average patterns or principles that apply across groups of individuals and can be used to develop treatment guidelines. An idiographic research approach focuses on the uniqueness and specific features of an individual. Especially within a psychotherapy context, both forms of research are necessary and helpful, though therapists state that receiving more specific information about individual patients (i.e., idiographic information) is a source of motivation for integrating these types of empirical methods into clinical practice (Burger et al., 2022a; Hall et al., 2024a; Hatfield & Ogles, 2007; Jensen-Doss & Hawley, 2010, 2011). A more idiographic approach, as established by ESM, may more closely align with tenants of personalized and precision medicine (Hayes et al., 2015; Herrman et al., 2022; Schiepek et al., 2015), thereby possibly filling the aforementioned gap in the literature and research on treatment nonresponse and lacking knowledge on what works for whom.

Earlier Research on Personalized ESM in Clinical Settings

There is evidence from nomothetic studies supporting the beneficial effects of ESM in clinical settings (Colombo et al., 2019; Kramer et al., 2014), although contradictory findings have been reported as well (Folkersma et al., 2021). Previous idiographic ESM-implemented research includes, among others, the work of Schiepek et al. (2015), wherein patients are supported in developing a fully personalized ESM questionnaire based on their case conceptualizations. This idiographic approach within the private inpatient clinical setting allowed patients to fully personalize ESM. Collected ESM data are visualized in a variety of graphs that reflect dynamic systems theory. The discussion of these connections is used to validate or update patients' and therapists' unique case conceptualizations. Though there have been some efforts to make personalized ESM more widely available in outpatient settings, successful implementation has been scarce, with much debate surrounding when and how to collect and present the ESM data. More consistent findings are needed to warrant its large-scale applications in regular psychotherapy (Bartels et al., 2023; Bos et al., 2022).

Our aim, to that end, is to present two ongoing innovative projects where personalized ESM is integrated into regular mental health care, to discuss their differences and similarities, and to provide a road map for future clinical research in this area. Recent research findings, from both the patient and therapist perspectives, stress the importance of personalizing ESM assessment by personalizing items monitoring affect, cognitions, behavior, and relevant (social) contexts, and presenting the resulting time-series data as intuitively as possible in feedback reports (Bartels et al., 2023; Bos, 2021; Hall et al., 2022; Piot et al., 2022). How to best present complex time-series data (i.e., so it is intuitive to understand and use in clinical practice) is still understudied. Data can be visualized using line graphs or bar graphs, for instance, showing the course of mood over a certain period or frequencies of activities, respectively. Furthermore, more dynamic visualizations, including network models, may represent a promising method for creating clinically useful visualizations of ESM data, when used thoughtfully (Bringmann et al., 2021; Frumkin et al., 2021; Hall et al., 2022; Wichers et al., 2021). The first findings suggest that ESM-based visualizations may aid in the process of psychoeducation, case conceptualization, and the prioritization of treatment targets through shared decisionmaking(Burger et al., 2022a; Hall et al., 2022, 2024a, 2024b; von Klipstein et al., 2020).

In sum, although there are studies that have used ESM-derived feedback in clinical practice, there are still some major gaps in this research field. To the best of our knowledge, the Therap-i and TheraNet randomized control trials (RCT) studies are the only two initiatives that have attempted to fill in this gap by studying the efficacy of personalized ESM and ESM-derived feedback during psychological treatment for depression in patients diagnosed with (complex forms of) depression. Next, we describe the similarities and unique features of both studies. We conclude with several lessons learned from performing these studies and suggestions for future research.

Filling a Similar Gap: The Therap-i and TheraNet Studies

The Therap-i and TheraNet RCTs aim to answer similar questions; Is personalized ESM a useful add-on tool in psychological treatment of depressive symptoms in clinical practice? Both studies compare psychological treatment as usual (TAU) for depression against TAU with ESM as an add-on tool. Besides similarities, both projects have unique characteristics we will outline below.

The ongoing Dutch Therap-i study is a pragmatic RCT that investigates whether adding personalized ESM and ESM-based feedback, collectively named the Therap-i module, to psychological treatment for depression is effective in reducing depressive symptomatology, as well as improving psychological functioning, the therapeutic working alliance, illness perception, and self-management (Riese et al., 2021; von Klipstein et al., 2023a, 2023b). The aim of the Therap-i module is to support the process of case conceptualization and to better understand the unique (contextual) factors triggering and maintaining depressive symptoms for a specific individual patient. The Therap-i project focuses on individuals diagnosed with a major depressive disorder (MDD), who received previous psychological treatment for depression from which they did not recover or relapsed, and utilizes a personalized ESM diary developed collaboratively by the researcher, patient, and therapist, based on the patient's case conceptualization (Kuyken et al., 2009). Therap-i was created as an add-on module to the existing PETRA tool (PErsonalized Treatment by Real-time Assessment; www.petrapsy.nl). Patients are asked to complete the ESM diary five times a day for eight weeks during psychological treatment. Subsequently, feedback is provided by the researcher and discussed collaboratively with the patient and therapist during three regular sessions. The feedback consisted of line graphs (course plots), qualitative contextual text information, and person-specific network models. During the feedback session, notes based on the discussions and lessons learned can be added to the feedback report, which afterward is sent to the patient and therapist as reference work.

The German TheraNet study is a pragmatic RCT that investigated whether receiving ESM-based feedback, particularly in the form of a person-specific network model, helped to improve therapy outcomes for outpatients suffering from mood and anxiety symptomatology (Hall & Rubel, 2022; Hall et al., 2022). The sample was recruited prior to formal diagnostic procedures and therefore ended up with a wide range of disorders, though all patients reported symptoms of anxiety and/or depression at intake. The feedback provided within TheraNet, once at the beginning of therapy, was based upon two weeks of ESM data collection, with patients being asked to fill out the ESM diary four times a day. The resulting feedback was always composed of the same three sections: a network model, a line diagram of the patient's subjective sleep quality, and a list of stressful events as reported by the patient. The study has thus far focused primarily on how therapists intuitively used, or chose not to use, this type of feedback in their therapies when they are not explicitly prompted to do so (Hall et al., 2024a, 2024b).

Although there are many similarities between the Therap-i and TheraNet studies, the two studies also differ in several ways, namely in their recruitment procedure, study design, ESM tool, feedback used, and study outcomes, which are described in more detail in Fig. 8.1. To showcase both studies, we now present two typical cases from each study.

Case 1 (Therap-i Study[1])

George, a 27-year-old man, was diagnosed with MDD and had been struggling with depressive symptoms since adolescence. Within the Therap-i study, a structured diagnostic interview confirmed the diagnosis. He experienced depressed mood, anhedonia, anxiety, internal restlessness, low energy, and a negative outlook on the future. He also had low self-esteem, struggled with criticism, and had a perfectionistic streak. In addition, he had to deal with the loss of a loved one within his household and was bullied in school, which made him feel alone and like an outsider. He also had to come to terms with his homosexuality and reconcile it with his religion. Three previous attempts at seeking therapeutic help in the last eight years had no persistent beneficial effects on his depression. George was starting outpatient cognitive-behavioral therapy, when enrolled in the Therap-i study, and together with his therapist, in close collaboration with a researcher, participated in the project. The ESM questionnaire included, besides a fixed set of items on mood/cognitions/behavior, personalized items on the topics of low self-esteem (feeling insecure about his capabilities, feeling judged by others, feeling a sense of belonging), his open versus withdrawn behavior (being open about his feelings, speaking his mind, avoiding activities), as well as the option to enter free text (e.g., specific thoughts or context information) at the end of each assessment. Both the patient and therapist evaluated the module through questionnaires, and George also participated in a semi-structured evaluation interview.

Collaborative discussions, between the patient, therapist, and researcher during the feedback sessions, focused on two core themes. First, George's low energy level was further explored regarding his sleep, medication, and activity patterns. The therapist and psychiatrist decided, also based on information from the Therap-i module, to prescribe medication for George's continuing low energy level and long-lasting sleep problems. So far, George had put off medication, because he was hesitant about its side effects. Second, his low sense of self-esteem led to an in-depth exploration of his social interactions and thinking patterns. These two themes can also be observed as two separate clusters in the network (see Fig. 8.2a). The two most important insights for George and his therapist were that (i) side effects of the medication initially increased but also always decreased again over time after every

[1] This case study is a summary published earlier. Further information, including a film clip of the Therap-i feedback module in the Supplementary Materials, can be found in von Klipstein et al. (2023a, 2023b).

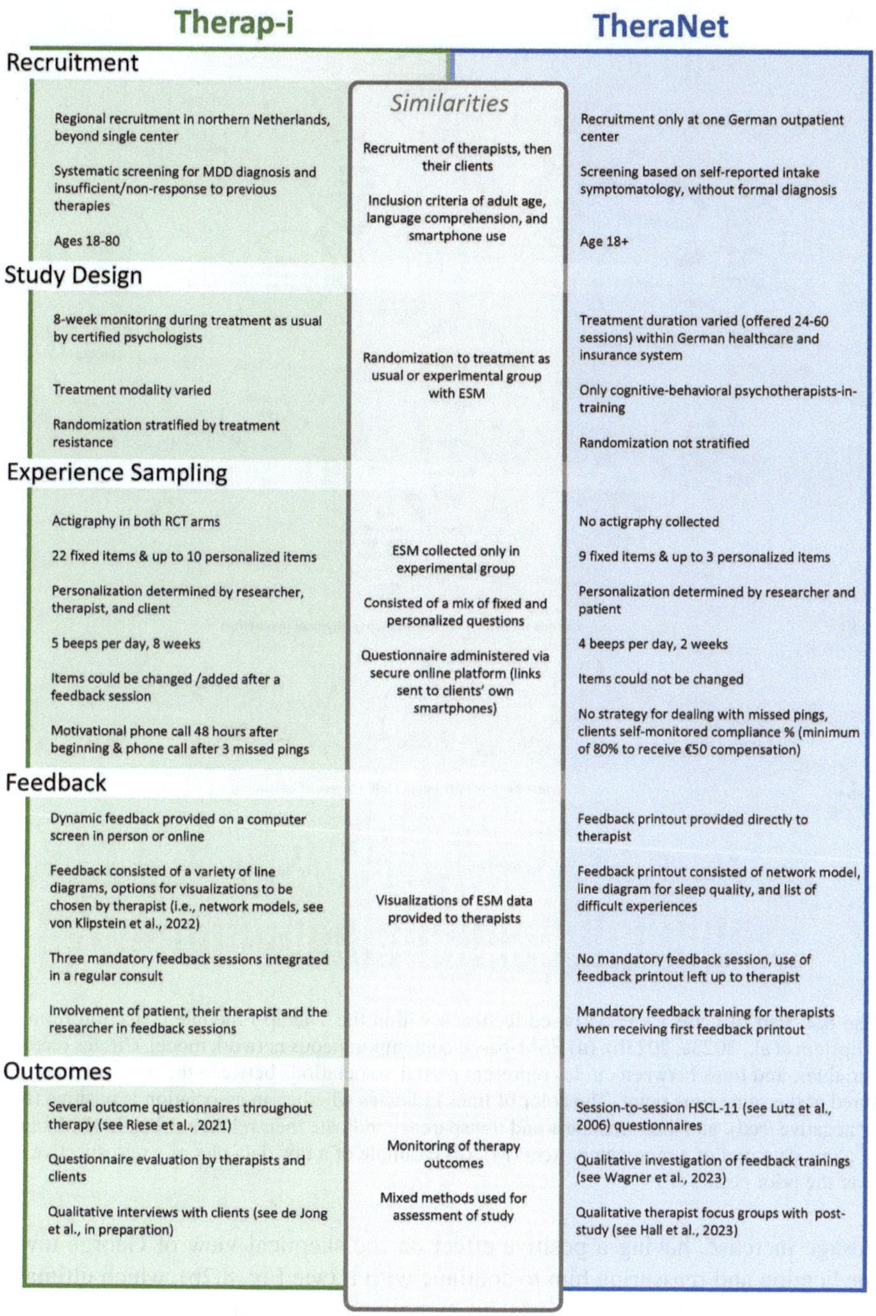

Fig. 8.1 Comparison of the Therap-i and TheraNet studies (see text for further details)

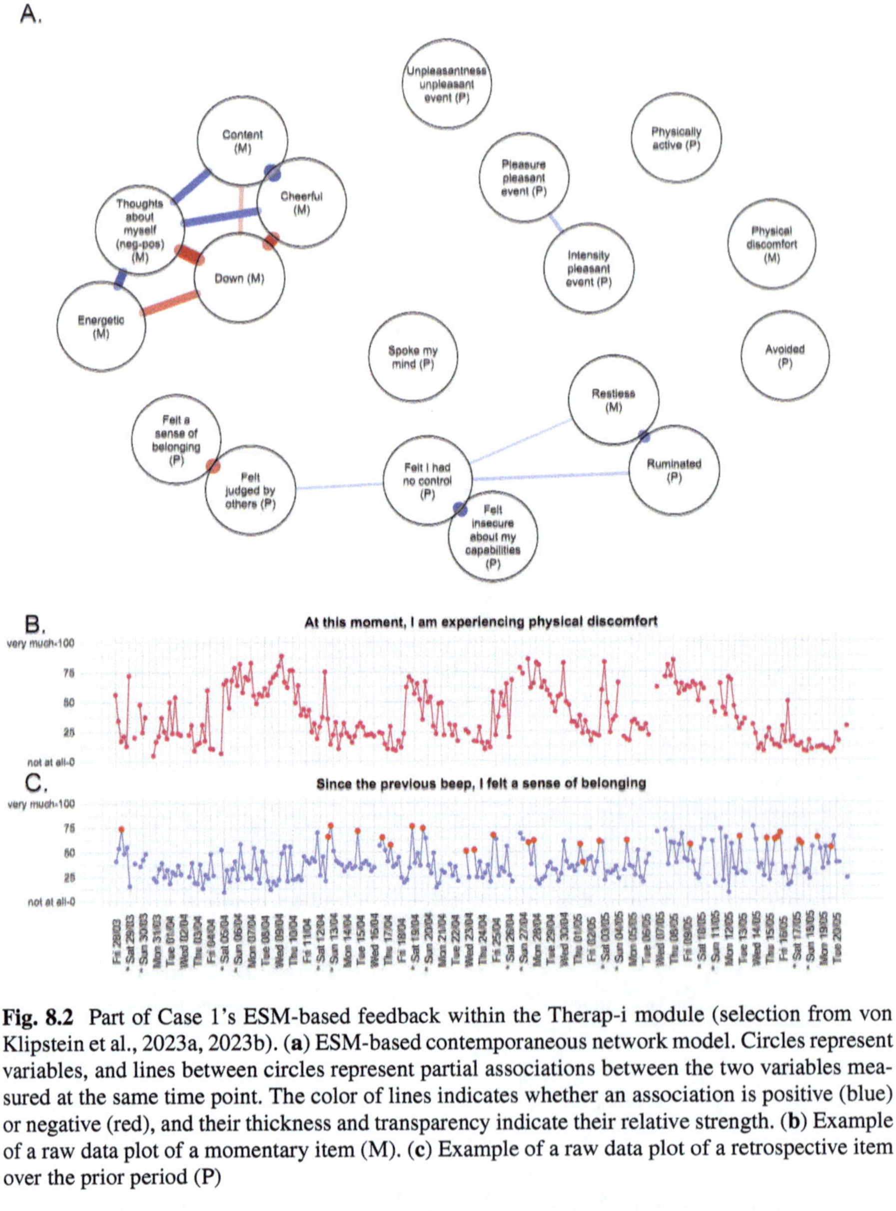

Fig. 8.2 Part of Case 1's ESM-based feedback within the Therap-i module (selection from von Klipstein et al., 2023a, 2023b). (**a**) ESM-based contemporaneous network model. Circles represent variables, and lines between circles represent partial associations between the two variables measured at the same time point. The color of lines indicates whether an association is positive (blue) or negative (red), and their thickness and transparency indicate their relative strength. (**b**) Example of a raw data plot of a momentary item (M). (**c**) Example of a raw data plot of a retrospective item over the prior period (P)

dosage increase, having a positive effect on the skeptical view of George toward medication and reassuring him to continue with it (see Fig. 8.2b), which ultimately had a positive effect on his depressive symptoms; (ii) social interactions that were not functional or formal and wherein George could be and express himself were specifically healing for him (see Fig. 8.2c). The red dots in Fig. 8.2c mark moments when George entered text descriptions of pleasant events in which he was in direct contact with other people. George and his therapist talked about this contextual information and came to the abovementioned insight about his social interactions. George and his therapist found the Therap-i ESM module to be useful and insightful; for instance, George found "ESM to function as a mirror," thereby increasing his awareness of and insights into his psychiatric complaints.

As a downside, George felt like the insights he gained could have been translated better into behavioral strategies improving self-management. He attributed this shortcoming to the fact that treatment sessions in between the Therap-i feedback sessions had been sparse and mostly via telephone due to the COVID-19 pandemic. However, altogether, George found the Therap-i module a useful tool, which he would recommend to others and would like to use again in the future (for the full case study, see von Klipstein et al., 2023a, 2023b).

Case 2 (TheraNet Study)

Carol, a 40-year-old woman, was diagnosed with MDD using a structured diagnostic interview, which was further supported by the results of several self-report questionnaires. Carol arrived at the outpatient center with a recent diagnosis of attention deficit hyperactivity disorder (ADHD), as determined by a specialized clinic using extensive diagnostic testing and interviewing. Symptoms of both diagnoses had been noticeable since her youth, but she had never sought outpatient psychotherapeutic help before. Her mood took a particularly negative turn over the previous eight months. She was no longer able to enjoy the things she used to enjoy, developed sleep difficulties, and frequently overwhelmed by negative, ruminative thoughts. At the age of 18, she survived a very severe horse-riding accident which resulted in multiple serious injuries, which were treated with over 30 operations under general anesthesia. This accident also led to intense and debilitating pain with unpredictable flare-ups. As a result, she gained weight and began to struggle with some unhealthy eating habits. She came to therapy with the goal of learning how to deal with her negative, ruminative thoughts and in the hopes of winning back some sense of joy, as well as dealing with work-related stress.

Carol and her therapist participated in the TheraNet study. She selected three personalized questions to add to the predetermined ESM questionnaire, which referred to the time since the last questionnaire: (1) To what extent did I have food cravings? (2) How often did I think about my (physical) illnesses? (3) How listless did I feel? The ESM time-series data were then used to calculate a contemporaneous network model, the sleep quality item was displayed as a line diagram, and stressful events were reported as Carol herself wrote them (for more methodological and design details, see Hall et al., 2022).

This feedback, particularly the network model (see Fig. 8.3), was used for psychoeducative purposes in one of the early therapy sessions. The network model was used as a starting point for discussing how her symptoms may be related to one another. Here, the connection between bodily tension ("TEN") and positive emotion

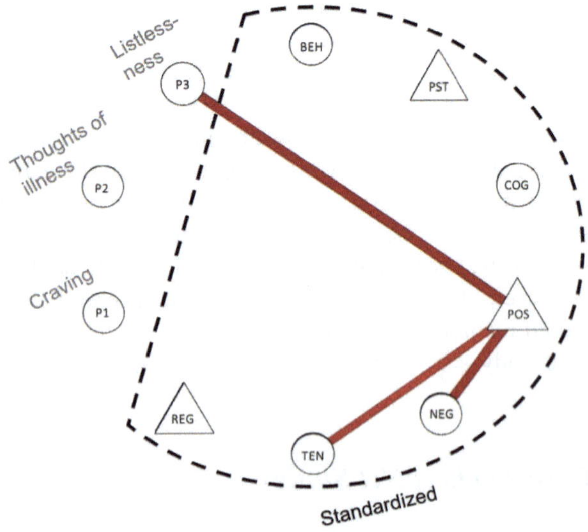

Fig. 8.3 Part of Case 2's ESM-based feedback within TheraNet (network model). Each node represents a single item in the ESM. BEH: Behavior you want to work on in therapy. PST: Positive activities. COG: Negative ruminative cognitions/ thoughts. POS: Positive emotions. NEG: Negative emotions. TEN: Tension. REG: Emotion regulation. P1: Cravings. P2: Thoughts of illness. P3: Listlessness. (Further details on the ESM procedure are given in Hall et al., 2022)

("POS") was clinically interesting, as her experienced pain often played a central role in her therapy sessions. Seeing that more tension was related to less positive emotions and feeling more listlessness to fewer positive emotions, provided tangible support that reaching one of her therapy goals (to feel more joy in life) might require working on managing her physical tension and/or reducing her listlessness. Here, the therapist used the feedback to provide more empirical backing to a mostly already formulated case conceptualization, while still providing the patient with the opportunity to voice that she viewed things differently.

After discussing these connections with Carol, she and her therapist agreed to focus on targeting her mood. They planned to work on this by trying to expand on the positive activities ("PST") she engaged in. PST did not share any edges with other variables in Carol's ESM-derived network, which, upon further exploration in-session, came about because Carol had not reported many (if any at all) during her ESM. However, increasing positive activities in her life became challenging as work-related stress fluctuated, and somatic flare-ups with associated pain spikes occurred suddenly. Based on these changes, the therapeutic focus shifted to acceptance-commitment therapy-based interventions to help her manage acute stress and chronic pain. Additionally, a heavy focus was placed on validating Carol's frustrations regarding the limitations she faced due to her chronic pain.

Overall, Carol's therapist saw the TheraNet feedback as a valuable starting point for the therapeutic work. However, the therapist was not involved in selecting the ESM items, which might have enhanced the clinical utility of the feedback. Moreover, the network visualization was challenging to interpret and explain to Carol. In particular, based on the therapist's anecdotal recollections, Carol would report different symptoms as her main concern each week in therapy partly due to her somatic flare-ups. As a result, the time frame in which the ESM was collected may not have been entirely representative or relevant. These and other related challenges, tied to the clinical utility of the TheraNet feedback, are discussed in more detail in Hall et al. (2024a).

Discussion

ESM shows promise as an add-on tool in mental health care, particularly when personalized. Specifically, this chapter explores its application in the treatment of depressive symptoms through two personalized ESM studies, as well as the perceived usefulness by patients and therapists when integrated into psychological treatment. Here, we reflect on the studies, compare them with other scientific endeavors, and share our experience-based recommendations for implementing ESM into regular psychological treatment.

Lessons Learned and Recommendations for Clinical Research

First, it is important to involve stakeholders (also named end-users) in the design of ESM tools to develop applications that are tailored to their individual needs and wishes (Kip et al., 2024). In the Therap-i and TheraNet studies, patients and therapists participated in focus groups to gather information on their needs and wishes to make ESM clinically meaningful and useful. Klintwall et al. (2023) approach to collaborative ESM design within their Perceived Causal Network (PECAN) approach is another noteworthy example of thoughtful and meaningful co-creation. Skipping this step may lead to a top-down design approach from a researcher's perspective, which may bias design decisions and lead to unsuccessful sustained use of tools based on such designs. Involving stakeholders encourages co-designed research to obtain clinical applications that are better supported and accepted by all involved parties (Bos et al., 2019; Labib et al., 2023; van Gemert-Pijnen et al., 2011).

Second, personalization of ESM items seems key for implementation in clinical practice, but the degree to which ESM diaries should be personalized is an open-ended question. We acknowledge the delicate balance between personalization and standardization. Standardization is often preferred in quantitative, nomothetic research, and sometimes clinical practice, for comparability purposes across patients. On the other hand, recent qualitative studies show that therapists and patients wish more personalization in ESM tools used in clinical practice, in line with more ideographically oriented clinical goals. For example, in the TheraNet study, retrospective focus groups revealed that therapists made many suggestions related to increasing personalization overall and therapists' involvement in that personalization (Hall et al., 2024a, 2024b). Ultimately, deciding to what extent ESM requires personalization remains an individual choice. This decision should ideally be informed by the intended clinical goals (e.g., whether ESM should provide more general information on negative affect or more specific information on personal factors triggering and maintaining psychiatric complaints; see, e.g., Janssens et al., 2018; Myin-Germeys & Kuppens, 2022).

Third, the process of designing ESM questionnaires should be well thought out. It is essential to consider patient burden, including balancing the number of items, sampling frequency, and monitoring duration with the amount of resulting work for the patient (Vachon et al., 2019; Myin-Germeys & Kuppens, 2022). This should be kept in mind when adding personalized items, but also when adding items capturing qualitative information, as it generally takes longer to fill in. Integrating quantitative and qualitative assessments is considered beneficial, as context-specific measures are critical for clinical utility as this may be helpful to generate working hypotheses on a patient's psychiatric complaints (Hill et al., 2013; von Klipstein et al., 2023a, 2023b; Stadel et al., 2023). For instance, patients should report on their context (e.g., "at a party" or "after a stressful work conversation") to capture how social situations affect their mental health. In the Therap-i study, a maximum of 10 personalized items could be added to the fixed set of 22 standard items, including three qualitative items. In general, it took individuals, after getting used to the ESM in general, two to three minutes to fill out the diaries.

Given all these decisions to be made, it can be beneficial to consult researchers in the design of ESM. Furthermore, there are some additional, general points to consider. First, transferring cross-sectional questionnaires directly into ESM items should be avoided, since their validity and reliability is not verified for this use (Fried et al., 2022; Flake & Fried, 2020). Second, there are large differences in how ESM tools have been designed, and the extent to which items/design aspects were reported, making it difficult to establish a gold standard (Hall et al., 2021). Third, steps taken to preprocess ESM data have an influence on the resulting feedback, where different mobile applications have vastly different approaches (see Bastiaansen et al., 2020 for a powerful clinical example). Overall, as there is no gold standard for designing and using ESM in mental health care, experienced researchers may be able to help in the design decision-making process. We recommend being intentional about the ESM design, to use scientifically based and co-designed applications and consider ESM-derived feedback as a conversation starter or facilitator for the case formulation, rather than an "objective truth."

Benefits of Using ESM in Clinical Use

In a qualitative study in patients and therapists, Bos et al. (2019) found several advantages of ESM, including the enhancement of awareness and insight, increasing self-management, the possibility to personalize interventions and to provide alerts in case of elevated scores on negative variables, improving the therapeutic relationship, less retrospectively biased data, and the possibility to provide visualized feedback. However, concerns were mentioned as well about the burden of self-monitoring, worsening of symptoms, and its suitability for certain patients. These concerns are common concerns from therapists about using ESM in clinical practice (see Addis et al., 1999; Burger et al., 2022b; Ellison, 2020; Frumkin et al., 2021; Kroeze et al., 2017; Zimmermann et al. 2019; Zuidersma et al., 2023). However, these fears may be unwarranted given that patients often report more favorable perceptions of ESM than their therapists (Folkersma et al., 2021; Frumkin et al. 2021). Though there has been some conflicting scientific evidence, most studies report positive effects of using ESM-derived feedback (Bastiaansen et al., 2022; Colombo et al., 2019; de Jong et al., in preparation; Folkersma et al., 2021; Kramer et al., 2014), in line with a recent meta-analysis (Linardon et al., 2024). In our experience with the Therap-i and TheraNet studies, ESM-derived (network) feedback is especially useful as a communication tool between the patient and therapist. Specifically, deciding on which ESM items to include and puzzling together on the meaning of the feedback results is evaluated to i) stimulate insight into psychopathological patterns, ii) strengthen the therapeutic alliance, iii) improve the communication of problems to the therapist, iv) increase mutual understanding, and v) empower patients (they feel taken seriously and heard) (de Jong et al., in preparation).

Although ESM is applied during treatment in the Therap-i and TheraNet studies, we advocate that ESM can be useful in different treatment phases. During the diagnostic phase, ESM can be used as a tool to get acquainted with each other, to strengthen the therapeutic relationship, and to obtain information for case conceptualization. During the treatment phase, ESM can be used to test clinical working hypotheses about the patients' psychopathology by gaining insight into context specificity of psychopathology and to enhance shared decision-making on intervention selection (Epskamp et al., 2018; Piot et al., 2022; Bartels et al., 2023). During the follow-up phase after treatment, ESM can be used for relapse prevention (Bringmann et al., 2021). Although, notably, alerts derived from increasing scores on negative affect ESM items were rated least useful in a survey on the utility of ESM in mental health care (Piot et al., 2022). Currently, ESM-derived early warning signals have not been deemed ready for implementation in clinical practice yet (Helmich et al., 2024). The next step for further integration of ESM in clinical practice, in our opinion, is to integrate ESM tools into existing specific clinical procedures and clinical tasks within psychological treatments. As an example of the latter, ESM might be an ideal tool to capture information for thought records in cognitive-behavioral therapy (Beck, 2011; Linardon et al., 2024) or schema diaries in schema therapy (Young et al., 2003).

Design and Implementation in Clinical Practice

Even if studies contain several innovative, potentially groundbreaking ideas surrounding the clinical effectiveness of ESM tools in clinical practice, its implementation is still a challenge. Innovative studies on ESM's clinical effectiveness must be paired with strong implementation strategies. We will discuss several practical considerations here and refer to the "Implementation" chapter of this book for further specific details.

Using Existing ESM-Based Tools

If therapists would like to use existing ESM-based tools, they must do so mindfully. There are many options on the market, with several options to tweak the methodology and make it your own. If the goal is to use an existing ESM tool, we would recommend those that have been co-created with relevant stakeholders (i.e., patients, their relatives, therapists, researchers, and clinical supervisors). Collaborating with researchers can provide insights into the complexities of selecting the best suitable ESM designs with regard to your aim, support in the data analysis process, and choosing which mobile applications to use. If this type of collaboration is not an option, applications like PETRA (Bos et al., 2022) can be used, because it was co-designed with relevant stakeholders. However, PETRA is only available to institutions that use RoQua (which includes eight mental health care institutions in the Netherlands).

Developing a New ESM-Based Tool

If therapists would like to develop a new ESM-based tool, we recommend considering the involvement of researchers. Research and clinical practices may have very different goals, which may at times compete with one another (Meehl, 1954). For example, ESM-based feedback spearheaded by researchers may not sufficiently match the goals of therapists who may seek specific, actionable insights for psychotherapy from that feedback (Fried, 2020). Ideally, the collaborating researcher would also be clinically trained, so they can advise on statistical, methodological, and clinical topics. When designing an ESM tool, minimizing the burden it places on its intended users is essential. Adding more steps to routine care procedures negatively impacted the behaviors of the nursing staff implicated (i.e., "felt more stressed," "spent more time on administration tasks and spent less time with patients"; Florisse & Delespaul, 2020). Therefore, carefully balancing the number of stakeholder involvement and honoring their boundaries herein is important.

One way researchers can motivate therapists in using these kinds of systems is to find ways to reduce their burden by integrating ESM feedback into existing software systems (as suggested by Piot et al., 2022). PETRA's integration into the electronic patient record can ease access and encourage adoption of the tool (Bos et al., 2022). However, building this kind of software to be compatible with existing health care systems requires a large budget and much patience, not only in the development and implementation but also in the maintenance thereof (i.e., safe data storage, software updates, business plans, customer service, etc.).

Conclusions

We conclude that personalized ESM holds immense potential to create empirically supported tools to be used in psychotherapy. By presenting two examples, along with case examples, we provided an illustrative overview of possible future implementations. More scientific clinical research and collaboration (i.e., between therapists and researchers, but also with insurance companies and entrepreneurs/business model developers) are needed before large-scale implementation of personalized ESM in clinical practice is feasible. However, therapists wishing to use ESM clinically can use the information provided in the discussion to decide whether they would like to use existing tools, build something novel, and/or involve researchers in this endeavor.

References

Addis, M. E., Wade, W. A., & Hatgis, C. (1999). Barriers to dissemination of evidence-based practices: Addressing practitioners' concerns about manual-based psychotherapies. *Clinical Psychology: Science and Practice, 6*(4), 430–441. https://doi.org/10.1093/clipsy.6.4.430

Bartels, S. L., Van Zelst, C., Melo Moura, B., Daniëls, N. E. M., Simons, C. J. P., Marcelis, M., Bos, F. M., & Servaas, M. N. (2023). Feedback based on experience sampling data: Examples of current approaches and considerations for future research. *Heliyon, 9*(9), e20084. https://doi.org/10.1016/j.heliyon.2023.e20084

Bastiaansen, J. A., Kunkels, Y. K., Blaauw, F. J., Boker, S. M., Ceulemans, E., Chen, M., Chow, S.-M., de Jonge, P., Emerencia, A. C., Epskamp, S., Fisher, A. J., Hamaker, E. L., Kuppens, P., Lutz, W., Meyer, M. J., Moulder, R., Oravecz, Z., Riese, H., Rubel, J., Ryan, O., et al. (2020). Time to get personal? The impact of researcher's choices on the selection of treatment targets using the experience sampling methodology. *Journal of Psychosomatic Research, 137*, 110211. https://doi.org/10.1016/j.jpsychores.2020.110211

Bastiaansen, J. A., Ornée, D. A., Meurs, M., & Oldehinkel, A. J. (2022). An evaluation of the efficacy of two add-on ecological momentary intervention modules for depression in a pragmatic randomized controlled trial (ZELF-i). *Psychological Medicine, 52*(13), 2731–2740. https://doi.org/10.1017/S0033291720004845

Beck, J. S. (2011). *Cognitive behavior therapy: Basics and beyond* (2nd ed., p. xix, 391). Guilford Press.

Bos, F. (2021). *Ecological momentary assessment as a clinical tool in psychiatry: Promises, pitfalls, and possibilities* [University of Groningen]. https://doi.org/10.33612/diss.177817937

Bos, F. M., Snippe, E., Bruggeman, R., Wichers, M., & van der Krieke, L. (2019). Insights of patients and clinicians on the promise of the experience sampling method for psychiatric care. *Psychiatric Services, 70*(11), 983. https://doi.org/10.1176/appi.ps.201900050

Bos, F. M., Von Klipstein, L., Emerencia, A. C., Veermans, E., Verhage, T., Snippe, E., Doornbos, B., Hadders-Prins, G., Wichers, M., & Riese, H. (2022). A web-based application for personalized ecological momentary assessment in psychiatric care: User-centered development of the PETRA application. *JMIR Mental Health, 9*(8), e36430. https://doi.org/10.2196/36430

Bringmann, L. F., van der Veen, D. C., Wichers, M., Riese, H., & Stulp, G. (2021). ESMvis: A tool for visualizing individual experience sampling method (ESM) data. *Quality of Life Research, 30*(11), 3179–3188. https://doi.org/10.1007/s11136-020-02701-4

Burger, J., Epskamp, S., van der Veen, D. C., Dablander, F., Schoevers, R. A., Fried, E. I., & Riese, H. (2022a). A clinical PREMISE for personalized models: Towards a formal integration of case formulations and statistical networks. *Journal of Psychopathology and Clinical Science, 131*(8), 906–916. https://doi.org/10.1037/abn0000903

Burger, J., Ralph-Nearman, C., & Levinson, C. A. (2022b). Integrating clinician and patient case conceptualization with momentary assessment data to construct idiographic networks: Moving toward personalized treatment for eating disorders. *Behaviour Research and Therapy, 159*, 104221. https://doi.org/10.1016/j.brat.2022.104221

Colombo, D., Fernández-Álvarez, J., Patané, A., Semonella, M., Kwiatkowska, M., García-Palacios, A., Cipresso, P., Riva, G., & Botella, C. (2019). Current state and future directions of technology-based ecological momentary assessment and intervention for major depressive disorder: A systematic review. *Journal of Clinical Medicine, 8*(4), 465. https://doi.org/10.3390/jcm8040465

Csikszentmihalyi, M., & Larson, R. (1987). Validity and reliability of the experience-sampling method. *The Journal of Nervous and Mental Disease, 175*(9), 526–536. https://doi.org/10.1097/00005053-198709000-00004

Cuijpers, P., Sijbrandij, M., Koole, S. L., Andersson, G., Beekman, A. T., & Reynolds, C. F., 3rd. (2013). The efficacy of psychotherapy and pharmacotherapy in treating depressive and anxiety disorders: A meta-analysis of direct comparisons. *World Psychiatry, 12*(2), 137–148. https://doi.org/10.1002/wps.20038

Cuijpers, P., Karyotaki, E., Weitz, E., Andersson, G., Hollon, S. D., & van Straten, A. (2014). The effects of psychotherapies for major depression in adults on remission, recovery and improvement: A meta-analysis. *Journal of Affective Disorders, 159*, 118–126. https://doi.org/10.1016/j.jad.2014.02.026

Daniëls, N. E. M., Verhagen, S. J. W., van Bokhoven, M. A., Beurskens, A. J., & Delespaul, P. A. E. G. (2023). How to use experience-sampling technology to understand daily functioning: A practical guide for mental health professionals. *Clinical Psychology & Psychotherapy, 30*(2), 357–372. https://doi.org/10.1002/cpp.2798

deVries, M., Delespaul, P. A., & Dijkman-Caes, C. (1992). Consequences of depression for the experience of anxiety in daily life. In M. deVries (Ed.), *The experience of psychopathology: Investigating mental disorders in their natural settings* (pp. 141–147). Cambridge University Press.

Ebner-Priemer, U. W., Kuo, J., Welch, S. S., Thielgen, T., Witte, S., Bohus, M., & Linehan, M. M. (2006). A valence-dependent group-specific recall bias of retrospective self-reports: A study of borderline personality disorder in everyday life. *Journal of Nervous & Mental Disease, 194*(10), 774–779. https://doi.org/10.1097/01.nmd.0000239900.46595.72

Ellison, W. D. (2020). An initial study of practicing psychologists' views of the utility of ecological momentary assessment for difficult psychotherapy cases. *Administration and Policy in Mental Health and Mental Health Services Research, 48*, 597–607. https://doi.org/10.1007/s10488-020-01093-4

Epskamp, S., van Borkulo, C. D., van der Veen, D. C., Servaas, M. N., Isvoranu, A.-M., Riese, H., & Cramer, A. O. J. (2018). Personalized network modeling in psychopathology: The importance of contemporaneous and temporal connections. *Clinical Psychological Science, 6*(3), 416–427. https://doi.org/10.1177/2167702617744325

Flake, J. K., & Fried, E. I. (2020). Measurement schmeasurement: Questionable measurement practices and how to avoid them. *Advances in Methods and Practices in Psychological Science, 3*(4), 4. https://doi.org/10.1177/2515245920952393

Florisse, E. J. R., & Delespaul, P. A. E. G. (2020). Monitoring risk assessment on an acute psychiatric ward: Effects on aggression, seclusion and nurse behaviour. *PLoS One, 15*(10), e0240163. https://doi.org/10.1371/journal.pone.0240163

Folkersma, W., Veerman, V., Ornée, D. A., Oldehinkel, A. J., Alma, M. A., & Bastiaansen, J. A. (2021). Patients' experience of an ecological momentary intervention involving self-monitoring and personalized feedback for depression. *Internet Interventions, 26*, 100436. https://doi.org/10.1016/j.invent.2021.100436

Fried, E. I. (2020). Theories and models: What they are, what they are for, and what they are about. *Psychological Inquiry, 31*(4), 336–344. https://doi.org/10.1080/1047840X.2020.1854011

Fried, E. I., Flake, J. K., & Robinaugh, D. J. (2022). Revisiting the theoretical and methodological foundations of depression measurement. *Nature Reviews Psychology, 1*(6), 358–368. https://doi.org/10.1038/s44159-022-00050-2

Frumkin, M. R., Piccirillo, M. L., Beck, E. D., Grossman, J. T., & Rodebaugh, T. L. (2021). Feasibility and utility of idiographic models in the clinic: A pilot study. *Psychotherapy Research, 31*(4), 520–534. https://doi.org/10.1080/10503307.2020.1805133

Hall, M., & Rubel, J. (2022). *[TheraNet] using personalized assessment and network model feedback in psychotherapy*. [Preregistration]. https://doi.org/10.17605/OSF.IO/QUPTY

Hall, M., Scherner, P. V., Kreidel, Y., & Rubel, J. A. (2021). A systematic review of momentary assessment designs for mood and anxiety symptoms. *Frontiers in Psychology, 12*, 642044. https://doi.org/10.3389/fpsyg.2021.642044

Hall, M., Wagner, A. A., Scherner, P., Michael, K. L., Lawyer, G., Lutz, W., & Rubel, J. (2022). Using personalized assessment and network model feedback in psychotherapy: Proof of principle for the TheraNet project [preprint]. *PsyArXiv*. https://doi.org/10.31234/osf.io/8deyj

Hall, M., Lappenbusch, L. M., Wiegmann, E., & Rubel, J. A. (2024a). To use or not to use: Exploring therapists' experiences with pre-treatment EMA-based personalized feedback in the TheraNet project. *Administration and Policy in Mental Health and Mental Health Services Research*. https://doi.org/10.1007/s10488-023-01333-3

Hall, M., Wagner, A. A., Scherner, P., & Rubel, J. (2024b). If you give a therapist a network: A qualitative analysis of therapists' reactions to their patients' EMA-based network models. *Clinical Psychology and Psychotherapy, 31*(6), e70013. https://doi.org/10.1002/cpp.70013

Hanley, G. P., Iwata, B. A., & McCord, B. E. (2003). Functional analysis of problem behavior: A review. *Journal of Applied Behavior Analysis, 36*(2), 147–185. https://doi.org/10.1901/jaba.2003.36-147

Hatfield, D. R., & Ogles, B. M. (2007). Why some clinicians use outcome measures and others do not. *Administration and Policy in Mental Health, 34*(3), 283–291. https://doi.org/10.1007/s10488-006-0110-y

Hayes, A. M., Yasinski, C., Ben Barnes, J., & Bockting, C. L. H. (2015). Network destabilization and transition in depression: New methods for studying the dynamics of therapeutic change. *Clinical Psychology Review, 41*, 27–39. https://doi.org/10.1016/j.cpr.2015.06.007

Hehlmann, M. I., Schwartz, B., Lutz, T., Gómez Penedo, J. M., Rubel, J. A., & Lutz, W. (2021). The use of digitally assessed stress levels to model change processes in CBT - A feasibility study on seven case examples. *Frontiers in Psychiatry, 12*, 613085. https://doi.org/10.3389/fpsyt.2021.613085

Helmich, M. A., Schreuder, M., Bringmann, L. F., Riese, H., Snippe, E., & Smit, A. C. (2024). Slow down and be critical before using early warning signals in psychopathology. *Nature Reviews Psychology, 3*, 767.

Herrman, H., Patel, V., Kieling, C., Berk, M., Buchweitz, C., Cuijpers, P., Furukawa, T. A., Kessler, R. C., Kohrt, B. A., Maj, M., McGorry, P., Reynolds, C. F., Weissman, M. M., Chibanda, D., Dowrick, C., Howard, L. M., Hoven, C. W., Knapp, M., Mayberg, H. S., et al. (2022). Time for united action on depression: A Lancet-World Psychiatric Association Commission. *The Lancet, 399*(10328), 957–1022. https://doi.org/10.1016/S0140-6736(21)02141-3

Hill, C. E., Chui, H., & Baumann, E. (2013). Revisiting and reenvisioning the outcome problem in psychotherapy: An argument to include individualized and qualitative measurement. *Psychotherapy, 50*(1), 68–76. https://doi.org/10.1037/a0030571

Janssens, K. A. M., Bos, E. H., Rosmalen, J. G. M., Wichers, M. C., & Riese, H. (2018). A qualitative approach to guide choices for designing a diary study. *BMC Medical Research Methodology, 18*(1), 140. https://doi.org/10.1186/s12874-018-0579-6

Jensen-Doss, A., & Hawley, K. M. (2010). Understanding barriers to evidence-based assessment: Clinician attitudes toward standardized assessment tools. *Journal of Clinical Child & Adolescent Psychology, 39*(6), 885–896. https://doi.org/10.1080/15374416.2010.517169

Jensen-Doss, A., & Hawley, K. M. (2011). Understanding clinicians' diagnostic practices: Attitudes toward the utility of diagnosis and standardized diagnostic tools. *Administration and Policy in Mental Health and Mental Health Services Research, 38*(6), 476–485. https://doi.org/10.1007/s10488-011-0334-3

Khan, A., Faucett, J., Lichtenberg, P., Kirsch, I., & Brown, W. A. (2012). A systematic review of comparative efficacy of treatments and controls for depression. *PLoS One, 7*(7), e41778. https://doi.org/10.1371/journal.pone.0041778

Kip, H., Beerlage de Jong, N., van Gemert-Pijnen, L., Sanderman, R., & Kelders, S. M. (Eds.). (2024). *EHealth research theory and development: A multidisciplinary approach* (2nd ed.). Routledge. https://doi.org/10.4324/9781003302049

Kirtley, O. J., Hiekkaranta, A. P., Kunkels, Y. K., Eisele, G., Verhoeven, D., Van Nierop, M., & Myin-Germeys, I. (2020). *The experience sampling method (ESM) item repository*. https://doi.org/10.17605/OSF.IO/KG376

Klintwall, L., Bellander, M., & Cervin, M. (2023). Perceived causal problem networks: Reliability, central problems, and clinical utility for depression. *Assessment, 30*(1), 73–83. https://doi.org/10.1177/10731911211039281

Kramer, I., Simons, C. J., Hartmann, J. A., Menne-Lothmann, C., Viechtbauer, W., Peeters, F., Schruers, K., van Bemmel, A. L., Myin-Germeys, I., Delespaul, P., van Os, J., & Wichers, M. (2014). A therapeutic application of the experience sampling method in the treatment of depression: A randomized controlled trial. *World Psychiatry, 13*(1), 68–77. https://doi.org/10.1002/wps.20090

Kroeze, R., Van Der Veen, D. C., Servaas, M. N., Bastiaansen, J. A., Oude-Voshaar, R. C., Borsboom, D., Ruhe, H. G., Schoevers, R. A., & Riese, H. (2017). Personalized feedback on symptom dynamics of psychopathology: A proof-of-principle study. *Journal for Person-Oriented Research, 3*(1), 1–11. https://doi.org/10.17505/jpor.2017.01

Kuyken, W., Padesky, C. A., & Dudley, R. (2009). *Collaborative case conceptualization: Working effectively with clients in cognitive-behavioral therapy* (p. xvii, 366). The Guilford Press.

Labib, K., Pizzolato, D., Stappers, P. J., Evans, N., Lechner, I., Widdershoven, G., Bouter, L., Dierickx, K., Bergema, K., & Tijdink, J. (2023). Using co-creation methods for research integrity guideline development—How, what, why and when? *Accountability in Research, 31*(6), 531–556. https://doi.org/10.1080/08989621.2022.2154154

Lamiell, J. T. (1998). 'Nomothetic' and 'idiographic': Contrasting Windelband's understanding with contemporary usage. *Theory & Psychology, 8*(1), 23–38. https://doi.org/10.1177/0959354398081002

Linardon, J., Torous, J., Firth, J., Cuijpers, P., Messer, M., & Fuller-Tyszkiewicz, M. (2024). Current evidence on the efficacy of mental health smartphone apps for symptoms of depression and anxiety. A meta-analysis of 176 randomized controlled trials. *World Psychiatry, 23*(1), 139–149. https://doi.org/10.1002/wps.21183

Meehl, P. E. (1954). *Clinical versus statistical prediction: A theoretical analysis and a review of the evidence*. University of Minnesota Press. https://doi.org/10.1037/11281-000

Myin-Germeys, I., & Kuppens, P. (Eds.). (2022). *The open handbook of experience sampling methodology: A step-by-step guide to designing, conducting, and analyzing ESM studies* (2nd ed.). Center for Research on Experience Sampling and Ambulatory Methods Leuven.

Myin-Germeys, I., Kasanova, Z., Vaessen, T., Vachon, H., Kirtley, O., Viechtbauer, W., & Reininghaus, U. (2018). Experience sampling methodology in mental health research: New insights and technical developments. *World Psychiatry, 17*(2), 123–132. https://doi.org/10.1002/wps.20513

Piot, M., Mestdagh, M., Riese, H., Weermeijer, J., Brouwer, J. M. A., Kuppens, P., Dejonckheere, E., & Bos, F. M. (2022). Practitioner and researcher perspectives on the utility of ecological momentary assessment in mental health care: A survey study. *Internet Interventions, 30*, 100575. https://doi.org/10.1016/j.invent.2022.100575

Riese, H., von Klipstein, L., Schoevers, R. A., van der Veen, D. C., & Servaas, M. N. (2021). Personalized ESM monitoring and feedback to support psychological treatment for depression:

A pragmatic randomized controlled trial (Therap-i). *BMC Psychiatry, 21*(1), 143. https://doi.org/10.1186/s12888-021-03123-3

Rosmalen, J. G., Wenting, A. M., Roest, A. M., de Jonge, P., & Bos, E. H. (2012). Revealing causal heterogeneity using time series analysis of ambulatory assessments: Application to the association between depression and physical activity after myocardial infarction. *Psychosomatic Medicine, 74*(4), 377–386.

Schiepek, G., Eckert, H., Aas, B., Wallot, S., & Wallot, A. (2015). *Integrative psychotherapy: A feedback-driven dynamic systems approach.* Hogrefe.

Schuler, K., Ruggero, C. J., Mahaffey, B., Gonzalez, A., Callahan, J. L., Boals, A., Waszczuk, M. A., Luft, B. J., & Kotov, R. (2019). When hindsight is not 20/20: Ecological momentary assessment of PTSD symptoms versus retrospective report. *Assessment, 107319111986982.* https://doi.org/10.1177/1073191119869826

Shiffman, S., Stone, A. A., & Hufford, M. R. (2008). Ecological momentary assessment. *Annual Review of Clinical Psychology, 4*(1), 1–32. https://doi.org/10.1146/annurev.clinpsy.3.022806.091415

Simons, C. J. P., Drukker, M., Evers, S., van Mastrigt, G. A. P. G., Höhn, P., Kramer, I., Peeters, F., Delespaul, P., Menne-Lothmann, C., Hartmann, J. A., van Os, J., & Wichers, M. (2017). Economic evaluation of an experience sampling method intervention in depression compared with treatment as usual using data from a randomized controlled trial. *BMC Psychiatry, 17*(1), 415. https://doi.org/10.1186/s12888-017-1577-7

Solhan, M. B., Trull, T. J., Jahng, S., & Wood, P. K. (2009). Clinical assessment of affective instability: Comparing EMA indices, questionnaire reports, and retrospective recall. *Psychological Assessment, 21*(3), 425–436. https://doi.org/10.1037/a0016869

Stadel, M., Stulp, G., Langener, A. M., Elmer, T., van Duijn, M. A. J., & Bringmann, L. F. (2023). Feedback about a person's social context—Personal networks and daily social interactions. *Administration and Policy in Mental Health, 51*, 476. https://doi.org/10.1007/s10488-023-01293-8

Stone, A. A., Schwartz, J. E., Neale, J. M., Shiffman, S., Marco, C. A., Hickcox, M., Paty, J., Porter, L. S., & Cruise, L. J. (1998). A comparison of coping assessed by ecological momentary assessment and retrospective recall. *Journal of Personality and Social Psychology, 74*(6), 1670–1680. https://doi.org/10.1037/0022-3514.74.6.1670

Strauss, B., Gawlytta, R., Schleu, A., & Frenzl, D. (2021). Negative effects of psychotherapy: Estimating the prevalence in a random national sample. *BJPsych Open, 7*(6), 6. https://doi.org/10.1192/bjo.2021.1025

Tanious, R., Manolov, R., Onghena, P., & Vlaeyen, J. W. S. (2024). Single-case experimental designs: The importance of randomization and replication. *Nature Reviews Methods Primers, 4*, 27. https://doi.org/10.1038/s43586-024-00312-8

Trull, T. J., & Ebner-Priemer, U. W. (2009). Using experience sampling methods/ecological momentary assessment (ESM/EMA) in clinical assessment and clinical research: Introduction to the special section. *Psychological Assessment, 21*(4), 457–462. https://doi.org/10.1037/a0017653

Vachon, H., Viechtbauer, W., Rintala, A., & Myin-Germeys, I. (2019). Compliance and retention with the experience sampling method over the continuum of severe mental disorders: Meta-analysis and recommendations. *Journal of Medical Internet Research, 21*(12), e14475. https://doi.org/10.2196/14475

Van Gemert-Pijnen, J. E., Nijland, N., Van Limburg, M., Ossebaard, H. C., Kelders, S. M., Eysenbach, G., & Seydel, E. R. (2011). A holistic framework to improve the uptake and impact of eHealth technologies. *Journal of Medical Internet Research, 13*(4), e111. https://doi.org/10.2196/jmir.1672

von Klipstein, L., Riese, H., van der Veen, D. C., Servaas, M. N., & Schoevers, R. A. (2020). Using person-specific networks in psychotherapy: Challenges, limitations, and how we could use them anyway. *BMC Medicine, 18*(1), 345. https://doi.org/10.1186/s12916-020-01818-0

von Klipstein, L., Servaas, M., Schoevers, R. A., van der Veen, D. C., & Riese, H. (2023a). Integrating personalized experience sampling in psychotherapy: A case illustration of the Therap-i module. *Heliyon, 9*(3), e14507.

Von Klipstein, L., Stadel, M., Bos, F. M., Bringmann, L. F., Riese, H., & Servaas, M. (2023b). Opening the contextual black box: A case for idiographic experience sampling of context for clinical applications [preprint]. *PsyArXiv*. https://doi.org/10.31234/osf.io/nv7c6

Wichers, M. (2014). The dynamic nature of depression: A new micro-level perspective of mental disorder that meets current challenges. *Psychological Medicine, 44*(7), 1349–1360. https://doi.org/10.1017/S0033291713001979

Wichers, M., Riese, H., Hodges, T. M., Snippe, E., & Bos, F. M. (2021). A narrative review of network studies in depression: What different methodological approaches tell us about depression. *Frontiers in Psychiatry, 12*, 719490. https://doi.org/10.3389/fpsyt.2021.719490

Widdershoven, R. L. A., Wichers, M., Kuppens, P., Hartmann, J. A., Menne-Lothmann, C., Simons, C. J. P., & Bastiaansen, J. A. (2019). Effect of self-monitoring through experience sampling on emotion differentiation in depression. *Journal of Affective Disorders, 244*, 71–77. https://doi.org/10.1016/j.jad.2018.10.092

Young, J. E., Klosko, J. S., & Weishaar, M. E. (2003). *Schema therapy: A practitioner's guide* (p. xii, 436). Guilford Press.

Zimmermann, J., Woods, W. C., Ritter, S., Happel, M., Masuhr, O., Jaeger, U., Spitzer, C., & Wright, A. G. C. (2019). Integrating structure and dynamics in personality assessment: First steps toward the development and validation of a personality dynamics diary. *Psychological Assessment, 31*(4), 516–531. https://doi.org/10.1037/pas0000625

Zuidersma, M., Riese, H., Snippe, E., Booij, S. H., Wichers, M., & Bos, E. H. (2020). Single-subject research in psychiatry: Facts and fictions. *Frontiers in Psychiatry, 11*, 539777. https://doi.org/10.3389/fpsyt.2020.539777

Zuidersma, M., Müller, F., Snippe, E., Zuidema, S. U., & Oude Voshaar, R. C. (2023). Feasibility, usability and clinical value of intensive longitudinal diary assessments in older persons with cognitive impairment and depressive symptoms. *Aging & Mental Health, 27*(8), 1466–1475. https://doi.org/10.1080/13607863.2022.2102143

Chapter 9
Feedback in the Treatment of Suicidality

Andrew C. Page, Michael J. Kyron, and Geoff R. Hooke

Randomized controlled trials (RCTs) can create the misperception that this structure characterizes routine clinical practice (Castonguay et al., 2021). The requirements of RCTs are needed to demonstrate the causal impact of a particular intervention. Specific patients are allocated to conditions and delivered predetermined treatments according to fixed schedules. Assessments occur according to a pre-determined schedule, such as at pre-treatment, post-treatment, and follow-up. While clinical practice can be informed by the strong causal evidence that an RCT may provide, the orderly schedule of an RCT rarely corresponds to naturalistic settings. Clinical presentations do not always fit neatly into diagnostic categories, and the delivery of treatment rarely follows a linear sequence of assessment and a single intervention followed by a post-treatment evaluation. Additionally, considering the impact of specific behaviours, such as self-harm and suicidal acts, generates ever-increasing complexity. Self-harm and suicide risk might not have been the main target of treatment and given the relatively low base rates of self-harm and suicidal behaviours (compared with other clinical presentations, such as elevated anxiety and depression), routine assessments may not include detailed examination of all relevant variables. Therefore, the present chapter will outline a particular case example (see Hooke et al., 2022) with the goal of demonstrating the value of monitoring and feedback in an agile manner. Additionally, the case formulation of the client's clinical presentation and associated suicidal risk will be separated into two sections for the purposes of discussion. The key theme will be that monitoring and

A. C. Page (✉) · M. J. Kyron
School of Psychological Science, University of Western Australia, Perth, WA, Australia
e-mail: andrew.page@uwa.edu.au

G. R. Hooke
School of Psychological Science, University of Western Australia, Perth, WA, Australia

Perth Clinic, Perth, WA, Australia
e-mail: GeoffH@perthclinic.com.au

J. A. Rubel, W. Lutz (eds.), *Feedback Informed Psychological Therapy*, CBT: Science Into Practice, https://doi.org/10.1007/978-3-031-90428-8_9

feedback provided a foundation for a common language of communication with the patient and among the treating team.

Suicidal behaviour describes actions that could cause a person to die and is typically preceded by a period of increased suicidal intention that may transition into action (Olson et al., 2022). The transition may not be a steady linear pathway but can involve the waxing and waning of the motivation and intention as a person struggles with potentially competing wishes to live and to die (Stritzke & Page, 2020). In addition to this ambivalence, an individual may exhibit suicidal behaviours through which they may acquire the capability to suicide (George et al., 2016). Self-harming behaviours are an instance of actions which increase this capability even if they are not accompanied by a current intention to die. That is, acts of self-harm may be carried out without an intention to kill oneself, but the process of engagement in the behaviour involves learning about potential life-ending actions (Mars et al., 2014). While there is no one-to-one correspondence between self-harming and suicidal acts, these sets of behaviours are related. It may be that the self-harm itself is a cause (e.g. via increasing the acquired capability for suicidal acts) or it may be that self-harm and suicide are correlated variables that share common causes (Chan et al., 2016). Future research will clarify these relationships, but proactive clinical management is needed to reduce the occurrence of self-harm. The occurrence of self-harm is always of concern as the risk of suicide attempts and suicide rises among those who engage in non-suicidal self-injury (NSSI). The risk of death by suicide is elevated in the six months after NSSI (Cooper et al., 2005) and among people who have an incident of NSSI, 70% will go on to attempt suicide (Nock et al., 2006).

For the clinician, there are a variety of challenges in preventing self-harm. First, prevention requires a priori identification of clients who are at risk, so that interventions can be delivered ahead of self-harm. Second, self-harm can be associated with a sense of shame, and clients may avoid discussion of the topic. One way to address these challenges has been with the extensions to Routine Outcomes Monitoring (ROM) systems (Douglas et al., 2023). ROM seems to support clinical engagement by identifying when symptom reduction is not tracking against the expected trajectory of improvement (Davis et al., 2006; de Jong et al., 2021; Delgadillo et al., 2017, 2018). ROM systems involve the repeated collection of quantitative clinically relevant data (e.g. well-being and symptom assessments) and the regular presentation to clients and/or therapists to facilitate evidence-based conversations about treatment progress. Tracking a client's current therapeutic progress against the ratings of similar individuals undergoing treatment allows a real-time conversation informed by data the client has provided (Kia et al., 2024). ROM stands to be beneficial to clinical practice by identifying clients who are "not on track" and facilitate a conversation enabling staff and patient to work collaboratively towards a positive outcome (de Jong et al., 2021; Delgadillo et al., 2018). Furthermore, to the extent that the ROM system includes questions about self-harm, suicidal behaviours, and risk predictors, it can facilitate conversations by bringing these topics "to the table".

ROM feedback permits both a self-comparison across time and a group-based comparisons (Hooke et al., 2018). The group-based feedback can use a "traffic light" system where the regular scores with each occasion of care are presented against clinical significance categories of recovered (blue), improved (green), no change (amber), and deteriorated (red; Ronk et al., 2012, 2016) or a "flight path" system where a client's routine scores across time are plotted against the personalized expected trajectory of change.

Perth Clinic initiated progress monitoring and feedback within the closed Cognitive Behaviour Therapy (CBT) group programmes (Newnham et al., 2010a, 2010b). This CBT programme was provided in the context of an acute inpatient psychiatric clinic, and therefore we developed a briefer measure than typically used in outpatient and daypatient settings (Andrews & Page, 2005; Lambert et al., 2001). This permitted the same instrument to be used in both inpatient and outpatient contexts, setting the stage for the seamless monitoring of patients who used both types of treatment. The World Health Organization's five-item Well-Being Index (WHO-5; Bech et al., 2018) was selected as it asked clients to rate the frequency over the last day that they have felt cheerful and in good spirits, felt calm and relaxed, felt active and vigorous, felt fresh and rested, and that their daily life has been filled with things that interest them. A complementary symptom measure was developed, the five-item Distress Index (DI-5; Dyer et al., 2014). The DI-5 instrument asks patients to report "Over the last day….." to rate the frequency that they have, felt anxious, felt depressed, felt that worthless, had thoughts about killing self, and felt that they are not coping. Importantly in the context of suicidality, the DI-5 included a question about suicidal thoughts; the Suicide Question (SQ).

The ROM system monitored progress during an inpatient hospital stay and also during closed therapy groups. To assess the client's progress during a therapy group, the client's individual scores are presented against a background of the trajectory of expected recovery based on the average therapy progress of similar clients. The presentation of well-being and symptom scores permitted identification of when progress was on-track (i.e. within tolerance of typical progress) and off-track (i.e. when outside the tolerance band; Hooke et al., 2018). While these trajectories are useful in the context of a treatment group with a discrete start and end, they are less useful for inpatient care. Many inpatients transfer from open to closed psychotherapy groups, and they can move between inpatient and daypatient care. This movement is challenging to capture within a single trajectory of improvement (typically used in outpatient treatment; Delgadillo et al., 2018). Furthermore, by their nature, open groups mean that individuals enter at different points during their therapeutic journeys. There is not a fixed number of sessions, and this makes it challenging to estimate the expected duration of treatment. To accommodate this flexibility, we adapted ROM feedback system that included four ranges, shown in the left-hand side of the graphs (see Fig. 9.1). Both of these types of feedback were used with the individual who is the focus of the present chapter.

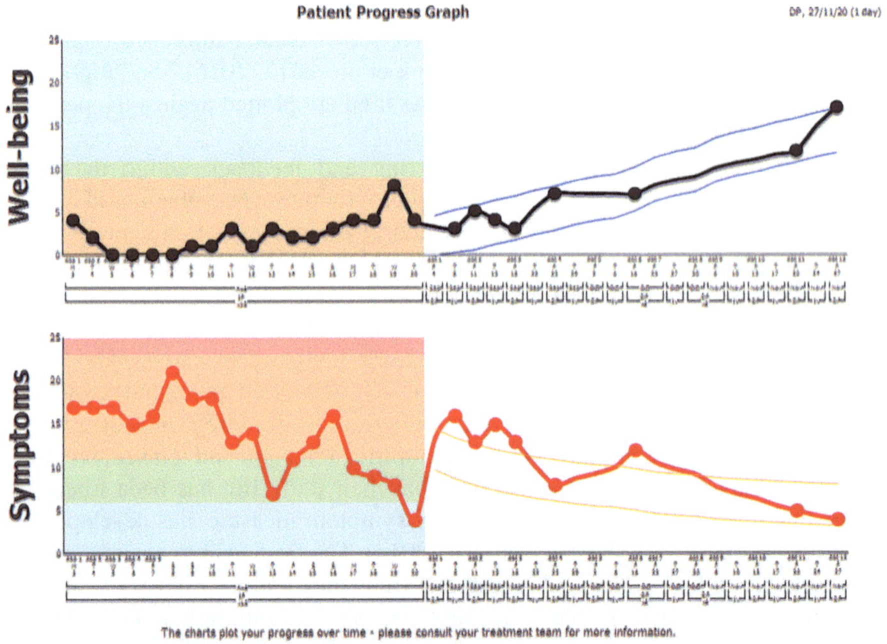

Fig. 9.1 Routine Outcome Monitoring of Well-Being scores (upper panel) and Symptom scores (lower panel) during an inpatient admission (left-hand side) and daypatient (right-hand side) phases of treatment. Reproduced from and used with permission from Hooke et al. (2022). *Journal of Clinical Psychology, 78*(10), 2041–2053)

Case Description and Clinical Formulation: Phase 1

Terri was an 18-year-old female with a history of major depression and borderline personality disorder. In addition, to symptoms of low mood, low self-esteem, perceived worthlessness, chronic emptiness, emotional instability, and instability of self, Terri had thoughts of suicide and incidents of self-harm. A case formulation developed across her contact with the hospital and different elements in the clinical profile came into greater focus during the initial inpatient and subsequent daypatient treatment delivery modes. The self-harm behaviours were perceived by Terri to be impulsive in nature. The precipitants of the behaviours included thoughts of self-loathing and the belief that she was a "bad person". Treatment goals, agreed between Terri and the inpatient treatment team, were to: reduce self-harm, clarify and settle upon daily routines, and stabilize her mood so that the fluctuations were less frequent and less intense. Terri then used her time as an inpatient to address these identified goals by enrolling in a treatment programme was embarked upon that prioritized the self-harm, by encouraging Terri to start her inpatient admission by participating in, and completing, a one-week Dialectical Behaviour Therapy (DBT) Primer programme (see Seow et al., 2022). The DBT group targeted emotional instability and episodes of self-harm, and she enrolled in this programme due to

address therapy-interfering behaviours early during her admission. The goals of improved routine and mood stabilization were further addressed in a Cognitive Behaviour Therapy (CBT)-based mood management programme.

Monitoring and Feedback: Phase 1

Terri was admitted to hospital with scores in the clinical range; with elevated symptom scores (17/25) and a low well-being (4/25) on the DI-5 (DI-5; Dyer et al., 2014) and WHO-5 (Newnham et al., 2010a, 2010b), respectively. The DI-5 symptom scores peaked at times when Terri commented she struggled to manage her emotions and these events provided a basis for conversations anchored in her reports of therapy progress. The well-being scores demonstrated relatively smaller changes, dropping within the first two days of being an inpatient, but increasing steadily in the second week of the inpatient admission. Routinely, the opening of each day's therapy groups begins with a "check-in" that allows a reflection on symptoms, well-being, and support seeking. The therapist was able to highlight changes in the symptoms and well-being, to encourage reflective practice and increase insight into the impact of Terri's actions on her experiences. In addition, the reflection provides an opportunity to review the scores on the Suicide Question of the DI-5.

In Terri's case, the DI-5 enabled therapy staff to discuss changes in suicidal ideation or urges. The hospital's database presents the score on the SQ for the current day as well as the preceding four days. This allowed the therapist to reflect upon changes in this score and use the self-report measure (that Terri entered into the computer earlier in the morning) provides another mechanism for clients to provide this information. During Terri's progress through treatment, the use of the graphical presentation of the symptoms and well-being was able to validate her challenges and also to point to areas where treatment was beginning to have positive outcomes.

In the current clinical context, the scores during the inpatient stay (left-hand side of Fig. 9.1) provided a vehicle to validate Terri's experience. Terri's symptoms had fluctuations (15–17/25) during her time in the DBT Primer group, however, her well-being index dropped completely (0/25). Thus, the scores provided data for therapists to share the observation that symptoms were fluctuating. These fluctuations are common among people with borderline symptoms, and they could be used to reflect the emotional instability and validate this experience.

Another point for Terri during her inpatient admission and during the DBT Primer programme is that her symptoms and well-being were in the amber (or unchanged) range. The boundaries of the unchanged category are set individually for each person, based upon the admission score. Importantly, for Terri, this enabled staff to convey acceptance of Terri's experiences by validating that this is where the client's symptoms are. The therapist was able to convey an understanding of the level of the symptoms and the fluctuations around the mean.

Furthermore, it was possible to validate Terri's experience by noting that the reduction in WHO-5 well-being index reflected a frequent experience observed among clients, as they begin to reflect on their problems and adapt to an inpatient setting. While patients may hope that progress after admission is going to be steady linear improvement, this is rarely the case. Furthermore, the relative stability of symptoms in the first week was consistent with Terri's presentation being distracted by her own thoughts during group sessions. She described being caught in rumination which began to give way to a spirally upwards in symptoms towards the end of the week. The depiction of these symptoms in her graphs both provided a platform for discussion of how her inner experiences translated into her emotional experiences and allowed validation of Terri's experience.

Terri's symptoms peaked (21/25) at the end of her first week as an inpatient, as she started to confront challenging problems, albeit supported by the safety net afforded by the hospital environment and team. At this time of elevated symptoms, Terri interpreted some otherwise innocuous comments from hospital staff as a perceived criticism. Ruminating upon this perceived criticism was filtered through the thought that she was a "bad person", and this led to increases in urges to self-harm (although Terri did not disclose these urges to staff). The elevation in DI-5 scores highlighted to staff that progress was not as expected and highlights the potential value of staff using these data to foster conversations about the client's feelings. Even though Terri was not prepared to disclose the increases in her self-harm urges, the potential therapeutic benefits of validating the observable increases in symptoms can serve to validate the emotional distress. One possible benefit to these discussions could be that the groundwork is laid for greater openness in the future. Following from this supposition, Terri did later note that her attempts to manage her self-harm urges using grounding and distraction were insufficient. She described how her thoughts of self-loathing increased in intensity and ultimately culminated in a self-harm incident. Following the incident, her symptoms dropped marginally (18/25), and she worked with staff to take steps to stay safe.

After completion of the closed DBT programme, which had been aimed at providing some skills to address self-harm tendencies, Terri remained as an inpatient but entered an open CBT-based psychotherapy group. The mood management group focussed on teaching skills to help clients to better manage symptoms of depression and anxiety. Sessions involved a check-in with each patient about their emotional experiences with the goal of increasing their reflective practice as well as skills training in CBT mood management skills, such as relaxation, cognitive restructuring, and exposure. Terri reported an improvement in her mood after a few days of these CBT-informed sessions, and this was evident in her symptom score, which had decreased (6/25).

At this point, Terri prepared to be discharged from the hospital, and care could continue to be delivered in an outpatient context. Terri began to reflect on previous relationships and her feelings of loneliness and emptiness rose accordingly (16/25); accompanied by thoughts of self-loathing. The spike in symptoms is further explainable by the anxiety Terri experienced concerning discharge, a common concern for inpatients. After working through the concerns with Terri, her symptoms reduced to the healthy range (3/25). Her well-being index remained unchanged (4/25) from admission, and daypatient care was provided to assist to consolidate her gains and to ensure generalization of the skills acquired within hospital to a wider range of contexts.

A presentation of the scores to this point reflected the journey of improvement (chiefly in symptoms), but also validated that Terri's experience of well-being had shifted little during her inpatient stay. Hence, there was an agreement about continuing to engage with therapy.

Case Description and Clinical Formulation: Phase 2

Following discharge from hospital, the therapy team identified with Terri a set of therapy targets. Key themes were (i) an elevated sensitivity to criticism, (ii) low self-worth accompanied by a tendency to seek external validation from others to confirm that she was "good", and (iii) a sense of emptiness associated with a lack of clarity around her self-identity (as she felt this was psychologically eclipsed by her symptoms) that extended into her perception that she was not fully known by others. Key therapeutic goals included management of self-harm behaviour and suicidal thoughts. These themes were addressed within a 12-week DBT programme that involved weekly manualised group therapy sessions interspersed with individual sessions (Seow et al., 2022).

Despite the progress during her inpatient admission, a fortnight later, the intake assessment for the group programme revealed her symptoms had risen (15/25) and well-being had declined. As part of the case formulation, Terri identified that when she perceived that she was a "failure" or felt anxious about success or failure, she felt increased urges to self-harm behaviour. Her perceived unworthiness manifest itself in a view that she "deserved to feel pain". Thus, in addition to being encouraged to implement DBT skills and strategies, Terri was also encouraged to take a self-compassionate attitude towards herself in DBT skills coaching sessions.

Monitoring and Feedback: Phase 2

The initial week of DBT was accompanied by an increase in Terri's self-harm, and in the first two weeks of treatment she did not report using the skills being covered in the treatment programme. The symptom and well-being scores were used to frame a homework task of weighing up the pros and cons of using DBT skills. Furthermore, the scores on these two indices depicted changes and fostered a conversation about the value of psychotherapy. With hindsight, Terri described the process of completing the daily questionnaires as "a helpful way to check in with yourself". She noted that it provided an occasion to reflect upon her mood and means of coping. As part of that reflection, Terri commented that her urges to self-harm two weeks into the DBT programme accompanied her fears of the implications of "getting better", and self-harm was a coping strategy that was in her "comfort zone", albeit a maladaptive one.

During the group, the Suicide Question (SQ) provided a helpful vehicle for allowing Terri to communicate her thoughts about suicide and self-harm. Knowing that her therapist would be aware of the responses and ready to discuss (and validate) any thoughts and feelings, provided a safe context for a two-way, respectful communication. More broadly, inclusion of the question enables group members struggling with increased suicide risk to be identified and offered support without taking time away from the group's psychotherapeutic intent.

A common question that our team receives about the monitoring and feedback system and general and the SQ in particular, relates to a client's willingness to honestly complete the items. Given that all the Clinic's patients are voluntary admissions, our typical response is to note that the questionnaires are no different to any communication by a client. The therapist needs to evaluate all that is said and to create an environment of supportive, non-judgmental acceptance. However, Terri's responding highlights the value of this environment and also the danger of treating the numerical scores generated as an absolute indication of risk. That is, Terri's SQ score was consistently low (0–1/5) throughout the programme, but nevertheless, Terri began to entertain suicidal thoughts during a group session. Interestingly, she did not complete the questionnaires and nor did she raise this issue with her therapist, but self-harmed during a break between sessions without discussing the incident. When reviewing her diary cards at her next individual session Terri noted the self-harm incident and was able to discuss the event. The conversation with the individual therapist and the validation she received put her in a place where the incident could be raised in the group session, and Terri was able to express her sense of hopelessness she had felt regarding her own future well-being as she listened to the other group members' concerns.

Following this self-harm incident and the undisclosed elevation in symptoms, Terri's symptom measure then proceeded to demonstrate an increase in symptoms and a reduction in well-being. In part, this could be seen as reflecting shame and discomfort in acknowledging her recent behaviour, but it also could reflect a willingness to disclose how she was feeling in a context of validation and supportive encouragement to use the therapeutic skills to avoid the use of maladaptive coping and to constructively address problems.

Terri's symptom measure and reported distress began to decline as she cultivated greater acceptance of her emotions and began to evaluate herself as a worthy individual. Terri's engagement in learning and practising mindfulness skills appeared to provide a sound foundation for her to reconnect with her physical self. She commented on her self-harm behaviour's past role to "feel" and to "release" emotions. During the programme, she explored opportunities to implement skills as an alternative to self-harm. Terri explored distress tolerance strategies, including active distraction, sensory soothing, and radical acceptance. Terri reflected on building her understanding and acceptance of emotions, particularly exploring the "feeling behind the urge" associated with her self-destructive behaviour and striving to self-validate more effectively.

The preceding case illustrates the extension of ROM to monitor self-harm, in addition to general monitoring and feedback of well-being and symptoms. It highlights the complexity of monitoring in routine clinical practice, as the clinician needs to use the outputs as an element in their case formulation. As with all information, the clinician needs to constantly weigh up the information provided and continue to provide an environment where clients are supported with skills to understand and communicate their feelings, but also to ensure that the clinical context is accepting and validating so that clients can openly and accurately depict their progress. However, Terri's case does highlight the challenges in a clinical context when clients sometimes cannot and at other times do not wish to disclose their feelings and intentions.

New Developments in Monitoring and Feedback

While ROM is traditionally used to gauge treatment progress, our ongoing research programme seeks to leverage routinely collected patient data for addressing various prevalent clinical concerns (Restifo et al., 2015). Given that clinical environments frequently attend to individuals grappling with acute mental health challenges, there is a propensity for adverse events to emerge during both inpatient and outpatient care. Although the frequency and nature of events vary based on the hospital and patient population, self-harm is prevalent across most psychiatric settings (Bowers et al., 2010).

The effective prevention of self-harm within clinical settings can be enhanced by understanding which individuals are more susceptible and when they are particularly vulnerable, which guides staff in efficiently allocating limited clinical resources. However, conventional risk assessments often rely on data collected at the outset of treatment, despite that the risk of non-suicidal self-injury and suicidal thoughts and behaviours can fluctuate rapidly over short-term periods, such as hours or days (Kyron et al., 2018; Kleiman et al., 2017).

Predicting self-injurious thoughts and behaviours over short time spans necessitates a comprehensive understanding of the factors most strongly associated with such occurrences. Sudden fluctuations in both negative and positive affect over periods of hours and days correlate with increased and decreased risks of non-suicidal self-injury, respectively (Kiekens et al., 2020, 2023; Kyron et al., 2023a). Consequently, there exists significant potential in using ROM to forecast current or short-term self-injury risks. Moreover, suicidal ideation and interpersonal difficulties serve as reliable predictors of both non-suicidal self-injury and suicide attempts on a day-to-day basis (Kyron et al., 2023a, 2023b). Hence, for instances where clients, such as Terri, indicate the absence of suicidal thoughts, the responses to other items may still end up with that person being flagged as being at risk of self-harm or suicide.

The capacity to pinpoint reliable short-term predictors of self-harm and suicide attempts has spurred the development of a predictive algorithm that forecasts the likelihood of self-harm events within a 7-day time frame. Based on these probabilities, nursing staff receive a spectrum of recommendations aligned with nursing guidelines, including intensified or routine observations. While traffic light systems are commonly employed to indicate risk levels, nursing terminology was opted for due to its familiarity, and low probability does not signify the absence of the risk of suicide or non-suicidal self-injury as prediction is not perfect (i.e. a green light may be interpreted as no risk).

Using self-reported assessments to anticipate the immediate risk of self-injurious behaviours encounters several obstacles. Foremost among these is the reluctance of patients to candidly disclose current suicidal ideation (Høyen et al., 2022; Kyron et al., 2023a, 2023b) as highlighted in Terri's case. Individuals who opt not to disclose suicidal ideation tend to exhibit mental health profiles more closely aligned with those who do report ideation (Kyron et al., 2020). However, suicidal ideation represents just one facet among a spectrum of factors predictive of self-injury, and aspects such as interpersonal challenges, feelings of hopelessness, and protective factors may also play a part in contributing to the move from ideation-to-action (Klonsky et al., 2018; Kyron et al., 2023a, 2023b).

At Perth Clinic, instances have arisen where patients reporting no suicidal ideation were flagged by the algorithm due to elevated scores on other risk or protective factors associated with self-injury. During discussions about potential self-harm risk with these patients, many have eventually disclosed experiencing suicidal ideation despite initially denying it. In one specific case, a patient reported high interpersonal difficulties and hopelessness, and during discussions with nursing staff they queried how staff knew they were experiencing suicidal ideation. Importantly, by assessing co-occurring difficulties with cognitive-affective states, clinical staff can also identify issues relevant to each patient that can be targeted during brief interventions to predict imminent risk of self-injury.

The issues with self-report can, in part, be circumvented by the integration of objective assessments into routine monitoring of patients. For example, on-body or near-body wearable technology is currently a cost-effective solution to obtain real-time data from patients that could be used to identify shifts in well-being and psychological distress. In particular, monitoring sleep quality may be of appeal to clinical settings, as negative sleep patterns have consistently been shown to cause and be caused by mental health difficulties (Littlewood et al., 2016, 2019; Mayers & Baldwin, 2006). Thus, in absence of self-reported well-being and distress, sleep quality could be used to identify patients at risk of deteriorating symptoms. Take, for instance, the patient presented in Fig. 9.2, who entered Perth Clinic with high suicidal ideation. The shift in their daily suicidal ideation scores from day four to six are mirrored by co-occurring increases in the sleep quality (represented by a combination of total sleep time, sleep depth, and disruptions). When ideation subsequently increases, there are associated drops in sleep quality.

Figure 9.2 presents an idealized relationship whereby sleep acts as a strong proxy for mental health, in which case biometric readings can be a useful method to infer

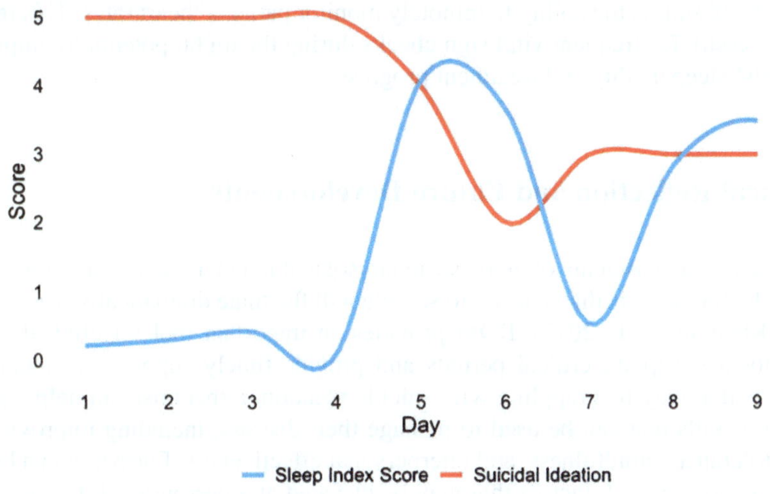

Fig. 9.2 Example data for a patient admitted with high ideation, with their sleep quality from the prior night presented

patient progress. However, it is anticipated that these readings will also contribute to new information about patients' mental and physical states that can facilitate treatment efforts. For instance, if sleep predicts suicide risk beyond known factors, it suggests that sleep is a construct worth targeting in its own regard. This routine assessment of sleep can help in monitoring patients' responses to pharmacological interventions and target psychological interventions (e.g. CBT for Insomnia; Taylor & Pruiksma, 2014).

The challenge within clinical settings lies in accurately assessing sleep while ensuring patient motivation to use monitoring devices. For example, polysomnography, the gold standard for diagnosing sleep issues, is hindered by its obtrusive nature and lack of cost-effectiveness, limiting its widespread clinical application. In our preliminary trials, we discovered that under-mattress sleep mat devices present a viable compromise between accuracy and feasibility (Edouard et al., 2021). These devices can monitor total sleep time and overnight sleep apnoea, while also offering assessments of resting heart rate, which has been linked to potential mental health challenges.

Other on-body wrist-worn devices have the potential to track heart rate and physical activity throughout the day, both of which have been correlated with well-being and suicidal ideation (Chan et al., 2019; Littlewood et al., 2016; Strasser & Fuchs, 2015). For example, patients who exhibit reduced physical activity compared to their usual patterns may be experiencing a decline in well-being during their hospitalization. While the burden of incorporating these devices is minimal, they may encounter a broader range of challenges, such as patients removing, misplacing, or even stealing the devices. However, these limitations may offset by the improvements to monitoring patient well-being. Further, an advantage of wrist-worn devices for nursing staff is the ability to remotely monitor patients' heart rates. This reduces the necessity for frequent vital sign checks during the night, potentially improving patients' sleep quality and treatment progress.

Critical Reflection and Future Developments

Suicide risk assessments often occur in an isolated manner, yet a consistent finding from the literature is that a desire to suicide will fluctuate dramatically from day-to-day (Kleiman et al., 2017). ROM provides an important tool for clinical staff to monitor and capture critical periods and provide timely support. By identifying patients that may be grappling with suicide ideation, a therapist can help a patient develop skills that can be used to manage their distress, including improving distress tolerance, mindfulness, and interpersonal effectiveness. Further, it can be used to target specific risk factors that may be elevated at a person-level that may often coincide with increases in ideation, helping therapists pinpoint potential targetable factors.

Relatedly, ROM offers the added benefit of dynamically developing crisis response plans in collaboration with patients, using personalized information collected. These plans outline warning signs for suicide, recommended coping strategies, available supports, and pathways to access professional help (Rudd et al., 2006). In its original use, this was as simple as developing a handwritten note to give specific instructions outlining sequential steps to follow when distress or suicidal intent increases, with the final stage being to seek external professional services. Recent studies suggest that these approaches reduce the incidence of suicidal behaviour (Bryan et al., 2017, 2018, 2024; Miller et al., 2017). However, it is critical that response plans are routinely revisited with patients to capture the shifting nature of circumstances and needs over time.

ROM data can assist the development of crisis response plans, identifying specific risk factors, triggers, and protective factors for each patient, especially on days when suicidal ideation is heightened. Therapists can monitor patients reporting increased intent to act on their suicidal thoughts, as well as instances of self-injurious behaviours. By revisiting crisis response plans and evaluating the effectiveness of implemented strategies, therapists can adjust response plans accordingly. This iterative process allows for plans to remain responsive to patients' evolving needs.

To enhance patient outcomes, a key step involves bolstering post-discharge communication with mental health professionals. This entails implementing regular check-ins at specified intervals, such as weekly or monthly, to promptly detect any escalation in suicidality. This proactive strategy underscores the importance of maintaining continuity of care and delivering personalized support that aligns with the individual's specific requirements. By doing so, the risk of adverse outcomes, including completed suicide, can be mitigated effectively.

In tandem with conventional therapeutic sessions, it is essential to empower patients to actively engage in managing their mental health and well-being between appointments. This involves not only fostering self-awareness regarding their mental state but also integrating practices that promote physical well-being, as previously discussed. Leveraging wearable technology to incorporate assessments of sleep patterns and physical activity can enhance this approach. By providing individuals with actionable insights into their overall well-being, such technology facilitates the monitoring of changes over time, including fluctuations in suicidal ideation or psychological distress levels. In response to these indicators, tailored recommendations can be offered, spanning from self-help resources to facilitating connections with relevant care providers. Thus, routine monitoring of general well-being need not be an approach that fits only the immediate needs of therapists, it could be used more proactively to prevent readmissions and acute risk of suicide.

The information collected during these intervals provides important insights into well-being in daily life that are usable for by therapy staff at subsequent sessions (Hehlmann et al., 2021). Evidence suggests that individuals who self-harm experience higher intensity and greater variability of negative affect, rumination, and self-criticism from within-and-across days (Kiekens et al., 2023). By leveraging these data, therapy staff can tailor interventions to address the specific needs and challenges of their clients, ultimately supporting them in achieving improved emotional well-being and reducing the risk of self-harm.

The integration of prediction algorithms, wearable technology, and various non-invasive methodologies, such as natural language processing and facial analysis, marks a significant advancement in providing therapists with real-time, high-quality information to better manage patient suicide risk. These innovative tools offer promising avenues for intervention and support, revolutionizing the way therapists engage with their patients. However, the effectiveness of these tools ultimately hinges on their adoption and use by clinicians (Boswell et al., 2015). To maximize their potential impact, it is imperative to ensure co-design, easy access to information, seamless integration within standard clinical practice, and minimal barriers to usage. Therapists must be empowered to leverage these resources fully, enabling them to make informed decisions and provide timely interventions when necessary.

Streamlining access to these tools within the clinical workflow is paramount. This includes incorporating them into existing electronic health record systems or providing dedicated platforms that seamlessly integrate with therapists' daily routines. By eliminating logistical hurdles and simplifying the user experience, therapists can more readily incorporate these technologies into their practice, enhancing their ability to assess and address patient suicide risk effectively. Moreover, ongoing training and support are essential to optimize the use of these tools. Clinicians should receive comprehensive education on how to interpret and act upon the data provided by prediction algorithms and wearable devices. Additionally, continuous updates and refinements to these technologies based on user feedback and emerging research can further enhance their efficacy and relevance in clinical settings.

References

Andrews, G., & Page, A. C. (2005). Outcome measurement, outcome management, and monitoring. *Australian and New Zealand Journal of Psychiatry, 39*(8), 649–651. https://doi.org/10.1080/j.1440-1614.2005.01648.x

Bech, P., Lindberg, L., & Moeller, S. B. (2018). The Reliable Change Index (RCI) of the WHO-5 in primary prevention of mental disorders: A measurement-based pilot study in positive psychiatry. *Nordic Journal of Psychiatry, 72*(6), 404–408. https://doi.org/10.1080/08039488.2018.1463393

Boswell, J. F., Kraus, D. R., Miller, S. D., & Lambert, M. J. (2015). Implementing routine outcome monitoring in clinical practice: Benefits, challenges, and solutions. *Psychotherapy Research, 25*(1), 6–19. https://doi.org/10.1080/10503307.2013.817696

Bowers, L., Banda, T., & Nijman, H. (2010). Suicide inside: A systematic review of inpatient suicides. *The Journal of Nervous and Mental Disease, 198*(5), 315–328. https://doi.org/10.1097/NMD.0b013e3181da47e2

Bryan, C. J., Mintz, J., Clemans, T. A., Leeson, B., Burch, T. S., Williams, S. R., Maney, E., & Rudd, M. D. (2017). Effect of crisis response planning vs. contracts for safety on suicide risk in US army soldiers: A randomized clinical trial. *Journal of Affective Disorders, 212*, 64–72. https://doi.org/10.1016/j.jad.2017.01.028

Bryan, C. J., Mintz, J., Clemans, T. A., Burch, T. S., Leeson, B., Williams, S., & Rudd, M. D. (2018). Effect of crisis response planning on patient mood and clinician decision making: A clinical trial with suicidal US soldiers. *Psychiatric Services, 69*(1), 108–111. https://doi.org/10.1176/appi.ps.201700157

Bryan, C. J., Bryan, A. O., Khazem, L. R., Aase, D. M., Moreno, J. L., Ammendola, E., Bauder, C. R., Hiser, J., Daruwala, S. E., & Baker, J. C. (2024). Crisis response planning rapidly reduces suicidal ideation among US military veterans receiving massed cognitive processing therapy for PTSD. *Journal of Anxiety Disorders, 102*, 102824. https://doi.org/10.1016/j.janxdis.2023.102824

Castonguay, L. G., Barkham, M., Youn, S. Y., & Page, A. C. (2021). Practice-based evidence—Findings from routine clinical settings. In M. Barkham, W. Lutz, & L. G. Castonguay (Eds.), *Bergin and Garfield's handbook of psychotherapy and behavior change* (7th ed.). Wiley.

Chan, M. K., Bhatti, H., Meader, N., Stockton, S., Evans, J., O'Connor, R. C., Kapur, N., & Kendall, T. (2016). Predicting suicide following self-harm: Systematic review of risk factors and risk scales. *The British Journal of Psychiatry, 209*(4), 277–283. https://doi.org/10.1192/bjp.bp.115.170050

Chan, J. S., Liu, G., Liang, D., Deng, K., Wu, J., & Yan, J. H. (2019). Special issue–therapeutic benefits of physical activity for mood: A systematic review on the effects of exercise intensity, duration, and modality. *The Journal of Psychology, 153*(1), 102–125. https://doi.org/10.1080/00223980.2018.1470487

Cooper, J., Kapur, N., Webb, R., Lawlor, M., Guthrie, E., Mackway-Jones, K., & Appleby, L. (2005). Suicide after deliberate self-harm: A 4-year cohort study. *American Journal of Psychiatry, 162*(2), 297–303. https://doi.org/10.1176/appi.ajp.162.2.297

Davis, S., Hooke, G. R., & Page, A. C. (2006). Identifying and targeting predictors of drop-out from group cognitive behaviour therapy. *Australian Journal of Psychology, 58*(1), 48–56. https://doi.org/10.1080/00049530500504096

de Jong, K., Conijn, J. M., Gallagher, R. A., Reshetnikova, A. S., Heij, M., & Lutz, M. C. (2021). Using progress feedback to improve outcomes and reduce drop-out, treatment duration, and deterioration: A multilevel meta-analysis. *Clinical Psychology Review, 85*, 102002. https://doi.org/10.1016/j.cpr.2021.102002

Delgadillo, J., Overend, K., Lucock, M., Groom, M., Kirby, N., McMillan, D., Gilbody, S., Lutz, W., Rubel, J. A., & de Jong, K. (2017). Improving the efficiency of psychological treatment using outcome feedback technology. *Behaviour Research and Therapy, 99*(12), 89–97. https://doi.org/10.1016/j.brat.2017.09.011

Delgadillo, J., de Jong, K., Lucock, M., Lutz, W., Rubel, J., Gilbody, S., Ali, S., Aguirre, E., Appleton, M., Nevin, J., O'Hayon, H., Patel, U., Sainty, A., Spencer, P., & McMillan, D. (2018). Feedback-informed treatment versus usual psychological treatment for depression and anxiety: A multisite, open-label, cluster randomised controlled trial. *The Lancet Psychiatry, 5*(7), 564–572. https://doi.org/10.1016/S2215-0366(18)30162-7

Douglas, S., Page, A. C., Moltu, C., Kyron, M., & Satterthwaite, T. (2023). The connections matter: Bi-directional learning in program evaluation and practice-oriented research. *Administration and Policy in Mental Health and Mental Health Services Research, 51*, 318. https://doi.org/10.1007/s10488-023-01304-8

Dyer, K., Hooke, G., & Page, A. C. (2014). Development and psychometrics of the five item daily index in a psychiatric sample. *Journal of Affective Disorders, 152*(1), 409–415. https://doi.org/10.1016/j.jad.2013.10.003

Edouard, P., Campo, D., Bartet, P., Yang, R.-Y., Bruyneel, M., Roisman, G., & Escourrou, P. (2021). Validation of the withings sleep analyzer, an under-the-mattress device for the detection of moderate-severe sleep apnea syndrome. *Journal of Clinical Sleep Medicine, 17*(6), 1217–1227. https://doi.org/10.5664/jcsm.9168

George, S., Page, A. C., Hooke, G. R., & Stritzke, W. G. K. (2016). Multi-facet assessment of capability for suicide: Development and prospective validation of the acquired capability with rehearsal for suicide scale. *Psychological Assessment, 28*(11), 1452–1464. https://doi.org/10.1037/pas0000276

Hehlmann, M. I., Schwartz, B., Lutz, T., Gómez Penedo, J. M., Rubel, J. A., & Lutz, W. (2021). The use of digitally assessed stress levels to model change processes in CBT - A feasibility study on seven case examples. *Frontiers in Psychiatry, 12*, 613085. https://doi.org/10.3389/fpsyt.2021.613085

Hooke, G. R., Sng, A. A. H., Cunningham, N. K., & Page, A. C. (2018). Methods of delivering progress feedback to optimise patient outcomes: The value of expected treatment trajectories. *Cognitive Therapy and Research, 42*(2), 204–211. https://doi.org/10.1007/s10608-017-9851-z

Hooke, G. R., Savani, P., Stewart, B., Araujo, S., & Page, A. C. (2022). Illustrating routine outcomes monitoring at different points in a patient's journey: Inpatient then daypatient treatment of a patient with depressive and borderline symptoms. *Journal of Clinical Psychology, 78*(10), 2041–2053. https://doi.org/10.1002/jclp.23426

Høyen, K. S., Solem, S., Cohen, L. J., Prestmo, A., Hjemdal, O., Vaaler, A. E., Galynker, I., & Torgersen, T. (2022). Non-disclosure of suicidal ideation in psychiatric inpatients: Rates and correlates. *Death Studies, 46*(8), 1823–1831. https://doi.org/10.1080/07481187.2021.1879317

Kia, S. A., Wittkampf, L., van Lankeren, J., & Janse, P. (2024). Motives of therapists for using Routine Outcome Monitoring (ROM) and how it is used by them in clinical practice: Two qualitative studies. *Administration and Policy in Mental Health and Mental Health Services Research*. https://doi.org/10.1007/s10488-024-01374-2

Kiekens, G., Hasking, P., Nock, M. K., Boyes, M., Kirtley, O., Bruffaerts, R., Myin-Germeys, I., & Claes, L. (2020). Fluctuations in affective states and self-efficacy to resist non-suicidal self-injury as real-time predictors of non-suicidal self-injurious thoughts and behaviors. *Frontiers in Psychiatry, 11*, 214. https://doi.org/10.3389/fpsyt.2020.00214

Kiekens, G., Hasking, P., Nock, M. K., Kleiman, E., Kirtley, O. J., Houben, M., Boyes, M., Bruffaerts, R., Myin-Germeys, I., & Claes, L. (2023). A comparison of affective-cognitive states in daily life between emerging adults with and without past-year nonsuicidal self-injury. *Behavior Therapy, 55*(3), 469–484. https://doi.org/10.1016/j.beth.2023.08.004

Kleiman, E. M., Turner, B. J., Fedor, S., Beale, E. E., Huffman, J. C., & Nock, M. K. (2017). Examination of real-time fluctuations in suicidal ideation and its risk factors: Results from two ecological momentary assessment studies. *Journal of Abnormal Psychology, 126*(6), 726–738. https://doi.org/10.1037/abn0000273

Klonsky, E. D., Saffer, B. Y., & Bryan, C. J. (2018). Ideation-to-action theories of suicide: A conceptual and empirical update. *Current Opinion in Psychology, 22*, 38–43. https://doi.org/10.1016/j.copsyc.2017.07.020

Kyron, M. J., Hooke, G. R., & Page, A. C. (2018). Daily assessment of interpersonal factors to predict suicidal ideation and non-suicidal self-injury in psychiatric inpatients. *Journal of Consulting and Clinical Psychology, 86*(6), 556–567. https://doi.org/10.1037/ccp0000305

Kyron, M. J., Podlogar, M. C., Joiner, T. E., McEvoy, P. M., Page, A. C., & Lawrence, D. (2020). Allowing nondisclosure in surveys with suicide content: Characteristics of nondisclosure in a national survey of emergency services personnel. *Psychological Assessment, 32*(12), 1106–1117. https://doi.org/10.1037/pas0000949

Kyron, M. J., Hooke, G. R., Bryan, C. J., Kiekens, G., Chen, W., Hasking, P., & Page, A. C. (2023a). Daily prediction of nonsuicidal self-injury among inpatients: The roles of suicidal thoughts, interpersonal difficulties, hopelessness, and affect. *Journal of Consulting and Clinical Psychology, 91*(6), 323–336. https://doi.org/10.1037/ccp0000812

Kyron, M. J., Hooke, G. R., Bryan, C. J., Kiekens, G., Chen, W., Udupa, N., Joiner, T., & Page, A. C. (2023b). Daily prediction of inpatient suicide attempts using routinely collected theory-driven data. *Journal of Psychopathology and Clinical Science, 133*(2), 208–222. https://doi.org/10.1037/abn0000880

Lambert, M. J., Whipple, J. L., Smart, D. W., Vermeersch, D. A., Nielsen, S. L., & Hawkins, E. J. (2001). The effects of providing therapists with feedback on patient progress during psychotherapy: Are outcomes enhanced? *Psychotherapy Research, 11*(1), 49–68. https://doi.org/10.1080/713663852

Littlewood, D. L., Gooding, P., Kyle, S. D., Pratt, D., & Peters, S. (2016). Understanding the role of sleep in suicide risk: Qualitative interview study. *BMJ Open, 6*(8), e012113. https://doi.org/10.1136/bmjopen-2016-012113

Littlewood, D. L., Kyle, S. D., Carter, L.-A., Peters, S., Pratt, D., & Gooding, P. (2019). Short sleep duration and poor sleep quality predict next-day suicidal ideation: An ecological momentary assessment study. *Psychological Medicine, 49*(3), 403–411. https://doi.org/10.1017/S0033291718001009

Mars, B., Heron, J., Crane, C., Hawton, K., Kidger, J., Lewis, G., Macleod, J., Tilling, K., & Gunnell, D. (2014). Differences in risk factors for self-harm with and without suicidal intent: Findings from the ALSPAC cohort. *Journal of Affective Disorders, 168*, 407–414. https://doi.org/10.1016/j.jad.2014.07.009

Mayers, A. G., & Baldwin, D. S. (2006). The relationship between sleep disturbance and depression. *International Journal of Psychiatry in Clinical Practice, 10*(1), 2–16. https://doi.org/10.1080/13651500500328087

Miller, I. W., Camargo, C. A., Arias, S. A., Sullivan, A. F., Allen, M. H., Goldstein, A. B., Manton, A. P., Espinola, J. A., Jones, R., & Hasegawa, K. (2017). Suicide prevention in an emergency department population: The ED-SAFE study. *JAMA Psychiatry, 74*(6), 563–570. https://doi.org/10.1001/jamapsychiatry.2017.0678

Newnham, E. A., Hooke, G. R., & Page, A. C. (2010a). Monitoring treatment response and outcomes using the World Health Organization's Wellbeing Index in psychiatric care. *Journal of Affective Disorders, 122*(1–2), 133–138. https://doi.org/10.1016/j.jad.2009.06.005

Newnham, E. A., Hooke, G. R., & Page, A. C. (2010b). Progress monitoring and feedback in psychiatric care reduces depressive symptoms. *Journal of Affective Disorders, 127*(1–3), 139–146. https://doi.org/10.1016/j.jad.2010.05.003

Nock, M. K., Joiner, T. E., Gordon, K. H., Lloyd-Richardson, E., & Prinstein, M. J. (2006). Non-suicidal self-injury among adolescents: Diagnostic correlates and relation to suicide attempts. *Psychiatry Research, 144*(1), 65–72. https://doi.org/10.1016/j.psychres.2006.05.010

Olson, M. A., McNulty, J. K., March, D. S., Joiner, T. E., Rogers, M. L., & Hicks, L. L. (2022). Automatic and controlled antecedents of suicidal ideation and action: A dual-process conceptualization of suicidality. *Psychological Review, 129*(2), 388–414. https://doi.org/10.1037/rev0000286

Restifo, E., Kashyap, S., Hooke, G. R., & Page, A. C. (2015). Daily monitoring of temporal trajectories of suicidal ideation predict self-injury: A novel application of patient progress monitoring. *Psychotherapy Research, 25*(6), 705–713. https://doi.org/10.1080/10503307.2015.1006707

Ronk, F. R., Hooke, G. R., & Page, A. C. (2012). How consistent are clinical significance classifications when calculation methods and outcome measures differ? *Clinical Psychology: Science and Practice, 19*(2), 167–179. https://doi.org/10.1111/j.1468-2850.2012.01281.x

Ronk, F. R., Hooke, G. R., & Page, A. C. (2016). Validity of clinically significant change classifications yielded by Jacobson-Truax and Hageman-Arrindell methods. *BMC Psychiatry, 16*(187), 1–9. https://doi.org/10.1186/s12888-016-0895-5

Rudd, M. D., Mandrusiak, M., & Joiner, T. E., Jr. (2006). The case against no-suicide contracts: The commitment to treatment statement as a practice alternative. *Journal of Clinical Psychology, 62*(2), 243–251. https://doi.org/10.1002/jclp.20227

Seow, L. L., Collins, K., Page, A. C., & Hooke, G. R. (2022). Outcomes of brief versions of dialectical behaviour therapy for diagnostically heterogeneous groups in a routine care setting. *Psychotherapy Research, 32*(2), 179–194. https://doi.org/10.1080/10503307.2021.1933240

Strasser, B., & Fuchs, D. (2015). Role of physical activity and diet on mood, behavior, and cognition. *Neurology, Psychiatry and Brain Research, 21*(3), 118–126. https://doi.org/10.1016/j.npbr.2015.07.002

Stritzke, W. G. K., & Page, A. C. (2020). Suicide is about life. In A. C. Page & W. G. K. Stritzke (Eds.), *Alternatives to suicide: Beyond risk and toward a life worth living* (pp. 3–16). Elsevier.

Taylor, D. J., & Pruiksma, K. E. (2014). Cognitive and behavioural therapy for insomnia (CBT-I) in psychiatric populations: A systematic review. *International Review of Psychiatry, 26*(2), 205–213. https://doi.org/10.3109/09540261.2014.902808

Chapter 10
Feedback in Rehabilitation Settings

Johannes Knauer, Yannik Terhorst, and Harald Baumeister

Introduction

In rehabilitation medicine, the integration of sophisticated psychodiagnostic tools and real-time feedback mechanisms has the potential of fundamentally changing the landscape of patient care. Digital innovations are not just improving the accuracy of psychodiagnostic assessments but are transforming how personalized care can be delivered. By leveraging cutting-edge technology to tailor treatments to individual needs, rehabilitation professionals can optimize recovery pathways, thereby increasing the efficacy of interventions and improving patient quality of life. This chapter explores the profound impact of these technologies on treatment outcomes in rehabilitation settings, emphasizing their role in enhancing the precision and personalization of the rehabilitation process.

We plan to do so by outlining different settings of rehabilitation, that is, rehabilitation for patients with somatic diseases. Delving into patient-reported outcome measures as one basis of psychological diagnostic assessments, we will introduce computer-adaptive testing (CAT) strategies as well as advanced psychodiagnostic technologies (especially sensing frameworks). Drawing on new research findings and practical implementations, we will exemplarily introduce the web-based computer adaptive psychodiagnostic system RehaCAT and the accompanying case study, to provide a foundation for understanding how feedback-informed strategies

J. Knauer (✉) · H. Baumeister
Department of Clinical Psychology and Psychotherapy, Institute of Psychology and Education, University Ulm, Ulm, Germany
e-mail: johannes.knauer@uni-ulm.de; harald.baumeister@uni-ulm.de

Y. Terhorst
Department of Psychological Methods and Assessment, Ludwigs-Maximilian University Munich, Munich, Germany
e-mail: yannik.terhorst@psy.lmu.de

J. A. Rubel, W. Lutz (eds.), *Feedback Informed Psychological Therapy*, CBT: Science Into Practice, https://doi.org/10.1007/978-3-031-90428-8_10

are driving significant improvements in rehabilitation practices through routine outcome monitoring. This chapter will close with a general discussion on challenges and possibilities of the introduced technologies.

Patient Profile and Rehabilitation Needs

The International Classification of Functioning, Disability, and Health from the WHO uses a biopsychosocial model as a framework of health (World Health Organization, 2001). Thereby, functional health represents a core concept which can be viewed as a result of health problems linked to body functions and structures on the one hand and activity and participation level on the other hand moderated by environmental and personal factors.

Rehabilitation settings cater to a highly diverse patient population, each presenting unique physical and psychosocial challenges. In these environments, patients frequently exhibit a range of comorbidities, including mental health conditions such as depression and anxiety, which can significantly impact their physical rehabilitation processes. Numerous studies show high prevalence rates of mental disorders in different medical settings. For example, recent longitudinal studies found prevalence rates at 12 months of 29.0% (Shelley et al., 2021) and point prevalence rates of 36.0% (95% CI 31.1–40.3) (Srahbzu et al., 2018) for depressive symptoms in orthopedic care. A retrospective cohort study of $N = 5908$ patients in cardiac rehabilitation found point prevalence rates of 18%, 28%, and 13% for moderate depression, anxiety, and stress symptoms, respectively (Rao et al., 2020). A systematic review and meta-analysis including $N = 5951$ patients with 24 different rare chronic diseases (such as amyotrophic lateral sclerosis) found pooled lifetime prevalence estimates of 39.3% (95% CI 31.7–47.4%; $I2 = 84\%$, $p < 0.001$) for major depressive disorder, 46.1% (95% CI 35.8–56.8%; $I2 = 90\%$, $p < 0.001$) for affective disorders, and 44.2% (95% CI 27.0–62.9%; $I2 = 94\%$, $p < 0.001$) for anxiety disorders (Uhlenbusch et al., 2021).

This not only showcases the individual psychosocial burden and decreased quality of life of patients with comorbid somatic diseases and mental disorders (Baumeister et al., 2011a; Hutter et al., 2010, 2011) but also hints at the sequential societal consequences (Baumeister et al., 2012; Hutter et al., 2010, 2011). A meta-analysis of indirect costs of depression alone showed an associated doubled increase of costs compared to nondepressed participants (Ratio of means = 2.28 [1.75–2.98], $p < 0.001$) (König et al., 2020). Coexisting symptoms of mental disorders with somatic problems often lead to less effective standard somatic care (Leo et al., 2022), negatively influencing somatic outcomes (Strube et al., 2019). A meta-analysis on hospital readmission rates found a statistic increase for cardiac rehabilitation patients with comorbid mental disorders (SMD = 0.34 [0.17_0.51]) (Baumeister et al., 2015).

If mental burden is recognized in time, clinical practitioners might be able to appropriately choose treatment strategies. Studies on transdiagnostic rehabilitation

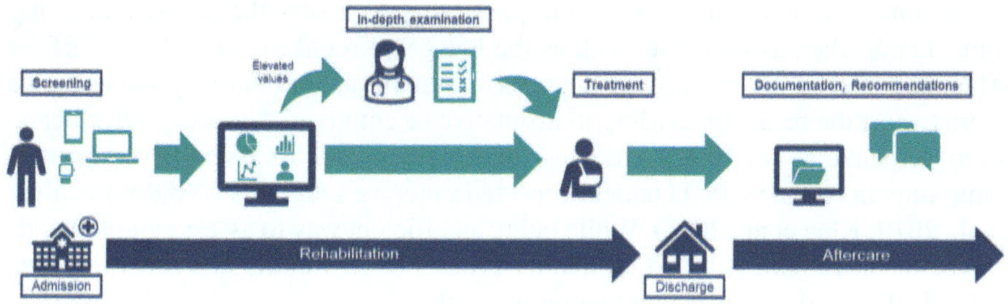

Fig. 10.1 Psychodiagnostics in Rehabilitation

programs found promising findings for (re)entry to work (Hara et al., 2018). These programs are accompanied by reduced costs in comparison to delivering multiple different programs targeted at specific disorders by efficiently using rehabilitation personnel and an increased access of comorbidity related rehabilitation services (Hara et al., 2018).

Summarizing, the effective management of these complex needs requires a precise but time-efficient psychosocial diagnostic procedure (Baumeister, 2016). Psychodiagnostics is thereby a fundamental prerequisite for needs-based treatment planning. Recommendations for psychodiagnostics in rehabilitation settings suggest an implementation strategy in stages: (1) routine screening at or before admission; (2) in-depth psychodiagnostic examination of all patients showing elevated screening values; (3) indication and treatment; (4) documentation with recommendations for post-rehabilitation treatment (Baumeister et al., 2011b) (Fig. 10.1).

Digital-Based Routine Assessments and Advanced Monitoring Technologies

Psychodiagnostics can be distinguished into categorical and dimensional approaches. Categorical psychodiagnostics are criteria-orientated and based on the current classification systems ICD-10/11 (World Health Organization, 2016, 2019) or DSM-5 (American Psychiatric Association, 2013). In the case of mental disorders, they check for time criteria, progression criteria, and impairment criteria, on the basis of which the presence of a mental disorder can be assessed and thereby diagnosed. Their strength lies in the comparability and reference to the specific therapy. However, the dichotomy of the approach often falls short in the case of mental burden, which has been shown to be rather a dimensional than a categorical concept (Haslam et al., 2020). Furthermore, the categorical diagnosis of mental disorder is time-consuming, particularly if—in the best-case scenario—a structured clinical interview is used (Münster, 1999), which is why it is not frequently conducted in clinical practice in general (Dubovsky, 2024) and in somatic rehabilitation with its focus on the somatic diseases in particular.

Dimensional assessments offer the possibility to assess the severity of symptoms. Established assessments such as the PHQ-9 (Kroenke et al., 2001) or BDI-II (Hautzinger et al., 2006) assess depressive symptoms and severity using a total score to sort the results according to normative or empirical categories (Beck et al., 1996; Kroenke et al., 1999). The most feasible approach to assess psychosomatic symptoms in routine care is patient-reported outcome measures (PROMs) (Calvert et al., 2019; Klag et al., 2008). While being an efficient way to assess symptoms, the choice of instrument is based on quality criteria (e.g., validity and reliability) and individual cut-off scores depending on the scale.

Both categorical and dimensional systems are necessary; however, in routine practice, there is a difference in where and when to use them most efficiently. With regard to the recommendations for psychodiagnostics in a medical rehabilitation setting, PROMs in particular can be used to economically identify individuals at risk based on screening results. Studies have shown that PROMs can lead to an improved communication, patient satisfaction, and decision-making in health care (Field et al., 2019; Howell et al., 2015). PROMs excel especially in the context of routine outcome monitoring, allowing for an efficient broad initial diagnostic coverage.

Although psychodiagnostics is generally an established routine procedure at some point during the rehabilitation process, there is a widespread concern about what is assessed and when assessments take place. While physical diagnostics are prioritized in somatic rehabilitation, the prevalence rates of mental comorbidities make it imperative to at least screen for mental burden. Low-threshold screening procedures (e.g., PROMs) constitute an efficient selection process, so further psychodiagnostics can focus on relevant individuals. Furthermore, the methodology of psychodiagnostic assessment in rehabilitation settings is often not contemporary (Baumeister et al., 2017). Current standard practice still involves the usage of paper-pencil measurement tools with numerous inherent disadvantages. Problems include the length of questionnaires to achieve a satisfactory reliability as well as problems with incomplete assessments. Processing these data requires a considerable workload for clinic personnel to evaluate and upload assessments into the clinics information system (Gibbons et al., 2008) (Fig. 10.2).

The implementation of digital psychodiagnostics within rehabilitation settings offers significant advantages by providing efficient and timely feedback, deleting the need to analyze measures on a paper-pencil basis, and guaranteeing complete data (Calvert et al., 2019). Digital psychodiagnostics leverage platforms to integrate patient-reported outcomes efficiently, allowing to focus on patient needs and minimizing delays in treatment adjustments. The benefits of such systems are evident in their ability to support clinical decisions with robust data on patient progress and treatment efficacy. Psychometrically speaking, the use of standardized tools ensures that the feedback collected is reliable and valid. Furthermore, a digital environment enables usage of advanced psychodiagnostic systems. For example, computer-adaptive tests (CAT) offer reliable, time-efficient psychodiagnostic assessments for a broad symptomatologic range (Abberger et al., 2013; Cella et al., 2007; Forkmann et al., 2009). CATs are based on the item response theory (Embretson & Yang,

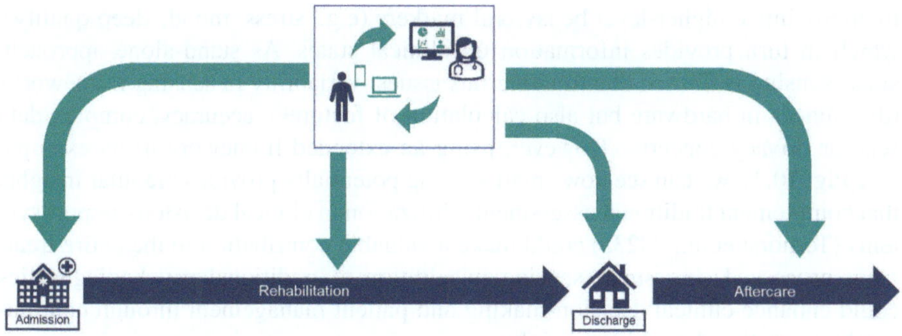

Fig. 10.2 Digital Psychodiagnostics

2006). The algorithm selects the items providing the maximum information about the patient. This reduces the burden of the assessment by requiring fewer items (compared to static procedures) and asking questions perceived as more relevant by patients (personalizing), thereby leading to more acceptance of the psychodiagnostic procedure (Gamper et al., 2019). Compared to static and nonadaptive usage of PROMs, CATs use the most efficient questions to achieve a reliable final score.

Sensing Framework and Decision-Support Systems

The aforementioned International Classification of Functioning, Disability, and Health (World Health Organization, 2001) provides a structured approach to understanding the impact of conditions on patients' lives and vice versa. Assuming that one has a perfect psychodiagnostic overview of all relevant factors, this assessment is nevertheless limited to fixed points in time. This brings the risk of missing potential significant symptom changes happening between assessments. Furthermore, traditional assessments require active input of patients, which might be biased due to the nature of self-reports (Ben-Zeev & Young, 2010; Gorzelitz et al., 2018; Paulhus, 2017). In today's world, where smartphones and digital devices are an integral part of life, the usage of this sensing data offers great opportunities (Cornet & Holden, 2018). The most prominent approach is referred to as digital phenotyping and smart sensing (Montag & Baumeister, 2023). This involves collecting data through digital devices and sensors to track and analyze patient behavior and symptoms in real-time, providing an unobtrusive and continuous monitoring of a patient's condition. Smartphones, in particular, are carried on near us most of the time (Mohr et al., 2017; Montag et al., 2020), which leads to a wide array of possible sensors (Garatva et al., 2023). Mohr et al. (2017) summarized an exemplary overview for sensing frameworks: On the basis of hardware and software sensor data (e.g., GPS, voice call, messages, app usage), lower-level features (e.g., home stay, activity, social communication) can be derived. In a next step, this information can be used to approximate higher-level behavioral markers (e.g., stress, mood, sleep quality), which in turn provides information on clinical states. As stand-alone approach, smart sensing is limited due to numerous issues: variability in sensing frameworks (differences in hardware but also calculation of features), accuracy, complex data sets, or privacy concerns. However, using an extended framework as an example (see Fig. 10.3), we can see how smart sensing potentially provides granular insights that complement traditional assessment. Utilization in clinical decision-support systems (Terhorst et al., 2023a) could make a valuable contribution to the entire treatment process. Using smart sensing in addition to traditional psychodiagnostics could enhance clinical decision-making and patient management through continuous high-quality, data-driven insights.

Potential applications include:

- Assistance in differential psychodiagnostics: low-threshold identification of potential patients at risk, which in turn leads to an efficient handling of which patients to further investigate.
- Based on predicted symptom trajectories, just-in-time interventions (Schulte-Strathaus et al., 2023) can be prompted for the respective clinicians or patients themselves. This could lead to timely interventions or preventive measures for patients potentially at risk.
- Due to the complexity and continuity of data, just-in-time adaptive approaches can support personalized clinical decision-making and potential treatment adaptions.
- Through general monitoring treatment response, adherence and relapse risk can be tracked.

Sensing technologies and advanced technological frameworks could enable clinicians to dynamically adapt treatment plans, ensuring that care strategies are responsive to the changing conditions of patients. Integration of these technological frameworks into the ICF model allows for a comprehensive evaluation of health

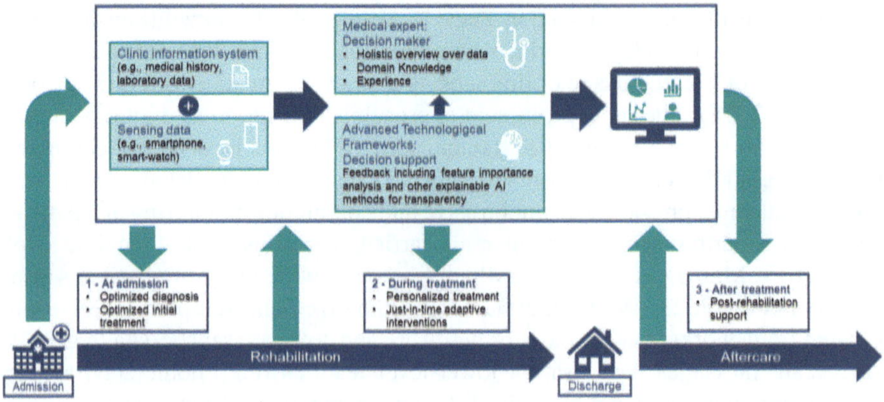

Fig. 10.3 Extension of Digital Psychodiagnostics

status, aligning with informed practices and leading to interventions that are not only holistic but also targeted.

Case Study: RehaCAT

In order to illustrate some of the aforementioned digital possibilities of enhancing psychodiagnostics in medical rehabilitation, we are introducing RehaCAT, a web-based platform for outcome assessment in clinical routine practice. The pragmatic implementation of this system represents a significant advancement in the integration of technology for standard psychodiagnostic procedures within rehabilitation settings. RehaCAT was designed as a toolbox with the primary goal of optimizing the psychosocial diagnostic and treatment processes for patients within rehabilitation facilities. Based on many years of rehabilitation research, RehaCAT combines a patient-centered economic psychodiagnostic assessment with insights into psychodiagnostic results for treating personnel, enabling an efficient routine outcome monitoring approach to support clinical practice. This is achieved by a role-specific framework. The platform was developed independently according to the open-source principle, taking into account standards such as the IEC 62304 standard (safety class B), GAMP5 (category 4), General Principles of Software Validation, PIC/S 11-3, and the requirements of the Medical Devices Regulation. The functionality, reliability, performance, and safety requirements are very high in order to enable high-quality and safe research.

The system itself offers the opportunity to schedule assessments with time frames corresponding to the individual rehabilitation timeline of patients (Fig. 10.4). Ideally, psychodiagnostic results are used for treatment planning at the beginning of rehabilitation, as well as to track the reaction to measures during and at the end of rehabilitation through continuous psychodiagnostics or to record aftercare-specific data. The current implementation is creating awareness for mental comorbidities in somatic rehabilitation, that is, rehabilitation for patients with cardiac and musculoskeletal diseases. It is aiming to capture a comprehensive picture of patients' functional health in a time- and resource-saving manner, by using state-of-the-art CAT scales, in this case the PROMIS item banks for CAT on depression, anxiety, satisfaction with participation in social roles and activities, pain impairment, fatigue, sleep, and physical functioning. The implementation also allows the use of questionnaires based on classical test theory as well as additional cut-off triggered questionnaires for patients with elevated screening results.

Fig. 10.4 Patient Management

For Clinicians

The low-threshold screening procedures can be used to routinely identify mentally distressed patients at an early stage. If the first assessment is completed before admission, clinicians can react accordingly and are provided with a groundwork for individualized treatment planning as well as first decision-support suggestions. Assessments during the rehabilitation process can be used to monitor if the treatment is on track or if treatment plans need to be adapted. The results at every assessment point provide a comprehensive picture of patients' functional health in a time- and resource-saving manner. The standardized reporting of psychodiagnostic results with easy-to-understand interpretation aids and automatically generated discharge report modules can reduce the documentation workload for hospital staff. Especially, at the end of rehabilitation, clinicians are able to evaluate the treatment based on assessment results (Fig. 10.5). The function for generating patient-orientated reports strengthens patient empowerment through involvement and furthermore supports discussions with patients with an informational basis. Depending on implementational strategies, the system can trigger recommendations for action depending on cut-off scores. Aftercare assessments can help to understand long-term treatment effects and thereby strengthen individualized approaches.

For Patients

Psychodiagnostic assessments during rehabilitation routine care can be completed on any digital device. Furthermore, patients can be automatically invited to aftercare surveys via email. Aftercare data can be used by clinics to record the need for follow-up care. At the same time, patients can be informed about their assessment results, thus leading to motivation and self-empowerment of patients to seek professional care when problems arise (e.g., by recommending relevant support services). Additionally, this allows for initiation of potential preventive measures. Utilizing easy-to-understand psychodiagnostic reports with additional general symptomatic information, patients can be informed about their health status (Fig. 10.6).

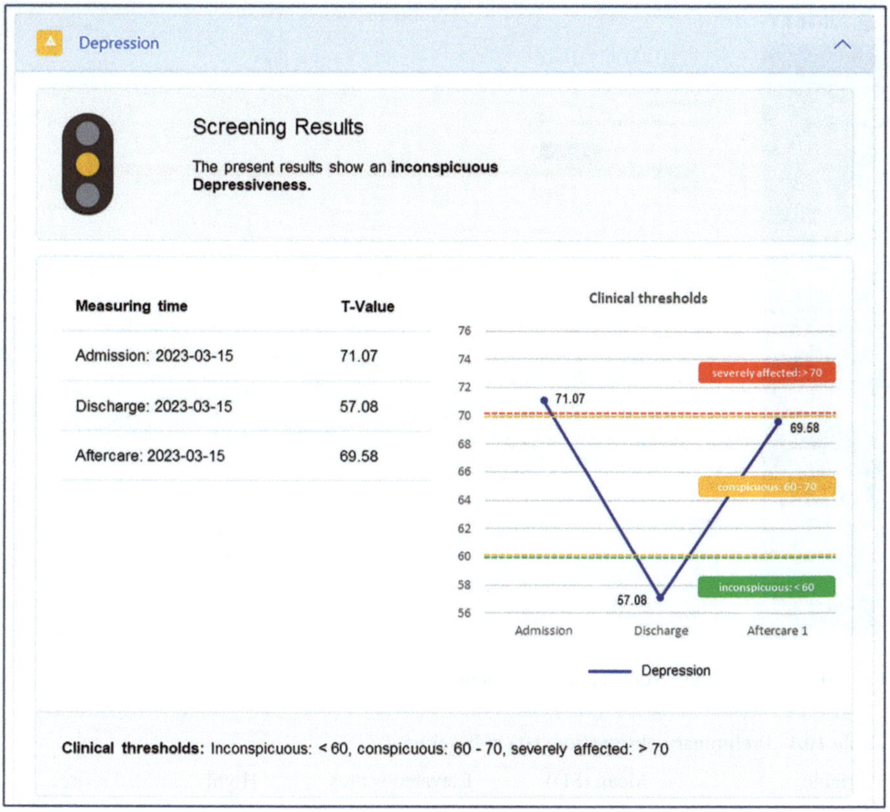

Fig. 10.5 Psychodiagnostic Report

RehaCAT Study

In a pragmatic study setting, an advanced version of RehaCAT was compared to the standard system (Knauer et al., 2022). Conducted across 12 rehabilitation clinics in Germany, the study employed a two-arm, cluster-randomized controlled trial design. The study not only explores the operational aspects of the RehaCAT system but also evaluates its impact on clinical outcomes such as depression severity, anxiety levels, and overall patient well-being over a 12-month period. It showcases how systematic feedback and recommendations for action can lead to significant improvements in treatment plans, demonstrating the potential of feedback-informed practices to enhance rehabilitation. Exploratively, as part of an optional sub-study, smart sensing data were collected actively and passively via a mobile application for smartphones.

Preliminary data on routine assessments show promising findings concerning utilization of the system. Monitoring and feedback are central to the RehaCAT approach, with currently over 25,000 routine assessments conducted to track patient

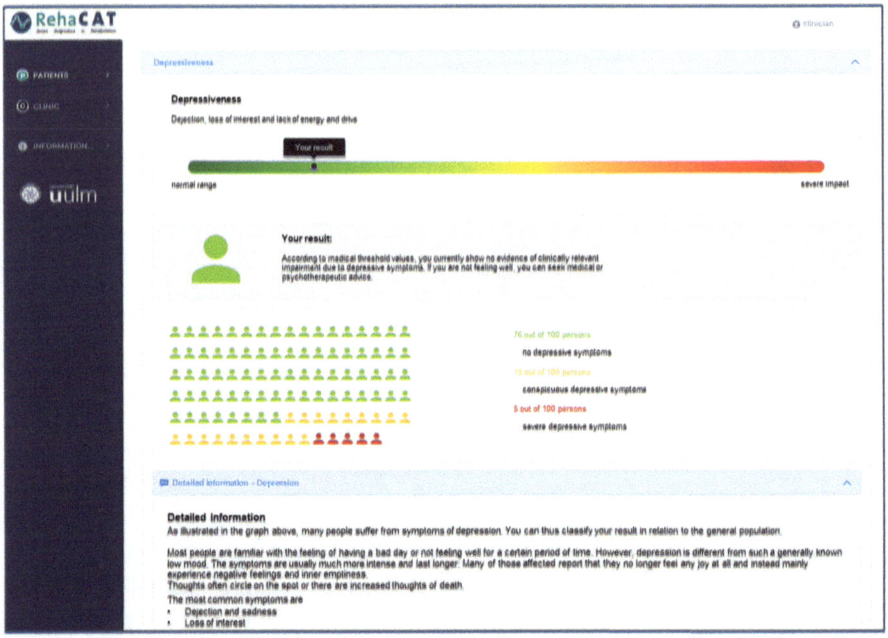

Fig. 10.6 Psychodiagnostic Report for Patients

Table 10.1 Preliminary observation data at baseline

Variable	Mean (SD)	Elevated scores	Highly elevated scores
Depression	0.55 (0.74)	28%	2%
Anxiety	0.62 (0.70)	27%	2%
Pain	1.01 (0.68)	55%	5%
Physical function	0.87 (0.74)	45%	6%
Sleep	0.50 (0.86)	30%	4%
Fatigue	0.64 (0.83)	37%	4%

Note. N = 12,670; Scores follow a normal distribution with a mean value of 0 and a standard deviation of 1; Elevated scores > 1; Highly elevated scores > 2; utilized scales: PROMIS® Emotional Distress—Depression, Emotional Distress—Anxiety, Pain Interference, Physical Function, Sleep Disturbance, and Fatigue

progress. Due to the pragmatic nature of the trial, implementation strategies differed between clinics. Integration of the system into routine practice for both patients and clinicians emerged as a major predictive factor for general adherence rates (up to 81%) as well as dropout at all following assessment points. Overall, there was a significant improvement in survey duration from first time using the system to the second time (22 min to 14 min). Additional qualitative interviews pointed at the same trend of implantation strategies and general utilization and acceptance. Symptom severity was elevated for most variables highlighting the need for routine screening (see Table 10.1).

Table 10.2 Preliminary data for pre–post rehabilitation effects

Dimension	M_0 (SD)	M_1 (SD)	Cohens d	β (95%-CI)
Depression	0.50 (0.74)	−0.04 (0.82)	0.69	−0.66 (−0.68, −0.64)
Anxiety	0.59 (0.69)	0.06 (0.81)	0.70	−0.66 (−0.68, −0.64)
Pain	0.97 (0.7)	0.66 (0.74)	0.43	−0.42 (−0.43, −0.40)
Physical function	0.85 (0.75)	0.63 (0.79)	0.29	−0.28 (−0.30, −0.27)
Sleep	0.46 (0.85)	0.19 (0.89)	0.31	−0.30 (−0.32, −0.28)
Fatigue	0.59 (0.83)	0.15 (0.91)	0.51	−0.50 (−0.52, −0.48)

Note. $N = 6497$; Scores follow a normal distribution with a mean value of 0 and a standard deviation of 1

Furthermore, quality assurance and aftercare assessment emerged as particularly relevant topics. Given the broad range of data, clinics are able to evaluate treatment effectiveness and monitor symptom trajectories (Table 10.2). Additionally, automation of aftercare assessment gives insight into symptom trajectories in rehabilitation aftercare, thereby offering valuable data on potential long-term effects of rehabilitation treatment. It also offers the possibility to preventively reintroduce persons with elevated symptoms after rehabilitation back into the health care systems.

Critical Reflection

The insights gathered from digital assessment systems like RehaCAT, along with the discussed advanced monitoring technologies, provide a comprehensive framework on the possibilities and challenges in integrating such technologies into rehabilitation routine.

Digitalization of psychodiagnostics is the contemporary approach to routinely assess patients' psychosocial symptomatology. This can streamline the treatment process, increasing efficiency by filtering out patients in need for further attention and potentially personalizing the procedure. Advanced digital frameworks have potential to support the decision-making process. Real-time data collection enhances the ability to make immediate adjustments to therapy, potentially leading to better patient outcomes and increased efficiency in rehabilitation settings.

However, acceptance of technologies, implementation, and thereby utilization play crucial roles in the potential gain digital systems can offer. This is especially relevant for less widely known and acknowledged approaches such as monitoring or further developed clinical decision-support systems. Even the most ideally planned systems is of no use if it is not utilized by the target group. Therefore, the acceptance toward technologies is a prerequisite toward the impact of this technology. With many different factors influencing acceptance of technologies (Blut et al., 2021), it is important to understand the determinants and take them into account during implementation (Hennemann et al., 2016; Philippi et al., 2021). For example, in the case of smart sensing, studies in different settings found the expected personal benefit to be an important determinant of acceptance (Knauer et al., 2024; Rottstädt et al., 2024; Terhorst et al., 2023b). Furthermore, the attitude of different groups involved needs to be differentiated (Gao et al., 2020; Montag et al., 2020). Acceptance of new technologies is a major barrier for both patients and caregivers.

This leads to implementational aspects as a core challenge for routine outcome monitoring systems such as RehaCAT in rehabilitation settings. A robust implementation involves training of healthcare personnel. This includes informing health care professionals about technological advancements as a necessity for optimizing the use of these tools in everyday clinical practice. Technological literacy as well as the willingness to use the technology are main obstacles. Related to this the implementation strategy needs to be considered. In our pragmatic case study, we found clinics that opted for a broad implementation of the system in clinical routine practice to profit more compared to clinics with less strict implementational strategies.

Next, data quality and the related topic of standardization need to be addressed. In order to effectively utilize psychodiagnostic data, we need reliable measures, consistent assessment strategies, as well as appropriate use. In the context of PROMs, we are confronted with a multitude of developed and well-established instruments for psychodiagnostics assessment. Consequently, scale-specific metrics impair the comparability between different instruments for similar symptomatology (Wahl et al., 2014). Well-established PROMs, that is, scales developed by PROMIS (Cella et al., 2010; van Muilekom et al., 2021), are setting a high standard in a multitude of settings. When it comes to advanced technological frameworks or other innovative digital procedures, standardization is of equal importance (Mohr et al., 2017). In the context of sensors, we find a broad array of used frameworks, calculations and algorithms for features, as well as varying research designs and general low quality in reporting (Garatva et al., 2023; Mohr et al., 2017). In order to correctly evaluate and realize the full potential of these technologies, there is a need for standardization to make measures comparable. In contrast to other fields, like assessment of people in organizational settings (ISO 10667-1:2020), or suitability assessments (e.g., DIN 33430), we are lacking normative approaches for reporting psychodiagnostic results in rehabilitation context. This makes it difficult to interpret and compare results, thereby hindering the overall utilization in health care systems.

Privacy and ethical considerations are another important topics to consider in view of sensitive patient data, especially in the context of new technologies. On an individual level, studies found the willingness of patients to share data to be dependent on the type of data as well as the recipient of data (Nicholas et al., 2019). This supports the need for transparency concerning topics like data usage, processing, storage, as well as access. Related to this, medical device regulations, including data safety and prevention of misuse of data, address this issue on a political level (The European Parliament & The Council of the European Union, 2018). Additionally, the potential for depersonalization of care needs to be taken into account. For clinicians in rehabilitation settings, integrating these technologies involves a careful consideration of both the potential benefits and the inherent risks. Health care practitioners are encouraged to maintain an active role in decision-making processes, using technology as a complementary tool on top of their clinical expertise.

However, we are living in a quickly changing digital landscape. This not only concerns what technologies we use but also how we use them. For example, digital frameworks that depend on algorithms are relatively short lived with frequent technological updates and also the permanently evolving way people use and interact with digital devices and platforms. Promising sensor data and features derived from smartphone usage are ultimately dependent on setting variables (e.g., how we interact with out smartphone, where we carry it with us). Promising different fields, for example, large language models like Chat GPT, show enormous potential for behavioral health care ranging from automation of clinical administration, measuring treatment fidelity, offering feedback between sessions to decision aids for existing evidence-based practices (Stade et al., 2024).

Conclusion

Throughout this chapter, the critical examination of feedback-informed treatment strategies within rehabilitation settings has highlighted both the transformative potential and the challenges of integrating advanced psychodiagnostic and digital technologies. The discussion underscored the necessity of balancing technological innovation with clinical feasibility to enhance patient care without compromising the human interaction. As rehabilitation settings continue to evolve, the integration of such technologies promises significant advances in patient outcomes, provided that these tools are used appropriately and embedded in routine therapeutic approaches. This reaffirms the importance of continued research and development in this area to fully realize the benefits while addressing the ethical and practical challenges posed by technological dependence.

References

Abberger, B., Haschke, A., Wirtz, M., Kroehne, U., Bengel, J., & Baumeister, H. (2013). Development and evaluation of a computer adaptive test to assess anxiety in cardiovascular rehabilitation patients. *Archives of Physical Medicine and Rehabilitation, 94*(12), 2433–2439. https://doi.org/10.1016/J.APMR.2013.07.009

American Psychiatric Association. (2013). *Diagnostic and statistical manual of mental disorders*. American Psychiatric Association. https://doi.org/10.1176/appi.books.9780890425596

Baumeister, H. (2016). Diagnostik und Indikationsstellung bei psychischen Belastungen und Störungen. In *Psychologie in der medizinischen Rehabilitation* (pp. 39–49). Springer. https://doi.org/10.1007/978-3-662-47972-8_4

Baumeister, H., Hutter, N., Bengel, J., & Härter, M. (2011a). Quality of life in medically ill persons with comorbid mental disorders: A systematic review and meta-analysis. *Psychotherapy and Psychosomatics, 80*(5), 275–286. https://doi.org/10.1159/000323404

Baumeister, H., Jahed, J., Vogel, B., Härter, M., Barth, J., & Bengel, J. (2011b). *Diagnostik, Indikation und Behandlung von psychischen Störungen in der medizinischen Rehabilitation (DIBpS): Ein Leitfaden zur Implementierung eines psychodiagnostischen Stufenplans in der medizinischen Rehabilitation*. DRV M4 - Citavi.

Baumeister, H., Knecht, A., & Hutter, N. (2012). Direct and indirect costs in persons with chronic back pain and comorbid mental disorders - A systematic review. *Journal of Psychosomatic Research, 73*(2), 79–85. https://doi.org/10.1016/j.jpsychores.2012.05.008

Baumeister, H., Haschke, A., Munzinger, M., Hutter, N., & Tully, P. J. (2015). Inpatient and outpatient costs in patients with coronary artery disease and mental disorders: A systematic review. *BioPsychoSocial Medicine, 9*(1), 11. https://doi.org/10.1186/s13030-015-0039-z

Baumeister, H., Lin, J., & Ebert, D. D. (2017). Internet- and mobile-based approaches: Psychosocial diagnostics and treatment in medical rehabilitation. *Bundesgesundheitsblatt - Gesundheitsforschung - Gesundheitsschutz, 60*(4), 436–444. https://doi.org/10.1007/s00103-017-2518-9

Beck, A. T., Steer, R. A., & Brown, G. (1996). Beck depression inventory–II. *APA PsycTests*. https://doi.org/10.1037/t00742-000

Ben-Zeev, D., & Young, M. A. (2010). Accuracy of hospitalized depressed patients' and healthy controls' retrospective symptom reports: An experience sampling study. *The Journal of Nervous and Mental Disease, 198*(4), 280–285. https://doi.org/10.1097/NMD.0b013e3181d6141f

Blut, M., Chong, A., Tsiga, Z., & Venkatesh, V. (2021). Meta-analysis of the unified theory of acceptance and use of technology (UTAUT): Challenging its validity and charting a research agenda in the Red Ocean. *Journal of the Association for Information Systems, 2021*, 1–128.

Calvert, M., Kyte, D., Price, G., Valderas, J. M., & Hjollund, N. H. (2019). Maximising the impact of patient reported outcome assessment for patients and society. *BMJ, 364*. https://doi.org/10.1136/bmj.k5267

Cella, D., Gershon, R., Lai, J.-S., & Choi, S. (2007). The future of outcomes measurement: Item banking, tailored short-forms, and computerized adaptive assessment. *Quality of Life Research, 16*(S1), 133–141. https://doi.org/10.1007/s11136-007-9204-6

Cella, D., Riley, W., Stone, A., Rothrock, N., Reeve, B., Yount, S., Amtmann, D., Bode, R., Buysse, D., Choi, S., Cook, K., DeVellis, R., DeWalt, D., Fries, J. F., Gershon, R., Hahn, E. A., Lai, J.-S., Pilkonis, P., Revicki, D., et al. (2010). The patient-reported outcomes measurement information system (PROMIS) developed and tested its first wave of adult self-reported health outcome item banks: 2005–2008. *Journal of Clinical Epidemiology, 63*(11), 1179–1194. https://doi.org/10.1016/j.jclinepi.2010.04.011

Cornet, V. P., & Holden, R. J. (2018). Systematic review of smartphone-based passive sensing for health and wellbeing. *Journal of Biomedical Informatics, 77*, 120–132. https://doi.org/10.1016/j.jbi.2017.12.008

Dubovsky, S. L. (2024). Will interviewing become a lost art? *Psychotherapy and Psychosomatics, 93*(2), 75–79. https://doi.org/10.1159/000537783

Embretson, S., & Yang, X. (2006). Item response theory. In J. L. Green, G. Camilli, & P. B. Elmore (Eds.), *Handbook of complementary methods in education research* (pp. 385–409). Lawrence Erlbaum Associates Publishers.

Field, J., Holmes, M. M., & Newell, D. (2019). PROMs data: Can it be used to make decisions for individual patients? A narrative review. *Patient Related Outcome Measures, 10*, 233–241. https://doi.org/10.2147/prom.s156291

Forkmann, T., Böcker, M., Norra, C., Eberle, N., Kircher, T., Schauerte, P., Mischke, K., Westhofen, M., Gauggel, S., & Wirtz, M. A. (2009). Development of an item bank for the assessment of depression in persons with mental illnesses and physical diseases using Rasch analysis. *Rehabilitation Psychology, 54*(2), 186–197.

Gamper, E. M., Martini, C., Petersen, M. A., Virgolini, I., Holzner, B., & Giesinger, J. M. (2019). Do patients consider computer-adaptive measures more appropriate than static questionnaires? *Journal of Patient-Reported Outcomes, 3*(1), 7. https://doi.org/10.1186/s41687-019-0096-3

Gao, S., He, L., Chen, Y., Li, D., & Lai, K. (2020). Public perception of artificial intelligence in medical care: Content analysis of social media. *Journal of Medical Internet Research, 22*(7), e16649. https://doi.org/10.2196/16649

Garatva, P., Terhorst, Y., Messner, E.-M., Karlen, W., Pryss, R., & Baumeister, H. (2023). Smart sensors for health research and improvement. In C. Montag & H. Baumeister (Eds.),

Digital phenotyping and mobile sensing (2nd ed., pp. 395–411). Springer. https://doi.org/10.1007/978-3-030-98546-2_23

Gibbons, R. D., Weiss, D. J., Kupfer, D. J., Frank, E., Fagiolini, A., Grochocinski, V. J., Bhaumik, D. K., Stover, A., Bock, R. D., & Immekus, J. C. (2008). Using computerized adaptive testing to reduce the burden of mental health assessment. *Psychiatric Services, 59*(4), 361–368.

Gorzelitz, J., Peppard, P. E., Malecki, K., Gennuso, K., Nieto, F. J., & Cadmus-Bertram, L. (2018). Predictors of discordance in self-report versus device-measured physical activity measurement. *Annals of Epidemiology, 28*(7), 427–431. https://doi.org/10.1016/j.annepidem.2018.03.016

Hara, K. W., Bjørngaard, J. H., Jacobsen, H. B., Borchgrevink, P. C., Johnsen, R., Stiles, T. C., Brage, S., & Woodhouse, A. (2018). Biopsychosocial predictors and trajectories of work participation after transdiagnostic occupational rehabilitation of participants with mental and somatic disorders: A cohort study. *BMC Public Health, 18*(1), 1014. https://doi.org/10.1186/s12889-018-5803-0

Haslam, N., McGrath, M. J., Viechtbauer, W., & Kuppens, P. (2020). Dimensions over categories: A meta-analysis of taxometric research. *Psychological Medicine, 50*(9), 1418–1432. https://doi.org/10.1017/S003329172000183X

Hautzinger, M., Keller, F., & Kühner, C. (2006). *Das Beck Depressionsinventar II. Deutsche Bearbeitung und Handbuch zum BDI-II*. Pearson.

Hennemann, S., Beutel, M. E., & Zwerenz, R. (2016). Drivers and barriers to acceptance of web-based aftercare of patients in inpatient routine care: A cross-sectional survey. *Journal of Medical Internet Research, 18*(12), e337. https://doi.org/10.2196/jmir.6003

Howell, D., Molloy, S., Wilkinson, K., Green, E., Orchard, K., Wang, K., & Liberty, J. (2015). Patient-reported outcomes in routine cancer clinical practice: A scoping review of use, impact on health outcomes, and implementation factors. *Annals of Oncology, 26*(9), 1846–1858. https://doi.org/10.1093/annonc/mdv181

Hutter, N., Schnurr, A., & Baumeister, H. (2010). Healthcare costs in patients with diabetes mellitus and comorbid mental disorders—A systematic review. *Diabetologia, 53*(12), 2470–2479. https://doi.org/10.1007/s00125-010-1873-y

Hutter, N., Knecht, A., & Baumeister, H. (2011). Health care costs in persons with asthma and comorbid mental disorders. *General Hospital Psychiatry, 33*(5), 443–453. https://doi.org/10.1016/j.genhosppsych.2011.06.013

Klag, M. J., MacKenzie, E. J., Carswell, C. I., & Bridges, J. F. P. (2008). The role of the patient in promoting patient-centered outcomes research. *The Patient: Patient-Centered Outcomes Research, 1*(1), 1–3. https://doi.org/10.2165/01312067-200801010-00001

Knauer, J., Terhorst, Y., Philippi, P., Kallinger, S., Eiler, S., Kilian, R., Waldmann, T., Moshagen, M., Bader, M., & Baumeister, H. (2022). Effectiveness and cost-effectiveness of a web-based routine assessment with integrated recommendations for action for depression and anxiety (RehaCAT+): Protocol for a cluster randomised controlled trial for patients with elevated depressive symptoms in r. *BMJ Open, 12*(6), e061259. https://doi.org/10.1136/bmjopen-2022-061259

Knauer, J., Baumeister, H., Schmitt, A., & Terhorst, Y. (2024). Acceptance of smart sensing, its determinants, and the efficacy of an acceptance-facilitating intervention in people with diabetes: Results from a randomized controlled trial. *Frontiers in Digital Health, 6*.

König, H., König, H.-H., & Konnopka, A. (2020). The excess costs of depression: A systematic review and meta-analysis. *Epidemiology and Psychiatric Sciences, 29*, e30. https://doi.org/10.1017/S2045796019000180

Kroenke, K., Spitzer, R. L., & Williams, J. B. W. (1999). Patient Health Questionnaire-9. *APA PsycTests*. https://doi.org/10.1037/t06165-000

Kroenke, K., Spitzer, R. L., & Williams, J. B. W. (2001). The PHQ-9. *Journal of General Internal Medicine, 16*(9), 606–613. https://doi.org/10.1046/j.1525-1497.2001.016009606.x

Leo, A. J., Schuelke, M. J., Hunt, D. M., Metzler, J. P., Miller, J. P., Areán, P. A., Armbrecht, M. A., & Cheng, A. L. (2022). A digital mental health intervention in an orthopedic setting for patients with symptoms of depression and/or anxiety: Feasibility prospective cohort study. *JMIR Formative Research, 6*(2), e34889. https://doi.org/10.2196/34889

Mohr, D. C., Zhang, M., & Schueller, S. M. (2017). Personal sensing: Understanding mental health using ubiquitous sensors and machine learning. *Annual Review of Clinical Psychology, 13*(1), 23–47. https://doi.org/10.1146/annurev-clinpsy-032816-044949

Montag, C., & Baumeister, H. (Eds.). (2023). *Digital phenotyping and mobile sensing* (2nd ed.). Springer. https://doi.org/10.1007/978-3-030-98546-2

Montag, C., Sindermann, C., & Baumeister, H. (2020). Digital phenotyping in psychological and medical sciences: A reflection about necessary prerequisites to reduce harm and increase benefits. *Current Opinion in Psychology, 36*, 19–24. https://doi.org/10.1016/j.copsyc.2020.03.013

Münster, R. D. (1999). Wittchen, H.-U., Zaudig, M. & Fydrich, T. (1997). SKID Strukturiertes Klinisches Interview für DSM-IV. Achse I und II. Göttingen: Hogrefe, DM 158,-. Hiller, W., Zaudig, M. & Mombour, W. (1997). IDCL Internationale Diagnosen Checklisten für DSM-IV und ICD-10. Göttingen: Hogrefe, DM 198,- bzw. DM 239,-. *28*(1), 68–70. https://doi.org/10.1026//0084-5345.28.1.68

Nicholas, J., Shilton, K., Schueller, S. M., Gray, E. L., Kwasny, M. J., & Mohr, D. C. (2019). The role of data type and recipient in individuals' perspectives on sharing passively collected smartphone data for mental health: Cross-sectional questionnaire study. *JMIR mHealth and uHealth, 7*(4), e12578. https://doi.org/10.2196/12578

Paulhus, D. L. (2017). Socially desirable responding on self-reports. In *Encyclopedia of personality and individual differences* (pp. 1–5). Springer. https://doi.org/10.1007/978-3-319-28099-8_1349-1

Philippi, P., Baumeister, H., Apolinário-Hagen, J., Ebert, D. D., Hennemann, S., Kott, L., Lin, J., Messner, E.-M., & Terhorst, Y. (2021). Acceptance towards digital health interventions—Model validation and further development of the unified theory of acceptance and use of technology. *Internet Interventions, 26*, 100459. https://doi.org/10.1016/j.invent.2021.100459

Rao, A., Zecchin, R., Newton, P., Phillips, J., DiGiacomo, M., Denniss, A., & Hickman, L. (2020). The prevalence and impact of depression and anxiety in cardiac rehabilitation: A longitudinal cohort study. *European Journal of Preventive Cardiology, 27*(5), 478–489. https://doi.org/10.1177/2047487319871716

Rottstädt, F., Becker, E., Wilz, G., Croy, I., Baumeister, H., & Terhorst, Y. (2024). Enhancing the acceptance of smart sensing in psychotherapy patients: Findings from a randomized controlled trial. *Frontiers in Digital Health, 6*. https://doi.org/10.3389/fdgth.2024.1335776

Schulte-Strathaus, J. C. C., Rauschenberg, C., Baumeister, H., & Reininghaus, U. (2023). Ecological momentary interventions in public mental health provision. In *Digital phenotyping and mobile sensing* (pp. 427–439). Springer. https://doi.org/10.1007/978-3-030-98546-2_25

Shelley, J. K., Roden-Foreman, J. W., Vier, D., McShan, E. E., Bennett, M. M., Jones, A. L., & Warren, A. M. (2021). Relation of length of stay and other hospital variables to posttraumatic stress disorder and depression after orthopedic trauma. *Baylor University Medical Center Proceedings, 34*(1), 28–33. https://doi.org/10.1080/08998280.2020.1801113

Srahbzu, M., Yigizaw, N., Fanta, T., Assefa, D., & Tirfeneh, E. (2018). Prevalence of depression and anxiety and associated factors among patients visiting orthopedic outpatient Clinic at Tikur Anbessa Specialized Hospital, Addis Ababa, Ethiopia, 2017. *Journal of Psychiatry, 21*(4). https://doi.org/10.4172/2378-5756.1000450

Stade, E. C., Stirman, S. W., Ungar, L. H., Boland, C. L., Schwartz, H. A., Yaden, D. B., Sedoc, J., DeRubeis, R. J., Willer, R., & Eichstaedt, J. C. (2024). Large language models could change the future of behavioral healthcare: A proposal for responsible development and evaluation. *npj Mental Health Research, 3*(1), 12. https://doi.org/10.1038/s44184-024-00056-z

Strube, P., Schöpe, T., Hölzl, A., Brodt, S., Matziolis, G., & Zippelius, T. K. (2019). Influence of anxiety and depression, self-rated return-to-work problems, and unemployment on the outcome of outpatient rehabilitation after shoulder arthroscopy. *American Journal of Physical Medicine & Rehabilitation, 98*(12), 1118–1124. https://doi.org/10.1097/PHM.0000000000001260

Terhorst, Y., Knauer, J., & Baumeister, H. (2023a). Smart sensing enhanced diagnostic expert systems. In C. Montag & H. Baumeister (Eds.), *Digital phenotyping and mobile sensing* (2nd ed., pp. 413–425). Springer. https://doi.org/10.1007/978-3-030-98546-2_24

Terhorst, Y., Weilbacher, N., Suda, C., Simon, L., Messner, E.-M., Sander, L. B., & Baumeister, H. (2023b). Acceptance of smart sensing: A barrier to implementation—Results from a randomized controlled trial. *Frontiers in Digital Health, 5*, 1075266. https://doi.org/10.3389/fdgth.2023.1075266

The European Parliament, & The Council of the European Union. (2018). Regulation (EU) 2016/679 on the protection of natural persons with regard to the processing of personal data and on the free movement of such data (General Data Protection Regulation – GDPR). *Official Journal of the European Union, 2014*(April), 958–981. https://doi.org/10.5771/9783845266190-974

Uhlenbusch, N., Swaydan, J., Höller, A., Löwe, B., & Depping, M. K. (2021). Affective and anxiety disorders in patients with different rare chronic diseases: A systematic review and meta-analysis. *Psychological Medicine, 51*(16), 2731–2741. https://doi.org/10.1017/S0033291721003792

van Muilekom, M. M., Luijten, M. A. J., van Oers, H. A., Terwee, C. B., van Litsenburg, R. R. L., Roorda, L. D., Grootenhuis, M. A., & Haverman, L. (2021). From statistics to clinics: The visual feedback of PROMIS® CATs. *Journal of Patient-Reported Outcomes, 5*(1), 55. https://doi.org/10.1186/s41687-021-00324-y

Wahl, I., Löwe, B., Bjorner, J. B., Fischer, F., Langs, G., Voderholzer, U., Aita, S. A., Bergemann, N., Brähler, E., & Rose, M. (2014). Standardization of depression measurement: A common metric was developed for 11 self-report depression measures. *Journal of Clinical Epidemiology, 67*(1), 73–86. https://doi.org/10.1016/J.JCLINEPI.2013.04.019

World Health Organization. (2001). *International classification of functioning, disability and health: ICF*. World Health Organization. Retrieved from https://apps.who.int/iris/handle/10665/42407

World Health Organization. (2016). *International statistical classification of diseases and related health problems* (10th ed.). Retrieved from https://icd.who.int/browse10/2016/en

World Health Organization. (2019). *International statistical classification of diseases and related health problems* (11th ed.). Retrieved from https://icd.who.int/

Chapter 11
Outcome and Therapeutic Relationship Feedback in Group Therapy

Tate M. Paxton, Derek Griner, Mark E. Beecher, and Gary M. Burlingame

Outcome and Therapeutic Relationship Feedback in Group Therapy

It is important to begin this chapter by acknowledging two important contextual factors that create the context for some of our later recommendations. First, the authors have worked extensively in the development, implementation, and research associated with the Outcome Questionnaire-45 (OQ-45) and its web-based routine outcome monitoring system—OQ-Analyst (OQ-A), described in this text (Erekson et al., 2025). In short, we are proponents of routine outcome monitoring (ROM) and have seen its benefits for the past 35 years through the multiple measures of outcome and treatment support found in the OQ-A. Second, the authors are strong proponents of group therapy having empirically documented it as an equally efficacious treatment when compared to individual therapy (Burlingame et al., 2016). However, we view multi-person treatment as very different than individual treatment and have documented the different mechanisms of change, challenges, and predictors of improvement (Burlingame & Strauss, 2021).

In contrast to the single patient-and-therapist work unit found in individual therapy, a group leader can have 8–15 patients in a group creating multiple work units. This complexity makes it nearly impossible to know who is improving, who may be stuck and, who is deteriorating when it comes to symptomatic distress in group therapy patients. Moreover, the therapeutic relationship which has been shown to be the best empirical predictor of patient improvement in group therapy (Burlingame,

T. M. Paxton · G. M. Burlingame (✉)
Department of Psychology, Brigham Young University, Provo, UT, USA
e-mail: gary_burlingame@byu.edu

D. Griner · M. E. Beecher
Counseling and Psychological Services, Brigham Young University, Provo, UT, USA

J. A. Rubel, W. Lutz (eds.), *Feedback Informed Psychological Therapy*, CBT: Science Into Practice, https://doi.org/10.1007/978-3-031-90428-8_11

2023). However, conceptualizing and measuring the therapeutic relationship in group treatment is far more complex including at least three structural components: member–leader, member–member, and member–group. Indeed, two special issues focused on therapeutic relationship ruptures and repair in group therapy were published in the same year (2021) by the *International Journal of Group Psychotherapy* and *Group Dynamics: Theory, Research and Practice* documenting the clinical, measurement, and methodological complexity. Our team has been tackling the clinical implementation of ROM in group treatment for 25 years, and there is much to be learned. Nonetheless, we believe the future is bright and promising, and ROM in group treatment may provide the leader with essential information to improve therapeutic relationships and symptoms of group members.

Routine Outcome Monitoring in Group Therapy

Routine outcome monitoring (ROM) and therapist feedback has become a key ingredient of evidence-based individual and group psychotherapy (Levine et al., 2017). This is due to a desire among clinicians to track client progress and evidence of clinician inaccuracy in predicting change and therapeutic relationship status among their clients based on clinical judgment alone (Lambert, 2017). In this chapter, we focus on the role of routine outcome and relationship monitoring in group therapy from both a research and clinical implementation perspective. Routine outcome monitoring is the repeated measurement of an individual member's self-reported symptomatic distress (outcome) and/or perception of the therapeutic relationship with the intent to improve both in real-time session interventions and across an episode of group therapy. This self-report data is scored, normed, and then provided as feedback to the therapist to help them track real-time change and make treatment interventions adjustments if progress is not being made.

In group treatments, clinicians can use routine outcome monitoring and feedback to assess several constructs. The most common focus includes outcome measures that assess general psychological distress, specific symptom status, progress since treatment initiation, and therapeutic relationships. For example, many clinicians treat patients presenting with a variety of clinical indications that may or may not meet a formal psychiatric diagnosis. Given this, the use of a general symptom or psychological distress measure can address many of the reasons a patient presents for treatment. In some instances, specialists who treat a specific disorder such as anxiety might choose an anxiety symptom assessment over general psychiatric distress.

Group practitioners who embrace group mechanisms of change are particularly interested in assessing a member's perception of the therapeutic relationships in group (Burlingame & Strauss, 2021). This allows them to track these relationships and gauge how group members are perceiving themselves in relation to others and to the group (Burlingame et al., 2018b). However, beyond this clinical interest, there is an empirical reason for tracking therapeutic relationships in group. It has been shown that individual therapists are not able to accurately predict when their clients are deteriorating (Hannan et al., 2005). A replication and extension of this study in group therapy showed that group leaders are also unable to accurately predict the outcome or therapeutic relationship status of the members in their group (Chapman et al., 2012). These findings are unsurprising, since group leaders are monitoring far more patients than individual therapists, who also cannot accurately predict. By measuring psychological distress, specific symptoms, and/or therapeutic relationships, clinicians do not have to rely on their own perception of therapeutic progress alone. This is particularly relevant in group settings, where even astute experienced clinicians can miss subtle interpersonal or verbal cues from clients. As will be documented below, ROM feedback can be used collaboratively with group members to address challenges in symptomatic improvement, therapeutic relationships, and other treatment issues.

Brief Review of Empirical Research

Multiple studies have examined the role of routine outcome monitoring in group therapy (Gleave et al., 2017; Burlingame et al., 2018a, 2018b). Here, we briefly outline these findings, organized by non-randomized and randomized reports. Readers will notice that studies of ROM impact on group therapy outcome have multiple approaches that make general inferences difficult to make or support. Studies have been conducted using different: samples, approaches to therapy, ROM measures, and approaches to feedback. Information about these studies is provided in the sections below to outline this heterogeneity. For brevity, we focus solely on quantitative research. Qualitative research is also helpful on this topic, and those interested should consult Solstad et al. (2019) and Koementas-de Vos et al. (2022).

Non-randomized Research

Multiple non-randomized studies have found that routine outcome monitoring enhances treatment effects for several disorders and symptom classes. For example, Newnham et al. (2010) tested feedback in a sample of 1308 inpatients and day patients in a day treatment program diagnosed with primarily depressive and anxiety disorders. They offered group cognitive behavioral therapy, with groups lasting 10 working days (2 weeks), conducted about 8 hours per day. The feedback measure used was the 5-item World Health Organization's Well-being Index (WHO-5), and feedback was provided to therapists once at the midpoint of treatment (day 5). They found that clients in the feedback condition had reduced depressive symptoms compared to no-feedback, but there was not a significant difference in well-being. Likewise, Hutson et al. (2020) examined the impact of feedback among 778 outpatients at a private psychiatric hospital in Western Australia. Their groups were a similar 2-week (10 day) format with 10 sessions total. They also employed the WHO-5 and provided feedback based on this measure but made feedback available to therapists before each session and included color-coded on-track and not-on-track (NOT) alerts based on expected recovery curves. They found that clients in the feedback condition had more consistent and faster recovery rates than those in the no-feedback condition. Furthermore, their findings indicated that clients who were deteriorating or staying stable experienced a boost toward recovery after feedback was provided.

Other studies have found that routine outcome monitoring did not have an effect on symptom improvement compared to active control conditions. Koementas-de Vos et al. (2018) studied feedback in a sample of 269 patients with major depressive and anxiety disorders using the OQ-45. The group treatment was cognitive behavioral or interpersonal, and groups were either open or half open, meaning that membership changed at some point during the group. They provided group therapy once per week, and sessions varied from 6 to 24 total. Feedback was provided weekly before each session, and clinicians were encouraged to discuss the results in group. They found that clients in both the feedback and no-feedback condition improved, with no significant differences between them. Still, some effects of feedback were suspected, as clients in the feedback condition required fewer sessions to improve (Koementas-de Vos et al., 2018). Fewer required sessions for a feedback condition parallel results from individual therapy ROM studies, suggesting that feedback might create a more efficient treatment experience, even if outcomes are equivalent (Delgadillo et al., 2017). With all of these findings, causal claims are more difficult to support due to the lack of randomized assignment to feedback or no-feedback conditions.

Randomized Research

The same heterogeneity that affects non-randomized results also impacts randomized studies, where samples, group treatments, feedback measures, and frequency vary substantially. Once again, some studies find that feedback enhances group therapy outcome, while others find no significant difference compared to active controls. These studies are outlined below to provide further context.

Schuman et al. (2015) tested the effect of feedback in groups comprised of soldiers in an Army Substance Abuse Outpatient Treatment Program (ASAP). They found that in a short (5-session) course of treatment with open groups, soldiers in the feedback condition had significantly more improvement than treatment-as-usual on a measure of general psychological functioning ($d = 0.28$). Slone et al. (2015) also found significant effects of feedback compared to no-feedback TAU in a college counseling center, with significantly higher post-therapy gains ($d = 0.41$). Both studies employed the Outcome Rating Scale (ORS; cite), a 4-item scale that was used to generate feedback that was based upon the OQ-45. Schuman et al. (2015) provided feedback after sessions, while Slone et al. (2015) provided it before which was paired with discussion of progress in the group. Both studies employed a 4-level alert system which identified ORS scores in the normal (non-clinical) range, adequate change, less than adequate change, and not expected level of progress.

Several researchers tested the effect of ROM and feedback in populations with higher distress or more serious diagnoses who received group treatment. Davidsen et al. (2017) used ROM and feedback in 159 patients diagnosed with eating disorders. The groups were open, with clients joining and leaving on a rolling basis. The average length was 20–25 sessions, and patients were also offered sessions with a physician, dietician, physiotherapist, and social worker, in addition to sessions with relatives as needed. They used the ORS to measure progress and provide feedback each session, and clinicians were encouraged to discuss results with clients. They found that the feedback condition did not differ from the no-feedback condition on attendance rates nor symptom improvement.

Wise and Streiner (2018) randomized 161 patients in an intensive outpatient program primarily treating depression to an ROM + feedback condition and a no-feedback TAU. A plurality of patients were African-American (40%). This study examined traditional process groups that had several treatment orientation approaches (interpersonal, cognitive behavioral, skills training, and motivational interviewing). Groups were held 3 days per week for 3 hours at a time (though patients could attend 5 days per week), and patients were also offered individual therapy. The treatment center created its own measure of progress monitoring focused on depressive symptoms and provided alerts and progress graphs based on empirically derived cutoffs. They provided feedback and alerts to clinicians weekly with recommendations for further intervention for patients who were deteriorating. They found no significant differences between feedback and no-feedback groups, though they noted that patients in both conditions made substantial improvement. They hypothesized that where clients are making significant improvement and there are few deteriorating clients, there may be a ceiling effect of feedback, meaning the effect of feedback may be attenuated.

Finally, Koementas-de Vos et al. (2022) studied the effect of adding feedback to cognitive behavioral and interpersonal therapy group treatments in a sample of 197 patients with anxiety or depressive disorders. Interpersonal groups were half open, while CBT groups were closed. Group therapy was held once per week for 5–24 sessions. They employed the OQ-45 as their outcome tracking and feedback tool. The authors reported that therapists were asked to take time before every group session to look at feedback results, then to discuss them with clients in the group setting. They found no significant differences in general psychological functioning between their feedback and no-feedback conditions. They also elaborated that attendance was lower in their feedback condition and that while therapists were optimistic about the usefulness of feedback, patients reported that it was used only 50% of the time and were less optimistic about its usefulness.

In this emerging area, there are many different signals from the research, ranging from clear positive effects to no significant differences between experimental groups. For now, it appears that ROM has positive benefit for heterogenous client samples in settings with less severe pathology (college counseling centers, general outpatient settings). However, effects of ROM and feedback are unclear for clients with more serious pathology, and more investigation is warranted.

Routine outcome monitoring has also been paired with relationship monitoring. Burlingame and colleagues (2018b) assigned participants in a college counseling center to an outcome feedback condition or an outcome + relationship feedback condition. A key finding of this experiment was that therapeutic relationships were linked to outcome and also amenable to feedback. Feedback helped clinicians intervene with relationship deterioration and failure, and lower relationship deterioration and failure was observed in the outcome + relationship feedback condition. However, results regarding outcome between the two conditions were mixed. While the combined relationship/outcome feedback condition had fewer outcome deterioration cases, the outcome-only condition had higher rates of improvement. More on this study and other studies examining the relationship will be elaborated later. First, a specific system of outcome monitoring will be outlined to aid in understanding the subsequent clinical vignette.

Systems of Routine Outcome Monitoring and Feedback: OQ-45 and GQ

The OQ-Analyst (OQ-A) is the first scientifically validated ROM system designed to provide feedback in individual therapy (Lambert et al., 2018). A separate chapter in this text introduces the OQ-45 and the web-based OQ-A, so the interested reader is directed to Erekson et al. (2025). In brief, the OQ-45 is a broad measure of psychological distress with a cutoff score based on clinically significant distress (Lambert et al., 2013). It is the original adult outcome measures in the OQ-A system (a shorter 30-item version is available) that provides normative scores from several clinical populations/settings that assists therapists in interpreting their client's initial score at intake. Feedback from the OQ-A is based upon the cutoff score that distinguishes clinical and non-clinical levels of distress. The routine outcome monitoring feedback system compares a client's session-by-session progress from initial distress with empirically derived change and five feedback alerts to inform the therapist if a client is "on-track" for a successful outcome, "not-on-track" based upon symptom deterioration, or a prediction of treatment failure unless treatment changes are made. NOT alerts are followed up with a separate measure, Assessment for Signal Cases (ASC), which assesses the therapeutic alliance, motivation for treatment, social support, or negative life events that might explain symptom deterioration. These four areas of assessment are related to common factors in individual therapy that empirically explain treatment outcome.

In group therapy, the best predictor of patient improvement is the therapeutic relationship (Burlingame & Strauss, 2021). A recent meta-analysis summarizing 55 studies showed that member–group and member–member therapeutic relationship (cohesion) predicted symptomatic improvement in group therapy (Burlingame et al., 2018a). A second meta-analysis summarizing 29 studies showed a similarly strong relationship between member–leader (alliance) and improvement (Alldredge et al., 2021). However, one of the limitations noted by these authors was that no single measure assessed all three structural components of the therapeutic relationship in group treatment except for the Group Questionnaire (GQ) which is described below.

A second reason we recommend therapeutic relationship feedback monitoring in group coupled with routine outcome monitoring are two studies that suggest deviation in OQ-45 alert patterns in group therapy. More specifically, in the randomized clinical trial of Burlingame et al. (2018b) described above, clients in group therapy had fewer not-on-track (NOT) progress alerts than individual therapy clients in early sessions of treatment. Furthermore, the frequency of these NOT alerts peaked at session 8 compared to individual therapy that peaked at session 2. Given the vital nature of timeliness in feedback-based intervention, this opened up the possibility that the lag in outcome alerts in group therapy may put group clinicians at a disadvantage, since the efficacy of OQ-45 feedback has been linked to having a sufficient number of sessions to correct an alert status (Shimokawa et al., 2010). A second study in a similar clinical setting conducted by Alldredge et al. (2020) found the same alert delay, underscoring the importance of relationship monitoring as a complement to outcome monitoring in group therapy.

Complementing ROM with Relationship Monitoring: The Group Questionnaire

The OQ-A system can simultaneously employ both routine outcome monitoring instruments (OQ-45) and relationship monitoring instruments. The Group Questionnaire (GQ) is an empirically validated measure of group therapeutic relationships, with factor validity in multiple languages (Burlingame et al., 2017; Krogel et al., 2013; Giannone et al., 2020). The GQ is a 30-item self-report measure that assesses the quality of the therapeutic relationship using three subscales: positive bond (positive affect), positive work (tasks/goals of group), and negative relationship (group conflict or alliance rupture). These quality subscales are crossed with three main relationship structures found in group—member–member, member–group, and member–leader (Thayer & Burlingame, 2014)—to capture the main therapeutic relationship constructs found in the group psychotherapy clinical and empirical literature (Table 11.1). As noted above, each of these relationship constructs have been shown to predict member improvement in group therapy in recent meta-analyses (Burlingame et al., 2018a, 2018b; Alldredge et al., 2021). The goal of routine relationship monitoring is to provide another avenue of understanding how clients are experiencing therapy and to intervene if problems arise. For example, if a specific client remains low in positive bond throughout the first four sessions of therapy, the group therapist may consider raising this with a member or with others

Table 11.1 Underlying relationship constructs assessed by GQ subscales crossed X relationships in group

GQ Subscales	Member–Member	Member–Leader	Member–Group
Positive bond	Cohesion	Alliance	Climate
Positive work	Task/goals	Task/goals	None
Negative relationship	Empathic failure	Alliance rupture	Conflict

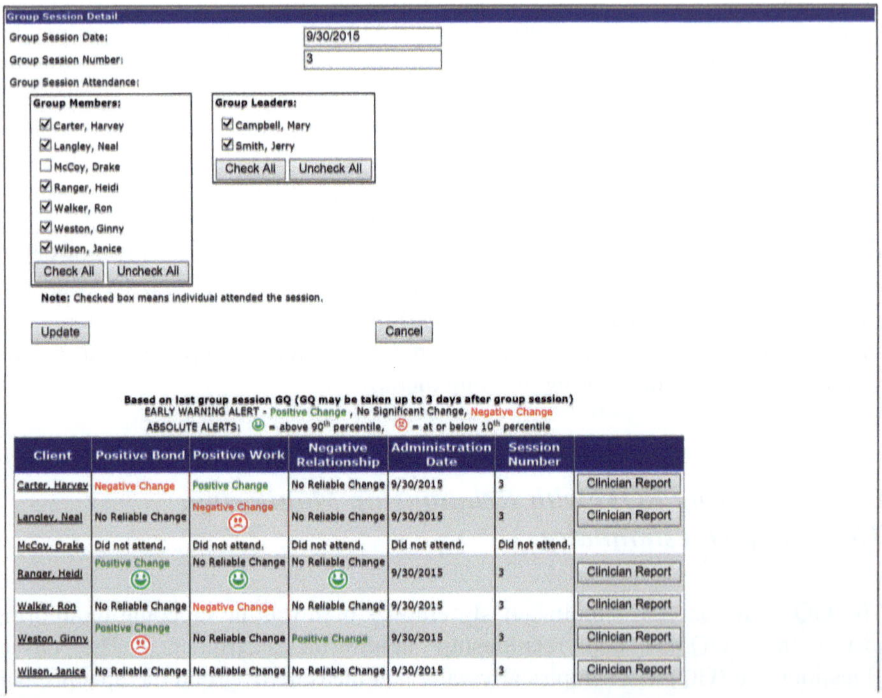

Fig. 11.1 First page of GQ/OQ® group report from OQ®-Analyst. *Note.* Used with permission from OQ Measures from the OQ®-Analyst. Reproduced with permission from Burlingame et al. (2017)

in the group. Conversely, if there is a spike in the negative relationship subscale, clinicians might pay attention to what happened in a specific session and address this with a client, when appropriate.

The initial GQ report produced by the OQ-A can be found in Fig. 11.1 that summarizes all members from an outpatient group with the upper left-hand box indicating which members were present at a particular session. A *change alert* identifies reliable relationship deterioration as *negative change* and reliable relationship improvement as *positive change* for each member and each GQ subscale. The report uses "early warning" to describe change alerts to emphasize that a member with negative change is at risk for a relationship failure alert in subsequent sessions. GQ *status alerts* indicate that a member's perception of the therapeutic relationship is exceptionally poor and define relationship rupture on the GQ. They are identified by a red frowning face icon (☹) reflecting rock-bottom scores or a green smiling face icon (☺) if a score is unusually high. Change patterns over time will be presented in the clinical example below.

Recent GQ Empirical Findings In addition to the evidence that GQ feedback can lead to rupture repair (Burlingame et al., 2018a, 2018b) and the importance of attention to relationship status, given the evidence for delayed outcome alerts in group (Alldredge et al., 2021), a few additional findings are useful to highlight. Arnold et al. (2022) found that higher scores on alliance, cohesion, and climate GQ items (see Table 11.1) were related to lower distress on the OQ-45. However, when linear trajectory change was examined, only alliance predicted change in the OQ-45 over time underscoring the important of the member–leader relationship. Rands (2022) found more evidence for a unilateral rather than reciprocal statistical relationship between outcome and therapeutic relationship change. More specifically, there was more evidence that improvement in the therapeutic relationship predicted subsequent improvement on the OQ-45. This provides further support for the importance monitoring the GQ and OQ-45.

Several other studies have examined how group members impact one another on the GQ relationship constructs positive bond, positive work, and negative relationship. Two recent studies tested how individuals impact the group and how other group members impact individuals over time (Lo Coco et al., 2019; Paxton & Burlingame, 2023). Both found that member ratings of group therapeutic relationships tend to converge over time, with more group members rating relationships similarly at later sessions. They also found that negative relationship in single members of the group can impact the rest of the group in later sessions. This was particularly true if individuals or other group members noted negative relationship in the middle sessions of group (Paxton & Burlingame, 2023). Gullo et al. (2021) conducted another study and found that group members' working ruptures disrupt their engagement and are a subject of interest to group leaders. In short, using the GQ to detect session-by-session changes in group therapeutic relationships can help group practitioners intervene in a timely manner.

Case Example

The following is a case vignette that is based on a semester-long, process-oriented, psychotherapy group in a university counseling center. Though this vignette is based on an amalgamation of real experiences, we have changed all identifying information. For the purposes of this case example, we highlight the background information of two group members who play a prominent role in our discussion of ROM feedback. While this is an illustration of one possible way ROM may be used, we invite clinicians to consider how they might best adapt ROM to their specific clinical settings.

Kenji is a 25-year-old, straight, married, cisgender, Japanese man who is currently applying for citizenship in the USA. He met his girlfriend (now married partner) five years ago at a Japanese club event that was held on campus during his first semester attending this university. They married about a year after meeting. His partner is a 24-year-old, White woman from a Southeastern state in the USA. During one of the first group sessions, Kenji told the group that he and his partner met due to her interest in Japanese culture. He also told the group that because of the stress (financial and emotional) he experienced when they were both attending school, he put aside his own schooling for two years and worked while she completed her degree. He is currently seeking to finish his undergraduate degree and has talked in group about his struggles straddling his own culture and U.S. culture.

Kenji reported struggles with symptoms consistent with major depressive disorder and generalized anxiety disorder in the past, but repeatedly told the group, "I don't have depression or anxiety." He told the group that he needed to "get over my worries on my own" and explained that this mentality was emphasized in his family and was culturally expected as well. During the first two weeks of group, he talked about having a younger brother and sister who both still live in Tokyo, Japan with his parents. He tearfully talked about being away from home while both his parents' health suffered. He shared that he felt guilty about not being home with his family and that as the eldest son he "should be there with them" as he had "the responsibility to take care of them."

During the first group therapy session, Kenji stated that he told his individual therapist that, "Since being in the USA, I only hang out with my wife, and I want to figure out how to connect with and spend time with other people." He reported that his therapist encouraged him to attend group, as she felt this would be an ideal setting to learn to connect with others.

Isabella is a 22-year-old, straight, single, cisgender, Latin(x) American woman. She grew up on the East coast and said that her parents immigrated to the USA before she was born. She reported that she spoke Spanish in her home growing up and English at school and "everywhere else." Like Kenji, she identified with the difficulties of straddling two distinct cultural worldviews.

During the third session of group, Isabella talked openly about the difficulties she experienced identifying as a feminist in a family culture that was "totally machismo." This was her first time attending group therapy, and she stated that she came to group at the encouragement of her individual therapist to "see if others may be able to relate to your experiences with your family."

As we have talked about in this paper, use of ROM is meant to enhance, not replace, psychotherapists' clinical judgment. Subsequently, there are many ways that therapists can approach their use of ROM in group treatment. During the first session of this group, the leader introduced the concept of ROM and discussed its potential benefits for the group. For contextual purposes, the leader of this group is a 48-year-old, straight, cisgender, White woman who has worked and run groups at this counseling center for 15 years. She presented several options for how she had used ROM in previous groups (i.e., leader could look at data and not show data to clients, could bring all group data to the group for everyone to see, or could give each group member their individual data without showing others' data). She further expressed that the group could change the way ROM was used as the group progressed if they wanted. This led to a discussion about the potential pros and cons of each option. Group members shared their thoughts and collectively decided that they would like to have access to their own data, but they did not necessarily want their data to be seen by everyone in the group.

During the fourth session, several group members expressed that hearing Isabella talk about her family the week before made them think about ways they too had been impacted by their own familial experiences. This sparked an emotional discussion in which several group members talked about difficulties navigating various aspects of their family dynamics. Isabella expressed gratitude that others were willing to listen to her last week and continued to talk about how much she loved her family and how frustrating it was to be a part of their lives. Others in the group seemed to join her, expressing similar sentiments, and reporting that they had experienced comparable complex feelings.

Throughout this session, Kenji was quieter than others in the group, but seemed engaged and nodded at many of the comments made. Other group members noticed this and checked in to see how he was doing. Kenji reported that he was doing well and appreciated the conversation; however, he said that he did not have much to add other than that he also cared deeply for his family. Following the session, the leader felt that the group members seemed to be connecting well with one another and that the group seemed to be in a working phase.

Following group, the leader reviewed the group's GQ scores for the session (Figs. 11.2, 11.3, and 11.4). She noted that most members showed increases in positive bond and positive work and decreases in negative relationship. However, she also noted significant decreases in Kenji's Positive Bond and Positive Work and a slight increase in his Negative Relationship. She began to feel curious about what

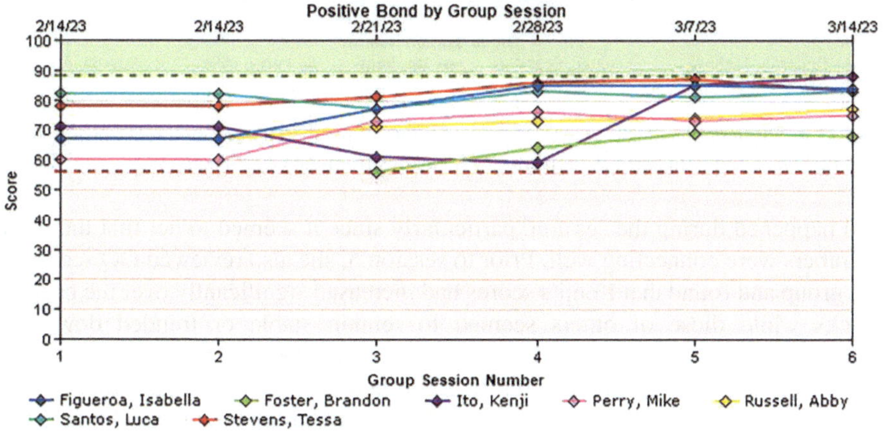

Fig. 11.2 Clinician feedback graph generated by OQ-A for the GQ positive bond at session 6. *Note*. Used with permission from OQ Measures from the OQ®-Analyst

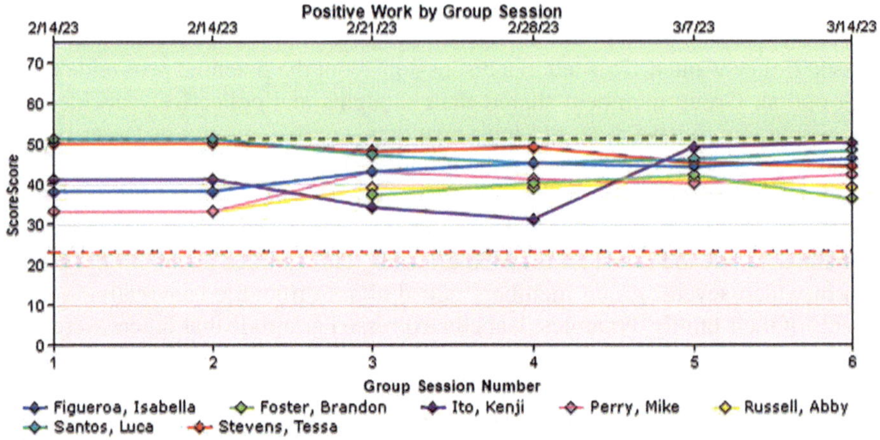

Fig. 11.3 Clinician feedback graph generated by OQ-A for the GQ positive work at session 6. *Note*. Used with permission from OQ Measures from the OQ®-Analyst

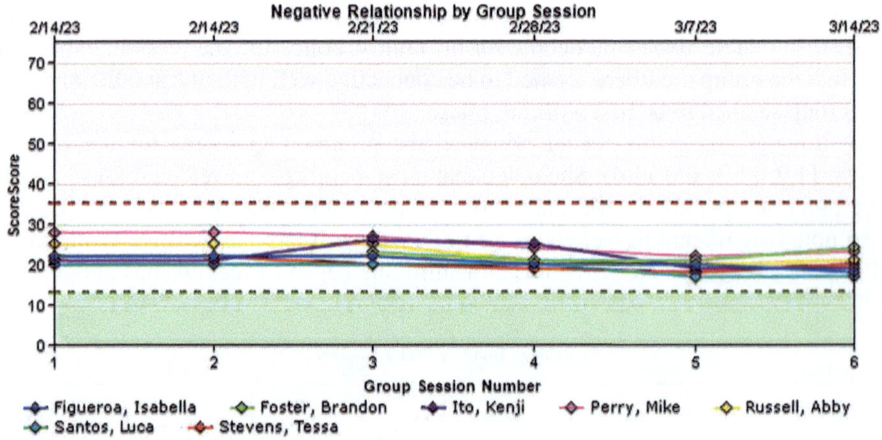

Fig. 11.4 Clinician feedback graph generated by OQ-A for the GQ negative relationship at session 6. *Note.* Used with permission from OQ Measures from the OQ®-Analyst

had happened during the session, particularly since it seemed to her that the group members were connecting well. Prior to session 5, she also reviewed OQ scores for the group and found that Kenji's scores had increased significantly over the past few weeks while those of others seemed to remain stable or trended downward (Fig. 11.5). She looked at the individual items on the OQ and found no safety concerns. She decided not to reach out to Kenji before group, but rather to begin the fifth session as she had done in the past by providing group members with access to their own scores.

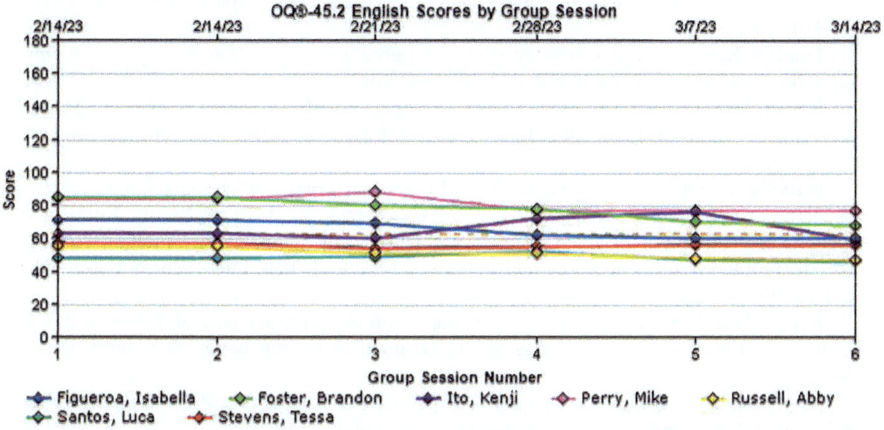

Fig. 11.5 Clinician feedback graph generated by OQ-A for the OQ-45.2 at session 6. *Note*. Used with permission from OQ Measures from the OQ®-Analyst

Leader: As you look over your scores, does anything stand out or surprise you today? Also, like we've talked about in each group, I want to stress that your lived experiences are much more important than what the scores may show.

Brandon: It's kind of cool to see my positive bond go up. I really enjoyed last week and feel like I know you guys better. I feel more comfortable than I have before. It's the first time I've ever really talked about my own family that way.

Tessa: Yeah, me too. I guess Isabella being so open about her family made it feel like I could talk about mine too.

Isabella: Thanks for saying that, Tessa. I'll be honest, that felt way scary to talk about at first. And afterwards, I felt closer to you all. It felt like I wasn't alone in family stuff. Thanks for giving me the space.

Others in the group continue to discuss feeling connected in various ways around this topic.

Leader: What about others?

Kenji: (smiling) It was nice to see people connecting.

Abby: (looking at Kenji) You don't have to answer, but you didn't share much about your family last week or your scores today. I guess I was just kind of wondering what's going on with you.

Kenji: I'm embarrassed that I didn't say anything at all about my family last week, and I don't even know where to begin with all of this.

Abby: I'm sad you feel embarrassed. I don't want to pressure you, but I'd love to hear more if you're willing.

Others in the group agree and encourage Kenji to share.

Leader: Kenji, it sounds like the group is really interested in hearing more about you. And I just want to emphasize that in this group you can absolutely choose when and how much you want to share. Also, I remember you talking early on about the difficulty of navigating two cultures. I know just enough about Japanese culture to be dangerous, and I can't help but wonder what it means for you to talk about your family with us given what you've shared about your background. Again, I really want you to feel free to share or not share.

Kenji: Thanks. It's nice to know people are interested. It helps me feel more confident to speak, and I'm still finding it hard to talk. In Japanese culture and especially in my family, we were taught to always respect family…especially parents. It feels weird to talk about family problems. I didn't feel that way when others were talking about their families last week. It's weird.

Leader: Kenji, "weird" can mean a lot of different things to different people. Can you say more about what it's like to talk with us about this?

Kenji: Growing up, I was taught to always respect my elders. It kind of feels like I'd be betraying my family if I talk about how I really feel. I guess "weird" is maybe a feeling of being scared.

Isabella: I know that feeling really well. I think that's part of what made it hard for me to share last week. Like, somehow if I say all of my feelings about my family, I'm disrespecting or betraying them. Even though it was hard to talk about, for me, it felt nice to not keep that all to myself. I'm totally not saying you need to do that; I just wanted to join you and say it was tough for me too.

Kenji: That feels really nice. I was actually talking with my wife about last week's group, and I'm thinking it probably would be good to try out being more open about this stuff.

Kenji talks about complicated feelings associated with his family and how he felt a sense of love and duty, coupled with disappointment and anger.

Several group members expressed relating to Kenji's fears of betraying family and having complicated feelings about those they love. They also expressed feeling closer to Kenji and understanding him more because of what he shared.

Following the session, the leader again pulled up the group's GQ scores. She noticed that Kenji's scores had changed significantly, with large increases in positive bond and positive work and a slight decrease in negative relationship. Prior to session 6, she also reviewed the group members' OQ scores and found that Kenji's score had decreased significantly. During the sixth session, she noticed that group members seemed to connect more with one another, and Kenji seemed more involved in the discussion.

Critical Reflection of Routine Outcome and Relationship Monitoring in Group Therapy

Given the information above, what should group clinicians do to best implement and benefit from ROM and relationship monitoring in group therapy? This section focuses on strengths and limitations of ROM and relationship monitoring in group treatments. These strengths and limitations are outlined from both research and clinical perspectives.

There are two major limitations in the extant empirical evidence testing ROM systems in group psychotherapy. As contributors to the ROM individual therapy research literature, which has a broad and rigorous empirical foundation, we are struck by the paucity of randomized clinical trials testing the efficacy of ROM systems for group treatment. This limited research base is particularly troubling given the recent empirical evidence documenting how a modest increase in group treatment offerings addresses the growing challenge of mental health access in North America (Whittingham et al., 2023). A second limitation with the small number of studies is the heterogeneity of ROM systems tested, clinical populations examined, and type of alerts tested. We have noted elsewhere (Burlingame & Strauss, 2021) that a reliable deterioration alert (i.e., change alert) sends a very different message to a therapist than one that suggests a client is on course for a treatment failure (i.e., progress alert). Perhaps the most parsimonious explanation for the mixed empirical findings summarized above is a combination of the paucity and heterogeneity of studies that produce an insufficient unitary signal for ROM applied to multi-person treatment. Our hope is the future decade will produce research that replicates past findings using the same ROM system and alerts with similar clinical populations to refine our empirical understanding.

We also see several strengths in the research literature that give us hope. While there are singular studies piloting unique ROM systems, we also see ROM systems that have a strong presence in the individual literature discussed in this book (e.g., OQ-A & Partners for Change Outcome Management System) being tested in the group format. While findings are mixed with these well-known ROM systems, some studies replicate the effectiveness of feedback in group therapy. A few studies suggest a delayed temporal alert pattern in outcome monitoring in group compared to individual therapy using one ROM system (OQ-A). This underscores the importance of pairing relationship and outcome monitoring in group treatment which resonates with both the clinical and empirical literature underscoring the importance of the multi-person therapeutic relationship in the group format.

A final strength supported by the empirical evidence is the difficulty of accurately tracking the symptom and relationship status of 8–10 members participating in a group. ROM provides a solution to this challenge when group members complete an outcome and relationship measure before and after each session. More specifically, our experience is that it is most useful to have a group member complete an outcome measure before a group session, so the therapist can review it for any significant symptomatic deterioration. At the end of each session, we invite group members to complete a relationship measure while their group experience is still fresh in their minds. The research evidence supports using the therapeutic relationship as an early predictor of group member improvement, and the repeated assessment of this relationship provides the therapist with real-time feedback to intervene early when problems arise.

From a clinical perspective, we have noted some limitations to using ROM in group psychotherapy. Unless a culture has been established in which therapists and clients regularly utilize ROM, we have seen that group members tend to resist completing measures, as doing so can feel onerous, time-consuming, and/or redundant. This is particularly true when clients do not feel that clinicians are using the results. If clinicians demonstrate that ROM results are important and useful, group members are typically far more willing to invest in completing them.

A second limitation is clinicians finding the time to review ROM. Many report that they are busy and that, given institutional constraints, they do not feel able to "add one more thing." Unless a therapist feels that ROM is beneficial, it is unlikely that they will make the time to review and use results.

It can also be difficult to know how to therapeutically use ROM results. We have experimented with just the clinician reviewing the results, having each group member see their own results individually, and sharing the results in ways that each client can view their own results and how they relate to those of others. As one might imagine, each of these options has its own strengths and weaknesses. The numerous ways in which feedback can potentially be provided could make it difficult for therapists who prefer a more structured or manualized approach.

That being said, the majority of therapists with whom we have worked have appreciated the flexibility in which they can provide feedback and have noted this as a particular strength of ROM. Being able to adjust the manner in which feedback is administered provides therapists with a myriad of ways in which they can adjust to the specific needs of the group. Again, this flexibility allows clinicians to use ROM to supplement rather than supplant their own clinical judgment.

As therapists, we tend to be optimistic about treatment progress and, as noted earlier, sometimes miss treatment failures (Chapman et al., 2012; Hannan et al., 2005). ROM provides alerts that enable therapists to better see potential treatment failures and observe trends that are occurring within an individual and within the group as a whole.

Finally, ROM provides clients another platform to share their internal experience that they may be reluctant to share in a group setting. ROM should not be seen as a substitute for engaging in the process of discussing difficult internal experiences in group, but it can certainly provide opportunities for reticent clients to bring such issues into the group. We have found this to be particularly true for many individuals from non-majority populations.

References

Alldredge, C., Burlingame, G., Olsen, J., & Van Epps, J. (2020). Outcome Questionnaire-45 (OQ-45) progress alert rates in group versus individual treatment: An archival replication. *Group Dynamics: Theory, Research, and Practice, 24*(4), 247–260. https://doi.org/10.1037/gdn0000121

Alldredge, C. T., Burlingame, G. M., Yang, C., & Rosendahl, J. (2021). Alliance in group therapy: A meta-analysis. *Group Dynamics: Theory, Research, and Practice, 25*(1), 13–28. https://doi.org/10.1037/gdn0000135

Arnold, R. A., Burlingame, G. M., & Olsen, J. A. (2022). The relationship of alliance, cohesion, and climate with outcome among college counseling populations. *Journal of Counseling Psychology, 69*(5), 722–731. https://doi.org/10.1037/cou0000613

Burlingame, G. M. (2023). The future of group therapy is bright! *International Journal of Group Psychotherapy, 73*(1), 1–19. https://doi.org/10.1080/00207284.2022.2133717

Burlingame, G. M., & Strauss, B. (2021). Efficacy of small group treatments: Foundation for evidence-based practice. In M. Barkham, W. Lutz, & L. G. Castonguay (Eds.), *Bergin and Garfield's handbook of psychotherapy and behavior change: 50th anniversary edition* (7th ed., pp. 583–624). Wiley.

Burlingame, G. M., Seebeck, J. D., Janis, R. A., Whitcomb, K. E., Barkowski, S., Rosendahl, J., & Strauss, B. (2016). Outcome differences between individual and group formats when identical and nonidentical treatments, patients, and doses are compared: A 25-year meta-analytic perspective. *Psychotherapy, 53*(4), 446–461. https://doi.org/10.1037/pst0000090

Burlingame, G. M., Gleave, R., Beecher, M., Griner, D., Hansen, K., Jensen, J., Worthen, V., & Svien, H. (2017). *Group Questionnaire OQ®-GQ*, p. 76.

Burlingame, G. M., McClendon, D. T., & Yang, C. (2018a). Cohesion in group therapy: A meta-analysis. *Psychotherapy, 55*(4), 384–398. https://doi.org/10.1037/pst0000173

Burlingame, G. M., Whitcomb, K. E., Woodland, S. C., Olsen, J. A., Beecher, M., & Gleave, R. (2018b). The effects of relationship and progress feedback in group psychotherapy using the Group Questionnaire and Outcome Questionnaire–45: A randomized clinical trial. *Psychotherapy, 55*(2), 116–131. https://doi.org/10.1037/pst0000133

Chapman, C. L., Burlingame, G. M., Gleave, R., Rees, F., Beecher, M., & Porter, G. S. (2012). Clinical prediction in group psychotherapy. *Psychotherapy Research, 22*(6), 673–681. https://doi.org/10.1080/10503307.2012.702512

Davidsen, A. H., Poulsen, S., Lindschou, J., Winkel, P., Tróndarson, M. F., Waaddegaard, M., & Lau, M. (2017). Feedback in group psychotherapy for eating disorders: A randomized clinical trial. *Journal of Consulting and Clinical Psychology, 85*(5), 484–494. https://doi.org/10.1037/ccp0000173

Delgadillo, J., Overend, K., Lucock, M., Groom, M., Kirby, N., McMillan, D., Gilbody, S., Lutz, W., Rubel, J. A., & de Jong, K. (2017). Improving the efficiency of psychological treatment using outcome feedback technology. *Behaviour Research and Therapy, 99*, 89–97. https://doi.org/10.1016/j.brat.2017.09.011

Erekson, D. M., Ogles, B. M., & Lambert, M. J. (2025). The OQ analyst. In J. A. Rubel, W. Lutz (Eds.), *Feedback informed psychological therapy: Science and practice*. Springer.

Giannone, F., Guarnaccia, C., Gullo, S., Di Blasi, M., Giordano, C., Lo Coco, G., & Burlingame, G. (2020). Italian adaptation of the group questionnaire: Validity and factorial structure. *Research in Psychotherapy: Psychopathology, Process, and Outcome, 23*(2), 443. https://doi.org/10.4081/ripppo.2020.443

Gleave, R. L., Burlingame, G. M., Beecher, M. E., Griner, D., Hansen, K., & Jenkins, S. A. (2017). Feedback-informed group treatment: Application of the OQ–45 and group questionnaire. In *Feedback-informed treatment in clinical practice: Reaching for excellence* (pp. 141–166). American Psychological Association. https://doi.org/10.1037/0000039-008

Gullo, S., Kivlighan, D. M., Giordano, C., Di Blasi, M., Giannone, F., & Lo Coco, G. (2021). Bond and work ruptures in group counseling. *Group Dynamics: Theory, Research, and Practice, 25*(1), 29–44. https://doi.org/10.1037/gdn0000136

Hannan, C., Lambert, M. J., Harmon, C., Nielsen, S. L., Smart, D. W., Shimokawa, K., & Sutton, S. W. (2005). A lab test and algorithms for identifying clients at risk for treatment failure. *Journal of Clinical Psychology, 61*(2), 155–163. https://doi.org/10.1002/jclp.20108

Hutson, J., Hooke, G. R., & Page, A. C. (2020). Progress monitoring and feedback delivered in routine psychiatric care: Beneficial but not reaching those thought to need it most. *Psychotherapy Research, 30*(7), 843–856. https://doi.org/10.1080/10503307.2019.1710305

Koementas-de Vos, M. M. W., Nugter, M. A., Engelsbel, F., & De Jong, K. (2018). Does progress feedback enhance the outcome of group psychotherapy? *Psychotherapy, 55*(2), 151–163. https://doi.org/10.1037/pst0000164

Koementas-de Vos, M. M. W., Van Dijk, M., Tiemens, B., De Jong, K., Witteman, C. L. M., & Nugter, M. A. (2022). Feedback-informed group treatment: A qualitative study of the experiences and needs of patients and therapists. *International Journal of Group Psychotherapy, 72*(3), 193–227. https://doi.org/10.1080/00207284.2022.2086557

Krogel, J., Burlingame, G., Chapman, C., Renshaw, T., Gleave, R., Beecher, M., & MacNair-Semands, R. (2013). The group questionnaire: A clinical and empirically derived measure of group relationship. *Psychotherapy Research, 23*(3), 344–354. https://doi.org/10.1080/10503307.2012.729868

Lambert, M. J. (2017). Maximizing psychotherapy outcome beyond evidence-based medicine. *Psychotherapy and Psychosomatics, 86*(2), 80–89. https://doi.org/10.1159/000455170

Lambert, M. J., Kahler, M., Harmon, C., Burlingame, G. M., Shimokawa, K., & White, M. M. (2013). *Outcome questionnaire OQ-45.2 administration and scoring manual*. OQ Measures.

Lambert, M. J., Whipple, J. L., & Kleinstäuber, M. (2018). Collecting and delivering progress feedback: A meta-analysis of routine outcome monitoring. *Psychotherapy, 55*(4), 520–537. https://doi.org/10.1037/pst0000167

Levine, J., Cruz, R., Cooper, L., Murphy, H., Peterson, P., Hurd, L., & Feldner, M. (2017). Integrating routine outcome monitoring into graduate training clinics to advance evidence-based practice. *The Behavior Therapist, 40*, 17–22.

Lo Coco, G., Gullo, S., Profita, G., Pazzagli, C., Mazzeschi, C., & Kivlighan, D. M. (2019). The codevelopment of group relationships: The role of individual group member's and other group members' mutual influence and shared group environment. *Journal of Counseling Psychology, 66*(5), 640–649. https://doi.org/10.1037/cou0000349

Newnham, E. A., Hooke, G. R., & Page, A. C. (2010). Progress monitoring and feedback in psychiatric care reduces depressive symptoms. *Journal of Affective Disorders, 127*(1–3), 139–146. https://doi.org/10.1016/j.jad.2010.05.003

Paxton, T. M. & Burlingame, G. M. (2023, June 24). *Codevelopment of group therapeutic relationships in short-term therapy: A conceptual replication of Lo Coco et al. (2019). Taking the pulse of the group: The link between group relationships and therapy outcomes*. Society for Psychotherapy Research International Annual Meeting, Dublin, Ireland. Retrieved from https://cdn.ymaws.com/www.psychotherapyresearch.org/resource/resmgr/imported/events/annualmeeting_progs/spr_meeting_program_2023.pdf

Rands, A. M. (2022). *The reciprocal relationship between group therapeutic relationships and group member symptom improvement: An archival analysis* [Thesis]. Brigham Young University.

Schuman, D. L., Slóne, N. C., Reese, R. J., & Duncan, B. (2015). Efficacy of client feedback in group psychotherapy with soldiers referred for substance abuse treatment. *Psychotherapy Research, 25*(4), 396–407. https://doi.org/10.1080/10503307.2014.900875

Shimokawa, K., Lambert, M. J., & Smart, D. W. (2010). Enhancing treatment outcome of patients at risk of treatment failure: Meta-analytic and mega-analytic review of a psychotherapy quality assurance system. *Journal of Consulting and Clinical Psychology, 78*(3), 298–311. https://doi.org/10.1037/a0019247

Slone, N. C., Reese, R. J., Mathews-Duvall, S., & Kodet, J. (2015). Evaluating the efficacy of client feedback in group psychotherapy. *Group Dynamics: Theory, Research, and Practice, 19*(2), 122–136. https://doi.org/10.1037/gdn0000026

Solstad, S. M., Castonguay, L. G., & Moltu, C. (2019). Patients' experiences with routine outcome monitoring and clinical feedback systems: A systematic review and synthesis of qualitative empirical literature. *Psychotherapy Research, 29*(2), 157–170. https://doi.org/10.1080/10503307.2017.1326645

Thayer, S. D., & Burlingame, G. M. (2014). The validity of the group questionnaire: Construct clarity or construct drift? *Group Dynamics: Theory, Research, and Practice, 18*(4), 318–332. https://doi.org/10.1037/gdn0000015

Whittingham, M., Marmarosh, C. L., Mallow, P., & Scherer, M. (2023). Mental health care equity and access: A group therapy solution. *American Psychologist, 78*(2), 119–133. https://doi.org/10.1037/amp0001078

Wise, E. A., & Streiner, D. L. (2018). Routine outcome monitoring and feedback in an intensive outpatient program. *Practice Innovations, 3*(2), 69–83. https://doi.org/10.1037/pri0000064

Chapter 12
Feedback Technology for Practice and Research

Steffen T. Eberhardt, Antonia Vehlen, Fabienne Mink, Brian Schwartz, and Wolfgang Lutz

Feedback Technology for Practice and Research

In this chapter, we explore the technology essential for implementing routine outcome monitoring (ROM) and feedback systems in psychotherapy research and clinical practice. Recognizing that clinical settings vary widely in technical resources and expertise, ranging from mental health professionals in private practice to researcher-practitioners in research hubs, we address practitioners across this spectrum. In particular, the depth and precision of feedback measurements are linked to technical complexity. In private practices, systems need to be simple, user-friendly, and scalable, typically relying on a single data source like questionnaires due to limited time and resources. The goal is broad applicability and easy dissemination while providing essential outcome monitoring. In addition to traditional questionnaires, research hubs can integrate advanced data sources such as Ecological Momentary Assessment (EMA) and video analysis, allowing for more detailed studies of patient progress and treatment efficacy. Technological advancements aim to simplify the integration of these diverse data sources through better technical integration and automation, enabling broader use across various settings.

Using our university training clinic in Trier as an example, we illustrate how these technologies are incorporated into a therapeutic setting. We provide guidance for implementing sophisticated feedback systems in research hubs and offer practical advice for mental health professionals in private practice on adopting simpler systems without significant technical investment. We describe the necessary workflow and technical infrastructure, including hardware, software, secure data storage, and IT security measures to ensure data protection and privacy. Our goal is to encourage practitioners by demonstrating how small, incremental steps can lead to

S. T. Eberhardt (✉) · A. Vehlen · F. Mink · B. Schwartz · W. Lutz
Department of Clinical Psychology and Psychotherapy, Trier University, Trier, Germany
e-mail: eberhardt@uni-trier.de

J. A. Rubel, W. Lutz (eds.), *Feedback Informed Psychological Therapy*, CBT: Science Into Practice, https://doi.org/10.1007/978-3-031-90428-8_12

the development of a robust feedback system. In the following sections, we will discuss the feedback system and its technical specifications, practical implementation within therapy rooms, network and server infrastructures, the role of IT teams, and innovative approaches like EMA and video analysis.

Feedback System

A feedback system is an application or software that enables the collection of psychometric data for the routine monitoring of therapy progress and provides results to therapists, patients, and/or supervisors (Barkham et al., 2023; Lutz et al., 2022). In our clinic, we use the Trier Treatment Navigator (TTN), developed in the Department of Clinical Psychology and Psychotherapy at the University of Trier (Lutz et al., 2019). The TTN is a web application that runs on an Apache web server and is accessible via all common web browsers. The collected data is stored in a MariaDB database on the server (see section "Network and Server Infrastructure" for additional information).

The TTN provides various portals depending on the user role: the therapist portal, the patient portal, the supervisor portal, and the admin portal. In the therapist portal, clinicians can access session reports of their patients or release assessments after every fifth session. When therapists release questionnaires for their patients, these can be completed in the patient portal. Clinicians can not only open and release questionnaires but also view the results graphically, which aids in tracking patient progress over time. The TTN's structure and functionality have been designed to enhance the therapeutic process. For instance, a therapist can quickly identify areas where a patient is struggling and adjust treatment plans accordingly. Supervisors can also monitor these metrics to provide more targeted guidance to therapists in training. For a comprehensive understanding of how these technological tools impact clinical practice, see Chap. 3, where the TTN's application in practice, training, and supervision is discussed in detail. Understanding the core features of the TTN sets the foundation for exploring its different versions tailored to various clinical settings, which we discuss next.

Treatment Navigator Versions

The TTN is freely available under a Creative Commons license on GitHub. Two distinct versions are available to meet the specific needs of different environments: Treatment Navigator Hub (TN-HUB) and Treatment Navigator Pro (TN-PRO). TN-HUB is an open-source version designed for research hubs that have access to more technological resources. It is installed on the server of the research hub and serves as the central system for managing data. TN-HUB supports research, practice, training, and supervision, integrating advanced features. TN-HUBs can manage several TN-PROs, allowing multiple mental health professionals to be supported by a single hub. TN-PRO is the foundational version for mental health professionals in private practices or other settings with fewer technical resources. It is optimized for simplicity, scalability, and ease of use, making it feasible for routine outcome monitoring through more straightforward data sources, such as self-report questionnaires. Mental health professionals only need a TN-PRO account and a computer, as the data collected via TN-PRO is securely stored and pseudonymized on the server of a research hub using TN-HUB. Patients can conveniently fill out questionnaires on their mobile devices, making the system easy to use in daily practice. As part of a research project on the implementation of feedback systems in private practices, practicing mental health professionals and their patients can participate as study participants and use TN-PRO in their practice. With these versions in mind, it is essential to understand the technical specifications and data security measures necessary for their successful deployment.

Technical Specifications and Data Security

The TTN is programmed using PHP, JavaScript, HTML, CSS, and R, and uses the CodeIgniter and Bootstrap frameworks for development. Data is securely stored in a MariaDB database, and OpenSSL is used to encrypt data transmission. This ensures that all sensitive information is protected during transfer. To ensure confidentiality, no personal data (e.g., names, email addresses, phone numbers) is stored with the routinely collected psychometric data. Instead, pseudonymization is implemented using codes or identification numbers (IDs). The additional information needed to link the code to the patient is stored in the patient's file, which is kept securely. This pseudonymization technique aligns with the principle of data minimization, reducing the risk associated with potential data breaches. These technical foundations facilitate integration with other platforms, as discussed in the following section on technical interfaces.

Technical Interfaces

The TTN is integrated into a comprehensive technical system that facilitates integration and data exchange with various platforms. A central component is the shared database usage with the third-party software PsychoEQ. This software enables our department's documentation team to enter psychometric questionnaires, especially when they have been completed in paper format. This database structure ensures consistent data collection and management across different systems. For the development and versioning of the TTN, we use Gitea, a platform for collaborative software development. The integration of Gitea allows our development team to work on various stages of development and continuously improve the code. Integration with Visual Studio Code provides additional support for effective programming and development. Furthermore, we have linked the TTN with the Meeting Room Booking System (MRBS). This system is used by therapists in training to book therapy rooms for their sessions. This integration facilitates the scheduling and organization of therapy sessions.

To track and analyze user behavior on the platform, we use the open-source web analytics platform Matomo (formerly Piwik). This integration provides valuable insights into user behavior and helps to continuously optimize the user experience. Moreover, it facilitates the exploration of the relationship between the actual use of feedback and therapy outcomes. Currently, we are working on integrating interactive R Shiny web apps into the TTN to seamlessly incorporate feedback from EMA. This extension simplifies the presentation of complex data and enables user-friendly interaction with the feedback, further enhancing treatment dynamics (see section "Ecological Momentary Assessment" for additional information).

Therapy Rooms

Technical Requirements for ROM

To collect questionnaires efficiently as part of ROM, it is helpful to have a computer available in the therapy room. In our clinic, we use a simple setup: a standard computer with either a touch screen or a mouse (see Fig. 12.1). Therapists and patients

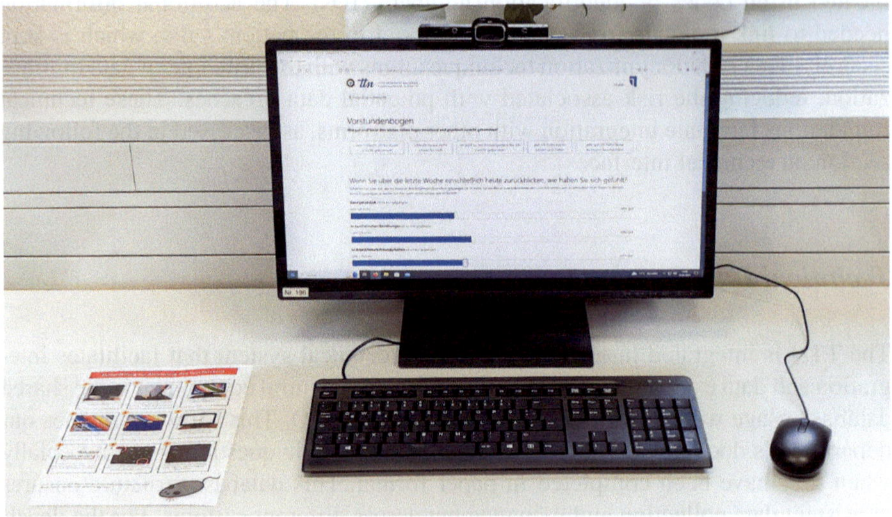

Fig. 12.1 Feedback computer. *Note.* Computer with touch screen for entering routine data collection with an open pretreatment session report in the Trier Treatment Navigator (TTN) feedback system and enclosed brief instructions. The webcam also enables online therapy

can easily access the TTN through a link on the desktop. This allows patients to complete session reports quickly before or after sessions, integrating seamlessly into the therapy workflow. To prepare for the session, the therapist logs into the TTN using his or her therapist profile and starts the session report for that patient. The patient is then invited into the therapy room and fills out the presession report on the PC. Once the presession report has been completed, the therapy session begins. At the end of the session, the therapist starts the post-session report for the patient. This is filled out again on the PC and the patient then leaves the therapy room. After the patient has left the room, the therapist can complete the therapist's post-session report on the PC. Alternatively, the therapist can activate the session report so that the patient can complete it in their patient profile in TTN. In this way, the patient can also complete the questionnaire on their device, such as a smartphone. However, the PC in our outpatient clinic is also used for other purposes, such as video therapy. The computers are equipped with a webcam for this purpose. Having established the requirements for ROM, we now turn to the technical setup necessary for video recordings, which could further enhance the feedback system, especially in research hubs.

Technical Requirements for Video Recordings

Recording therapy sessions on video can offer several benefits in research and training contexts. In training, the videos can be used for supervision purposes; in research, video recordings open up a whole range of possibilities (see section "Video Analysis" for additional information). For the video recordings, we use two cameras that record the patient and the therapist crosswise (see Fig. 12.2). Our video setup is therefore intended for individual therapy. The cameras are connected to a timer to switch them off overnight. This avoids continuous operation, saves electricity, and increases the cameras' lifespan. If the cameras switch off automatically, they have to be automatically repositioned and aligned correctly after start-up. Depending on the camera model, it is possible to program certain default or idle settings into the cameras for this purpose. The conversation is also recorded via a ceiling microphone. Installing two microphones may make it easier to automatically separate the patient and therapist at a later stage. However, it is also possible to separate the speakers automatically, if there is only one audio signal (see "Video Analysis" for additional information).

The video cameras and microphone are connected to an additional computer, where videos are recorded using Open Broadcaster Software (OBS). This computer should be distinct from the one used for the feedback system, since usage rights on the recording computer need to be restricted to ensure that therapists cannot accidentally make system changes or access videos of other therapists or patients they are not treating. We use a specialized software setup called a "kiosk system" (Wieland, 2024), which restricts the computer's functions to only what is necessary for video recording. This prevents accidental changes to the system.

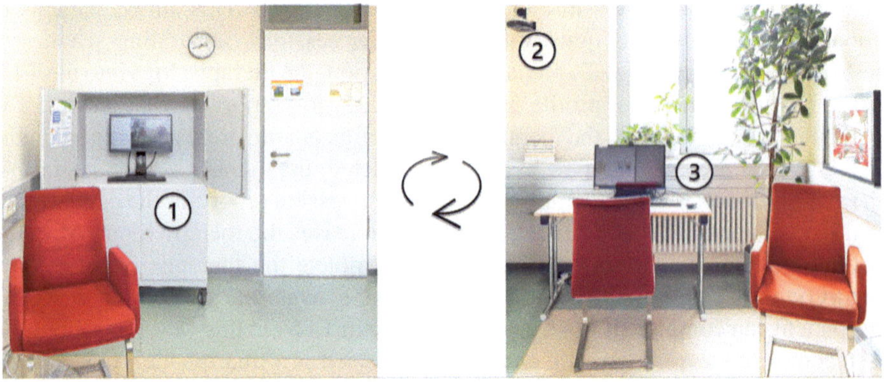

Fig. 12.2 Depiction of a therapy room. *Note.* (1) shows the computer cabinet for the video recordings. In addition to the monitor and keyboard for starting and stopping the video recording, the cabinet contains the computer, mouse, and mixer in the lower area, which is locked away. (2) Shows one of two full HD cameras in the therapy room that are aligned crosswise. Each camera is aimed at one of the two therapy chairs. The microphone is not visible as it is embedded in the ceiling above the two therapy chairs. (3) Shows the computer for the feedback system, which can be operated using a mouse or touch screen

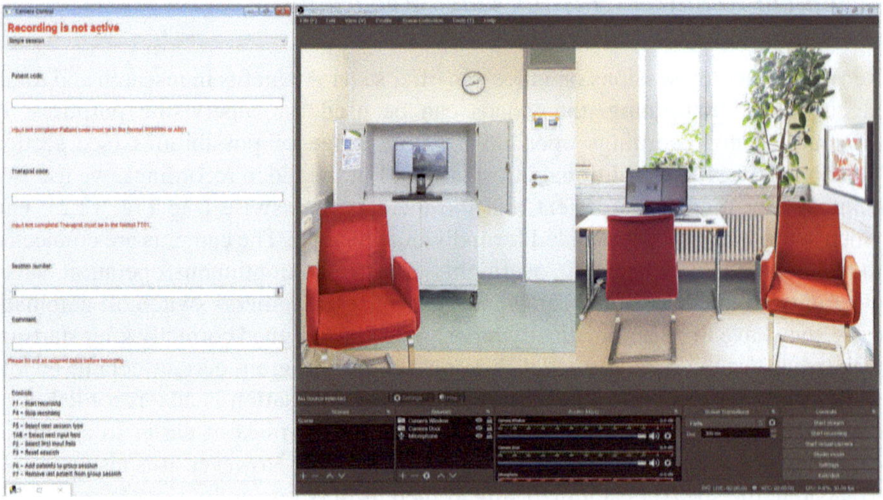

Fig. 12.3 Camera Control user interface. *Note.* Illustration of Camera Control (left) for starting (F1) and stopping (F4) video recordings by the therapists

To facilitate this, we have developed a software called Camera Control, which provides an input interface allowing therapists to enter their therapist code, the patient code, and the session number before starting and stopping the recording (see Fig. 12.3). The input interface is entirely keyboard-operated, with the computer mouse locked away in the computer cabinet to reduce the chance of therapists making unintended changes to the PC settings. Once the relevant session information is entered, therapists can start the recording with a keystroke (e.g., F1), and Camera Control will automatically start the recording in OBS in the background. After the session, therapists can stop the recording using another keystroke (e.g., F4). Camera Control then stops the recording in OBS, automatically names the video file according to a predefined naming convention (e.g., therapist code_patient code_session number_date.mp4), and saves it to the hard drive. To protect the videos, file sharing is not enabled for playing the videos on the recording PC itself (write access only, no read access). However, file sharing is enabled for the central Linux server, where a cron job runs daily to automatically transfer the videos from the PCs in the therapy rooms to the central server and subsequently delete them from the PC. A cron job is an automated task that runs on the server at specified times (see section "Network and Server Infrastructure" for additional information). An internet connection is not required for the video recording computer. It is crucial, however, that the computer is part of the domain, so that the Linux server can access the videos.

The BIOS settings ensure the computer boots up automatically, and the Windows Task Scheduler is used to shut down the PC automatically. The kiosk system ensures that instead of the Explorer, the relevant programs for video recording (e.g., OBS and Camera Control) are started automatically. This approach not only saves power and extends the computer's lifespan but also resolves many potential system errors through the frequent automatic restart routine.

Additional Equipment in Therapy Rooms

If the video recordings and therapy rooms are intended for use not only in therapy but also for supervision as part of training, it can be beneficial to equip some rooms with a TV display or Smart Board. These devices can be used to view therapy videos and for presentation purposes during therapy sessions. The TV display or Smart Board should be connected to the PC used for the feedback system, not the video recording PC. Additionally, it is advisable to have paper-pencil versions of the questionnaires available as a backup in case of technical issues. This ensures that routine outcome monitoring is not interrupted if technical problems prevent the use of the feedback system for data entry. The specific hardware and software setup used in the therapy rooms of the psychotherapy outpatient clinic in Trier for both feedback and video recording purposes is detailed in Table 12.1. While both ROM and video recordings depend on network connectivity, each has specific server requirements due to the nature of the data handled.

Table 12.1 Technology in the therapy rooms of the psychotherapy outpatient clinic in Trier

1x computer for feedback (and video therapy)	1x computer for video recording
Hardware: • Screen (optional with touch screen) • Keyboard and mouse • Internet connection (ideally via LAN for stable connection) • Webcam (optional)	**Hardware:** • Mini-PC Esprimo G558 (i7, 16GB RAM, 1xDP) for camera control • Mixer Behringer XENYX Q802 USB • PC screen 22" Iiyama ProLite (display port connection)
Software: • Link to the feedback system in the web browser • Access to video therapy software (optional) • OBS and camera control for video recording of online therapy	**Software:** • OBS for video recording • Camera control (custom-developed) • Kiosk system (Wieland, 2024)
Other equipment: • 1x TV monitor, e.g., for supervision or presentation purposes in therapy • All necessary cables and adapters	**2x video cameras** • 2x Telycam TLC-700-S-R • 2x timer switches **1x microphone** • Beyerdynamic BM 32 W

Network and Server Infrastructure

Network and Server for ROM

The feedback system in our clinic is a web application running on a self-hosted Apache web server, accessible over the internet via a port release with a TLS security certificate through a domain. Given that patients sometimes need to fill out questionnaires from home, we decided to provide internet access to the TTN. However, the feedback system could theoretically be operated offline. For offline use, the Apache server would need to be installed locally on a computer to run PHP and MySQL databases. We strongly advise against storing data on externally hosted servers by third-party providers to ensure that patient data does not leave the premises and to maintain data security. While there are affordable offers for web servers with preinstalled PHP and MySQL databases, it is worthwhile to establish your own server infrastructure. This approach provides better control over access and processing of sensitive data, eliminating the risk of unauthorized access by third parties. Utilizing an in-house server structure allows for additional security measures to be implemented, ensuring the confidentiality and integrity of the data and compliance with data protection regulations.

It is crucial to create regular backups of the databases. In our clinic, for instance, cron jobs automatically back up the entire database to another hard drive in the server. We use a staggered backup system where hourly, daily, and weekly backups are saved. After one day, the hourly backups are deleted, and after one week, the daily backups are deleted to manage storage space effectively. Additionally, the latest hourly and daily backups are encrypted and copied to an external server to ensure dual backups. By implementing these practices, we ensure robust data management and security, maintaining high standards of confidentiality and integrity for patient data.

Network and Server for Videos

A more complex network and server structure is necessary for the video infrastructure. The video computers in the therapy rooms are connected via LAN to a server in the server room through the university network (see Fig. 12.4). Our server is equipped with high storage capacity to handle the large volume of therapy video data. Currently, it has three hard drives, each with 6 TB capacity. In nonuniversity settings, we recommend using an internal, isolated intranet. During transmission, Server Message Block 3 (SMB 3) network protocols with end-to-end encryption are used, ensuring that the videos are protected from unauthorized access during transfer to the server. The receiving server is a Linux server with Samba, a freely available server software, to provide shares for Windows computers and domain integration to simplify user management. The domain integration allows network shares to be linked to the university user IDs of the trainee psychotherapists. This setup enables, for example, the sharing of therapy videos with the respective therapist for supervision. Using a custom script and Windows Task Scheduler, a folder structure on the server is automatically created, with a folder for each therapy room generated weekly. Videos from the therapy rooms are automatically sorted into the

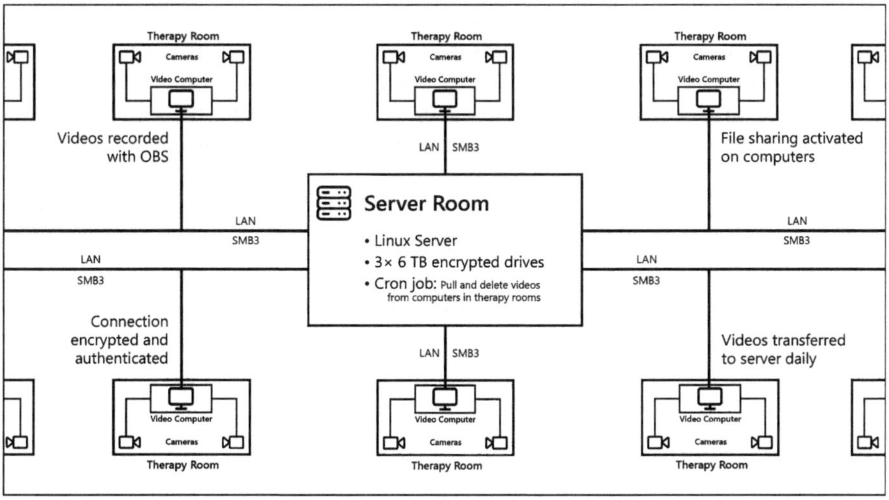

Fig. 12.4 Network and server room. *Note*. LAN = Local area network. RAID 1 = Redundant array of independent disks with an exact copy (mirror) of videos on two drives. SMB 3 = Samba Server Message Block version 3. TB = Terabyte

corresponding folders on the server daily and then deleted from the video computer in the therapy room.

For video backup, a RAID-1 system is employed, ensuring that each hard drive is mirrored. Additionally, a one-time backup is performed on another server using the synchronization software rsync, providing three copies of the videos at all times. VeraCrypt is used to encrypt the hard drives, ensuring compatibility with both Windows and Linux systems.

IT Teams and Technical Support

Implementing and maintaining this technological environment requires skilled IT teams to ensure seamless operation and address technical challenges. The maintenance effort for the system varies significantly depending on the specific setting. In educational and research contexts, having a dedicated technical team to oversee the IT infrastructure is beneficial. For instance, in our outpatient clinic, we have a team focused on improving the TTN feedback system. The TTN team handles regular updates and maintenance to ensure the system runs smoothly, addressing user inquiries, troubleshooting issues, and continuously enhancing the feedback system. This includes updating the syntax to match newer versions of programming languages and frameworks, implementing new features, and adding therapy tools such as feedback from EMA. They also developed versions of the TTN suitable for other contexts, such as the TN-PRO and TN-HUB.

Additionally, there is a technical team responsible for managing the technical infrastructure for recording therapy videos. This team ensures the video recording equipment functions correctly, oversees the secure transfer, storage, and backup of recorded videos, and regularly updates the video recording software (e.g., OBS and Camera Control) to ensure compatibility with the overall IT infrastructure. They also provide support to therapists and supervisors in operating the video recording systems, troubleshooting technical issues, and ensuring ease of use. Having specialized teams for both the feedback system and video recording infrastructure ensures that both systems operate efficiently and securely. The division of tasks between the TTN team and the technical team, covering responsibilities for system maintenance, video management, and infrastructure improvements, is outlined in Table 12.2. Beyond the core technologies, we are exploring innovative approaches like EMA and video analysis to further enhance feedback systems.

Innovative Technical Approaches

Beyond the technical requirements and interfaces for feedback systems and video recordings illustrated by the example of the Trier outpatient clinic, several advanced methods are increasingly gaining interest. In the following sections, we describe

Table 12.2 Tasks in the TTN team and the technical team

TTN team	Technical team
Maintenance of the feedback system – Adaptation to newer versions (e.g., change from PHP 7 to 8). – Installing updates – Fixing system errors (bug fixing) – Securing the system (e.g., backups, etc.) – Database backup via task scheduling and batch scripts – Documentation – Port shares – Gitea administration – User administration – Response to support requests – Database management and administration – Administration of Windows services Improvement of the system – Implementation of new evidence-based features – Improving the usability – Modernization of the design – Creating interfaces between programs	Maintenance of the IT infrastructure – Setting up computers (e.g., setting up and installing software) – Fixing system errors – Backing up the system (e.g., backups with FreeFileSync) – Updating security certificates – Installing updates – Expanding the storage capacity – IT support (e.g., responding to support requests by email) – Replacement of defective devices – Advice on technical acquisitions – Documentation – Ensuring IT security Management of therapy videos – Quality control of the videos – Monitoring the recording quality – Quality assurance in the therapy rooms – Provision of therapy videos at the request of the respective therapists – Backing up the therapy videos – Processing of deletion orders – Archiving of videos (on separate hard disk, no longer integrated) – Securing physical hard disks (encrypted, shockproof case, lockable cabinet) Improvement of the infrastructure – Automation of processes – Programming of scripts – Reduction of error sources – Optimization of processes

two approaches that are currently being integrated into feedback systems: EMA, which enables the collection of real-time patient data, and video analysis, which allows for the analysis of nonverbal behavior and communication patterns during therapy sessions.

Ecological Momentary Assessment

Ecological Momentary Assessment is a method for repeatedly assessing an individual's affective, cognitive, and behavioral experiences in real-time and real-world situations. According to Shiffman et al. (2008), EMA includes various methods, such as self-reports, where patients actively answer questions about their experiences multiple times per day, and passive sensing, which involves the passive assessment of individuals' physiological parameters (e.g., heart rate) or other characteristics (e.g., GPS, App usage data). Such intensive longitudinal data assessments supplement retrospective self-reports, such as questionnaires (e.g., Ben-Zeev et al., 2012), and are used in psychotherapy research, for example, to predict dropout rates (e.g., Lutz et al., 2018), treatment outcomes (e.g., Husen et al., 2016), or as a feedback tool within psychotherapy (e.g., Bos et al., 2022). Chapter 7 addresses the various applications of EMA extensively. In this chapter, we focus on describing the technical challenges specific to EMA.

To collect such EMA-based fine-granular information, various software systems are accessible for both active self-reports (e.g., m-Path or movisensXS) and passive sensing (e.g., Garmin Connect or Behapp). These applications are usually installed on the patient's hardware (i.e., Smartphones), with researchers getting access to the data through administrative accounts. Within self-report applications, these accounts also allow the generation and management of questionnaires and their assessment schemes (i.e., time-contingent or event-contingent). For passive sensing, for example, the measurement of heart rates or activity levels, separate hardware, such as wrist-worn wearables or chest strips, is often necessary. Whereas applications used for self-reports usually need an internet connection to receive the questionnaires and send the respective answers to the company's server, wearables can usually collect data offline since they have a certain storage capacity (up to 14 days). However, to get access to the wearables' data, an internet-supported synchronization is needed, to upload the data to the company's server. For both, self-report and passive sensing data, Application Programming Interfaces (APIs) are required to automatically transfer the collected data to one's own server systems. Several companies offer guidelines for programming such APIs, highlighting specific requirements for secure data transfer between servers.

Ecological Momentary Assessment, in general, allows the capture of large quantities of information. Imagine one would decide to implement a two-week EMA period at the beginning of treatment, with self-reports being requested six times per day and continuous passive measurement of physiological parameters (e.g., heart rate, stress, activity). For each person, 84 data points could be captured based on self-reports. According to passive sensing measures, the sampling rate differs from measure to measure and company to company. Garmin, for example, provides data on heart rates every 15 seconds. This would lead to 80,640 data points (i.e., rows) for each person. Since several people are usually part of an EMA study, one can imagine the amount of data being collected (e.g., 150 patients would produce 12.096.000 rows). Combining different measures with different sampling rates further increases the complexity. Therefore, handling EMA data is more challenging compared to less frequent questionnaire data. For instance, data storage capacity in databases needs to be sufficient. Through the implementation of APIs, it is possible to store the data pseudonymized within databases (e.g., MariaDB). Through various free software applications, such as HeidiSQL, data can be viewed and organized. EMA data are sensitive as they give real-time information about a patient's experiences. Therefore, secure data management plays a crucial role within EMA. Usually, third-party companies have to delete the data from their server after user accounts are deactivated. Through this, researchers can ensure that the data is stored long-term only on their own secure server. To access the data from databases, the data can be retrieved using, for example, Python and saved in a format suitable for further preprocessing. Usually, data can be exported in intuitive formats, such as comma-separated values (CSV). However, due to the amount of data points, datasets cannot be visually inspected. Moreover, reading and handling such large CSV files in R or Python can take a long time or may fail. R, for example, comprises specific packages, such as "data.table" (Barrett et al., 2024) that allow efficient data manipulation. Since databases, such as MariaDB, allow storage of different data sources, it is possible to directly create another interface from one database to feedback systems, such as TTN, through web-based applications such as Shiny or JavaScript. Figure 12.5 illustrates the different phases of EMA data handling.

To sum up, EMA comprises different methods for intensive longitudinal assessment, with several studies demonstrating its usefulness within psychotherapy research. However, several aspects need to be considered, with secure storage and the ability to handle huge datasets and create interfaces being three crucial aspects. In general, the high resolution of EMA data enables new forms of ROM, with real-world information that may improve measurement-based care. While EMA captures real-time data from patients' daily experiences, video analysis provides in-depth insights into therapy sessions themselves.

Video Analysis

In recent years, technological advances have transformed the analysis and interpretation of video recordings from psychotherapy sessions. One such innovative tool is the Nonverbal Behavior Analyzer (NOVA) user interface embedded in the DISCOVER software framework, designed specifically to import videos of therapy sessions and perform comprehensive analyses using a variety of models (Baur et al.,

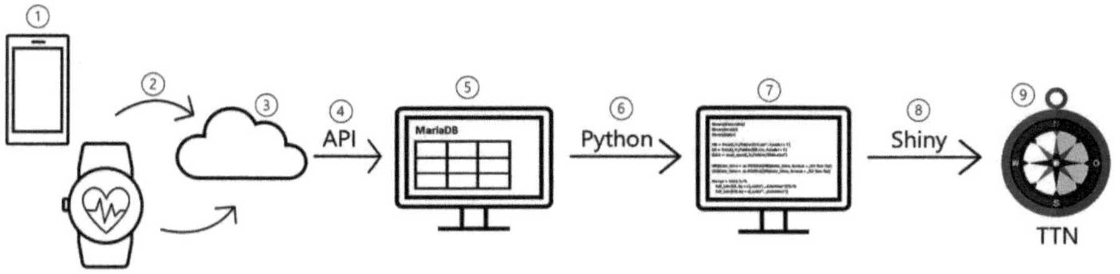

Fig. 12.5 Phases of EMA data handling. *Note*. (1) Collection of EMA data via smartphones for self-reports and wearables for example, heart rate monitoring, (2) automatic upload of EMA data to (3) the specific third-party server, (4) transformation of EMA data via an Application Programming Interface (API) into a (5) database (e.g., MariaDB) on an organization-owned server. (6) Download the EMA data stored in the database in a compatible format that allows for upload into (7) additional data handling software (e.g., R), (8) develop a web-based application using tools like Shiny to integrate the data into (9) a feedback system, such as the TTN

2020; Schiller et al., 2024; Terhürne et al., 2022). NOVA integrates models such as OpenFace and OpenPose to analyze facial expressions, body movements, and gestures within therapy sessions. A notable feature of NOVA is the integration of the Emonet model, which enables automatic analysis of emotions based on facial expressions captured in therapy videos. Using machine learning techniques, Emonet provides valuable insights into the emotional dynamics occurring during sessions.

While NOVA was originally designed as a nonverbal behavior analyzer, the evolution of the DISCOVER framework has led to significant expansions in functionality. One of the most notable advancements is the integration of WhisperX, which enables automatic transcription of therapy sessions. NOVA also includes SpeechBrain, a tool for automatic speaker diarization. These features not only streamline the process of transcribing sessions but also open up a variety of natural language processing (NLP) possibilities. Researchers can use the NLP models implemented in NOVA to identify key themes, extract meaningful insights from session transcripts, and analyze sentiment (Eberhardt et al., 2024). Figure 12.6 shows a screenshot of NOVA with different features extracted from a simulated therapy video, such as feature points on the face and body, as well as the automatically transcribed statements separated by patient and therapist.

NOVA also introduced the NOVA Assistant, a tool that uses the capabilities of large language models (LLMs) such as Generative Pretrained Transformers (GPTs, e.g., LLAMA). This assistant allows users to interact with therapy session transcripts through natural language prompts, facilitating access to specific information and increasing the efficiency of analysis processes.

An inherent advantage of the NOVA user interface and the DISCOVER software framework is their ability to perform all analysis locally or on-premises, eliminating

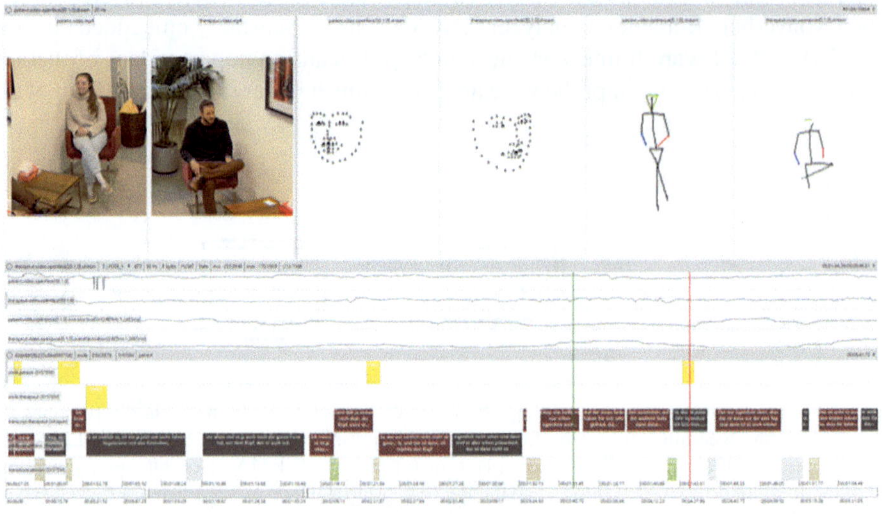

Fig. 12.6 Nonverbal Behavior Analyzer (NOVA) for automated analysis of therapy videos. *Note.* The video still frames show a simulated therapy situation

the need to transmit sensitive therapy session data to third-party cloud servers. This ensures the confidentiality and security of patient information, addressing critical privacy concerns in psychotherapy research and practice.

The NOVA software, along with the implementation of modern machine learning tools and large language models, is still in its early stages. However, the potential for using these advancements for feedback in psychotherapy practice is promising. Therapists and supervisors can leverage NOVA's analyses of nonverbal behaviors, emotional expressions, and linguistic patterns as a means of feedback. Therapists may use the insights provided by NOVA to gain a deeper understanding of their communication style, identify areas for improvement, and refine their therapeutic techniques. Supervisors, equipped with the data generated by NOVA, could offer targeted feedback and guidance to therapists under their supervision. Video-based feedback sessions facilitated by NOVA could become a standard practice in professional development, fostering self-reflection and enhancing the effectiveness of therapeutic interventions. Additionally, NOVA's transcription capabilities and linguistic analysis could enable supervisors to identify recurring themes, track therapeutic progress, and tailor supervision strategies accordingly. Finally, responses from LLMs could be integrated with data from questionnaires and ecological momentary assessments in a feedback system (see Fig. 12.7, for example).

Conclusion

The implementation of feedback systems for ROM involves various technical requirements that vary depending on the specific context in which the system will be used (i.e., private practice vs. research hub). Especially when multiple data sources, such as questionnaires, EMA, and video analysis, are involved, it is crucial to consider how different sampling rates, software systems, and data storage platforms can be accessed and meaningfully integrated into the system. While there may not be a single solution that integrates all tools simultaneously, we have outlined how interfaces can be developed to support final integration into platforms like the TTN. Separate feedback systems for different data sources are feasible, but combining them into a unified system offers significant advantages, such as enhanced usability and simplified maintenance.

We encourage both research hubs and mental health professionals to adopt feedback systems, as there are accessible options tailored to settings with varying levels of technical resources. For mental health professionals in private practice, user-friendly feedback systems are available that do not require extensive technical resources (e.g., TN-PRO). However, in research settings, the presence of dedicated technical teams plays a critical role in maintaining systems, troubleshooting, and ensuring secure data handling. Data security remains a priority for all users, and secure storage and transmission processes are an integral part of the system design. As the technology evolves, implementation will become easier, enabling both researchers and practitioners to improve therapeutic outcomes through effective feedback systems, regardless of their technical capacity.

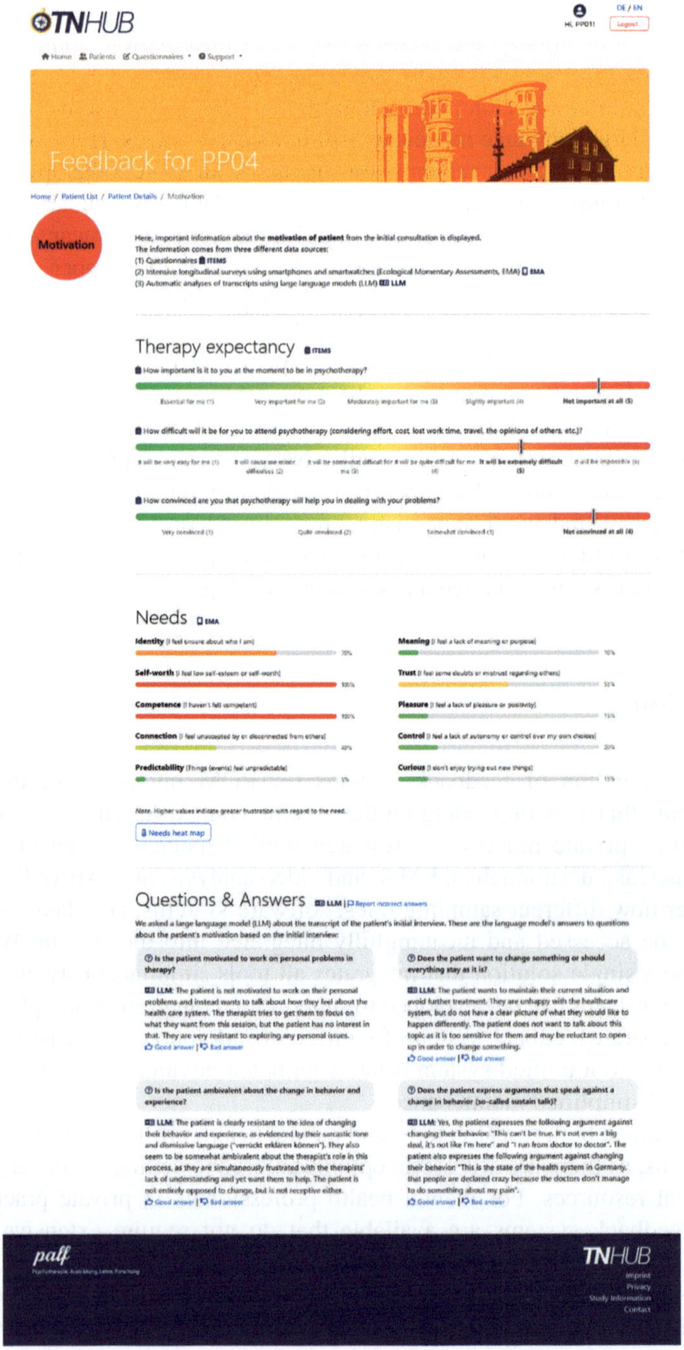

Fig. 12.7 Integration of data from different sources (Questionnaires, EMA, & Video Analysis) in the Treatment Navigator Hub (TN-HUB). *Note.* The data is from a simulated patient

Acknowledgments We would like to thank all employees and assistants who have worked on the development of the Trier Treatment Navigator (TTN) and the continuous improvement of the technical infrastructure and workflow over the years: Christopher Baumann, Niklas Becht, Stefan Braun, Benedikt Breitlauch, Markus Bruchertseifer, Robin Drees, Danny Engels, Christoph Fischer, Martin Jaehde, Rouven Martin, Martin Kock, Daniel Lider, Maxim Maier, Andreas Michels, Till Petro, Marisa Richter, Jessica Sander, Timur Sultanov, Andreas Wieland, Jochen Wiechmann, Simon Werner, Nicolai Wolters, Tobias Ziegelmayer, Dirk Zimmermann, and more.

References

Barkham, M., De Jong, K., Delgadillo, J., & Lutz, W. (2023). Routine outcome monitoring (ROM) and feedback: Research review and recommendations. *Psychotherapy Research, 33*(7), 841–855. https://doi.org/10.1080/10503307.2023.2181114

Barrett, T., Dowle, M., Srinivasan, A., Gorecki, J., Chirico, M., Hocking, T., & Schwendinger, B. (2024). *data.table: Extension of 'data.frame'.* https://doi.org/10.32614/CRAN.package.data.table

Baur, T., Clausen, S., Heimerl, A., Lingenfelser, F., Lutz, W., & André, E. (2020). NOVA: A tool for explanatory multimodal behavior analysis and its application to psychotherapy. In Y. M. Ro, W.-H. Cheng, J. Kim, W.-T. Chu, P. Cui, J.-W. Choi, M.-C. Hu, & W. de Neve (Eds.), *MultiMedia modeling: 26th international conference, MMM 2020, Daejeon, South Korea, January 5–8, 2020: Proceedings* (Vol. 11962, pp. 577–588). Springer. https://doi.org/10.1007/978-3-030-37734-2_47

Ben-Zeev, D., McHugo, G. J., Xie, H., Dobbins, K., & Young, M. A. (2012). Comparing retrospective reports to real-time/real-place mobile assessments in individuals with schizophrenia and a nonclinical comparison group. *Schizophrenia Bulletin, 38*(3), 396–404. https://doi.org/10.1093/schbul/sbr171

Bos, F. M., von Klipstein, L., Emerencia, A. C., Veermans, E., Verhage, T., Snippe, E., Doornbos, B., Hadders-Prins, G., Wichers, M., & Riese, H. (2022). A web-based application for personalized ecological momentary assessment in psychiatric care: User-centered development of the PETRA application. *JMIR Mental Health, 9*(8), e36430. https://doi.org/10.2196/36430

Eberhardt, S. T., Schaffrath, J., Moggia, D., Schwartz, B., Jaehde, M., Rubel, J. A., Baur, T., André, E., & Lutz, W. (2024). Decoding emotions: Exploring the validity of sentiment analysis in psychotherapy. *Psychotherapy Research, 35*(2), 174–189. https://doi.org/10.1080/10503307.2024.2322522

Husen, K., Rafaeli, E., Rubel, J. A., Bar-Kalifa, E., & Lutz, W. (2016). Daily affect dynamics predict early response in CBT: Feasibility and predictive validity of EMA for outpatient psychotherapy. *Journal of Affective Disorders, 206*, 305–314. https://doi.org/10.1016/j.jad.2016.08.025

Lutz, W., Schwartz, B., Hofmann, S. G., Fisher, A. J., Husen, K., & Rubel, J. A. (2018). Using network analysis for the prediction of treatment dropout in patients with mood and anxiety disorders: A methodological proof-of-concept study. *Scientific Reports, 8*(1), 7819. https://doi.org/10.1038/s41598-018-25953-0

Lutz, W., Rubel, J. A., Schwartz, B., Schilling, V., & Deisenhofer, A.-K. (2019). Towards integrating personalized feedback research into clinical practice: Development of the Trier Treatment Navigator (TTN). *Behaviour Research and Therapy, 120*, 103438. https://doi.org/10.1016/j.brat.2019.103438

Lutz, W., Deisenhofer, A.-K., Rubel, J., Bennemann, B., Giesemann, J., Poster, K., & Schwartz, B. (2022). Prospective evaluation of a clinical decision support system in psychological therapy. *Journal of Consulting and Clinical Psychology, 90*(1), 90–106. https://doi.org/10.1037/ccp0000642

Schiller, D., Hallmen, T., Don, D. W., André, E., & Baur, T. (2024). *DISCOVER: A data-driven interactive system for comprehensive observation, visualization, and exploration of human behaviour (Version 1)*. arXiv. Retrieved from https://doi.org/10.48550/ARXIV.2407.13408

Shiffman, S., Stone, A. A., & Hufford, M. R. (2008). Ecological momentary assessment. *Annual Review of Clinical Psychology, 4*(1), 1–32. https://doi.org/10.1146/annurev.clinpsy.3.022806.091415

Terhürne, P., Schwartz, B., Baur, T., Schiller, D., Eberhardt, S. T., André, E., & Lutz, W. (2022). Validation and application of the non-verbal behavior analyzer: An automated tool to assess non-verbal emotional expressions in psychotherapy. *Frontiers in Psychiatry, 13*. https://doi.org/10.3389/fpsyt.2022.1026015

Wieland, A. (2024). *Video computer kiosk system [Computer software]*. Retrieved from https://www.computer-wieland.de/

Chapter 13
Opportunities and Obstacles When Implementing Feedback-Informed Treatment into Practice: Learning from Experience with the Trier Treatment Navigator

Brian Schwartz, Antonia Vehlen, Steffen T. Eberhardt, and Wolfgang Lutz

Introduction

When the technical prerequisites of feedback-informed treatment (FIT) described in the previous chapter are in place, human factors still require consideration. During implementation, various stakeholders play a role. Implementation success centrally hinges on the patients and therapists who are supposed to use the technology, in particular, their attitudes, behaviors, and acceptance of the system, as well as their commitment to using it.

Implementation of FIT in Clinical Practice

Deisenhofer et al. (2024) have published a comprehensive model on the implementation of data-informed psychological therapies called the Implementing Precision Methods (IPM) Framework. This framework addresses implementation issues, obstacles, and possible solutions across four areas: context (including financial, societal, and ethical questions), statistics (including the generalizability of models and their practical usefulness), technical aspects (such as software and hardware; see Chap. 12 of this book), and clinical and practical application (such as patient needs and therapist concerns). This chapter primarily deals with the latter, that is, the clinical and practical application, though problems and solutions from other areas sometimes overlap and are then also discussed. Not all barriers and potential paths forward will be repeated in this text, as they have been discussed in detail

---

B. Schwartz (✉) · A. Vehlen · S. T. Eberhardt · W. Lutz
Department of Clinical Psychology and Psychotherapy, Trier University, Trier, Germany
e-mail: schwartzb@uni-trier.de

J. A. Rubel, W. Lutz (eds.), *Feedback Informed Psychological Therapy*, CBT: Science Into Practice, https://doi.org/10.1007/978-3-031-90428-8_13

elsewhere (e.g., Deisenhofer et al., 2024). Instead, we will present the specific challenges that arose at the university outpatient clinic at the University of Trier during the implementation and ongoing development of the Trier Treatment Navigator (TTN; Lutz et al., 2019, 2022a) as well as the strategies we applied to address them.

Assessments and Functionality

When implementing FIT into practice, continuous assessments are a critical aspect that requires careful consideration. It is necessary to decide when, where, and how questionnaires should be completed by patients and possibly also by therapists. For the sake of both patients and therapists, it is preferable to use short questionnaires and keep their number manageable (Lutz et al., 2021). So-called session reports can be filled out by patients both before (to assess current distress) and after the session (to evaluate the session). If therapists prefer not to take a few minutes out of the session time for this, patients can also complete questionnaires in the waiting room. A mobile device such as a tablet or laptop is preferable to paper-pencil, as this eliminates the need for manual data entry and allows automated processing. This way, the waiting time before the session can be used meaningfully, with the patient already engaging with relevant content without session time having to be reduced. This is particularly relevant as therapists often schedule hourly appointments lasting 50 minutes, with the remaining 10 minutes required as a time buffer for the previous session, for documentation, or a short break.

Longer regular questionnaires (e.g., every 4 or 5 sessions) can be given to patients as homework, either on paper or using an online form available through their web browser. In any case, it is essential that the psychometric assessments interfere as little as possible with the therapeutic process and practice workflow and consume minimal time for the sake of efficiency (Boswell et al., 2015). Another important factor is cost efficiency. Therefore, wherever possible, questionnaires with open licensing are preferable, as they are freely available and do not involve any additional costs that may be difficult to compensate for.

Even with a well-structured and efficient assessment plan, implementation still requires resources compared to omitting psychometric assessments and feedback. These primarily include the time spent on data collection and the review and interpretation of feedback. Therefore, the benefits of using feedback, which are extensively described in this book, must be made clear to users as a source of motivation (see section "A Rationale for Using ROM"). Even the collection of diagnostic information can be simplified, if questionnaires are completed digitally, automatically stored, evaluated, and graphically prepared for therapists. For example, manual scoring using scoring templates and the more complex classification of test results based on reference values or tables become unnecessary if the feedback system automatically generates color-coded graphs displaying reference values. The TTN, for example, displays intake assessments even before the first session to support therapists in their risk assessment, case conceptualization, and treatment planning.

Intermediate assessments and session reports are fed back to therapists as progress charts to monitor change and indicate the need of treatment adaptation (for details, see Chap. 2).

However, the most convincing argument for therapists will always be the potential to streamline their routine tasks, which are time-consuming and possibly disliked. For instance, modern developments that extract information from therapy recordings (video or audio) could, in the future, use large language models (LLMs; Eberhardt et al., 2024; Stade et al., 2023) to automatically generate session notes or reports, thereby providing valuable preliminary work for therapists. Such direct improvements to clinical practice will significantly increase potential users' motivation, the frequency of implementation, and ultimately support the adoption of these systems.

Validity of Prediction Models

For feedback to be used, users must be able to trust it. As soon as therapists feel that the system's recommendations are too often incorrect, they will be inclined to trust their intuition rather than the system. An important step in this direction is to ensure that prediction models are reliable and valid. The generalizability of prediction models, such as those used to predict treatment outcomes or dropout probability, is to be ensured by applying modern approaches from the field of machine learning (ML) and advanced validation methods. Such ML models include regularized regression models, like LASSO regression or elastic net (e.g., Bennemann et al., 2022), which shrink the coefficients of predictors to prevent the overestimation of associations (a phenomenon known as overfitting). Internal validation strategies are used to validate the algorithms, in which the models are repeatedly tested on parts of the data not used for model development. This increases the likelihood that the predictions will also hold for new data from future incoming patients. Initial attempts to test prediction models on data from other studies have so far highlighted the need for further refinement, as current models have not generalized to other populations and settings well (Tait et al., 2024; van Bronswijk et al., 2021), with only a few studies showing successful external validation (e.g., Moggia et al., 2023). Therefore, prediction models embedded in comprehensive feedback systems are better trained on comparable data, or updated as necessary, allowing the model to learn the associations in a specific setting. If predictions repeatedly prove to be biased, this is likely to decrease therapists' willingness to use the system and consider its recommendations in decision-making.

Presentation of Feedback

The presentation of feedback in Routine Outcome Monitoring (ROM) systems should focus on simplicity and clarity without oversimplifying the data to the point of losing scientific rigor. An example of this is differential predictions in treatment selection, where one of several alternative treatment approaches or strategies is recommended. Classical approaches in the literature tend to offer a clear recommendation for a specific treatment approach (Cohen & DeRubeis, 2018). However, research also shows that for approximately 40–50% of patients, the treatment alternatives are equally promising and only for the remaining patients does the choice significantly impact treatment success (DeRubeis et al., 2014; Moggia et al., 2023; Schwartz et al., 2021). It has been observed that the effect of treatment selection is greater for patients who are predicted to have a more substantial difference in outcome between treatment alternatives (e.g., Lutz et al., 2022a).

For this reason, in the TTN, we decided not to set an arbitrary threshold for the necessary difference between the predicted effect sizes of the three strategies (problem-focused, motivation-oriented, and mixed), beyond which a strategy would be categorically recommended. Instead, the therapists are shown the three effect sizes, so that they can decide for themselves whether the predicted differences (and the sample sizes they are based on) are large enough to pursue a specific strategy (Lutz et al., 2019). This way the therapists retain the final decision and can integrate the information into their clinical perspective without the system forcing them to interpret given numbers in a predetermined way. The strategy recommendation of the TTN is shown in Chap. 2, Fig. 2.1.

The Patient's Role

Patients interact with ROM feedback more indirectly, as feedback is typically provided to therapists, who are then expected to discuss it with their patients. Generally, there is no direct feedback given to the patients themselves. However, patient acceptance of FIT is crucial, as they bear the extra effort of regularly and conscientiously completing the questionnaires. If data quality is low, because patients are not accurately answering the questions, feedback systems cannot function properly and may even recommend contraindicated approaches.

A key factor for patients is the burden of completing the questionnaires. This factor has been investigated in more detail in the context of high-frequency Ecological Momentary Assessments (EMA) in patients' daily lives. It has been shown that it is not the frequency of the measurements, but the length of the questionnaires that can negatively impact both their subjective burden and the quantity and quality of the data (Eisele et al., 2022). Therefore, only relevant and primarily robust short forms of psychometric questionnaires should be used. However, acceptance is less of a problem, with around 90% of patients supporting thorough diagnostics and repeated questionnaires (Lutz et al., 2021). In our outpatient clinic, we have observed that patients respond positively to regular assessments, seeing them as a sign that their therapists are attentive and committed. The TTN, for example, was evaluated positively by 86% of more than 600 outpatients in our clinic and 70% of their treating therapists (Lutz et al., 2024). Additionally, studies on digital innovations in psychotherapy suggest that patients are usually more open to their use than therapists. For example, Frumkin et al. (2021) surveyed patients and therapists regarding the use of EMA and symptom networks for therapy planning and diagnostics. Patients were significantly more open than therapists and found the feedback to be helpful, while therapists were more skeptical about whether the models provided additional information and could support treatment. Therefore, more attention should be given to how ROM can be designed, so that therapists also find it feasible and beneficial. It seems to be much more challenging to achieve positive therapist attitudes, usage, and commitment (e.g., Barkham et al., 2023; de Jong et al., 2021).

Training Therapists

As systems become more complex and incorporate more data, therapists receive more information, enabling them to make more data-informed decisions (Lutz et al., 2022b, 2024). At the same time, the difficulty of implementing the system rises, as therapists need comprehensive psychometric and scientific training to understand and operate these complex systems. Therapists, and FIT users in general, need to be trained on different levels to ensure successful implementation. These levels include the rational level, that is, understanding the purpose and value of FIT and increasing motivation for its use; the methodological level, that is, enabling therapists to use the feedback system; and the content level, that is, understanding the content, such as the interventions recommended by the system. Central determinants of the successful implementation of technology are performance and effort expectancy as well as facilitating conditions, as highlighted by the Unified Theory of Acceptance and Use of Technology (UTAUT; Venkatesh et al., 2003). Performance and effort expectancy influence the behavioral intention, while facilitating conditions foster the usage behavior. Therefore, the expected benefits of FIT must be outlined (rational level), the feasibility of usage must be ensured (methodological and content levels), and necessary effort should be kept low (see sections “Assessments and Functionality” and “The Patient’s Role”).

A Rationale for Using ROM

As previously mentioned, therapists’ attitudes toward FIT in general and the specific system in use play a crucial role in its implementation. Therapists need a convincing rationale explaining why they should apply FIT and what the positive outcomes of its use will be. In a study by de Jong et al. (2012), feedback only affected treatment outcomes if it was actually used, and this effect was again moderated by therapists' commitment to use the feedback. Therefore, to motivate therapists to use it, it should be systematically communicated to them that FIT is associated with better treatment outcomes and fewer dropouts (de Jong et al., 2021). In addition to these findings from ROM evaluation studies, the theoretical background is also critical to provide a rationale.

Therapists should be aware that, like all human beings, they are prone to cognitive biases when making decisions and predictions about complex problems, which often lead to errors in clinical judgment. One key issue is that therapists tend to overestimate the effectiveness of their therapy in advance and are particularly biased against predicting negative outcomes (Walfish et al., 2012). Knowledge of this so-called positivity bias, or better-than-average effect, can help therapists understand the problem and recognize the need for external support. Another important finding is the superiority of statistical predictions over clinical judgments (Hannan et al., 2005; Lutz et al., 2006). These two aspects lead to the conclusion that ROM can be a valuable complement to therapists' own expertise. Just as in therapy, where cognitive preparation can clarify the rationale for challenging exercises (e.g., exposure exercises) and facilitate their implementation, FIT users need to understand why they should consult the system to use it. To this end, we have introduced a seminar on change mechanisms in psychotherapy at the University of Trier's outpatient clinic. This seminar covers key findings from psychotherapy research and provides the theoretical framework for FIT.

In addition to the lack of a solid rationale, therapists' negative emotions toward data collection, feedback, and technology also present significant barriers to the implementation of FIT. Common concerns include questions about what happens to the data, whether it could be used for external control, whether it might be used to evaluate therapists' performance, compare them to their colleagues, potentially reduce their fees, or even deny patients access to therapy based on the results (Boswell et al., 2015). To preempt or counter these concerns, transparent communication and disclosure of how the data will be used is essential. Therapists must be assured that neither they nor their patients will face any disadvantages from the implementation of FIT.

In our outpatient clinic, for example, feedback is used solely for clinical purposes and is only reported back to the respective therapists themselves. There is no personal identification of effective or less effective therapists, and the data is not used for evaluation or performance-based billing of clinicians. Such negative attitudes among therapists are critical and influential barriers to the implementation of FIT. These attitudes can now be assessed with validated instruments and are related to therapists' intentions and behavior regarding technology (Bagarić, & Jokić-Begić, 2020; Rye et al., 2019).

Practical Application of the FIT System

Even when therapists are motivated to use FIT because they see its value, this does not necessarily mean that they know how to use it. The likelihood of implementation increases when using the ROM system does not require unnecessary resources due to a lack of familiarity. For this reason, we have established a mandatory training course designed as a hands-on workshop to give therapists a practical introduction to the TTN. They learn about the system and all its functions, so that they know what is possible and what features are accessible in different sections of the system. Additionally, the individual functions and support tools are explained in detail, including their theoretical background, their development, the presentation and meaning of the data, as well as their interpretation and implications for therapeutic action. During the course, therapists explore parts of the system in small, independent groups, allowing them to engage with the system deeply. By the end of the course, they should feel confident navigating the system and know how to access and interpret information at various points. The goal is to develop skills in the cognitive (knowledge-based) and psychomotor (action-based) domains of Bloom's taxonomy for educational goals (Ormell, 1974) to use the feedback system effectively.

To run the feedback system smoothly, technical staff are at least helpful, if not essential. Details on the role of technical staff are given in Chap. 12. At this point, it should be emphasized that these technicians are not only necessary to develop and manage the software and maintain its functionality but also particularly valuable as a point of contact for therapists in the event of technical problems, questions about procedures, and other uncertainties not related to the therapeutic content.

Training in Therapeutic Content

The prospective evaluation of the TTN has shown that the feedback system's recommendations do not always lead to better outcomes, but they do when the therapeutic recommendations are followed (Lutz et al., 2022a). There are two plausible reasons why the recommendation does not consistently lead to better results. First, it could be that therapists received the recommendation, but either did not notice it or chose not to follow it. To reduce this obstacle, motivation to use the system and skills in practical application must be addressed, as mentioned in the two previous sections. Second, some therapists may have noticed the recommendations and wanted to follow them but lacked the knowledge to practically implement them. Therefore, the feedback system's recommendations should be as clear and understandable as possible. Simply pointing out a problematic treatment response that deviates from the statistically expected response curve is not enough. Therapists also need practical clinical guidance on how to adjust their treatment approach in the session to adapt to the individual patient.

Empirical evidence shows that FIT leads to better outcomes, especially when clinical support tools are provided during unexpected deviations in the treatment response. These tools provide individualized therapeutic strategies, methods, and techniques (Harmon et al., 2005; Schilling et al., 2021). In addition to learning how to use the ROM system, therapists must also develop appropriate therapeutic skills, so they can effectively implement the exercises recommended by the system. To improve the implementation of strategy recommendations in the TTN (e.g., motivation-oriented vs. problem-solving approaches in early sessions), we have also introduced clinical courses that teach motivational techniques (e.g., motivational interviewing) as well as problem-solving methods (e.g., behavioral activation or social skills training) and their various applications.

Timely Supervision for Critical Events

When continuous outcome and process measurements in the system indicate a critical change (e.g., a significant symptom worsening) during ongoing treatment, therapists may feel overwhelmed or struggle to adapt their treatment to the updated feedback. This can happen, for example, when a patient deteriorates and receives a "not-on-track" signal. In such cases, timely and appropriate action is needed to prevent a negative treatment outcome. To support therapists in responding promptly and appropriately, any such signal is reported to our background team, and the therapist is invited to a so-called *feedback meeting*. This is a regular meeting with experienced team members, in which therapists can discuss their cases that are not progressing as expected. The discussion covers how to understand and handle specific feedback and how to use the clinical support tools that have been provided. The goal is to sharpen therapists' skills at this crucial juncture in FIT and to increase the likelihood of successful implementation.

Involving Therapists and Expanding Reach

The primary users of FIT systems are therapists. Therefore, it makes sense to involve them in the development of the system and to adapt the system to their needs and preferences, rather than trying to force clinical practice to adapt to a theoretically developed system. For therapists in private practice in the larger Trier area, we are currently developing a streamlined version of the TTN, the Treatment Navigator Pro (TN-PRO), which includes the core functions for easier use and relies exclusively on open-source questionnaires, eliminating the need for users to budget for licensing fees for psychometric tools. To adapt the system in such a way that mental health professionals in private practice find it useful and easy to integrate into their workflow, we are conducting a pilot project, in which the TN-PRO is being tested by a few therapists in private practice. In the first phase, former trainees from our training clinic will use the new system, and eventually, more external therapists will join. These users will provide continuous feedback on problems and suggestions for improvements, which we will work to implement, creating a feedback–adjustment cycle. These informal feedback processes are accompanied by continuous measurement of constructs such as usability, acceptance, and trust as well as their evolution over time by users. This iterative process helps to continuously optimize the TTN for use in private psychotherapy practices. Successful implementation is more likely when users are given a say in shaping the feedback system so that it best meets their needs, helping them to perceive it as beneficial and actively use it.

In addition to involving the therapists as the main users in the development, aspects of sustainability are also important for implementation. Instead of constantly developing new approaches and systems independently of each other, which then do not make it into practical application, the focus should be on developing sustainable systems that can be used for a long time so that a certain routine can develop. The TTN is already a good example of this, as it has been in continuous use for over five years in its current form and over 15 years in the previous version, before it was dubbed TTN. This means that its applicability over a longer period of time and thus its sustainability can be regarded as established.

In addition to a version of the Therapy Navigator for private practitioners (TN-PRO), a research version is being developed that can be implemented at other research clinics and universities (TN-HUB). These clinics could serve as research hubs and points of contact for private practitioners in their region. This could lead to the development of local research-practice networks in various regions of Germany, which, in turn, could begin to collaborate with each other. International cooperation and alignment of FIT approaches are also desirable. To this end, the European Chapter of the Society for Psychotherapy Research (SPR) has initiated the formation of the European Psychotherapy Consortium (EPoC). One of its first steps was the introduction of a single item, the EPO-1, which has now been translated into 13 languages and is to be used in different clinics across Europe (Gonçalves et al., 2024; Schwartz et al., 2024). In addition to the shared item and the development of crosswalks between different psychometric measures, EPoC focuses on collaboration and support in the implementation of FIT.

Global Changes

In addition to the intrinsic motivation that arises when therapists understand the rationale and benefits of FIT, Boswell et al. (2015) also consider financial incentives as a potential external motivator in their recommendations for the future use of ROM. However, in many areas of healthcare, structural or environmental interventions are known to show larger effects than behavioral interventions (Honeycutt et al., 2015). Therefore, it could be fruitful to implement the use of ROM and the application of FIT nationwide for quality assurance. While this is mandatory in large parts of the United Kingdom as part of the NHS Talking Therapies for anxiety and depression program (formerly called Improving Access to Psychological Therapies, IAPT; Wakefield et al., 2021), where patients are required to complete selected questionnaires as standard practice, there is currently no quality assurance in Germany via the systematic collection of psychometric data and direct or indirect change assessments. Nevertheless, the routine use of FIT in German psychotherapy practices would be a desirable way to ensure the quality of psychotherapeutic treatments. However, implementing this on a large scale would pose even greater challenges than implementing it in a single clinic.

Regarding therapists' attitudes and their openness to FIT and data-informed support in clinical decision-making, there appears to be a generational effect. Therapists who have been working in their own private practices for many years or even decades tend to be more resistant to change and are more likely to reject the introduction of FIT. In contrast, younger colleagues, who have been more exposed to ideas of evidence-based predictions and recommendations during their studies as well as in their private lives, tend to show more interest. Our former trainees, for instance, increasingly inquire about the possibility of using the TTN in their own practices, for which TN-PRO is intended to serve in the future. Even therapists who are still in training in our clinic express a desire for similar feedback systems in the clinics where they complete the inpatient part of their training. During the German Research Foundation (DFG)-funded study on the prospective evaluation of the TTN in our outpatient clinic (Lutz et al., 2022a), some therapists even complained about being in the control group, as they had to treat their patients without the feedback they were used to receiving.

This means a key factor in the implementation of FIT and the likelihood of therapists adopting it is their socialization. To facilitate implementation, therapists should be exposed to the concepts of FIT early on, during their training or even undergraduate studies, and trained in its scientific, psychometric, and clinical aspects (Lutz et al., 2022b). The goal should be for FIT to become an integral part of their therapeutic identity, where they see themselves as therapists who benefit from data collection, technology, feedback, and data-informed recommendations and view these as a normal component of evidence-based psychological practice. This new generation of therapists can be expected to be more open to and confident in handling feedback, significantly contributing to the implementation of feedback research findings into clinical practice.

References

Bagarić, B., & Jokić-Begić, N. (2020). Measuring therapists' attitudes toward integration of technology in psychotherapy and predicting their use of technology. *Journal of Clinical Psychology, 76*(6), 1151–1172. https://doi.org/10.1002/jclp.22967

Barkham, M., De Jong, K., Delgadillo, J., & Lutz, W. (2023). Routine outcome monitoring (ROM) and feedback: Research review and recommendations. *Psychotherapy Research, 33*(7), 841–855. https://doi.org/10.1080/10503307.2023.2181114

Bennemann, B., Schwartz, B., Giesemann, J., & Lutz, W. (2022). Predicting patients who will drop out of out-patient psychotherapy using machine learning algorithms. *The British Journal of Psychiatry, 220*(4), 192–201. https://doi.org/10.1192/bjp.2022.17

Boswell, J. F., Kraus, D. R., Miller, S. D., & Lambert, M. J. (2015). Implementing routine outcome monitoring in clinical practice: Benefits, challenges, and solutions. *Psychotherapy Research, 25*(1), 6–19. https://doi.org/10.1080/10503307.2013.817696

Cohen, Z. D., & DeRubeis, R. J. (2018). Treatment selection in depression. *Annual Review of Clinical Psychology, 14*(1), 209–236. https://doi.org/10.1146/annurev-clinpsy-050817-084746

de Jong, K., van Sluis, P., Nugter, M. A., Heiser, W. J., & Spinhoven, P. (2012). Understanding the differential impact of outcome monitoring: Therapist variables that moderate feedback effects in a randomized clinical trial. *Psychotherapy Research, 22*(4), 464–474. https://doi.org/10.1080/10503307.2012.673023

de Jong, K., Conijn, J. M., Gallagher, R. A. V., Reshetnikova, A. S., Heij, M., & Lutz, M. C. (2021). Using progress feedback to improve outcomes and reduce drop-out, treatment duration, and deterioration: A multilevel meta-analysis. *Clinical Psychology Review, 85*, 102002. https://doi.org/10.1016/j.cpr.2021.102002

Deisenhofer, A.-K., Barkham, M., Beierl, E. T., Schwartz, B., Aafjes-van Doorn, K., Beevers, C. G., Berwian, I. M., Blackwell, S. E., Bockting, C. L., Brakemeier, E.-L., Brown, G., Buckman, J. E. J., Castonguay, L. G., Cusack, C. E., Dalgleish, T., de Jong, K., Delgadillo, J., DeRubeis, R. J., Driessen, E., Ehrenreich-May, J., et al. (2024). Implementing precision methods in personalizing psychological therapies: Barriers and possible ways forward. *Behaviour Research and Therapy, 172*, 10443. https://doi.org/10.1016/j.brat.2023.104443

DeRubeis, R. J., Cohen, Z. D., Forand, N. R., Fournier, J. C., Gelfand, L. A., & Lorenzo-Luaces, L. (2014). The personalized advantage index: Translating research on prediction into individualized treatment recommendations. A demonstration. *PLoS One, 9*(1), e83875. https://doi.org/10.1371/journal.pone.0083875

Eberhardt, S. T., Schaffrath, J., Moggia, D., Schwartz, B., Jaehde, M., Rubel, J. A., Baur, T., André, E., & Lutz, W. (2024). Decoding emotions: Exploring the validity of sentiment analysis in psychotherapy. *Psychotherapy Research, 35*, 174. https://doi.org/10.1080/10503307.2024.2322522

Eisele, G., Vachon, H., Lafit, G., Kuppens, P., Houben, M., Myin-Germeys, I., & Viechtbauer, W. (2022). The effects of sampling frequency and questionnaire length on perceived burden, compliance, and careless responding in experience sampling data in a student population. *Assessment, 29*(2), 136–151. https://doi.org/10.1177/1073191120957102

Frumkin, M. R., Piccirillo, M. L., Beck, E. D., Grossman, J. T., & Rodebaugh, T. L. (2021). Feasibility and utility of idiographic models in the clinic: A pilot study. *Psychotherapy Research, 31*(4), 520–534. https://doi.org/10.1080/10503307.2020.1805133

Gonçalves, M. M., Lutz, W., Schwartz, B., Oliveira, J. T., Saarni, S. E., Tishby, O., Rubel, J. A., Boehnke, J. R., Montesano, A., Paiva, D., Ceridono, D., Zech, E., Willemsen, J., Saarni, S. I., Kompan Erzar, K., Janeiro, L., Gelo, O. C. G., Errázuriz, P., Holas, P., Styła, R., et al. (2024). Developing a European psychotherapy consortium (EPoC): Towards adopting a single-item self-report outcome measure across European countries. *Clinical Psychology in Europe, 6*(3), 1–15. https://doi.org/10.32872/cpe.13827

Hannan, C., Lambert, M. J., Harmon, C., Nielsen, S. L., Smart, D. W., Shimokawa, K., & Sutton, S. W. (2005). A lab test and algorithms for identifying clients at risk for treatment failure. *Journal of Clinical Psychology, 61*(2), 155–163. https://doi.org/10.1002/jclp.20108

Harmon, C., Hawkins, E. J., Lambert, M. J., Slade, K., & Whipple, J. S. (2005). Improving outcomes for poorly responding clients: The use of clinical support tools and feedback to clients. *Journal of Clinical Psychology, 61*(2), 175–185. https://doi.org/10.1002/jclp.20109

Honeycutt, S., Leeman, J., McCarthy, W. J., Bastani, R., Carter-Edwards, L., Clark, H., Garney, W., Gustat, J., Hites, L., Nothwehr, F., & Kegler, M. (2015). Evaluating policy, systems, and environmental change interventions: Lessons learned from CDC's prevention research centers. *Preventing Chronic Disease, 12*, 150281. https://doi.org/10.5888/pcd12.150281

Lutz, W., Lambert, M. J., Harmon, S. C., Tschitsaz, A., Schürch, E., & Stulz, N. (2006). The probability of treatment success, failure and duration—What can be learned from empirical data to support decision making in clinical practice? *Clinical Psychology & Psychotherapy, 13*(4), 223–232. https://doi.org/10.1002/cpp.496

Lutz, W., Rubel, J. A., Schwartz, B., Schilling, V., & Deisenhofer, A.-K. (2019). Towards integrating personalized feedback research into clinical practice: Development of the Trier Treatment Navigator (TTN). *Behaviour Research and Therapy, 120*, 103438. https://doi.org/10.1016/j.brat.2019.103438

Lutz, W., De Jong, K., Rubel, J. A., & Delgadillo, J. (2021). Measuring, predicting and tracking change in psychotherapy. In M. Barkham, W. Lutz, & L. G. Castonguay (Eds.), *Bergin and Garfield's handbook of psychotherapy and behavior change* (7th ed., pp. 89–133). Wiley.

Lutz, W., Deisenhofer, A.-K., Rubel, J., Bennemann, B., Giesemann, J., Poster, K., & Schwartz, B. (2022a). Prospective evaluation of a clinical decision support system in psychological therapy. *Journal of Consulting and Clinical Psychology, 90*(1), 90–106. https://doi.org/10.1037/ccp0000642

Lutz, W., Schwartz, B., & Delgadillo, J. (2022b). Measurement-based and data-informed psychological therapy. *Annual Review of Clinical Psychology, 18*(1), 71–98. https://doi.org/10.1146/annurev-clinpsy-071720-014821

Lutz, W., Vehlen, A., & Schwartz, B. (2024). Data-informed psychological therapy, measurement-based care, and precision mental health. *Journal of Consulting and Clinical Psychology, 92*(10), 671–673. https://doi.org/10.1037/ccp0000904

Moggia, D., Saxon, D., Lutz, W., Hardy, G. E., & Barkham, M. (2023). Applying precision methods to treatment selection for moderate/severe depression in person-centered experiential therapy or cognitive behavioral therapy. *Psychotherapy Research, 34*(8), 1035–1050. https://doi.org/10.1080/10503307.2023.2269297

Ormell, C. P. (1974). Bloom's taxonomy and the objectives of education. *Educational Research, 17*(1), 3–18. https://doi.org/10.1080/0013188740170101

Rye, M., Rognmo, K., Aarons, G. A., & Skre, I. (2019). Attitudes towards the use of routine outcome monitoring of psychological therapies among mental health providers: The EBPAS–ROM. *Administration and Policy in Mental Health and Mental Health Services Research, 46*, 833–846. https://doi.org/10.1007/s10488-019-00968-5

Schilling, V. N. L. S., Zimmermann, D., Rubel, J. A., Boyle, K. S., & Lutz, W. (2021). Why do patients go off track? Examining potential influencing factors for being at risk of psychotherapy treatment failure. *Quality of Life Research, 30*, 3287–3298. https://doi.org/10.1007/s11136-020-02664-6

Schwartz, B., Cohen, Z. D., Rubel, J. A., Zimmermann, D., Wittmann, W. W., & Lutz, W. (2021). Personalized treatment selection in routine care: Integrating machine learning and statistical algorithms to recommend cognitive behavioral or psychodynamic therapy. *Psychotherapy Research, 31*(1), 33–51. https://doi.org/10.1080/10503307.2020.1769219

Schwartz, B., Gonçalves, M. M., & Lutz, W. (2024). Wie ein neues Mit- statt Nebeneinander in der Psychotherapieforschung Wissenschaft, Praxis und Weiterbildung verbessern kann. *PPmP-Psychotherapie· Psychosomatik· Medizinische Psychologie, 74*(01), 7–9. https://doi.org/10.1055/a-2170-7467

Stade, E. C., Stirman, S. W., Ungar, L. H., Boland, C. L., Schwartz, H. A., Yaden, D. B., Sedoc, J., DeRubeis, R., Willer, R., & Eichstaedt, J. C. (2023, April 24). *Large language models could change the future of behavioral healthcare: A proposal for responsible development and evaluation*. https://doi.org/10.31234/osf.io/cuzvr

Tait, J., Kellett, S., Saxon, D., Deisenhofer, A.-K., Lutz, W., Barkham, M., & Delgadillo, J. (2024). Individual treatment selection for patients with post-traumatic stress disorder: External validation of a personalised advantage index. *Psychotherapy Research, 11*, 1–14. https://doi.org/10.1080/10503307.2024.2360449

van Bronswijk, S. C., Bruijniks, S. J. E., Lorenzo-Luaces, L., Derubeis, R. J., Lemmens, L. H. J. M., Peeters, F. P. M. L., & Huibers, M. J. H. (2021). Cross-trial prediction in psychotherapy: External validation of the personalized advantage index using machine learning in two Dutch randomized trials comparing CBT versus IPT for depression. *Psychotherapy Research, 31*(1), 78–91. https://doi.org/10.1080/10503307.2020.1823029

Venkatesh, V., Morris, M. G., Davis, G. B., & Davis, F. D. (2003). User acceptance of information technology: Toward a unified view. *MIS Quarterly, 27*(3), 425–478. https://doi.org/10.2307/30036540

Wakefield, S., Kellett, S., Simmonds-Buckley, M., Stockton, D., Bradbury, A., & Delgadillo, J. (2021). Improving access to psychological therapies (IAPT) in the United Kingdom: A systematic review and meta-analysis of 10-years of practice-based evidence. *British Journal of Clinical Psychology, 60*(1), 1–37. https://doi.org/10.1111/bjc.12259

Walfish, S., McAlister, B., O'Donnell, P., & Lambert, M. J. (2012). An investigation of self-assessment bias in mental health providers. *Psychological Reports, 110*(2), 639–644. https://doi.org/10.2466/02.07.17.PR0.110.2.639-644

Chapter 14
Transforming Data into Action: A Case Study on Progress Feedback in Youth Mental Health

Susan Douglas, Grace Woodard, Jordan Zahora, Tasha Love, and Amanda Jensen-Doss

Transforming Data into Action: A Case Study on Progress Feedback in Youth Mental Health

> I believe the greatest gift I can conceive of having from anyone is to be seen by them, heard by them, to be understood and touched by them. The greatest gift I can give is to see, hear, understand and to touch another person. When this is done, I feel contact has been made.—Virginia Satir (1916–1988)

The practice of using patient-reported measures to track outcomes over the course of treatment has developed considerably, since it was first proposed two decades ago (Bickman, 2008; Lambert et al., 2003). While the notion of using measures to inform treatment progress seems simple, it is a complex intervention that requires shifts in how patients engage with their clinicians, how clinicians accomplish their work, and how the ecosystem of the organization supports and embeds these changes. Perhaps that complexity has contributed to the lack of agreement in naming the intervention, with terms focused on the monitoring aspect of using measures (routine outcome monitoring, or ROM), the measures themselves (measurement-based care, or MBC), or the interpreted results (progress feedback). For the purposes of this chapter, we use "progress feedback," in part due to our bias toward the alchemical process of transforming data (as signal) to information (interpreted for meaning making) to knowledge (actionable insights). It is that latter step that is

S. Douglas (✉) · J. Zahora
Department of Leadership, Policy, and Organizations, Vanderbilt University, Peabody College, Nashville, TN, USA
e-mail: susan.douglas@vanderbilt.edu

G. Woodard · A. Jensen-Doss
Department of Psychology, University of Miami, Coral Gables, FL, USA

T. Love
Health Connect America, Columbia, TN, USA

J. A. Rubel, W. Lutz (eds.), *Feedback Informed Psychological Therapy*, CBT: Science Into Practice, https://doi.org/10.1007/978-3-031-90428-8_14

perhaps the most profound and relevant to how we implement this intervention. Ultimately, the interpreted signals must be organized through the human lens of experience and learning to inform actionable insights (Weinberger, 2010).

Progress feedback is regarded as an evidence-based practice, reflected in professional practice guidelines for evidence-based practice (American Psychological Association, 2021), support for its own professional practice guideline (Boswell et al., 2023), and the consensus of 37 professional organizations (Coalition for the Advancement and Application of Psychological Science, 2018). Meta-analyses have concluded that progress feedback decreases treatment dropout and increases symptom reduction (e.g., De Jong et al., 2021), and individual studies suggest that these effects are most pronounced when it is implemented with fidelity (e.g., Bickman et al., 2011, 2016; Sale et al., 2021; van Sonsbeek et al., 2021, 2023).

Progress feedback is generally regarded as a multicomponent practice that includes patients (and associated others, such as caregivers) routinely completing measures of treatment target mechanisms (e.g., alliance, engagement) and/or clinical outcomes, clinicians then viewing the feedback from the measures, sharing and acting on that feedback with patients, and using the feedback to guide clinical case conceptualization and adaptive treatment planning (e.g., Barber & Resnick, 2022; Barkham et al., 2023; Jensen-Doss et al., 2020; Lewis et al., 2019). There is some evidence that the mechanisms by which progress feedback works include focusing the attention of the clinician, changing clinician expectations, providing new information, and enhancing patient–clinician communication (De Jong et al., 2024; Herzog et al., 2023). In youth community mental health settings, there is an additional layer of complexity introduced by the inclusion of caregivers and families into the treatment model. On the one hand, this means greater difficulty because the clinician must engage with more than one key actor to encourage the completion of measures and use of progress feedback. On the other hand, the feedback has uniquely useful information with the new element of youth- and caregiver-score comparisons on measures used.

This chapter will briefly review the evidence for effectiveness and implementation in community mental health settings serving youths and their caregivers. We will focus on implementation and include a richly descriptive case example to highlight salient points.

Brief Review of Progress Feedback in Youth Mental Health

Most studies supporting progress feedback have been conducted in adult samples, but the studies that have been conducted in youth samples show comparable effect sizes to studies in adults (De Jong et al., 2021). This finding is promising, given that implementing progress feedback with youth patients can be more complex than with adult patients. Unlike adult treatment, which typically involves one patient participating in treatment alone, youth therapy usually involves one or more caregivers in addition to the youth patient, and progress feedback therefore should involve multiple informants (Jensen-Doss et al., 2020). Decades of research have shown that different informants provide distinct information about treatment targets and outcomes (De Los Reyes et al., 2023), including in the literature on the effectiveness of progress feedback, where studies have found different impacts of progress feedback based on youth versus caregiver report (e.g., Bickman et al., 2011, 2016). While this information can be highly useful in providing a well-rounded picture of how youth are functioning to inform case conceptualization (De Los Reyes et al., 2022; Jensen-Doss & McLeod, 2020), it does require additional effort on the part of the clinician to integrate these perspectives. Shared decision-making strategies may need to be integrated into the use of progress feedback with youth to incorporate discrepant perspectives into a treatment plan (Fitzpatrick et al., 2023).

Implementation Matters

Progress feedback implementation is dynamic and complex (Douglas et al., 2023). Poor implementation at one level (e.g., infrequent feedback viewing by clinicians) can contribute to challenges at another level (e.g., lower measure completion by patients and caregivers). van Sonsbeek et al. (2021) called this the "vicious cycle," where the multiple components of progress feedback practice are likely interdependent. Here, we will focus on three key aspects of implementation drawn from the literature and our own experience supporting the implementation of progress feedback in youth community mental health settings. The first is to create a "golden thread" of reinforcing feedback loops from the bottom-up and top-down by attending to the unique value and use that progress feedback represents to patients and their families, clinicians, supervisors, clinical leaders, and executive leaders. Next, we zoom into the clinician's experience with progress feedback and the notion of cognitive dissonance as a critical lever of change. Finally, we propose an approach to indexing implementation to create clarity in performance metrics for measure completion and feedback viewing.

Focus on Value to Promote Use

We believe that progress feedback is a key strategy to realizing integrated data-informed decision-making at every level of a youth mental health care organization. We call this the "golden thread" of feedback (Douglas et al., 2016), where the use of real-time data in the form of feedback creates value for the users, thereby creating a positive reinforcement loop that promotes greater use. At the individual level, patient goals are linked to real-time data resulting from patient- and caregiver-reported measures. Data are then aggregated at the clinician level to inform supervision, at the program level to inform service planning, and the organization level to inform executive strategy.

Level	Potential to Inform	Potential to Improve
Encounter	Clinical conversation & actions	Shared understanding and therapeutic alliance (Brattland et al., 2019; Chen et al., 2018; Connors et al., 2023; De Jong et al., 2023a; Jensen-Doss et al., 2020)
Client	Clinical hypotheses & treatment approach	Collaborative treatment planning, case conceptualization, and goal attainment (Connors et al., 2023; Douglas et al., 2015; Jensen-Doss et al., 2020; Jensen-Doss & McLeod, 2020)
Clinician	Professional development	Clinical supervision and ongoing learning and development (Connors et al., 2021; Fortney et al., 2017; Lyon, Stanick, & Pullman, 2018)
Program	Service planning	Quality improvement efforts, such as adopting and sustaining evidence-based practices (Connors et al., 2021; Douglas et al., 2016; 2023b; Jensen-Doss et al., 2020)
Organization	Executive strategy	Organizational learning and performance metrics, external reporting to funders and reimbursement agencies (Connors et al., 2021; Jensen-Doss et al., 2020)
Health System	Generation of practice-based evidence	Spread of practice-level structures and policies for data use and documentation, adaptations of EBPs to local contexts and cultures, and rapid-cycle innovation and translation methods (Connors et al., 2021; Youn et al., 2023)

Fig. 14.1 The golden thread of feedback: focusing on value to promote use

The golden thread approach can create more data and better data for use at all levels by focusing attention on the value it creates, which differs by level. Figure 14.1 presents a simple framework for how the golden thread approach can guide the focus on value at each level of care. For example, at the point of service, or encounter level, the value lies in the potential of feedback to inform the conversation, thereby improving shared understanding and therapeutic alliance (Brattland et al., 2019; Chen et al., 2018; Connors et al., 2024). Another example is at the service planning level. In a case study presented by Douglas et al. (2024), measures of sleep problems and other predictors of self-harm were added to a service to guide treatment improvement efforts when working with suicidal patients (Kyron et al., 2021, 2022).

A critical aspect of the golden thread approach to guide implementation of progress feedback is the notion of multiple and overlapping reinforcement loops across levels of the system. Positive (or negative) influences on feedback use can come from any level. In our experience across multiple research studies on progress feedback over the past two decades (e.g., Bickman et al., 2011, 2016; Douglas et al., 2023; Jensen-Doss et al., 2018; Jensen-Doss & Douglas, 2020 November–2024 May), key actors in creating positive reinforcement loops to promote greater and ongoing feedback use are clinicians, supervisors, and clinical and executive leaders. Leaders and supervisors are critical to feedback use, because they carry the responsibility of creating structures, establishing processes and policies, and setting expectations to guide performance. However, the linchpin actor is likely the clinician, who operates within the performance setting established by their managers and is the "face" of the intervention for their patients.

Supporting Clinicians New to Progress Feedback to Reach the "Aha Moment"

We know from research on common factors of treatment that clinician beliefs in the value of the interventions they use influence patient perceptions and outcomes (see review in Douglas Kelley et al., 2010a). Figure 14.2 shows an image we use in our

Fig. 14.2 Zeroing in on the clinician's developmental experience: getting to the "Aha moment"

feedback education that represents what we called the "progress feedback learning curve." The figure was developed over many years of training and supporting clinical staff in the use of progress feedback to show the reinforcement loops in action. It is intended to educate leaders and supervisors about the need for ongoing support long past the initial training. It is also intended as a form of inoculation for clinicians, so they may expect that there can be a dip in enthusiasm or actual use of feedback as they begin to shift in their clinical workflow and their lived experience of communicating with patients using progress feedback.

In the figure, the curved line represents the clinician's comfort with and confidence in using progress feedback with their patients. Early after being introduced to progress feedback, clinicians may expect to experience high motivation and feelings of support through initial training. However, once the novelty has worn off and the intensity of support has waned, clinicians may begin to experience the challenges that come with instituting a new practice into their existing clinical workflow and changing how they engage with patients and their families. We believe this is a crucial time for supervisors and clinical leaders to increase their efforts to provide support, which can range from encouragement and problem-solving to decrease barriers and increase ease of use, to clear expectations for feedback use as a clinic service like any other.

The "aha moment" refers to the intrinsic and/or extrinsic motivation that stems from the first time the clinician experiences the difference that progress feedback can make in a session. According to the contextual feedback intervention theory (CFIT; Riemer & Bickman, 2011), this corresponds to a time when the clinician recognizes a discrepancy between their case conceptualization and what they see in the feedback measures, leading to a feeling of cognitive dissonance. It may be a time when they learn something they didn't already know about a patient, or when sharing a feedback graph in a session leads to a meaningful clinical conversation. Importantly, the feeling of cognitive dissonance is uncomfortable and constitutes a moment of vulnerability for the clinician, where they will either accept the feedback or dismiss it as invalid, incorrect, or not applicable. It is critical for supervisors and clinical leaders to create an environment supportive of openness and self-efficacy in response to feedback, and for clinicians to be aware of their own biases in response to positive or negative feedback (Riemer & Bickman, 2011). When they can remain open to feedback and accept it as useful information for insight and action, the clinician experiences the value that progress feedback can bring. Once that "aha moment" occurs, the clinician's comfort and confidence in use may increase along with their belief in progress feedback as a useful intervention.

As of this writing, the progress feedback learning curve is anecdotal, supported by our experience working with clinicians across different settings using different forms of progress feedback. While useful as a general concept to progress feedback training efforts, it lacks specificity in what level of use would shift someone into the "We've got this!" level. The field of progress feedback sorely lacks an understanding of what expectations should be set to guide implementation efforts. In other words, what is "good enough" feedback use?

Getting to "Good Enough"

As stated earlier, our practice model of progress feedback in youth community mental health settings consists of four components: completion of patient- and other-reported measures, viewing of feedback reports by clinicians, addressing feedback in sessions, and using feedback to guide clinical actions, such as treatment planning. However, research on understanding fidelity to progress feedback has primarily focused on measure administration and feedback viewing, with significantly less attention paid to how feedback is used within and outside of treatment sessions (Casline et al., 2022; Holliday et al., 2021). There is a critical need for research that can identify the practices that are and are not essential for progress feedback to be effective to help implementation efforts focus on training and monitoring essential clinician behaviors. That said, there is some literature that can help us think about "good enough" use of progress feedback.

How often should we measure? This is a question that has been raised repeatedly in the feedback literature, with some evidence for linking the frequency of measure administration to the session schedule (Barkham et al., 2023; Bickman et al., 2011, 2016; De Jong et al., 2021; Janse et al., 2020), while also accounting for the stability of the measured construct and the measure's sensitivity to change (Connors et al., 2024; Douglas Kelley & Bickman, 2009). Another critical question is: *When patient-reported measures have been completed, how often should the clinician be expected to view the resulting feedback report with interpreted information to inform treatment?* In the ideal world, it would be 100% of the time. Clinicians would view every feedback report and, in the process, address the feedback in sessions. However, this expectation fails to account for the dynamic and complex environment of mental health treatment, where priorities may shift based on patient presentation and clinician judgment. While data do support the notion that more frequent feedback viewing is associated with better outcomes, we don't yet know how much feedback viewing is needed to tip the scales for better outcomes.

For example, after the intention-to-treat (ITT) analyses were completed for their randomized controlled trials (RCTs), Bickman et al. (2011, 2016) conducted dose-response analyses, where they examined the proportion of feedback reports viewed using hierarchical linear models. While dose analyses are correlational, meaning that it is possible for non-feedback variables (e.g., clinician characteristics) to account for any relationships observed, they help us to better understand the cumulative effects of feedback viewing by clinicians on patient outcomes. For their 2011 RCT, with 144 clinicians who treated 340 youth over the course of the study, one-third of the clinicians in the feedback group did not view any feedback. After those cases were eliminated from analyses, effect sizes grew to 0.27 (from 0.18) for self-reported youth symptoms and 0.40 (from 0.24) for clinician-reported youth symptoms, increases of 50% and 66%, respectively. There was no increase in effect size for caregiver-reported youth symptoms, which remained at 0.27. Thus, the dose-response curve shows us that feedback may have a stronger effect on the rate of clinical progress when clinicians view more of the available reports.

Bickman and colleagues took a different approach with their 2016 RCT, where the ITT analyses found an effect of feedback at only one of two clinics, and only for clinician-reported outcomes. For patients in the feedback condition, they calculated a composite implementation index to estimate whether and how much youth patients' improvement increased with the amount of feedback reports viewed by clinicians. In other words, the implementation index captures the potential amount of the feedback intervention that could have been received by the clinician. The algorithm to calculate the index is shown in Fig. 14.3, with a more detailed discussion available in Bickman et al. (2016). The utility of the implementation index to estimate the dose of feedback intervention appears promising, with a mode of 0% for the clinic with a failed implementation and a mode of 50% (mean of 34%) for the clinic where feedback had a small effect on youth patient outcomes. In addition,

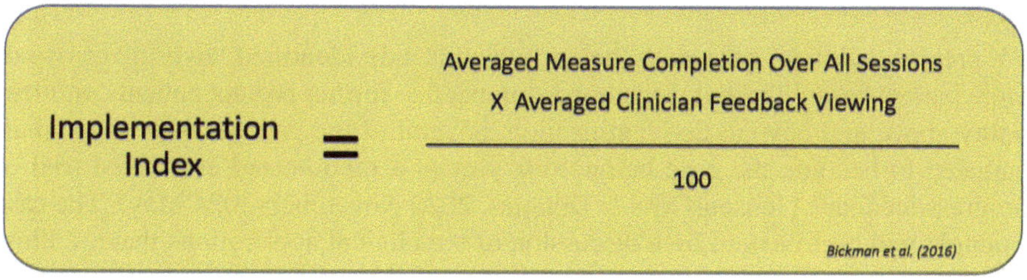

Fig. 14.3 Implementation index to estimate the potential for the clinician to apply progress feedback

when the implementation index was applied as a covariate in hierarchical linear model analyses, there was no dose effect for the clinic with an implementation failure (i.e., youth patients improved over the course of treatment regardless of the dose of feedback). For the other clinic, there was a dose effect of feedback for the youth self-report and clinician-report of youth symptoms, indicating that the higher the implementation index, the faster youth outcomes improved.

The field has made little progress toward identifying what is "good enough" completion of measures by patients and caregivers and feedback viewing by clinicians. Feedback researchers need to increase reporting of basic implementation rates of measure completion and feedback viewing, and ideally provide dose-response estimates using a strategy like the implementation index. In addition, there are other critical questions to ask, such as *How often should progress feedback be addressed in sessions and used to inform clinical actions?* There is likely a "sweet spot" of good enough implementation where the use of feedback becomes a self-sustaining reinforcement loop. Knowing this information is necessary to create realistic and attainable expectations for organizational leaders and clinicians to use when setting performance goals related to progress feedback.

Finally, for all these practices, we know from the treatment fidelity research that a focus on perfection (i.e., 100% feedback viewing rates) may be ineffective or even harmful to good care (Hagermoser Sanetti & Kratochwill, 2014). To paraphrase the French writer and activist, Voltaire, "The perfect is the enemy of good." In the case of progress feedback implementation, it is essential to go beyond more traditional concepts like "reliable" and "valid" measurement to include a focus on clinical utility. McLeod et al. (2022) lay out a framework for clinical utility for progress feedback approaches grounded in *implementability* (i.e., whether the approach can be used in a particular clinical setting) and *usefulness in aiding clinical activities* (i.e., whether the approach has the potential to improve care in a meaningful way). The "right" way to use progress feedback is going to depend on the characteristics and goals of the practice setting where it is being used, and the focus should always be on using it to improve care.

Clinical Case Example: Using Feedback for Improved Family Communication and Shared Understanding

We present a clinical case study below, which is a de-identified "hybrid" of two or more patient cases. The hybridization is intended to further protect patient confidentiality above and beyond de-identification. Several of the patients who were amalgamated to become the case below took part in a randomized controlled trial of progress feedback (Jensen-Doss & Douglas, 2020 November–2024 May). The case example will be followed by a discussion of the clinical applications that are illustrated here.

Youth Patient and Family Characteristics

In June 2020, Stella, a 14-year-old, Non-Hispanic White, non-binary adolescent, began home-based therapy at a community mental health clinic. They were diagnosed with Major Depressive Disorder and Generalized Anxiety Disorder. Their treatment goals included (1) sharing their gender identity[1] with their family, (2) learning healthy coping skills, and (3) improving grades at school. In-home services were provided three times a week in the family home, with treatment tailored to meet the needs of the patient and family's unique situation. Services could include crisis intervention and treatment, individual and family counseling, communication skills, and case management.

At the time of referral, Stella lived with their mother, Penny, stepfather, and older sister in a rural area in the Northwestern United States. Their father died by suicide when Stella was a young child after many years of depression and substance use. There was no other family history of psychiatric illness reported by Stella's mother. Since her late husband's death, Penny felt detached from her children. Penny remarried when Stella was in middle school, and at the time of referral, she was spending much of her time playing video games or with her husband.

Stella attended a small, public high school and had several friends at school with whom they shared interests. Historically, Stella performed in the average range at school with mostly B's and some A's in language arts and C's in mathematics. While Stella was shy and slow-to-warm up, they made several friends through the robotics club at their high school. Most of Stella's interactions with their friends were at school or via social media. Stella rarely saw their friends outside of school and hardly ever brought them home. During the intake, Stella said they did not feel close to their family and felt embarrassed to bring their friends to a small house that is cluttered. Stella had no reported health issues and had regular checkups and vaccinations as recommended by their pediatrician.

Presenting Problems and Diagnoses

Stella began to exhibit symptoms of depression and anxiety, as they started questioning their gender identity during the COVID-19 pandemic. Stella spent more time online at that time, and they noticed a feeling of detachment from being associated with traditionally feminine interests and appearance. Stella began to feel uncomfortable in traditionally feminine clothes, so they began to dress in a more androgynous way. As Stella's appearance began to shift, they were faced with community and internalized transphobia. Their stepfather wondered if they were

[1] At the beginning of treatment, Stella was still using she/her pronouns, but during the course of treatment revealed they felt their pronouns were actually they/them. They/them will be used throughout this discussion to be consistent with Stella's identity.

"gaining weight" since they started wearing "baggy clothes." As school began in person again, Stella's peers mocked their appearance, which prompted the beginning of self-critical thoughts about their appearance and wondering if their gender dysphoria was because they were "permanently messed up" by their father's death by suicide.

Stella began to have difficulty falling and staying asleep, reporting that they would stay up worrying about whether their family would still love them if they knew how they felt. Stella felt like a failure who was disappointing their family, had a depressed mood almost every day, and withdrew from activities they enjoyed (e.g., robotics club). Stella began to spend more time online, where they developed new online friendships with people who identified as non-binary. While it felt fulfilling to find friends with whom they could share their identity, they were envious of the support their non-binary friends had from friends and family as most of them lived in more urban areas of the United States. Stella's grades began to suffer, and they began to receive C's and D's in several classes (e.g., mathematics, science). As Stella thought about how many years they had left hiding who they were from their family and friends at school, they began to feel despair and hopelessness. They began to wish they would not wake up from sleep, and then started to have more active thoughts about self-harming and dying by suicide. As these thoughts became more specific and more frequent, they asked Penny and their stepfather to enroll them in outpatient therapy. While their parents were reluctant to enroll them in therapy, Stella discussed their fears based on their father's death by suicide. Stella's parents then agreed to help them find treatment if it was convenient and affordable.

Treatment Course Informed by Progress Feedback

The community mental health clinic where Stella received care used a progress feedback technology called Mirah. Mirah is software-as-a-service (SAAS) with all measures completed online, and once submitted, available as interpreted information presented in clinical feedback reports. The feedback protocol included the Symptoms and Functioning Severity Scale (SFSS; Athay et al., 2012), which is part of the Peabody Treatment Progress Battery (PTPB; Bickman et al., 2010). The SFSS is a brief and psychometrically sound measure of youth internalizing and externalizing symptoms that was specifically created for use in feedback. It can be completed by multiple respondents, including youths, their caregivers, clinicians, and teachers. The youth self-report and caregiver report were utilized by the clinic where Diana worked. Because the SFSS can be administered as frequently as once a week, the measure was automatically set to be sent out to respondents in conjunction with the first session within a given week for patients receiving in-home services.

At the intake appointment, Diana oriented the family to the services they would receive, which included progress feedback. In addition to giving them a flier with more information, Diana introduced progress feedback to Stella and Penny as a tool to improve communication among all of them and to ensure treatment was focused on their agreed upon goals. While Stella seemed open to trying this tool, Penny voiced some frustration with being asked to "do paperwork" each week. Because they lived in an area with adequate cell coverage, administration of measures was available online. To complete their measures, Stella and Penny each received clickable links in text messages to their respective mobile telephone numbers. The links were sent out 48 hours before a scheduled session, with reminders to complete up to the time of the session. If needed, Diana could also manually send out links or offer her tablet computing device for data entry. Once measures were completed, Diana was able to pull up clinical feedback reports on her tablet for visual reference when addressing feedback in sessions.

As can be seen in Fig. 14.4, near the beginning of treatment, Stella reported moderate-to-severe impairment for themself, while Penny indicated that her daughter experienced mild-to-no impairment. When viewing feedback reports with their clinician, Stella voiced frustration to Diana that their mother could not see the pain they were in. Stella noted that they stay in their room all the time at home, their grades have dropped, and they stopped attending robotics club, which were all behaviors they thought their mother should notice. Stella was motivated to review the feedback graphs with Diana each week to see if their mother's report had become more aligned with their own. When asked about their experience completing the feedback measures, Stella noted that they wished there were more questions about their gender dysphoria. When Diana suggested telling Penny about how much they were suffering, Stella was reluctant, saying they were afraid that their mother would be invalidating and transphobic. Stella and Diana decided to begin using they/them pronouns, which Stella used with their friends online, to help them feel affirmed in session.

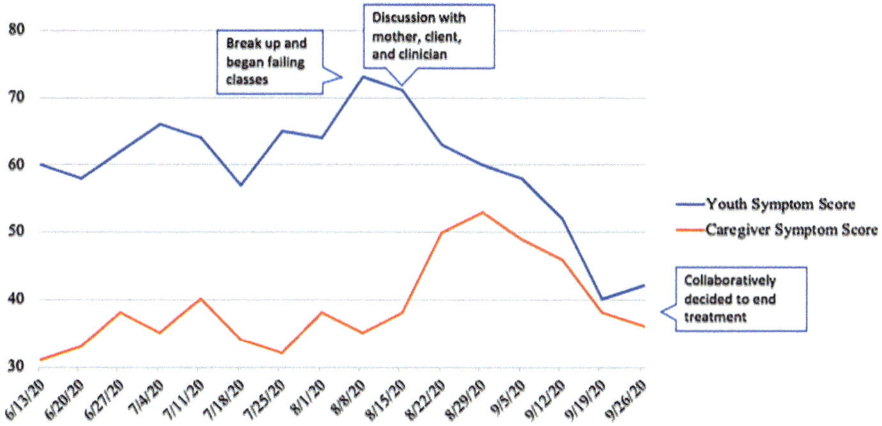

Fig. 14.4 Progress feedback data with significant clinical events for the clinical case of Stella: Youth- and caregiver-reports from the Symptoms and Functioning Scale (SFSS; Athay et al., 2012)

Diana initiated a family session with Stella and Penny to review the progress feedback report together. Penny seemed distracted and left part of the way through the session to play video games, saying that therapy was for her child and thus she didn't need to be there. Stella shared feelings of disappointment and that it felt like their mother did not care about them. Three months into treatment, around their 15th birthday in August, Stella ended a relationship with a significant other and began to make failing grades in several classes, which triggered the school to call Penny. In the next session, Stella and Diana were reviewing the feedback graphs when Stella's mother joined the session, which was being held in the family's living room. Penny began to voice frustration and anger at Stella over their failing grades. Stella responded by asking if their mom could see the difference in how they each responded on the measures and if she could see how much Stella was struggling. Diana showed Penny the feedback graph (see Fig. 14.4) with the difference in their scores. Also, she clicked around on the interactive feedback report to show Penny how Stella had responded to individual items, including one that indicated Stella was having suicidal ideation.

Penny looked saddened, said she felt surprised, and subsequently became more engaged in the therapy session. At that moment, Stella decided to tell their mother that they did not feel like a girl, or like a boy, and identified as non-binary and wanted to use "they" pronouns instead of "she." Stella's mother initially pushed back, saying that she herself had dressed like a boy sometimes growing up but it didn't mean she wasn't a girl. However, with support from Diana after seeing how her statements impacted Stella, Penny stopped arguing and stated that she didn't understand but she loved Stella and saw that this conversation was important to them. Penny said she was going to try to do a better job being there for Stella and was going to love them anyway.

After this session, Penny agreed to engage in regular family sessions in addition to Stella's regular individual sessions with Diana. Notably, Penny began rating her child's symptoms in the more severe range, indicating greater awareness of Stella's anxious and depressive symptoms. After the initial increase in Penny's ratings, both Stella and their mother began reporting steady improvements in Stella's symptoms. Stella's grades improved, they started attending robotics club again, and they felt freer to dress in a more androgynous way. A few weeks after the session, in September 2020, Diana, Stella, and Penny collaboratively decided to end treatment.

Reflections on Using Progress Feedback with Stella

Stella's case illustrates several important concepts of how progress feedback can be used to transform care for youth and their families. Here, we highlight four salient takeaways, focused on: (1) using informant discrepancies, (2) using feedback reports as a visual tool in session, (3) approaching progress feedback with openness and curiosity, and (4) gathering progress feedback beyond just standardized symptom measures.

Use Discrepancies as Guideposts for Shared Understanding and Better Collaboration

As stated earlier, a useful feature of progress feedback for youth patients is to shine a light on the youth mental health ecosystem from different perspectives, allowing clinicians to understand the subjective experience of each respondent (e.g., youths, caregivers, and teachers). Connors et al. (2024) call these discrepancies among respondents "diamonds-in-the-rough" that can assist clinicians with helping youths and caregivers come to a shared understanding of the problems being faced, which then contributes to collaborative goal setting. In addition to promoting greater understanding of multiple perspectives, respondent discrepancies can be useful opportunities to explore internal factors (e.g., previously held motivations and beliefs) and external factors (e.g., cultural values, norms) that may influence how we interpret and subsequently act (or not) on new information. This type of exploratory discussion can be well suited to the therapy setting and contribute to greater propensity to update beliefs in light of reliable information (Herzog et al., 2023).

In our example, the feedback report highlighted the lack of awareness of Stella's symptoms by their mother, Penny. Early in the course of treatment, there were several behaviors that seemed to indicate disengagement by Penny, including a reluctance to start treatment for Stella and dismissing progress feedback as just more paperwork. In addition, during the first few months of treatment when she was reporting low scores for Stella's internalizing and externalizing problems, Penny frequently became distracted or left treatment sessions, particularly around the discussion of feedback data. It is possible that the in-home treatment setting may have exacerbated the potential for Penny to disengage from sessions in a way that would have been more challenging in a clinic-based treatment session. However, it is also possible that Stella's mother would not have even entered the clinic or agreed to Stella beginning treatment if it had been clinic-based..

Notably, Penny's ratings of her child's symptoms abruptly increased in severity following the session where she engaged in a conversation with Diana and Stella about the feedback and Stella's challenges. The two respondents' ratings of Stella's symptoms converged, serving as an indicator of shared understanding throughout the remainder of treatment as both respondents reported improvement over time until discharge. This pattern of disengagement (and discrepancy) followed by engagement (and convergence) is consistent with research evidence that discrepancies in symptom ratings between youths and caregivers predict poorer treatment engagement, while convergence in ratings is associated with better treatment outcomes (see Connors et al., 2024 for more detail).

Use Visuals as Props for Validation and Voice

Stella consistently asked to view the feedback reports in treatment sessions. As seen in Fig. 14.4, the graph of symptom scores by both respondents showed Stella's scores being much more severe than those of their mother. Thus, the graphs seemed to validate the distance Stella felt from their mother and provided visual evidence to communicate this experience with their therapist, Diana. When Diana created opportunities to view the data together in sessions, it set the stage for a therapeutic conversation that incorporated and expanded on the feedback data. During those discussions, Stella was able to express their sadness toward their mother's disengagement and disclosed their gender identity as non-binary, which contributed to the development of treatment goals.

Given the power dynamics within families, children and adolescents may experience a lack of being heard, which is a common focus of family-oriented treatment models (Broder, 2010; Gammer, 2009; Moore & Seu, 2011). Perhaps, the visual nature of progress feedback allows youths to displace their internal and external conflicts, leading to greater comfort in the neutrality of discussing them in the context of a graph or other visual feedback element (e.g., item ratings). This could be similar to the play therapy technique of supporting a child to displace feelings connected to a person or a situation to an object, like a stuffed animal, to encourage voice for what is uncomfortable (Senko & Harper, 2019). This may also be related to the suggested utility of progress feedback in telemedicine, where clinicians value the visual information to engage youth clients in conversation when they lack the physicality of an in-person session (Donelan et al., 2024; Douglas et al., 2020).

Connors et al. (2024) suggest that progress feedback can help to surface difficult conversations between youths and their families, which is consistent with what we found in the case example shared above. Stella expressed some fears about their mother's reactions to their struggles and movement toward a non-binary gender identity. It is possible that viewing the feedback reports, where their symptom scores continued to deteriorate and their mother's ratings of their symptoms largely remained low and stable, served as a motivation to initiate a conversation. The therapist's facilitation of the conversation between Stella and Penny may have helped Stella feel safer to disclose and may have shaped their mother's willingness to accept the disclosure. Importantly, this highlights the need for discussion of the limits of confidentiality and informed consent to share feedback when working with youths and their caregivers. We recommend that decisions about sharing feedback be an explicit and collaborative decision among all who are involved in the youth's treatment to respect individual and family preference (Connors et al., 2024). This is consistent with best practices for professional ethics around confidentiality when working with youth patients, where boundary negotiations around privacy are an important part of treatment (Behnke & Warner, 2002).

Remain Open to Feedback and Stay Curious

A critical role for the clinician in facilitating conversations to improve communication and shared understanding of youth symptoms among the youth and their family members is to hold the mindset that *feedback suggests rather than tells*. For example, in Stella's case, someone who was not familiar with their treatment could look at the feedback report and interpret the increase in parent-reported symptoms as evidence of Stella deteriorating. However, Stella's therapist Diana was able to incorporate that feedback with her case conceptualization to understand that this reflected Penny's increased understanding of Stella's true symptom levels and therefore represented a positive shift.

Connors et al. (2024) suggest that this mindset shift can decentralize the data just enough to elevate the human perspective that puts the context around the information being conveyed. Although more research is needed, we think that the displacement effect of visual feedback suggested in the section above may be just as useful to helping clinicians take action by generating hypotheses from the data (De Jong et al., 2023; Jensen-Doss et al., 2020). By remaining open, curious, and eager to explore together with a patient and their family, it may be easier for a clinician to "think out loud" to allow ideas to emerge rather than waiting to "get it right." Feedback has been shown to benefit clinicians with high self-efficacy more than those with low self-efficacy (Janse et al., 2023), which may indicate a corrective effect of feedback to alert clinicians to patient problems (Douglas et al., 2015). As Shunryu Suzuki (2020) says, "In the beginner's mind there are many possibilities, in the expert's mind there are few." Learning to hold a beginner's mindset might be particularly important to shed light on clinician bias, or general style in how they approach the treatment process (Douglas Kelley et al., 2010b).

Anecdotally, we have been struck by the profound influence of an attitude of openness and curiosity on the part of the clinician, especially when confronted with challenging feedback. T. Love, a highly skilled clinician and co-author of this chapter, shared that using progress feedback has helped her surface assumptions that she made about parental attitudes toward a patient's non-binary gender identity, thereby opening up possibilities for using the feedback as described in the case above. In another example shared by N.E. Gomez (a clinician and co-author on Jensen-Doss et al., 2020), drastically declining scores on an alliance measure helped her question assumptions she had made about a child patient's use of video games for coping, which opened up possibilities for greater patient voice in determining treatment tasks and goals.

When we train clinicians to use progress feedback, we coach them to engage with the feedback data from a place of active curiosity and even playfulness, rather than simply information-seeking. The data can serve as a prompt for powerful questions (Heron, 2001), even simple ones where a clinician shows a feedback report and asks, "What do you notice?". A pilot of our coaching model was adapted for the use of progress feedback in group therapy. Developed with Edith De Wolf and Marjolein Koementas-de Vos, the coaching model was highly rated by clinicians (average of 7.7 out of 10) and contributed to clinician experimentation with using feedback in group therapy (Koementas-de Vos et al., 2024). However, although patients reported experiencing a greater frequency of feedback discussions that were rated as useful compared to patients whose clinicians had not gone through the training, there was less improvement on outcome measures. It is unclear whether this lack of improvement was due to the nature of the group treatment, the clinicians' approach to using feedback in group treatment, or the relevance of the measures themselves.

Think Beyond Standardized Symptom Measures

We have written elsewhere (Connors et al., 2021, 2024; Douglas Kelley & Bickman, 2009; Jensen-Doss et al., 2020) about the benefits of using multiple measures, including standardized (nomothetic) and individualized (ideographic) measures. Standardized measures, including broad-band measures to capture new or emerging symptoms, and narrow-band measures to focus specifically on patient presenting problems, allow clinicians to assess patient progress using clinical norms and organizations to easily aggregate data for program planning. However, as shown in the case example above, such measures don't always capture what is important to the patient and thus what would be most meaningful and relevant to inform clinical conversations and actions.

Stella stated that the feedback measure captured most of the symptoms important in understanding their mental health, but that they wished the measures had included questions about their gender identity. This case shows the power of nomothetic measurement, in being able to compare Stella's and their mother's scores to those of similar-aged youths but suggests that care may have been further enhanced by use of ideographic measurement of their gender dysphoria and discriminatory experiences. However, it would have been critical to take care not to show such items or ratings to Penny to avoid "outing" Stella to their mother.

Another way that progress feedback could have been expanded to support Stella's care would be by incorporating additional measures of treatment processes, such as the therapy alliance or engagement, or potential moderators of outcome, such as motivation for treatment, to help make feedback more "actionable" (Jensen-Doss et al., 2020; Connors et al., 2024). Bickman et al. (2016) have proposed that such measures can facilitate a "precision mental health approach," tailored to the specific needs, preferences, and characteristics of patients. In Stella's case, measures like the Motivation for Youth's Treatment Scale (MYTS; Breda & Riemer, 2012) could have been used to identify and monitor their mother's low motivation for being involved early in treatment, and it could have been helpful to monitor both Stella and their mother's alliance with the therapist throughout care to identify and address potential alliance ruptures (Chen et al., 2018; Rubel et al., 2018).

Where Do We Go from Here?

The quantification of deeply personal human stories represented in graphical form can mistakenly contribute to a sense that the data override the lived experience. We believe this is one of the most critical barriers to successful implementation of progress feedback and is at the heart of the cognitive dissonance that clinicians will experience when they begin to use progress feedback. There is an inherent tussle between "objective" data and "subjective" experience where the patient-reported measure scores are translated through the creative and complex human mind. Weinberger (2010, 2019), who writes about knowledge management in the age of big data, cautions that knowledge generation is not just about filtering out the noise to get clean data. Instead, actionable knowledge is "a far more complex process that is social, goal-driven, contextual, and culturally-bound" (p. 3, Weinberger, 2010).

The messiness of actionable knowledge has great implications for how clinicians learn to practice the clinical skill of using feedback, and for how organizations can reliably utilize aggregated data for quality improvement and performance. As a field, we should continue to focus on the *what* of progress feedback, such as measure content and frequency, and how the resulting interpreted information is displayed. However, we believe that better implementation will come only from widening our aperture to focus more on the patient, clinician, and system-level factors that influence *how* progress feedback improves mental health outcomes.

Acknowledgments Dr. Douglas' and Dr. Jensen-Doss' time on this manuscript was supported by R34 MH118316.

Conflict of Interest Disclosures Vanderbilt University and Susan Douglas receive compensation related to the Peabody Treatment Progress Battery (PTPB); and Susan Douglas has a financial relationship with MIRAH, and both are Measurement-Based Care (MBC) tools. The author declares a potential conflict of interest. There is a management plan in place at Vanderbilt University to monitor that this potential conflict does not jeopardize the objectivity of Dr. Douglas' research.

References

American Psychological Association. (2021). *Professional practice guidelines for evidence-based psychological practice in health care.* Retrieved from https://www.apa.org/about/policy/psychological-practice-health-care.pdf

Athay, M. M., Riemer, M., & Bickman, L. (2012). The symptoms and functioning severity scale (SFSS): Psychometric evaluation and discrepancies among youth, caregiver, and clinician ratings over time. *Administration and Policy in Mental Health, 39*(1–2), 13–29. https://doi.org/10.1007/s10488-012-0403-2

Barber, J., & Resnick, S. G. (2022). Collect, share, act: A transtheoretical clinical model for doing measurement-based care in mental health treatment. *Psychological Services.* https://doi.org/10.1037/ser0000629

Barkham, M., De Jong, K., Delgadillo, J., & Lutz, W. (2023). Routine outcome monitoring (ROM) and feedback: Research review and recommendations. *Psychotherapy Research, 33*(7), 841–855. https://doi.org/10.1080/10503307.2023.2181114

Behnke, S. H., & Warner, E. (2002). Confidentiality in the treatment of adolescents. *Monitor on Psychology, 33*(3), 44. Retrieved from https://www.apa.org/monitor/mar02/confidentiality

Bickman, L. (2008). A measurement feedback system (MFS) is necessary to improve mental health outcomes. *Journal of the American Academy of Child & Adolescent Psychiatry, 47*(10), 1114–1119. Retrieved from http://dx.doi.org.proxy.library.vanderbilt.edu/10.1097/CHI.0b013e3181825af8

Bickman, L., Athay, M., Riemer, M., Lambert, E. W., Douglas Kelley, S., Breda, C., Tempesti, T., Dew-Reeves, S. E., Brannan, A. M., & Vides de Andrade, A. R. (2010). *Manual of the Peabody treatment progress battery* (2nd ed.). Vanderbilt University.

Bickman, L., Kelley, S. D., Breda, C., de Andrade, A. R., & Riemer, M. (2011). Effects of routine feedback to clinicians on mental health outcomes of youths: Results of a randomized trial. *Psychiatric Services, 62*(12), 1423–1429. https://doi.org/10.1176/appi.ps.002052011

Bickman, L., Douglas, S. R., De Andrade, A. R., Tomlinson, M., Gleacher, A., Olin, S., & Hoagwood, K. (2016). Implementing a measurement feedback system: A tale of two sites. *Administration and Policy in Mental Health and Mental Health Services Research, 43*(3), 410–425. Retrieved from http://dx.doi.org.proxy.library.vanderbilt.edu/10.1007/s10488-015-0647-8

Bickman, L., Lyon, A. R., & Wolpert, M. (2016). Achieving precision mental health through effective assessment, monitoring, and feedback processes: Introduction to the special issue. *Administration and Policy in Mental Health and Mental Health Services Research, 43*(3), 271–276. https://doi.org/10.1007/s10488-016-0718-5

Boswell, J. F., Hepner, K. A., Lysell, K., Rothrock, N. E., Bott, N., Childs, A. W., Douglas, S., Owings-Fonner, N., Wright, C. V., Stephens, K. A., Bard, D. E., Aajmain, S., & Bobbitt, B. L. (2023). The need for a measurement-based care professional practice guideline. *Psychotherapy, 60*, 1–16. https://doi.org/10.1037/pst0000439

Brattland, H., Koksvik, J. M., Burkeland, O., Klöckner, C. A., Lara-Cabrera, M. L., Miller, S. D., Wampold, B., Ryum, T., & Iversen, V. C. (2019). Does the working alliance mediate the effect of routine outcome monitoring (ROM) and alliance feedback on psychotherapy outcomes? A secondary analysis from a randomized clinical trial. *Journal of Counseling Psychology, 66*(2), 234–246. https://doi.org/10.1037/cou0000320

Breda, C. S., & Riemer, M. (2012). Motivation for youth's treatment scale (MYTS): A new tool for measuring motivation among youths and their caregivers. *Administration and Policy in Mental Health and Mental Health Services Research, 39*(1–2), 118–132.

Broder, E. (2010). The child's voice in family therapy: A systemic perspective. *Journal of the Canadian Academy of Child and Adolescent Psychiatry, 19*(1), 56. Retrieved from https://www.ncbi.nlm.nih.gov/pmc/articles/PMC2809452/

Casline, E., Woodard, G., Patel, Z. S., Phillips, D., Ehrenreich-May, J., Ginsburg, G. S., & Jensen-Doss, A. (2022). Characterizing measurement-based care implementation using therapist report. *Evidence-Based Practice in Child and Adolescent Mental Health, 8*(4), 549–559. https://doi.org/10.1080/23794925.2022.2124555

Chen, R., Atzil-Slonim, D., Bar-Kalifa, E., Hasson-Ohayon, I., & Refaeli, E. (2018). Therapists' recognition of alliance ruptures as a moderator of change in alliance and symptoms. *Psychotherapy Research, 28*(4), 560–570. https://doi.org/10.1080/10503307.2016.1227104

Coalition for the Advancement and Application of Psychological Science. (2018). *Evidence-based practice decision-making for mental and behavioral health care*. Retrieved from https://www.caaps.co/consensus-statement

Connors, E. H., Douglas, S., Jensen-Doss, A., Landes, S. J., Lewis, C. C., McLeod, B. D., Stanick, C., & Lyon, A. R. (2021). What gets measured gets done: How mental health agencies can leverage measurement-based care for better patient care, clinician supports, and organizational goals. *Administration and Policy in Mental Health and Mental Health Services Research, 48*(2), 250–265. https://doi.org/10.1007/s10488-020-01063-w

Connors, E. H., Childs, A. W., Douglas, S., & Jensen-Doss, A. (2024). Data-informed communication: How measurement-based care can optimize child psychotherapy. *Administration and Policy in Mental Health*. https://doi.org/10.1007/s10488-024-01372-4

De Jong, K., Conijn, J. M., Gallagher, R. A. V., Reshetnikova, A. S., Heij, M., & Lutz, M. C. (2021). Using progress feedback to improve outcomes and reduce drop-out, treatment duration, and deterioration: A multilevel meta-analysis. *Clinical Psychology Review, 85*, 102002. https://doi.org/10.1016/j.cpr.2021.102002

De Jong, K., Delgadillo, J., & Barkham, M. (2023). *Routine outcome monitoring and feedback in psychological therapies*. McGraw-Hill Open University Press.

De Jong, K., Douglas, S., Wolpert, M., Delgadillo, J., Aas, B., Bovendeerd, B., Carlier, I. V. E., Compare, A., Edbrooke-Childs, J., Janse, P. D., Lutz, W., Moltu, C., Nordberg, S., Poulsen, S., Rubel, J., Schiepek, G. K., Schilling, V., van Sonsbeek, M., & Barkham, M. (2024). Using progress feedback to enhance treatment outcomes: A review. *Administration and Policy in Mental Health and Mental Health Services Research*. https://doi.org/10.1007/s10488-024-01381-3

De Los Reyes, A., Talbott, E., Power, T. J., Michel, J. J., Cook, C. R., Racz, S. J., & Fitzpatrick, O. (2022). The needs-to-goals gap: How informant discrepancies in youth mental health assessments impact service delivery. *Clinical Psychology Review, 92*, 102114. https://doi.org/10.1016/j.cpr.2021.102114

De Los Reyes, A., Epkins, C. C., Asmundson, G. J. G., Augenstein, T. M., Becker, K. D., Becker, S. P., Bonadio, F. T., Borelli, J. L., Boyd, R. C., Bradshaw, C. P., Burns, G. L., Casale, G., Causadias, J. M., Cha, C. B., Chorpita, B. F., Cohen, J. R., Comer, J. S., Crowell, S. E., Dirks, M. A., et al. (2023). Editorial statement about JCCAP's 2023 special issue on informant discrepancies in youth mental health assessments: Observations, guidelines, and future directions grounded in 60 years of research. *Journal of Clinical Child and Adolescent Psychology, 52*(1), 147–158. https://doi.org/10.1080/15374416.2022.2158842

Donelan, J., Douglas, S., Willson, A., Lester, T., & Daly, S. (2024). Implementing measurement-based care in a youth partial hospital setting: Leveraging feedback for sustainability. *Administration and Policy in Mental Health*. https://doi.org/10.1007/s10488-024-01358-2

Douglas Kelley, S., & Bickman, L. (2009). Beyond outcomes monitoring: Measurement feedback systems in child and adolescent clinical practice. *Current Opinion in Psychiatry, 22*(4), 363–368. Retrieved from http://dx.doi.org.proxy.library.vanderbilt.edu/10.1097/YCO.0b013e32832c9162

Douglas Kelley, S., Bickman, L., & Norwood, E. (2010a). Evidence-based treatments and common factors in youth psychotherapy. In B. L. Duncan, S. D. Miller, B. E. Wampold, & M. A. Hubble (Eds.), *The heart and soul of change* (2nd ed., pp. 325–355). American Psychological Association.

Douglas Kelley, S., de Andrade, A. R. V., Sheffer, E., & Bickman, L. (2010b). Exploring the black box: Measuring youth treatment process and progress in usual care. *Administration and Policy in Mental Health and Mental Health Services Research, 37*(3), 287–300. https://doi.org/10.1007/s10488-010-0298-8

Douglas, S., Jonghyuk, B., de Andrade, A. R. V., Tomlinson, M. M., Hargraves, R. P., & Bickman, L. (2015). Feedback mechanisms of change: How problem alerts reported by youth clients and their caregivers impact clinician-reported session content. *Psychotherapy Research, 25*(6), 678–693. https://doi.org/10.1080/10503307.2015.1059966

Douglas, S., Button, S., & Casey, S. E. (2016). Implementing for sustainability: Promoting use of a measurement feedback system for innovation and quality improvement. *Administration and Policy in Mental Health and Mental Health Services Research, 43*(3), 286–291. https://doi.org/10.1007/s10488-014-0607-8

Douglas, S., Jensen-Doss, A., Ordorica, C., & Comer, J. S. (2020). Strategies to enhance communication with telemental health measurement-based care (tMBC). *Practice Innovations, 5*(2), 143–149. https://doi.org/10.1037/pri0000119

Douglas, S., Bovendeerd, B., van Sonsbeek, M., Manns, M., Milling, X. P., Tyler, K., Bala, N., Satterthwaite, T., Hovland, R. T., Amble, I., Atzil-Slonim, D., Barkham, M., de Jong, K.,

Kendrick, T., Nordberg, S. S., Lutz, W., Rubel, J. A., Skjulsvik, T., & Moltu, C. (2023). A clinical leadership lens on implementing progress feedback in three countries: Development of a multidimensional qualitative coding scheme. *Administration and Policy in Mental Health and Mental Health Services Research*. https://doi.org/10.1007/s10488-023-01314-6

Douglas, S., Page, A., Moltu, C., Kyron, M., & Satterthwaite, T. (2024). The connections matter: Bi-directional learning in program evaluation and practice-oriented research. *Administration and Policy in Mental Health and Mental Health Services Research, 51*, 318–335. https://doi.org/10.1007/s10488-023-01304-8

Fitzpatrick, O. M., Holcomb, J. M., Weisz, J. R., & Langer, D. A. (2023). Shared decision-making as a tool for navigating multi-stakeholder discrepancies in youth psychotherapy. *Journal of Clinical Child & Adolescent Psychology, 52*(1), 95–107. https://doi.org/10.1080/15374416.2022.2127105

Gammer, C. (2009). *The child's voice in family therapy: A systematic perspective*. W. W. Norton & Company. Retrieved from https://wwnorton.com/books/The-Childs-Voice-in-Family-Therapy

Hagermoser Sanetti, L. M., & Kratochwill, T. R. (2014). *Treatment integrity: A foundation for evidence-based practice in applied psychology*. American Psychological Association.

Heron, J. (2001). *Helping the client: A creative practical guide* (5th ed.). Sage.

Herzog, P., Kube, T., & Rubel, J. (2023). Why some psychotherapists benefit from feedback on treatment progress more than others: A belief updating perspective. *Clinical Psychology: Science and Practice, 30*(4), 468–479. https://doi.org/10.1037/cps0000174

Holliday, S. B., Hepner, K. A., Farmer, C. M., Mahmud, A., Kimerling, R., Smith, B. N., & Rosen, C. (2021). Discussing measurement-based care with patients: An analysis of clinician-patient dyads. *Psychotherapy Research, 31*(2), 211–223. https://doi.org/10.1080/10503307.2020.1776413

Janse, P. D., de Jong, K., Veerkamp, C., van Dijk, M. K., Hutschemaekers, G. J. M., & Verbraak, M. J. P. M. (2020). The effect of feedback-informed cognitive behavioral therapy on treatment outcome: A randomized controlled trial. *Journal of Consulting and Clinical Psychology, 88*(9), 818–828. https://doi.org/10.1037/ccp0000549

Janse, P. D., Veerkamp, C., de Jong, K., van Dijk, M. K., Hutschemaekers, G. J. M., & Verbraak, M. J. P. M. (2023). Exploring therapist characteristics as potential moderators of the effects of client feedback on treatment outcome. *Clinical Psychology & Psychotherapy, 30*(3), 690–701. https://doi.org/10.1002/cpp.2828

Jensen-Doss, A., & Douglas, S. (2020, November–2024 May). *Improving measurement-based care in youth mental health: A comparison of unidimensional and multidimensional approaches*. Identifier NCT04369924. Retrieved from https://clinicaltrials.gov/study/NCT04369924

Jensen-Doss, A., & McLeod, B. D. (2020). Evidence-based case conceptualization/evidence-based clinical decision making. In R. G. Steele & M. C. Roberts (Eds.), *Handbook of evidence-based therapies for children and adolescents: Bridging science and practice* (pp. 39–52). Springer. https://doi.org/10.1007/978-3-030-44226-2_4

Jensen-Doss, A., Ehrenreich-May, J., Nanda, M. M., Maxwell, C. A., LoCurto, J., Shaw, A. M., Souer, H., Rosenfield, D., & Ginsburg, G. S. (2018). Community study of outcome monitoring for emotional disorders in teens (COMET): A comparative effectiveness trial of a transdiagnostic treatment and a measurement feedback system. *Contemporary Clinical Trials, 74*, 18–24. https://doi.org/10.1016/j.cct.2018.09.011

Jensen-Doss, A., Douglas, S., Phillips, D. A., Gencdur, O., Zalman, A., & Gomez, N. E. (2020). Measurement-based care as a practice improvement tool: Clinical and organizational applications in youth mental health. *Evidence-Based Practice in Child and Adolescent Mental Health, 5*(3), 233–250. https://doi.org/10.1080/23794925.2020.1784062

Koementas-de Vos, M. M. W., Tiemens, B., Engelsbel, F., de Jong, K., Witteman, C. L. M., & Nugter, M. A. (2024). Renewed feedback-informed group treatment for patients with anxiety and depressive disorders. *Administration and Policy in Mental Health and Mental Health Services Research, 52*, 88. https://doi.org/10.1007/s10488-023-01338-y

Kyron, M. J., Hooke, G. R., & Page, A. C. (2021). Prediction and network modelling of self-harm through daily self-report and history of self-injury. *Psychological Medicine, 51*(12), 1992–2002. https://doi.org/10.1017/S0033291720000744

Kyron, M. J., Hooke, G. R., Bryan, C. J., & Page, A. C. (2022). Distress tolerance as a moderator of the dynamic associations between interpersonal needs and suicidal thoughts. *Suicide & Life-Threatening Behavior, 52*(1), 159–170. https://doi.org/10.1111/sltb.12814

Lambert, M. J., Whipple, J. L., Hawkins, E. J., Vermeersch, D. A., Nielsen, S. L., & Smart, D. W. (2003). Is it time for clinicians to routinely track patient outcome? A meta-analysis. *Clinical Psychology: Science and Practice, 10*(3), 288–301. https://doi.org/10.1093/clipsy.bpg025

Lewis, C. C., Boyd, M., Puspitasari, A., Navarro, E., Howard, J., Kassab, H., Hoffman, M., Scott, K., Lyon, A., Douglas, S., Simon, G., & Kroenke, K. (2019). Implementing measurement-based care in behavioral health: A review. *JAMA Psychiatry, 76*(3), 324–335. https://doi.org/10.1001/jamapsychiatry.2018.3329

McLeod, B. D., Jensen-Doss, A., Lyon, A. R., Douglas, S., & Beidas, R. S. (2022). To utility and beyond! Specifying and advancing the utility of measurement-based care for youth. *Journal of Clinical Child & Adolescent Psychology, 51*(4), 375–388. https://doi.org/10.1080/15374416.2022.2042698

Moore, L., & Seu, I. B. (2011). Giving children a voice: Children's positioning in family therapy. *Journal of Family Therapy, 33*(3), 279–301. https://doi.org/10.1111/j.1467-6427.2011.00556.x

Riemer, M., & Bickman, L. (2011). Using program theory to link social psychology and program evaluation. In M. M. Mark, S. I. Donaldson, & B. Campbell (Eds.), *Social psychology and evaluation*. Guilford Press.

Rubel, J. A., Zilcha-Mano, S., Feils-Klaus, V., & Lutz, W. (2018). Session-to-session effects of alliance ruptures in outpatient CBT: Within- and between-patient associations. *Journal of Consulting and Clinical Psychology, 86*(4), 354–366. https://doi.org/10.1037/ccp0000286

Sale, R., Bearman, S. K., Woo, R., & Baker, N. (2021). Introducing a measurement feedback system for youth mental health: Predictors and impact of implementation in a community agency. *Administration and Policy in Mental Health and Mental Health Services Research, 48*(2), 327–342. https://doi.org/10.1007/s10488-020-01076-5

Senko, K., & Harper, B. (2019). Play therapy: An illustrative case. *Innovations in Clinical Neuroscience, 16*(5–6), 38–40. Retrieved from https://www.ncbi.nlm.nih.gov/pmc/articles/PMC6659989/

Suzuki, S. (2020). *Zen mind, beginner's mind* (T. Dixon, Ed.; 50th anniversary edition). Shambhala.

van Sonsbeek, M. A. M. S., Hutschemaekers, G. J. M., Veerman, J. W., Vermulst, A., Kleinjan, M., & Tiemens, B. G. (2021). Challenges in investigating the effective components of feedback from routine outcome monitoring (ROM) in youth mental health care. *Child & Youth Care Forum, 50*(2), 307–332. https://doi.org/10.1007/s10566-020-09574-1

van Sonsbeek, M. A. M. S., Hutschemaekers, G. J. M., Veerman, J. W., Vermulst, A., & Tiemens, B. G. (2023). The results of clinician-focused implementation strategies on uptake and outcomes of measurement-based care (MBC) in general mental health care. *BMC Health Services Research, 23*(1), 326. https://doi.org/10.1186/s12913-023-09343-5

Weinberger, D. (2010, February 2). The problem with the data-information-knowledge-wisdom hierarchy. *Harvard Business Review*. Retrieved from https://hbr.org/2010/02/data-is-to-info-as-info-is-not

Weinberger, D. (2019). *Everyday chaos: Technology, complexity, and how we're thriving in a new world of possibility*. Harvard Business Review Press.

Index

J. A. Rubel, W. Lutz (eds.), *Feedback Informed Psychological Therapy*, CBT: Science Into Practice, https://doi.org/10.1007/978-3-031-90428-8

MIX
Papier aus verantwortungsvollen Quellen
Paper from responsible sources
FSC® C105338

FSC
www.fsc.org

If you have any concerns about our products,
you can contact us on
ProductSafety@springernature.com

In case Publisher is established outside the EU,
the EU authorized representative is:
Springer Nature Customer Service Center GmbH
Europaplatz 3, 69115 Heidelberg, Germany

Printed by Libri Plureos GmbH
in Hamburg, Germany